SHAKESPEARE'S
SONNETS

Shakespeare's
SONNETS

Edited by

W. G. INGRAM M.A.

formerly Lector in English, Trinity College, Cambridge
Director of English Studies, Emmanuel College, Cambridge
and University Lecturer in Education

and

THEODORE REDPATH M.A. Ph.D.

Fellow, Senior Lecturer, and Director of English Studies, Trinity College,
Cambridge and University Lecturer in English
Sometime Charles Oldham Shakespeare Scholar

HODDER AND STOUGHTON
LONDON   SYDNEY   AUCKLAND   TORONTO

ISBN o 340 09080 4 Boards
ISBN o 340 22841 5 Paperback

Introductory matter, notes and commentary copyright © 1964, 1978
W. G. Ingram and Theodore Redpath
Third impression (with amendments) 1978

Printed in Great Britain for
Hodder and Stoughton Educational,
a division of Hodder and Stoughton Ltd,
Mill Road, Dunton Green, Sevenoaks, Kent,
by Fletcher & Son Ltd, Norwich

We dedicate
this edition to the memory of our Mothers,
who knew of and encouraged our work on it:

CLARA LOUISE INGRAM

died 9 October 1957

KITTY REDPATH

died 17 September 1957

CONTENTS

A NOTE ON THE SECOND IMPRESSION

IN revising our book for this impression we have corrected misprints and amended a few of the notes with whose wording in the first impression we have found ourselves dissatisfied. One or two additional notes have been added where we felt omission of comment was a defect. We have also added to the Bibliography a few titles of books published since this edition went to press in 1963. We have not, however, thought it desirable in a reprint to make any alterations in our commentary as a result of recent editors' annotations, though some may well be advisable should a second edition of our book eventually appear.

Cambridge, August 1966   W.G.I.
                                                                     T.R.

A NOTE ON THE THIRD IMPRESSION

WE have made some corrections to the text of the poems, and corrections and additions to the commentary; but sparingly, to keep down the price of the book. We have added to the bibliography a few important recent items, in particular the books by Professor Stephen Booth and Professor Giorgio Melchiori. We retain our modernized punctuation despite criticisms from devotees of the Quarto punctuation. Fuller justification of our views is given in an essay, 'The Punctuation of Shakespeare's Sonnets', in *New Essays on Shakespeare's Sonnets*, ed. Hilton Landry, AMS Press, New York, 1976. The fetish for the Quarto punctuation owes much to the maleficent influence of what Professor Booth has described as the 'notorious essay' by Laura Riding and Robert Graves in *A Survey of Modernist Poetry*, London, 1927. The Quarto punctuation has even been rashly described as 'Shakespeare's punctuation' (e.g. by M. Seymour-Smith in his edition of the *Sonnets* (1963), pp. 37, 38). There is no justification for this. The Quarto punctuation seems rather to be just an inferior example of normal printing-house practice at the time. It is worth noting that in the case of Donne the only extant autograph MS poem is punctuated very differently from its text in any early printed edition.

Cambridge, September 1977   W.G.I.
                                                                     T.R.

PREFACE

APART from mere reprints of the Sonnets, in various texts, about thirty fairly substantial editions have already appeared since the beginning of this century. We therefore feel some obligation to justify the present edition and to explain its main purposes.

We believe that most honest and intelligent readers of these poems admit that many of them are far from easy to understand. The difficulty is partly due to changes in the sense of particular words, and partly due to the elusiveness, in many places, of Shakespeare's thought. The poems were evidently already difficult for eighteenth-century readers. Certainly, the pioneer Shakespearean scholars of the late eighteenth century, Capell, Steevens, and Malone, considered it necessary to try to throw light on a fair number of words, phrases, and lines in the Sonnets, which they did mainly by paraphrasing or by citing passages from Shakespeare's plays or from his other poems. The reading of poetry has, however, during the last fifty years, become far closer than it seems to have been at least for some generations; and in fine and subtle work, such as the plays of Shakespeare, and the poems of the Metaphysical poets, Donne and Herbert, or the poetry of Pope, we have become aware of more than it seems likely readers and critics had been, at least since the time when those poets wrote. A full realization of a complex work will involve an awareness of relationships between its parts, and of implications of tone in its diction, and a sense of the development of its imagery, and of the pace of its movement. Now a considerable number of Shakespeare's Sonnets are works of this kind, and to direct attention to such features may often be useful. Even the bare sense, however, was often insufficiently or incorrectly elucidated by the older editors, and, even after much commentary, many dark or controversial passages remain.

Among modern editions of the Sonnets, which we may consider to have begun with Dowden's useful short edition in 1881, the majority have paid much attention to the questions of the identity of the Friend to whom it is generally believed the first 126 sonnets were addressed; of the 'Dark Lady' to whom some, at least, of the remainder seem to have been written; of the Rival Poet to whom some of the sonnets between 78 and 86 appear to refer; and of 'Mr. W. H.', who is named in the Dedication. This direction of attention, whatever its merits in itself, has resulted in not enough attention being paid to detailed meaning, and to the individual sonnets as works of art. Indeed, although there are some useful elucidatory notes in, for instance, the editions of Dowden (1881) and Tyler (1890), and still more in those of Wyndham (1898, including also the other poems), of Beeching (1904), of Pooler (1918, 1931, 1943), and of Tucker Brooke (1936), the only Commentary in which sufficient intellectual vigour is directed towards grappling with the many real difficulties of meaning is that of Tucker (1924), now out of print. The two large Furness Variorum editions, by Alden (1916) and Rollins (1944), are admirable, but could not, by their nature, concentrate on elucidation, and necessarily included many opinions of doubtful value. Rollins himself, in his Preface, writes as follows:

> 'Perhaps an ideal edition of the Sonnets would be devoted to facts, explanations of meaning, and esthetic criticism, giving little or no stress to theories about sonnet problems or to identifications of sonnet personages: but for such an edition the *New Variorum Shakespeare* is no place.'

It is somewhat hard to determine the scope of Rollins's term 'facts', but, for the rest, the ideal he describes forms a considerable part of the ideal we have aimed at in the present edition.

Apart from questions of identification there are two important 'sonnet problems' which we have deliberately refrained from tackling: (1) the problem of the date of composition,* and (2) the problem of correct sequence. Both problems have been much discussed, but neither has yet been satisfactorily settled. Rollins, after a thorough review of the various conjectures on dating, observes that the 'average of the guesses' indicates that Shakespeare began writing the sonnets about the middle of 1593, and 'laid aside his pen' about June 1599. It seems possible, however, that several may have been written after 1599. As to sequence, a fair number of scholars have regarded the Quarto order as unsatisfactory, and more than a few re-arrangements have been proposed. The vast majority of editors, however, have adopted the Quarto order, which has been defended as significant by various authorities. Whether there *is* a correct order, though (that is, an order intended by Shakespeare), and, if so, whether it is the Quarto order or some other, must be regarded as unsettled. Among recent re-arrangements the most interesting is perhaps that of Tucker Brooke, which was partly determined by his belief that the Friend was the Earl of Southampton. Yet, however interesting such re-arrangements may be, we have found that editions which do not preserve the Quarto order

---

* We have, however, indicated a number of proposed solutions in our notes to Sonnet 107.

are inconvenient to use. On this ground alone we should probably have decided to print the sonnets in that order, even had we felt strongly inclined to believe in the existence of a right order, different from that of the Quarto, and in our knowledge of it. It must be admitted, however, that it is always possible that if it were definitely known that there is a 'correct arrangement', and what that arrangement is, this might affect somewhat the interpretation of particular sonnets. On the other hand, we would claim that the great majority of our Commentary would still stand whatever the correct arrangement of the poems, and we would also urge that the Quarto order itself is sometimes an aid in interpretation, even if not to the degree that Dowden thought when he published his edition.

The question of the nature of the relationship between the poet and the Friend, as it emerges from the sonnets themselves, is clearly distinct from the question of the Friend's identity. We do not intend, in the present edition, to offer and argue for a view of that relationship, though in our notes on individual sonnets we have naturally tried to face particular aspects of it. It may, however, be in place to state our general impression, which is that the relationship was one of profound and at times agitated friendship, which involved a certain physical and quasi-sexual fascination emanating from the young Friend and enveloping the older poet, but did not necessarily include paederasty in any lurid sense. Elizabethan speech habits and literary conventions certainly encouraged a more fulsome and more frankly emotional style of expression in such relations than would prevail today (in England at least); and while this is emphatically no argument for belittling the intensity and even the sensuousness of the attraction, it suggests the need for considerable caution before supposing the existence of any consciously or overtly sexual quality in the relationship.

Our object in the present edition is twofold: first, to present as good a text as possible, in modern spelling and punctuation; and secondly, to offer a full and searching commentary. Our aims in the commentary are, more specifically: (1) to justify the text printed, where this could be controversial; (2) to gloss all words that might cause difficulty to a modern reader; (3) to attempt to tackle all really difficult problems of interpretation, whether these have already been given proper attention by commentators, or have been unduly neglected or perfunctorily treated; and (4) to make some contribution towards a fuller realization of the subtler features which characterize a considerable number of the poems and make for their excellence as artistic works. Some experts on the Sonnets may find that some of our notes add nothing to what they knew by scholarship or unaided intelligence; though we are sufficiently sceptical to doubt whether even experts have exhausted all the finer points of these poems, or even all those we have drawn attention to. Moreover, our edition is concerned in large measure to offer assistance to a far wider field of readers, and, in particular, to help the university student and the general reader, both here and abroad, who would not yet lay claim to expertise, but who wish to improve their understanding of the poems. The explicit offer of the interpretation of difficult words, phrases, or lines is, in any case, even for the expert, an offer of a point for comparison with his own interpretation. Indeed, in actual fact, readers can never be sure whether they are understanding the poems in the same way unless they indicate, as clearly as they can, *how* they *are* understanding them. Only by the free interchange of ideas on meaning can we further the desirable aim, which must essentially be a co-operative one, of achieving as full a realization as possible of the poems and of their characteristics as works of art.

Our first object—to present as good a text as possible, in modern spelling and punctuation—is in some ways easier to achieve than for much of the work of the older poets. There are no authoritative manuscripts to be collated. None of the seventeenth-century manuscripts of particular sonnets appears to be earlier in date than the Quarto of 1609, and none improves on its text.* Furthermore, except for two of the sonnets, printed in *The Passionate Pilgrim* (1599), there is only one text of these poems with any claim to authority (the Quarto of 1609), of which thirteen copies are known to survive.† There are, moreover, only very insignificant variations in any of the texts of these copies. On the other hand, apart from the problem of the order of the sonnets, already mentioned, there is another important problem facing editors who try to establish a satisfactory modern text: the problem of punctuation—how to punctuate in a modern edition so as to represent most accurately the poem Shakespeare wrote. It would readily become clear to any intelligent reader, even on a cursory inspection of the Quarto text, that to retain the Quarto punctuation (which, in so far as it follows any principle, follows one unfamiliar to the modern general reader) would be to spoil the poems for him. The Quarto punctuation has therefore (and, in our view, rightly) been much altered by almost all modern editors, even including Wyndham, who stoutly defended the Quarto punctuation on the ground that it often marked rhythmical and rhetorical as well as syntactical pauses. There are cases where the Quarto has no end-stops at all, but where some punctuation is imperative, at least in a modern recension, for instance in 24.10–14, where the Quarto prints:

* For an interesting list of seventeenth-century MSS of particular sonnets see Tucker Brooke's edition, pp. 66–9, which the editor acknowledges to be greatly indebted to the researches of Dr. Louise B. Osborn and Dr. Giles E. Dawson.
† For further details see p. xvii, below.

Mine eyes haue drawne thy shape, and thine for me
Are windowes to my brest, where-through the Sun
Delights to peepe, to gaze therein on thee
    Yet eyes this cunning want to grace their art
    They draw but what they see, know not the hart.

Again, the Quarto uses commas far more frequently than would be appropriate in a modern edition, where we should rightly print sometimes no stop at all, sometimes a colon or semi-colon, and sometimes even a full stop. On occasion, indeed, the Quarto punctuation would not simply impair the speed and timing of the lines for a modern reader, but would actually mislead as to the bare sense. A clear instance occurs in 72, where the Quarto prints lines 1–3 as follows:

    O least the world should taske you to recite,
    What merit liu'd in me that you should loue
    After my death (deare loue) for get me quite,

Capell saw that a comma was required at the end of line 2, since otherwise the implication would be that the love which 'the world' might challenge would be the Friend's love for the poet *after the poet's death*, whereas the adverbial phrase 'After my death' really modifies the verb 'forget'. The alterations in punctuation made by modern editors, however, have not always resulted in the punctuation that seems to be required by the sense and movement of the poems. Indeed, to achieve the best punctuation—the punctuation expressing most faithfully the sense and movement of the poems in all their life and subtlety—some devices additional to those generally used by modern editors seem to be needed. Useful devices of this kind are the dash, the comma–dash, the semi-colon–dash, and the colon–dash. We have made considerable use of the first two, and occasional use of the last two. In using the dash, either alone or combined with other stops, we are not, however, innovators. Wyndham himself uses the dash in a few places, either alone or combined with a comma or colon. Again, Beeching uses the dash several times, and the colon–dash once. It is Tucker, however, who really begins to exploit the device of the dash on a considerable scale, and he does so to very good effect. In our opinion, however, even Tucker does not make sufficient use of the device. Moreover, he does not employ it in combination with other stops. Whether, as we believe, the use of these devices more faithfully expresses the life of the poems than other, more traditional, punctuation, we must leave to the judgment of sensitive readers.

    With regard to controversial readings in the text, these arise where editors and scholars have emended the Quarto text in the belief that a

Quarto reading was unsatisfactory. A vast number of such emendations has been recorded by Rollins. In general, we have not found it necessary or advisable to do over again the work of collation which Rollins did so admirably. On the other hand, though a Variorum edition should record even emendations of comparatively trivial importance, a critical edition should record only those which are of sufficient importance to claim the attention of those readers for whom the edition is designed. Our general policy has been to record all proposed emendations, worth serious consideration, which would affect the meaning of the poem concerned. Moreover, in view of their effect on meaning, we have incorporated reference to these emendations into the body of the Commentary, instead of printing them in a separate textual apparatus. We believe that readers are thereby likely to gain a closer insight into the textual difficulties of the Sonnets, and we also believe that consideration of important controversial points in the text often results in a fuller grasp of the sense and movement of the poems.

As to the Commentary itself, this is fuller than any that has so far appeared, except those in the Variorum editions of Alden and Rollins, and in Tucker's edition. We do not pretend to have said the last word on all the difficult points of interpretation, but we do claim to have made some definite advances in the interpretation of a fair number of the poems. We have endeavoured to be scrupulous in acknowledging our debts to the many bright thoughts that have occurred to previous scholars and commentators. We have not, on the other hand, felt bound to search the commentaries in order to make ascriptions of first mention in cases where concordances, lexicons, glossaries, and dictionaries have made interpretations and parallels more readily available than they were to those who first thought of them. As to aesthetic, as contrasted with interpretative, comment, we have drawn attention in various places in the commentary to artistic features which we have noticed in our reading of the sonnets over the years. We have, however, after careful thought, come to believe that much of the critical material we have collected could be more effectively disposed in a number of critical essays on various aspects of the Sonnets than in the present edition, and we have therefore decided to reserve it for a future volume. What we are most concerned to do at present is to offer to readers of Shakespeare, in the quatercentenary year, our text and commentary, in the hope that these may make some contribution to a fuller and richer reading of the poems.

Trinity College, Cambridge, July 1963   W.G.I.
                                                                            T.R.

ACKNOWLEDGMENTS

WE wish to put on record our gratitude both to the work of previous scholars and to those friends who have made valuable comments on our work.

No Shakespearean editor can get far without J. Bartlett's *Concordance to Shakespeare* and A. Schmidt's *Shakespeare-Lexicon*, and any editor of the Sonnets needs to refer continually to Mrs. H. H. Furness's *Concordance to Shakespeare's Poems*. Among previous editions we have derived most assistance from those of R. M. Alden,* T. G. Tucker, and especially from that of H. E. Rollins, a mine of information on all aspects of the Sonnets.

Among our friends we owe particular thanks to Dr. T. R. Henn, C.B.E., President of St. Catharine's College, Cambridge, and Judith Wilson Lecturer on Drama in the University, for helpful comments on our Notes on the first thirty sonnets; to Mr. L. G. Salingar, M.A., Fellow of Trinity College, Cambridge, and University Lecturer in English, for detailed and constructive criticisms and suggestions on our notes on about half the poems; and, above all, to Mr. F. L. Lucas, O.B.E., M.A., Fellow of King's College, Cambridge, and lately Reader in English in the University, who has scrutinized almost all our edition with keen eye, saved us from some definite mistakes, and made a great number of perceptive suggestions which have vastly benefited the edition. We also wish to thank Professor Keith Walker of the University of New Brunswick for some meticulous, scholarly comments, and Mr. B. W. Vickers, B.A., of Trinity College, Cambridge, and Charles Oldham Shakespeare Scholar in the University for 1961, for one typically thorough piece of research, and for various items of useful information.

1963   W.G.I.
                                                                          T.R.

---

* An attempt to obtain a copy of this valuable edition was met, through the good offices of Mr. H. R. Creswick, M.A., Fellow of Jesus College and Librarian of the University of Cambridge, by a most generous gift to us of a copy from Professor W. A. Jackson, Professor of Bibliography at Harvard University.

ABBREVIATIONS AND REFERENCES

The following abbreviations have been used for the titles of books and periodical publications:

MLR: The Modern Language Review

MP: Modern Philology

OED: A New English Dictionary on Historical Principles ed. J. Murray and others, Clarendon Press, Oxford, 1883–1933

PMLA: Publications of the Modern Language Association of America

RES: The Review of English Studies

TLS: The Times Literary Supplement

Names of authors or editors (e.g. Beeching, Pooler, Rollins) refer to the books or editions listed on pp. xxiv–xxv and 374–5.

References to Shakespeare's plays adopt the scene and line numbering in *The Oxford Shakespeare* (ed. W. J. Craig), 1913.

A HISTORICAL NOTE ON THE TEXT OF THE SONNETS

No autograph manuscript of any of the sonnets has yet been discovered, and none of the extant seventeenth-century manuscripts of particular sonnets has any independent textual authority.

The only early printed texts with any valid claim to authority are: (1) the texts of Sonnets 138 and 144 printed in a collection of miscellaneous poems with Shakespeare's name on the title-page, called *The Passionate Pilgrim*, which was published by William Jaggard in 1599, and re-issued in 1612; (2) the first edition of the full text of all the 154 sonnets, published in 1609 by Thomas Thorpe. This is the basis of all subsequent texts. It is generally known as 'the Quarto' or 'Quarto', and will often be referred to in this edition by the usual abbreviation Q.

There are thirteen extant copies of Q. They are almost exactly alike except for their title-pages, four of which bear the imprint of William Aspley:*

SHAKE-SPEARES | SONNETS. | Neuer before Imprinted. | [Double rule] | AT LONDON | By *G. Eld* for *T.T.* and are | to be solde by *William Aspley.* | 1609.|

and seven the imprint of John Wright:†

[as above] by *Iohn Wright,* dwelling | at Christ Church gate. | 1609.|

The other two extant copies lack title-pages.‡

* The four copies with the Aspley imprint are in: (1) The British Museum (Grenville 11181). There is a facsimile by J. Cape, London, 1925. (2) The Bodleian Library, Oxford (Malone 34). There is a collotype facsimile by Sir Sidney Lee (1905). (3) The Huntington Library, California (Chalmers-Bridgwater). There is a photozincographic facsimile by Lovell Reeve and Co., London, 1862. (4) The Folger Shakespeare Library, Washington.
† The seven copies with the Wright imprint are in: (1) The Bodleian Library, Oxford (Caldecott, Malone 886). (2) The British Museum (B. H. Bright, C.21, C.44). There is a photolithographic facsimile by Charles Praetorius, *Shakespeare* Quarto Fascimiles, no. 30, London, 1886, with an introduction by T. Tyler; and a collotype fascimile by Noel Douglas, London, 1926 (reissued by Payson and Clarke, New York, 1927). (3) The John Rylands Library, Manchester. (4) The Elizabethan Club, Yale. (5) The Huntington Library, California. (6) The Folger Shakespeare Library, Washington. (7) a collection formerly a part of Dr. A. S. W. Rosenbach's private library. The copy has more recently been in Dr. Martin Bodmer's private collection in Geneva.
‡ The two copies without title-pages are in: (1) The Library of Trinity College, Cambridge. This copy lacks sigs. A1, A2, B, K2–L2, which Capell has written in, the title-page being given a Wright imprint. (2) The Harvard University Library. This copy has a facsimile title-page (with the Aspley imprint) and dedication page.

An entry in the Stationers' Register on 20 May 1609* of 'a Booke called Shakespeares *sonnettes*' identifies the publisher *T.T.* as Thomas Thorpe, who was active as a publisher between 1594 and 1624. He was the publisher of Ben Jonson's *Sejanus* (1605) and *Volpone* (1607). Thorpe was never, apparently, at the top of his profession, whereas his printer George Eld and his bookseller William Aspley were among the leading members of their trades. Aspley eventually became Master of the Stationers' Company, and in 1623 he joined the syndicate that printed the First Folio of Shakespeare's works. He was also a member of the new syndicate who printed the Second Folio in 1632. John Wright does not seem to have achieved such eminence. He printed mainly ballads and chapbooks, but occasionally a play (e.g. Marlowe's *Faustus* in 1609, and seven times more until 1631), and in 1626 he became co-owner of the rights to Shakespeare's *Venus and Adonis*.

What Thorpe's arrangement was with Aspley and Wright for the division of the sales we do not know. Moreover, on the question whether the publication was sanctioned by Shakespeare himself there is no external evidence.

Q printed the celebrated Dedication (see p. 2, below) by Thorpe 'to the onlie begetter of these insuing sonnets', which was to give rise to much speculation among scholars from the late eighteenth century until our own times.

Scholars and critics have differed widely in their estimates of the merits of the Quarto text. Its stoutest defender has been Wyndham (1898), who paid immense respect to its punctuation, and even considered its italics and capitals to be always significant. Wyndham's exaggerated respect for the Quarto text was attacked by Beeching (1904), Lee (1905), and Pooler (1918). Bullen (1907) held a medial position on the question. Tucker (1924), on the other hand, thought that Q's errors were so frequent as to shake confidence in its reliability, but Professor Dover Wilson in 1926 found it hard to believe that the printer's copy was not closely connected with Shakespeare's original, perhaps even by means of a transcript in a single hand. Sir Edmund Chambers (*William Shakespeare*, 1930, I, 559) passed the opinion that Q's text was not very good, that it might rest on a fairly authoritative manuscript, but contained enough misprints, including misprints of punctuation not explicable on any theory, to make it clear that the volume could not have been 'overseen' by Shakespeare. Rollins, in his Variorum Edition (1944), lists (II. 11–13) eighty-four cases (not including cases of punctuation) which one or more of the three editors, Beeching, Lee, and Tucker Brooke (1936) had held to be cases of misprints. He notes,

* Arber, *Transcript*, 1876, III, 410.

moreover, that fifty-three of the readings concerned had been emended or modernized (not always in the same way) in all the editions he had collated.* On the other hand, by further analysis he reduces the number by seventeen, by removing cases of certainly or possibly legitimate old spellings. The result would then be thirty-six strongly attested cases of misprints (apart from punctuation) out of 2,155 lines—one misprint in every sixty lines. As to Q's punctuation, its most notable defender, apart from Wyndham, has been the late Percy Simpson (*Shakespearian Punctuation*, Clarendon Press, Oxford, 1911), whose defence insists on rhythmical value. As Rollins points out, however, Simpson felt constrained to make many exceptions to his generalizations. Simpson's views were attacked by a number of scholars, including the earlier Variorum editor R. M. Alden (in *PMLA*, 1924, xxxix, 557–80), and it is quite certain that there are a number of instances (e.g. 113. 13, 118. 10, 129. 10, 11) where the punctuation of Q is indefensible.

Taken all in all, the present editors find it hard to believe that Shakespeare can have corrected the proofs of the Sonnets, even if (for which, as stated above, there is no external evidence) he sanctioned their publication.

The sonnets were printed for the second time in 1639 in a volume (bearing the date 1640) published by John Benson. The title-page reads:

POEMS: | WRITTEN | BY | WIL. SHAKE-SPEARE. | Gent. | — | [Device] | — | Printed at *London* by *Tho. Cotes*, and are | to be sold by *Iohn Benson*, dwelling in | *St. Dunstans* Church-yard. 1640.†

Many copies survive. Some slight variations have been detected between different copies. The printer Cotes is called by Lee (1905)‡ 'the most experienced of any in the trade in the production of Shakespearean literature'. Benson printed the Second Folio in 1632. He had been admitted to the Stationers' Company in 1631.

Benson's publication of Shakespeare's Poems was piratical. He reprinted (almost certainly from Q,§ except for the two sonnets 138 and 144, which he printed from the 1612 edition of *The Passionate Pilgrim*) 146 of the Sonnets, jumbling their order, and changing some pronouns and nouns, and inventing titles, all to suggest a mistress not a man. He also intermingled the Sonnets with *The Lover's Complaint*, the poems of the 1612 edition of

* A list of the editions collated by Rollins appears below on pp. xxiv–xxv.
† A modern reprint exists, by A. R. Smith (1885). This is quite good, but contains some errors.
‡ *Shakespeare's Sonnets*. A reproduction in facsimile of the first edition (1609). With Introduction and Bibliography by Sir Sidney Lee, Clarendon Press, Oxford, 1905, p. 55.
§ For convincing evidence drawn from a close examination of the texts of Q and Benson *see* R. M. Alden's article in *MP*, 14 (May 1916).

The Passionate Pilgrim, The Phoenix and the Turtle, and a number of poems by various other poets, including Ben Jonson and Milton. The sonnets are sometimes printed singly, sometimes in groups without spacing between one sonnet and the next, so as to look like continuous poems. They make up seventy-two 'poems', with titles provided, such as (for 46 and 47) *Two faithfull friends,* and (for 122) *Upon the receit of a Table Booke from his Mistris.*

Benson wrote a Preface, in which he had the cool impudence to pretend that he was publishing the poems by Shakespeare for the first time. This Preface reads as follows:

To the Reader.

I Here presume (under favour) to present to your view, some excellent and sweetely composed Poems, of Master William Shakespeare, Which in themselves appeare of the same purity, the Authour himselfe then living avouched; they had not the fortune by reason of their Infancie in his death, to have the due accomodatiō of proportionable glory, with the rest of his everliving Workes, yet the lines of themselves will afford you a more authentick approbation than my assurance any way can, to invite your allowance, in your perusall you shall finde them Seren, cleere and eligantly plaine, such gentle straines as shall recreate and not perplexe your braine, no intricate or cloudy stuffe to puzzell intellect, but perfect eloquence; such as will raise your admiration to his praise: this assurance I know will not differ from your acknowledgement. And certaine I am, your opinion will be seconded by the sufficiency of these ensuing Lines; I have beene somewhat solicitus to bring this forth to the perfect view of all men; and in so doing, glad to be serviceable for the continuance of glory to the deserved Author in these his Poems.

I.B.

Benson, it can be seen, to puff his publication, was willing to resort to deceit, and, no less, to misdescription.

Though Benson's text of the Sonnets cannot be regarded as having any independent authority, it does correct the evident mistakes of Q in about twenty cases. To compensate, however, it makes about fifty new and equally evident mistakes of its own.

It is an important fact that Benson (naturally) did not print the Dedication by T.T. This deliberate omission, and Benson's substitution in many cases of a mistress for the male friend, brought it about that theory-spinning as to the 'story' of the Sonnets, and the identity of its characters, did not begin until well after the 1609 text was re-introduced in the eighteenth century.

Gildon, the reputed editor of the first eighteenth-century edition of the Sonnets (1710),* followed Benson's text, but modernized the spelling and punctuation, and printed a fair number of new readings, some of which were evidently emendations and others simply errors. A revised edition of Gildon[1] appeared in 1714, as a supplement to Rowe's edition of Shakespeare's plays. This edition (Gildon[2]) contained further new readings, some of which were probably mistakes, though others were evidently conscious emendations.

The Benson tradition was continued by Sewell[1] (1725), which appeared as Volume VI of Pope's 1723–5 edition of the plays. This edition sometimes follows the text of Gildon[1], and sometimes that of Gildon[2], but also introduces some new readings. Sewell[2], published in 1728, was even closer to Gildon, especially to Gildon[2].

An undated volume (but possibly published in 1741) entitled *Poems on Several Occasions. By Shakespeare*, follows Sewell[2], but prints some new readings.

The editions of Ewing (1771), Gentleman (1774), and Evans (1775) continued the lineage of Benson's volume, and, even after Malone's editions of 1780 and 1790 had printed critically revised texts based on the 1609 Quarto, a few editors (e.g. Oulton in 1804) brought out texts in the Benson tradition, the last case, according to Rollins, being Durrell's New York edition of 1817–18, reissued several times early in the nineteenth century.

The text of the Quarto of 1609 had, however, been republished by Lintot in 1711. It is not known who the editor was, but he followed Q very faithfully, scarcely ever emending, even where emendation was required. Lintot's description of the volume, however, announcing it to contain 'One hundred and Fifty Four Sonnets, all of them in Praise of his Mistress', was clearly still under the influence of Benson's volume.

The 1609 text was reprinted by Steevens in his edition of twenty of the plays in 1766, without, however, any editorial or critical comments. Capell had been planning to edit Q, and had prepared a corrected copy of Lintot (1711) for the printer. This, known as the Capell MS, is in the Library of Trinity College, Cambridge. As far as is known, it was never set up. Capell wrote a preface, dated 1766, attacking the Benson text and the editions which had followed it, but this did not appear, and so did not have any direct effect on the continuance of the Benson tradition.

It was Malone, whose two editions appeared in 1780 and 1790, who firmly established the tradition of the 1609 Quarto which has continued until the present day. It is not known whether Malone had seen the 'Capell MS', but he attributes a number of his notes to a certain 'C', who was

* The volume appeared in 1709, but the general title-page is dated 1710.

almost certainly Capell, so that it is fair to conclude that Malone may have been indebted to Capell in a considerable degree.

Malone's 1780 edition was issued as a supplement to the 1778 edition of the plays for which Johnson and Steevens were jointly responsible. (Steevens himself thought little of the Sonnets, in which opinion he was by no means alone at the time.) In his Preface Malone alleges that Benson's text had been followed by all subsequent editors. Rollins suggests that this fact indicates that Malone did not know of Lintot's edition or of the Capell MS. It would certainly seem to favour the opinion that Malone did not know of Lintot's edition, but when he referred to subsequent editors it seems at least possible that he only had in mind those whose editions had actually appeared in print.

Malone's 1790 edition formed Volume X of his own edition of the plays and poems.

The texts in both volumes are excellent. Based on Q, they are the fruit of meticulous critical scholarship and intelligence. Malone also offered the first commentary on the Sonnets, in which he made use of notes by Steevens, and of the suggestions of a few other scholars, evidently including Capell.

Almost all early nineteenth-century texts were either reprints of one or other of Malone's texts (often that of 1780), or closely followed him. Dyce offered a newly revised text in the Aldine edition (1832), and again in his edition of Shakespeare's works (1857); but, though these texts are careful, the revisions are not great in number. They tend to re-establish Q readings in place of Malone's emendations.

More extensive was the textual work done by Clark and Aldis Wright, first for their Globe edition of 1864, and then for their two Cambridge editions, Cambridge[1] (1866) and Cambridge[2] (1893). Their texts are admirable, though their punctuation is sometimes rather heavy, and does not, in our view, always express the real movement and life of the poems. Their textual apparatus was limited to mentioning the first appearances of readings, and so did not indicate the weight of editorial opinion on textual points. Moreover, though fairly full, their apparatus was not really complete, and, though in general very accurate, contained some errors.

Wyndham (1898) restored many abandoned Q readings, and defended them vigorously, though often without convincing scholarly opinion. Butler (1899) went to the other extreme, offering many emendations which editors have felt little or no hesitation in rejecting.

Looking back over the last hundred years, we may perhaps say that editions have fallen textually into three main classes:

(1) those which have substantially followed the Globe or one of the Cambridge texts or that of some other standard edition;

(2) those which have, under antiquarian influences, or out of respect for Q, printed a text very close indeed to that of Q, with a minimum of corrections, e.g. the Clarendon Press's Tudor and Stuart Library reprint (1907), or even reprinted Q itself, e.g. the Nonesuch text established by Herbert Farjeon in 1929, and re-issued in 1953;

(3) those which, though not printing a text so close to Q as editions in class (2), have tried to draw closer to Q than did Malone, Dyce, or the Cambridge editors. Wyndham's edition belongs to this class, and so do the editions of Neilson (1906), Ridley (1934), Kittredge (1936), Harrison (1938), and Bush and Harbage (1961).

Outside all these classes lie the facsimiles of Q (see p. xvii, above). The two Variorum editions by Alden (1916) and Rollins (1944) form a class on their own. They rightly reprint Q's text and record variations from it. Each is the work of an excellent scholar. Even the textual apparatus of Rollins's edition, however, is not absolutely complete.

LIST OF EDITIONS COLLATED BY ROLLINS
IN HIS NEW VARIORUM EDITION (1944)

(Brackets indicate lack of date on title-page)

Name of Edition or Editor	Designation used in present edition	Date
First Quarto	Q	1609
John Benson (*Poems: Written by Wil. Shake-speare. Gent.*)	Benson	1640
Bernard Lintot (*Collection of Poems*, II)	Lintot	[1711]*
Charles Gildon (*Works*, VII)	Gildon[1]	1710
Charles Gildon (*Works*, IX)	Gildon[2]	1714
George Sewell (*Works*, VII)	Sewell[1]	1725
George Sewell (*Works*, X)	Sewell[2]	1728
A. Murden, R. Newton, etc. (*Poems*)	Murden	[1741]?
Thomas Ewing (*Poems*)	Ewing	1771
Francis Gentleman (*Poems*)	Gentleman	1774
Thomas Evans (*Poems*)	Evans	1775
Edmond Malone (*Supplement to the Edition of Shakespeare's Plays Published in 1778*, I)	Malone[1]	1780
Edmond Malone (*Plays and Poems*, X)	Malone[2]	1790
James Boswell (*Plays and Poems*, XX)	Boswell	1821
Alexander Dyce (*Poems*, Aldine Poets)	Aldine	1832
Charles Knight (*Works*, 'Tragedies', II)	Knight[1]	1841
J. P. Collier (*Works*, VIII)	Collier[1]	1843
Robert Bell (*Poems*)	Bell	1855
H. N. Hudson (*Works*, XI)	Hudson[1]	1856
Alexander Dyce (*Works*, VI)	Dyce[1]	1857
J. P. Collier (*Shakespeare's Comedies, Histories, etc.*, VI)	Collier[2]	1858
Howard Staunton (*Plays*, III)	Staunton	1860
Nicolaus Delius (*Werke*, VII)	Delius	1860
W. G. Clark and W. Aldis Wright (*Works*, Globe Edition)	Globe	1864
R. G. White (*Works*, I)	White[1]	1865
J. O. Halliwell-Phillipps (*Works*, XVI)	Halliwell-Phillipps	1865
W. G. Clark and W. Aldis Wright (*Works*, IX)	Cambridge[1]	1866

* The *Sonnets* are in Vol. II of the *Collection of Poems*, which, though ordinarily misdated 1709 or 1710, was actually published in 1711.

Alexander Dyce (*Works*, VIII)	Dyce[2]	1866
Charles Knight (*Works*, 'Tragedies', II)	Knight[2]	1867
Alexander Dyce (*Works*, VIII)	Dyce[3]	1876
J. P. Collier (*Plays and Poems*, VIII)	Collier[3]	1878
H. N. Hudson (*Works*, XX, Harvard Edition)	Hudson[2]	1881
Edward Dowden (*Sonnets*)	Dowden	1881
R. G. White (*Mr. William Shakespeare's Comedies . . . and Poems*, IV)	White[2]	1883
W. J. Rolfe (*Shakespeare's Sonnets*)	Rolfe	1883
Thomas Tyler (*Shakespeare's Sonnets*)	Tyler	1890
W. J. Craig (*Works*, Oxford Shakespeare)	Oxford	[1891]
W. Aldis Wright (*Works*, IX, Cambridge Shakespeare)	Cambridge[2]	1893
George Wyndham (*Poems*)	Wyndham	1898
Samuel Butler (*Shakespeare's Sonnets*)	Butler	1899
C. H. Herford (*Works*, X, Eversley Edition)	Herford	1899
H. C. Beeching (*Sonnets*)	Beeching	1904
W. A. Neilson (*Works*)	Neilson[1]	1906
A. H. Bullen (*Works*, X)	Bullen	1907
C. M. Walsh (*Sonnets*)	Walsh	1908
C. K. Pooler (*Sonnets*, Arden Shakespeare)	Pooler[1]	1918
E. B. Reed (*Sonnets*, Yale Shakespeare)	Yale	1923
T. G. Tucker (*Sonnets*)	Tucker	1924
C. K. Pooler (*Sonnets*, 2nd ed. Arden Shakespeare)	Pooler[2]	1931
M. R. Ridley (*Sonnets*)	Ridley	1934
T. Brooke (*Sonnets*)	Brooke	1936
G. L. Kittredge (*Works*)	Kittredge	1936
G. B. Harrison (*Sonnets*, Penguin Shakespeare)	Harrison	1938
W. A. Neilson and C. J. Hill (*Plays and Poems*)	Neilson[2]	1942

Note: The term 'modern editors' as used in our Commentary must be understood to mean the editors of all those editions since Malone's edition of 1790 which were collated by Rollins in his new Variorum Edition (1944), together with the third Arden Edition of C. K. Pooler, Methuen, London, 1943.

We have not collated the Pelican Edition of Bush and Harbage, Baltimore, 1961, since in their Note on the text the editors state that they have followed Q's text, except for 'obvious misprints', and for about forty other departures which they list on p. 19 of their edition.

Addendum to Third Impression

Since this is not a new edition, the above note still holds.

NOTES ON SOME PREVIOUS ANNOTATED
EDITIONS OF THE SONNETS

THE following are brief critical notes on some previous editions of the Sonnets containing Commentaries:

E. MALONE: *Supplement to the Edition of Shakespeare's Plays published in 1778 by Dr. Samuel Johnson and George Steevens*, 2 vols., London, 1780

Volume I contains *Advertisement, Additional Observations* (on the plays), *Venus and Adonis, The Rape of Lucrece*, the *Sonnets, The Passionate Pilgrim*, and *A Lover's Complaint*.

The first important textually critical and critically annotated edition, to which all subsequent editors are heavily indebted. On the Dedication Malone rejects William Harte as 'Mr. W. H.', and bases on a hint from Tyrwhitt concerning 20. 7 a (duly hesitant) conjecture that it was a 'W. Hughes'.

Text 120 pp., with notes at foot. Text based on Q, with a critically suspicious eye to possible errors. There is no proof that Malone had seen Capell's notes on a copy of Lintot's edition of 1711, but it appears that he had discussed the text with 'Mr. C.', who was almost certainly Capell. Malone finds the style, and passages reminiscent of the plays, convincing proof of the authenticity of the Sonnets. Notes, including a number by Steevens and a few other scholars, suggest numerous emendations of Q, and also interpret obscure lines and elucidate archaic usages. Though these notes lack the background of modern linguistic scholarship, they are acute, and though by no means all can be accepted, every subsequent editor has owed a great deal to Malone.

As an instance both of Malone's perceptiveness and of the limitations of eighteenth-century literary sympathies with the manner of the Sonnets, his comment on 132. 9, 'mourning eyes' may serve. He recognizes (despite a misprint 'mourning'—corrected in Malone[2], 1790—of Q's spelling, 'morning') the coincidence of sound, without seeing or admitting the legitimacy of a play between words, observing: 'The two words were, I imagine, in his time pronounced alike.'

The commentary on 127 takes shape as a dialogue between Malone and Steevens on the literary qualities of the sonnet form.

But such 'period' features cannot obscure the immense importance of Malone to later scholarship.

E. MALONE: *The Plays and Poems of William Shakespeare, Volume the Tenth,* Rivington and others, London, 1790

Contains *Venus and Adonis, The Rape of Lucrece,* the *Sonnets, The Passionate Pilgrim, A Lover's Complaint, Titus Andronicus, Romeo and Juliet,* an Appendix (of additional notes), and a Glossarial Index.

Many of the misprints of Malone[1] corrected, and a few conjectures and emendations altered.

E. DOWDEN: *The Sonnets of William Shakespere,* Kegan Paul, London, 1881

Introduction, Part I (35 pp.), gives a broadly non-committal account of the arguments to that date for identification of Southampton or Herbert as the Friend, and of candidatures for the Rival Poet, here favouring Chapman. Maintains the Shakespearean authorship and the reality of the subject-matter against Massey, asserting that 'Shakespeare's Sonnets express his own feelings in his own person'. Dates placed between 1594 and 1605. Part II (74 pp.) summarizes the main features of editions, critical comments, theories about identities, and re-arrangements of order, from Francis Meres (*Palladis Tamia,* 1598) to Mrs. Ashmead Windle (a Baconian) in 1881.

Dowden accepts the general order of Q (though seeing two groups or sequences), and prints in that order (which he thinks has significance), with spelling and punctuation modernized, and a number of emendations embodied in the text, or recorded in the notes. No full and separate *apparatus criticus.*

Notes at end of book (106 pp.), headed for each poem by a brief account of its theme and of its place in the sequence. Though very far from exhaustive, these notes are often acute.

The book is prefaced with a singularly wise 'counsel to a reader of Shakespeare': 'Notes are made to be used, and then cast aside. But the careful student knows how presumptuous a mistake it is to suppose that an offhand reader will always take up the meaning rightly.' And Dowden ends by commending 'the uses of the wary eye and slow approach'.

E. DOWDEN: *The Sonnets of William Shakspere,* in The Parchment Series, Kegan Paul, London, 1881

A shorter version of the above, with Part I of the Introduction very slightly abridged, Part II omitted, and somewhat briefer Notes.

T. TYLER: *Shakespeare's Sonnets, edited with Notes and Introduction*, Nutt, London, 1890

Introduction (154 pp.): 10 pp. on the intention, form, order, and poetical merit of the Sonnets; 3 pp. on criticism of the text. The rest on miscellaneous topics. Dates late 1598 to 1601. Southampton rejected in favour of Herbert as the Friend; Chapman chosen as Rival Poet; Mary Fitton proposed as the Dark Lady. Chapters include 'Shakespeare's Religion', 'Philosophy and Gloom in the Sonnets', 'The Scandal concerning Shakespeare in 1601' (see Sonnets 100–26), 'Seventeenth Century Editions', and 'A Sketch of the History of Interpretation of the Sonnets'. Brief notes below each poem, preceded by a comment on its subject and the situation involved. Very little textual criticism or notice of readings and emendations.

G. WYNDHAM: *The Poems of Shakespeare with an Introduction and Notes*, Methuen, London, 1898

Introduction (140 pp.) lively and discursive on Shakespeare's life and the background in court and literature; though 'dated' and lacking modern scholarship, this shows imaginative understanding of the period. The poems receive consideration as poems, their themes, imagery, and 'verbal melody' being discussed, and the 'problems' being relegated to the first Note. Wyndham attaches extreme significance to 'Platonisms' and Ideas in the Sonnets, a topic he somewhat overstresses. Text follows Q at every opportunity, Wyndham defending Q's readings vigorously.

Notes (130 pp., including 90 on Sonnets); limited in number and detail; some variants recorded, mostly to note where he has changed Q's spelling or (more rarely) punctuation, or to defend Q. About the 'problems' Wyndham eschews dogmatic assertion, but favours a date only a little earlier than 1599 for the earliest, and about 1601–3 for the last sonnets; Mary Fitton for the Dark Lady; Herbert for the Friend; and Drayton for the Rival Poet; but he admits the uncertainty of all evidence and theories. He attaches much importance to the typography of Q, whose italics and capitals he holds to be deliberate and to support his theory of Ideas in the Sonnets, and argues at length for the authenticity and purposive significance of Q's punctuation. Keeps Q's order.

SAMUEL BUTLER: *Shakespeare's Sonnets Reconsidered and in Part Rearranged, with Introductory Chapters, Notes, and a Reprint of the Original 1609 Edition*, Longmans, London, 1899

Introduction (122 pp.) dismisses all previous editors save Malone and Cambridge, ridicules Herbertites and Southamptonites. Rearranges poems to fit a story of his own devising, viz. that, written between 1585 and 1588 (Shakespeare being then between 21 and 24), they address one William Hughes (of whom nothing else is known). Hughes, handsome, and, though not nobly born, of wealthier standing than Shakespeare, is selfish, treacherous, and cruel—one brutal practical joke both shakes the poet's reputation and lames him physically. The poet's infatuation for so unworthy an object finally dies. Notes (at foot) few in number, citing few editions other than Malone and Cambridge, but recording Q where Butler freely and frequently prefers his own reading. Appendix with the Sonnets in Q's text and order, based on Tyler's facsimile, enables identification in Butler's rearrangement. An eccentric edition of small literary-critical value.

H. C. BEECHING: *The Sonnets of Shakespeare, with an Introduction and Notes*, Ginn and Co., Boston, and London, (Athenaeum Press Series), 1904

Introduction (53 pp.); restrained common sense on the subject (friendship for a younger man) and the 'Patron' and 'Literary Exercise' theories. ('The truth at which poetry aims is a truth of feeling, not of incident.') Summarizes the current arguments for Pembroke or Southampton as the Friend, and candidatures for the Rival Poet, without being convinced by any. Eleven pages on form and style of the Sonnets. Dismisses Wyndham's advocacy of the reliability of the Q text, but accepts Q's order as in general defensible, though considers a few poems misplaced. Text, divided into groups of poems, printed without variants or separate textual *apparatus criticus*.

Notes at end (30 pp.) comparatively brief and few in number, but often showing wise and perceptive understanding. Note appended (8 pp.) on Drayton's sonnets, rejecting the view that he was 'Shakespeare's master and not his pupil'.

R. M. ALDEN: *The Sonnets of Shakespeare from the Quarto of 1609 with variorum readings and commentary*, Houghton Mifflin, Boston and New York, 1916

Preface (8 pp.) summarizes history of text and editorial approaches both critical and interpretative, and defines own method. Text (373 pp.) Q, with some variants and emendations recorded below.

Notes printed below and following each sonnet, selected from commentators, with some added by the editor. These notes vary in extent, but contain much invaluable material.

Appendix (105 pp.) contains selected general criticism from Gildon to Mackail, a consideration of the respective merits of Q (1609) and Benson (1640), 16 pp. on the order of the poems, and 12 pp. on the date of composition; 25 pp. discuss Sources and Analogues, and theories regarding the

Friend and the Rival Poet. Five pages are given to *Willobie his Avisa*. Alden values finding himself 'still without a revelation' on Sonnet-problems as 'some evidence that he is still sane'. List of musical settings, and 38 pp. of Bibliography (1609–1916). A valuable edition by no means completely superseded by that of Rollins.

C. K. POOLER: *The Works of Shakespeare: Sonnets* (The Arden Edition), Methuen, London, 1918, revised 1931 and 1943

Includes *A Lover's Complaint*.

Introduction (32 pp.): 10 pp. on texts from Q to Evans (1775), but omitting a discussion of Steevens; 20 pp. outlining the Southampton, the Herbert, and 'Other Theories', but committing the editor on none; a brief note on metre, and an Appendix discussing some recent re-orderings and the date of events referred to in 107. Chief readings and emendations given beneath text; fairly full notes at foot. This has long been the principal student's edition, and has proved its value.

T. G. TUCKER: *The Sonnets of Shakespeare Edited from the Quarto of 1609 with Introduction and Commentary*, Cambridge University Press, London, 1924

Introduction (75 pp.) outlines the 'Problems', on which he remains non-committal, though favouring 1592–1601 for most of the sonnets, and Herbert for the Friend. Gives 20 pp. to the Sonnets 'as poetical compositions', their construction and themes, their imagery and Platonic echoes.

Text with a few variant readings at foot: varies Q's readings and punctuation, sometimes to conform with rather personal or over-ingenious interpretations.

Commentary (150 pp.) full and good, though, as already observed, at times too ingenious; gives more notice than earlier commentators to intricacies and ambiguities of diction, and to the nature and movement of the imagery. Follows Q's order of the poems: attaches little value to Q's typography and punctuation. Index to Notes, but no glossary.

An edition we have found most valuable, though we cannot accept all Tucker's subtleties of interpretation.

C. F. T. BROOKE: *Shakespeare's Sonnets Edited with Introduction and Notes*, Yale University Press and Oxford University Press, London, 1936

Chiefly devoted to rearranging the order of the poems. Introduction (81 pp.): 7 pp. on the Shakespearean Sonnet (some of its formal qualities); dates the poems 1592–6; 37 pp. on regrouping; 9 pp. of detailed criticism of Q as a text, containing valuable observations; a note (2½ pp.) on MS copies known; 7 pp. on the Poet, constructing a biography consonant with Brooke's own ordering of the poems. Southampton accepted as the Friend.

Text printed alone with Q's readings at foot where Brooke has not adopted them. Q's order rearranged.

Notes at back, limited in number and scope, largely citations of other commentators. No glossary.

Correspondences between Brooke's order and Q's printed at beginning, his own order first, which makes reference a trifle awkward, as there is no index of first lines.

H. E. ROLLINS: *A New Variorum Edition of Shakespeare: The Sonnets,* J. P. Lippincott, Philadelphia, 1944, 2 vols. 4to: pp. xix + 404, and 531

The indispensable edition for reference. A superb scholarly production collating the 13 known copies of Q, and 53 other editions from Benson (1640) to Neilson and Hill (1942). Twenty-seven others, not collated, are sometimes referred to, or represented by readings cited, in the Commentary and Appendices.

Volume I prints Q's text, with virtually all major and many less significant variant readings and conjectures beneath, followed by extensive citation of critical commentaries on the poems in question and cogent (and not infrequently pungent) comments by the editor.

Volume II gives the history of the text (41 pp.) and discusses the authenticity of Q (11 pp.). There follow discussions of the arrangement of the poems (with a table showing 20 of the many re-orderings), and detailed summaries, arranged chronologically, of commentators' theories on possible 'sources', the question of autobiography, the Dedication, identification of persons (the Friend, Dark Woman, Rival Poet, etc.), and on the question of homosexuality. Twelve pages are given to listing musical settings, 75 to discussing the vogue of the Sonnets in Britain and abroad, and 37 to representative quotations of general criticism of the Sonnets.

D. BUSH and A. HARBAGE: *Sonnets: William Shakespeare,* Penguin Books, Baltimore, 1961

Introduction (12 pp.) sanely factual on 'sonnet problems', brief notes on the sonnet tradition, Shakespeare's use of imagery, the structure and texture of the poems, and on universal emotions and values in the Sonnets.

Text in modern spelling and punctuation, but following Q closely, emending only 'obvious misprints' and about forty other readings. Very brief but well-considered glosses at foot.

M. SEYMOUR-SMITH: *Shakespeare's Sonnets, Edited with an Introduction and Commentary*, Heinemann, London, 1963

Introduction (39 pp.): 1 p. on the sonnet before Shakespeare; finds Daniel's *Delia* 'must have been one of Shakespeare's models'; 5 pp. on Q and Benson. Dates 1594 (for most); 6 pp. on theories of identity of Friend—'none, including those of Southampton and Herbert, is more than a guess'; Lucy Negro, prostitute, 'not impossible as the Mistress'. Favours Chapman as the Rival Poet. Two pages on *Willobie His Avisa*; 10 pp. on question of homosexuality, and Shakespeare's relation with the Friend.

Text Q verbatim save for 'obvious misprints', Q being 'emended only where the punctuation or spelling . . . is the undoubted result of a misprint'. The argument here a little confused: Q's punctuation referred to (pp. 37 and 38) as 'Shakespeare's punctuation' and 'the Shakespearian original', but p. 38 also states that 'the writer, if he thought about it at all, left the punctuation . . . to the printer'. Similar ambidexterous reasoning allows selection of readings and interpretations (69. 14 and 146. 2).

Brief Select Bibliography.

Notes (71 pp.) fairly full and often perceptive, though weakened by excessive reliance on Q's typography and some arbitrariness conflicting with the editor's objections (p. 38) to modernization.

J. DOVER WILSON: *The Sonnets* (The New Shakespeare), Cambridge University Press, Cambridge, 1966.

Introduction (110 pp.) outlines first publication, entertainingly dismisses Benson, but with borrowed inaccuracies; proposes the Dark Woman as provider of the MSS to Thorpe; 46 pleasantly discursive pages on relation of Poet to Friend; 20 pp. identifying Pembroke with Mr. W. H.; 12 pp. on possible influences on Shakespeare as sonneteer.

Text without variants on page follows Malone fairly closely for text and Q for punctuation, in our opinion overvaluing this aspect of Q.

Six and a half pages of Bibliography and 179 pp. of Notes at end of book, where many textual variants are noted, but many difficulties unclarified or even untouched. Interesting observations (often based on Dowden or borrowed from him) on the relations of individual sonnets to their neighbours. Summarizes Brents Stirling's argument for re-ordering nos. 127–54, and prints at end a List of the Sonnets in the Conjectured Order of Writing.

NOTE ON THE USE OF THE SLUR

FOLLOWING a practice common, in printing verse, at the time (and, indeed, till much later), Q generally prints an apostrophe for a vowel (usually 'e') to indicate either its complete suppression or a lightening or semi-elision of a syllable. This generally occurs in Q where '*the*' precedes an unaccented initial vowel, as in '*th'expence*' (30. 8, 129. 1) and '*th'account*' (58. 3); though a few cases of other kinds occur, e.g. '*th'course*' (115. 8), '*for't*' (101. 10), '*wer't*' (125. 1). Whether in fact the syllable was intended to be completely suppressed (as interestingly argued by Paul Ramsey in a recent article)* or simply lightened or semi-elided, is a controversial matter. On the other hand, we are quite clear that to print the apostrophe in a modern edition would often encourage a now unnatural reading, drawing attention away from the flow and meaning of the poem. We are convinced, indeed, that the large number of editors since the eighteenth century who have simply extracted the apostrophes and printed (for example) '*the expense*', '*the account*', '*the course*', and so on, have taken the right decision as against printing the apostrophe; and we are glad to see that Dame Helen Gardner, in her admirable new edition of *The Oxford Book of English Verse*, has taken this course for those Shakespeare sonnets she has selected to print. In the original printing of the present volume we were, however, apprehensive (perhaps unduly) that readers might separate the words too rigidly, and we therefore adopted in some fifteen cases the device of a slur below the line, joining the two words, e.g. '*The͜ expense*'. We now think that it may well be best to leave the method of reading in almost all cases to the good sense of the reader. We have, however, retained the slur in four cases, lest a reader might be tempted to misread the line by misplacing stress or unduly slowing the line. (See 101.10, 112.14, 120.6, 125.1.)

* 'The Syllables of Shakespeare's Sonnets', in *New Essays on Shakespeare's Sonnets*, ed. Hilton Landry, AMS Press, New York, 1976, pp. 193–215.

THE SONNETS

TEXT AND COMMENTARY

TO . THE . ONLIE . BEGETTER . OF .
THESE . INSVING . SONNETS .
Mr. W. H. ALL . HAPPINESSE .
AND . THAT . ETERNITIE .
PROMISED .

BY .

OVR . EVER-LIVING . POET .

WISHETH .

THE . WELL-WISHING .
ADVENTVRER . IN .
SETTING .
FORTH .

T. T.

A NOTE ON THE DEDICATION

THIS apparently straightforward dedication of a volume of poems, signed with the initials of the publisher (Thomas Thorpe), and seemingly addressed to somebody only indicated by initials, has raised a welter of ingenious speculations and conflicting interpretations. There is no evidence that the Dedication stimulated attention until very late in the eighteenth century, but since then it has been the playground of theorists who have allowed it to distract their interest from the poems as poems. As the late Professor Rollins wrote in 1944: 'No doubt the sonnets would be more often read for their poetry today if Thorpe had discarded his own thirty words!'

The chief enigmas embodied in the wording are as follows:

(1) What is a 'begetter'?
(2) What does 'onlie' mean?
(3) Who was Mr. W. H.?
(4) Who was the Well-wishing Adventurer?
(5) What is the meaning of 'setting forth'?
(6) What does 'promised' mean, and to whom was the 'eternitie' 'promised'?
(7) Who was T.T.?
(8) What is the syntax of the Dedication?

1 *Begetter*] The chief answers have been: (*a*) 'inspirer'; (*b*) 'procurer' (i.e. of the manuscript for the publisher).

Linguistic usage favours 'inspirer'. Although the *verb* 'beget' had earlier borne the sense 'to get, to acquire', no example is cited in *OED* after 1393, other than a sentence from Hamlet's advice to the players: 'You must acquire and beget a temperance that may give it smoothness', where the word does not mean *procuring* something external but *engendering* a quality in oneself. A further point is that the examples cited by *OED* always connote acquiring some thing or goods *for oneself*. This would argue against 'begetter' meaning 'procurer *for another person*', though it would still leave *possible* the sense 'procurer for himself'.

The passage from Dekker's *Satiromastix* often cited in support of the sense (of the *verb* 'beget') 'procure for another' is, in fact, as Samuel Butler

3

pointed out, spoken by a Welshman, Sir Rhys Ap Vaughan, who is held up to ridicule throughout the play by his travesties of English speech. The passage reads as follows: 'If I fall sansomely upon the Widdow, I have some cossens German at Court, shall beget you the reversion of the Master of the Kings Revels.' Other words in this very passage make it hardly respectable evidence of correct English usage.

Moreover, the *noun* 'begetter' is only cited by *OED* as having two senses: (1) 'a procreator'; (2) 'the agent that originates, produces or occasions'. This passage is cited under (2), where in all the other examples the word bears a figurative, theological sense, e.g. in Golding, *De Mornay's Work concerning the Trueness of the Christian Religion*, iii. 28: 'The onely one God . . . the Begetter of the Soules of the other Gods'. In no case cited there or elsewhere could the word mean 'procurer'.

Thus, whatever the dedicator may have intended the word to mean, it would not to the contemporary reader have conveyed the meaning 'procurer'. If the dedicator intended such a meaning he would, therefore, have been writing in a cryptic and private language. In any case, however, since he was himself of that time, the probability against his having even *intended* such a meaning is tremendous.

Against the meaning 'inspirer' it has been urged that the *Sonnets* are not all addressed to the same person. In answer, however, it has been pointed out that the first 126 sonnets (or, at all events, almost all of them) seem to be addressed to the same person, and that those addressed to a woman are printed at the end of the book; so that the allusion in the Dedication would be substantially accurate if 'begetter' meant 'inspirer'.

2 *Onlie*] This is taken by almost all commentators to mean 'sole', whether they think the reference is to the 'inspirer' or to the 'procurer'. There is, however, an alternative sense, namely, 'incomparable', 'peerless' (cf. *OED*, sense 5), and, as William Sharp, who has anticipated us in suggesting this meaning, points out (*Songs, Poems and Sonnets of Shakespeare*, Newcastle, 1885; Introduction, p. 23), the word is used in this sense in Sonnet 1, line 10. This meaning would possibly sort somewhat better with 'inspirer' than with 'procurer'.

3 *Mr. W. H.*] What Rollins called the 'guessing contest' about Mr. W. H. was started by Tyrwhitt and Farmer in the late eighteenth century. The chief candidates nominated by commentators for the honour of the designation have been: (*a*) William Herbert, Third Earl of Pembroke (1580–1630); (*b*) Henry Wriothesley, Third Earl of Southampton (1573–1624), whose initials would then be reversed; (*c*) William Hall, a piratical printer; (*d*) William Hervey, stepfather of the Earl of Southampton; (*e*) William Hathaway, Shakespeare's brother-in-law; (*f*) William Hughes

4

(Hewes), who has been variously identified; (*g*) William Himself. As stated in our Preface, we have no intention of adjudicating between their rival claims.

4 *The Well-wishing Adventurer*] There seems to be pretty general agreement that this was Thomas Thorpe, who, as the publisher of the *Sonnets*, was 'venturing' some capital.

5 *Setting forth*] The high-flown language of the Dedication is characteristic not only of the time but also, in particular, of Thorpe himself. Just as 'adventurer' would have suggested the enterprises of merchant venturers, so 'setting forth' would have suggested the sailing of one of their ships, though it would also have suggested the process of printing and publishing a book.

6 (*a*) *The meaning of 'promised'*] Two meanings are possible: (i) 'promised in the specific words of the poems' (e.g. in Sonnets 18 and 19); (ii) 'augured by the quality of the poet's work'.

(*b*) *To whom was the 'eternitie' 'promised'?*] (i) If Mr. W. H. was the *inspirer* it was 'promised' to him in whichever sense is the right one; (ii) if he was not the *inspirer* but only the *procurer*, it was 'promised' to him in sense (*a*)(ii), not in sense (*a*)(i), in which, indeed, it was 'promised' only to the *inspirer*.

7 *T.T.*] Undoubtedly Thomas Thorpe, the publisher of the *Sonnets*.

8 *The syntax of the Dedication*] The printing of the Dedication is lapidary, i.e. closely similar to that of many inscriptions in stone. It has a full stop after every word. The pointing, therefore, does not help in determining the syntax. Some scholars have seen 'wisheth' as concluding a sentence, and having 'Mr. W. H.' as its subject. The French scholar Chasles based this view on the leading between the central five lines, but, as Massey has pointed out, this no more divides them from what follows than from what precedes. It seems, indeed, pretty evident that the subject of 'wisheth' is 'T.T.'.

1 2 rose] Q: *Rose* (in italics). Interpreted by some editors emblematically as the 'Idea' beauty. (On Platonic echoes in the *Sonnets* see the editions of Wyndham, pp. cxvi ff and Tucker, pp. lxxx–lxxxii). Others, accepting Q, see a proper name here—a cue for biographical inquest. But 'rose' is a familiar figure for youthful beauty.

4 tender] Contrast 'riper' (line 3) and cf. line 12.

bear his memory] present a living memorial of him to others.

5 contracted] 'betrothed' (bound by exclusive contract). There may be a secondary sense of 'your attention restricted to'.

6 self-substantial] consuming its own substance, candle-like—so in the end destructive (cf. lines 13–14). In self-consuming contemplation of self, beauty, like Narcissus, dooms itself to barren brevity.

10 only] 'principal', 'chief' (Schmidt, *Shakespeare-Lexicon*); 'peerless', 'pre-eminent' (*OED*).

gaudy] 'joyously bedecked' (lacks the modern pejorative sense). 'Gauds' = jewels and finery. Cf. also Lat. *gaudia*.

11 Within . . . bud] The unexpanded flower betokens not only promise but incompletion. 'So longe is it called the budde of a rose, as it is not a perfyte rose.' Wynkyn de Worde.

content] probably (1) that which is contained, (2) contentment. Schmidt admits (1) only in the plural, but cf. the ambiguity in *T&C.* I. ii. 318–19: 'Then though my heart's content true love doth bear, Nothing of that shall from my eyes appear.' Sense (1) consorts closer with 'buriest', and might imply, partly, though not solely, progeny.

12 tender] as in 'tender years'. Cf. line 4.

churl] 'miser' (*OED.* 6). Cf. Coverdale, *Is.* xxxii. 5 (1535): 'then shal the nygarde be no more called gentle nor the churle liberall'. The resulting oxymoron with 'tender' would strike an Elizabethan, particularly in view of the other current sense of 'ill-bred fellow' (who will not breed!).

mak'st waste in niggarding] i.e. the Friend is wasting, by hoarding, what should be used for increase. Cf. 4. 5 and *R&J.* I. i. 223.

14 To eat] i.e. 'by being the kind of glutton who eats . . .'.

by the grave and thee] The world's due is propagation of the Friend's virtues in his heirs. His celibacy condemns these gifts to be twice devoured —ultimately by his death and meanwhile by himself alone.

6

I

FROM FAIREST creatures we desire increase,
That thereby beauty's rose might never die,
But as the riper should by time decease
His tender heir might bear his memory: 4
But thou, contracted to thine own bright eyes,
Feed'st thy light's flame with self-substantial fuel,
Making a famine where abundance lies,
Thyself thy foe, to thy sweet self too cruel: 8
Thou that art now the world's fresh ornament
And only herald to the gaudy spring
Within thine own bud buriest thy content,
And, tender churl, mak'st waste in niggarding: 12
    Pity the world, or else this glutton be—
    To eat the world's due, by the grave and thee.

2 1 *forty winters*] probably 'When you are pretty old' rather than 'in another forty winters'. See Elze (*Jahrbuch*, 1876, xi. 288–94) for examples of 'forty' used as an indefinite number.

1–4 *besiege . . . trenches . . . totter'd weed*] The sustained image is the ragged uniform of the long-besieged defender ('you' and beauty) of the city (youth and vigour) against time.

3 *proud livery*] splendid array of beauty. There are two metaphors: (1) clothing, and, derivatively from line 2, (2) flowers of beauty's field.

4 *totter'd*] So Q and often in Elizabethan usage (= 'tatter'd'). Cf. 26. 11.

weed] garment, but continuing the botanical metaphor of line 3.

3, 4] The contrasting metaphors are almost certainly those of the fine clothes of a nobleman's servant and the rags of a beggar.

6 *lusty*] 'full of animal spirits' (Schmidt), the commonest meaning in Shakespeare.

8] 'Would be a shameful admission of all-devouring greed, and self-praise given amiss for profitless living.' Such hypallagic adjectival usage is common in Shakespeare.

9 *use*] echoing 'thriftless' (line 8): investment instead of unprofitable idleness of capital (youth and beauty). *OED* sense I. 4 (abridged) is 'the act . . . of using . . . land or other property so as to derive revenue, profit, or other benefit from such'. There is also probably a sexual meaning.

11 *sum my count*] render a balanced audit, 'square my account'.

make my old excuse] not 'make my same old excuse' but 'in my old age justify by his existence my having lived'.

12 *by succession*] one of the many instances of the strict use of legal terms in the *Sonnets*.

2

WHEN FORTY winters shall besiege thy brow,
And dig deep trenches in thy beauty's field,
Thy youth's proud livery, so gaz'd on now,
Will be a totter'd weed of small worth held: 4
Then being ask'd where all thy beauty lies,
Where all the treasure of thy lusty days,
To say within thine own deep sunken eyes
Were an all-eating shame, and thriftless praise.   8
How much more praise deserv'd thy beauty's use
If thou couldst answer: 'This fair child of mine
Shall sum my count, and make my old excuse',—
Proving his beauty by succession thine!   12
 This were to be new made when thou art old,
 And see thy blood warm when thou feel'st it cold.

3 3 *fresh*] not faded or stale—for a somewhat similar use cf. 'fresh air'.

repair] 'condition'. Cf. 'to keep in good repair'. Not pleonastic with 'renewest'; nor evidence for identity-hunters that the Friend's house or family is in decline. Cf. 10. 7–8, note.

4 *unbless*] 'fail to bless' (with maternity).

5 *unear'd*] 'unploughed' (cf. Old English *erian*). Cf. *A&C.* I. iv. 49: 'Make the sea serve them, which they ear and wound With keels.' The figure is common enough with reference to fertility, and, as J. Q. Adams points out (*Life of William Shakespeare*, Houghton, Boston, and Constable, London, 1923), there is at least a suspicion of a pun on 'husband' in 'husbandry' (line 6).

7–8] 'Or who is so foolish (*OED* sense 3) (and/or 'infatuated' (*OED* sense 2)) as to make himself a living sepulchre of his self-love, as he will do if he denies himself the satisfaction of self-perpetuation?' Cf. *V & A*, 757–60.

9 *glass*] 'mirror', as usual in Elizabethan English. Cf. *Lucrece*, 1758, where Lucretius addresses his dead daughter: 'Poor broken glass, I often did behold In thy sweet semblance my old-age new-born!' The word itself probably suggested the transition to the image of 'windows' in line 11— the other 'frame' through which vision occurs.

11 *windows*] Though in Shakespeare's mature plays successive images grow out of one another—the second, suggested by some association of the first, leading in turn to others which may never return to the starting-point—in the *Sonnets* the progression is often (though not always, e.g. Sonnet 60) closer-knit, more recapitulatory, and cumulative in impact. (Cf. Sonnet 4, *General Note*.) Though 'windows' here may have grown out of 'glass', we do not turn our back on the mirror, and looking out through a lattice, forget entirely the earlier figure of speech. The man looks *through* the windows of old age—a figure not tied literally and restrictively to his eyes. In a mirror his wrinkled face would not show him to himself as he once was; but in that other 'mirror' of his child he can see his youth renewed. The expression parallels but does not merely repeat 'thy mother's glass' in line 9. Just as the windows are not simply the man's eyes, so the child is not merely the mirror into which he looks.

13 *remember'd*] 'commemorated'. Cf. *1H4.* V. iv. 100: 'Thy ignomy sleep with thee in the grave, But not remember'd in thy epitaph.'

14 *image*] There seems to be a threefold conceit, 'image' being (1) 'memorial', (2) 'mirror-image' (cf. line 1), (3) 'copy' (i.e. son, cf. 11. 14).

3

Look in thy glass, and tell the face thou viewest
Now is the time that face should form another,
Whose fresh repair if now thou not renewest
Thou dost beguile the world, unbless some mother.   4
For where is she so fair whose unear'd womb
Disdains the tillage of thy husbandry?
Or who is he so fond will be the tomb
Of his self-love to stop posterity?   8
Thou art thy mother's glass, and she in thee
Calls back the lovely April of her prime;
So thou through windows of thine age shalt see
Despite of wrinkles this thy golden time.   12
   But if thou live remember'd not to be,
    Die single, and thine image dies with thee.

4 *General Note:* The cumulative interlinked imagery of many groups in the *Sonnets*—one poem echoing the images of perhaps two or more preceding, while in its turn introducing a new image, itself echoed in those succeeding —is well illustrated here. The legacy of beauty to be held for the benefit of posterity, the contrast of capital put to profit or left idle, the account to be rendered, catch up themes from Sonnets 1 and 2, which will through their recombination here in terms of usury lead on to further development in Sonnet 6.

1 *unthrifty*] improvident for posterity. Cf. 'thriftless' in 2. 8.

2 *legacy*] Cf. 'the world's due' (1. 14), 'by succession' (2. 12) and line 6 below.

3 *Nature's . . . nothing*] Nature's bestowal of beauty (on you) is not an absolute gift.

In line 4 it becomes evident that it is only even a *loan* to those who are generous, which the Friend is not, since he 'beguiles the world' by not 'renewing' his beauty's 'fresh repair'.

3] 'Gives' carries a stress that contrasts it with 'lend'.

4 *frank*] 'liberal', 'bountiful'. Cf. *All's W.* I. ii. 20: 'Frank nature . . hath well compos'd thee'.

free] 'generous', 'open-handed'. The alliteration may reinforce a word-play which is both English and bilingual (cf. It. *franco* = 'free').

5 *niggard*] cf. 'waste in niggarding' (1. 12).

7 *Profitless*] cf. 'unthrifty' (line 1) and 'thriftless' (2. 8).

use] (1) 'use up', (2) 'employ profitlessly'—in paradox with 'usurer'. 6. 5 gives a further variation.

8 *live*] really benefit from living, as the childless niggard does not.

10 *deceive*] 'defraud'. Cf. the general sense of 2. 7–8.

12 *audit*] cf. 'sum my count' (2. 11).

13 *unus'd*] not invested.

13–14] There may be allusion to the Parable of the Talents, as also in Sonnets 6 and 9.

14 *executor*] clinching the testamentary image recurrent since Sonnet 1.

th'executor] So Q and many editors. Capell, Malone and some editors: *thy*. But Q text allows choice between 'thy' and 'the'.

4

Unthrifty loveliness, why dost thou spend
Upon thy self thy beauty's legacy?
Nature's bequest gives nothing, but doth lend,
And being frank she lends to those are free: 4
Then, beauteous niggard, why dost thou abuse
The bounteous largess given thee to give?
Profitless usurer, why dost thou use
So great a sum of sums, yet canst not live?   8
For having traffic with thyself alone
Thou of thyself thy sweet self dost deceive:
Then how when nature calls thee to be gone—
What acceptable audit canst thou leave?   12
    Thy unus'd beauty must be tomb'd with thee,
    Which usèd lives th'executor to be.

5 1 *hours*] a disyllable, as often. (Q: *howers*). The word refers, not to any one period of time past, but to 'never-resting time' in general. (Cf. line 5).

gentle] perhaps playing, as Tucker suggests, on (1) 'kindly', cp. the 'tyrants' (line 3), and (2) *gentil* = 'refined' (as the result of the work shows).

The wording of the line suggests the personification of 'hours 'as high-born ladies weaving a picture.

2 *lovely gaze*] 'the lovely object (of vision)'. See *OED*, sense 1.

4 *unfair*] 'deprive of beauty'.

fairly] probably 'in beauty', though Tucker suggests 'while still in its fair state', and quotes Sonnet 11. 3: 'youngly' = 'when young'.

6 *confounds*] 'ruins', 'utterly destroys' (cf. 60. 8, 64. 10).

9 *distillation*] The essence of summer distilled into perfume. The abstract concept of essence seems also to be implied here, and not merely the concrete product as in line 13.

11] 'The whole sensory impact and the fruit of beauty would be lost when the beauty itself faded.'

12] 'And we should have neither the beauty itself nor anything to remind us of it.' A similar ellipsis occurs in 65. 2. For 'remembrance' cf. *Oth*. III. iii. 291: 'This was her first remembrance from the Moor.'

14 *leese*] frequent enough for 'lose' until the seventeenth century, though Shakespeare uses it nowhere else.

5

THOSE HOURS that with gentle work did frame
The lovely gaze where every eye doth dwell
Will play the tyrants to the very same,
And that unfair which fairly doth excel: 4
For never-resting time leads summer on
To hideous winter and confounds him there,
Sap check'd with frost, and lusty leaves quite gone,
Beauty o'ersnow'd and bareness everywhere: 8
Then were not summer's distillation left
A liquid prisoner pent in walls of glass,
Beauty's effect with beauty were bereft,
Nor it nor no remembrance what it was.   12
    But flowers distill'd, though they with winter meet,
    Leese but their show: their substance still lives sweet.

6 1 *ragged*] 'rough', 'harsh', but also probably, as Tucker suggests, 'producing raggedness'.

The image involves the association of leaves torn from trees, which are left 'ragged'. This echoes the 'totter'd weed' of 2. 4, and contrasts with the 'proud livery' of youth (and of spring—cf. 'proud-pied April', 98. 2).

2 *distill'd*] cf. 5. 9 and 5. 13.

3 *some vial*] i.e. the womb of a mother.

treasure] fill with treasure (of beauty).

4 *self-kill'd*] cf. 3. 7 and 4. 13.

5 *use . . . usury*] Pooler suggests that this dates the sonnet before 1597. The statute 13 Eliz. cap. 8 (1571) revived a statute of Henry VIII making usury legal, while still calling it sinful (and so, presumably, 'forbidden' morally). 39 Eliz. cap. 18 (1597) admitted it as 'very necessary and profitable'. These facts may not, however, be reflected in this sonnet, whose imagery seems to refer simply to the general problem of the moral status of usury.

5–6] The construction is 'that use which happies . . . is not . . . usury'. Some modern editors retain Q's comma after usury, but this does not seem to be correct modern usage.

5–10] A difficult passage, surprisingly neglected by almost all commentators. A fair sense is made if Nature is taken as the usurer (cf. 4. 3), and the borrower as the Friend (see note on line 6, below). The usury would not be iniquitous if the rate of interest were a hundred or even a thousand per cent, for the borrower would be made happier in direct proportion. Ten children would make him ten times happier than one child would. Perhaps a still better sense, however, is given by taking 'use' as having its contemporary sexual meaning and as referring to the Friend's intercourse with a wife who would 'pay the willing loan' (bear him children).

6 *pay*] 'pay interest on' (viz. by begetting children).

willing] bounteously granted.

7 *That's*] meaning 'i.e.', the antecedent being either 'pay' or 'use' according to the interpretation of lines 5–10 (see note above).

8 *ten for one*] Pooler suggests a reference here to ten per cent as the highest rate of interest allowed by the Henry VIII statute (cf. line 5, note); but the rate suggested in line 8 is, surely, one thousand per cent!

10 *refigur'd*] repeated in facsimile.

12 *thee*] 'yourself'.

13 *self-will'd*] just possibly playing on (1) 'obstinate', (2) 'bequeathed to yourself alone.'

16

6

THEN LET not winter's ragged hand deface
In thee thy summer ere thou be distill'd:
Make sweet some vial; treasure thou some place
With beauty's treasure ere it be self-kill'd: 4
That use is not forbidden usury
Which happies those that pay the willing loan—
That's for thyself to breed another thee,
Or ten times happier be it ten for one;   8
Ten times thyself were happier than thou art,
If ten of thine ten times refigur'd thee:
Then what could death do if thou shouldst depart
Leaving thee living in posterity?   12
    Be not self-will'd, for thou art much too fair
    To be death's conquest and make worms thine heir.

14 *conquest*] The 'inheritance' images in these early sonnets suggest
much less the sense 'spoils of war' than the meaning in Scottish law, 'real
estate acquired otherwise than by inheritance . . . as opposed to "heri-
tage"' (*OED*). The military in place of the legal sense here would weaken
any antithesis with 'heir'.

7 1 *gracious*] a richer word than in current modern usage, involving simultaneously the senses (1) regal or sovereign, (2) emanating and bestowing beauty, and (3) spiritually beneficent.

light] not just daylight, but the sun itself (cf. *Gen.* i. 16: 'And God made two great lights').

2 *under*] (1) 'earthly', 'from below', (2) 'of his subjects', as Tucker alone among editors observes.

4 *Serving*] (1) 'worshipping', (2) 'paying a subject's homage'. Both senses anticipate 'sacred majesty'.

5 *steep-up*] 'high and precipitous' (Schmidt). Cf. *The Passionate Pilgrim*, 9. 4. Pooler (who omits the hyphen) suggests that this images the Ptolemaic conception of the sun's sphere, as distinct from its Copernican orbit. Phoebus would be driving his chariot up the steep convex slope of the sphere.

6] Either (1) 'Though now (at noon) middle-aged, the sun still has the strength and splendour of a young god'; or (2), taking (with Tucker) *his* = 'its', i.e. 'strong youth's', 'Looking now as youth, once strong, will look in middle age.'

7 *Yet*] pleonastic with 'still' (i.e. of time, not 'nevertheless').

9 *highmost pitch*] more probably just 'the very highest point' than a hawking metaphor.

weary] conveying the composite image of an exhausted driver and team.

9–12] Several editors refer to the old superstition of worshipping the rising but not the setting sun. It is natural to ask whether the Elizabethans did not admire sunsets less than the Romantics were to do.

11 *converted*] merely 'turned'.

12 *tract*] 'path'.

13] 'So you, outlasting your prime . . .'. For 'outgoing' = 'outlasting' cf. *A & C.* III. ii. 60–61: 'The time shall not outgo my thinking on you.' To take 'outgoing' as intransitive (= (1) dying or (2) declining) would be unsatisfactory. (1) would not fit the simile of lines 1–12, where Phoebus outlasts his prime; (2) would require '*from* thy noon'.

14 *son*] The whole tenour of the sonnet suggests the conceit 'son/sun'.

7

Lo, in the orient when the gracious light
Lifts up his burning head, each under eye
Doth homage to his new-appearing sight,
Serving with looks his sacred majesty;   4
And having climb'd the steep-up heavenly hill,
Resembling strong youth in his middle age,
Yet mortal looks adore his beauty still,
Attending on his golden pilgrimage: 8
But when from highmost pitch, with weary car,
Like feeble age he reeleth from the day,
The eyes ('fore duteous) now converted are
From his low tract, and look another way: 12
    So thou thyself out-going in thy noon,
    Unlook'd on diest unless thou get a son.

8 1 *Music to hear*] Vocative. 'O you, to hear whom is to hear music . . .'. Cf. 129. 4: 'rude, cruel, not to trust'.

hear'st] either referring (1) as Tucker suggests, to the Friend's general attitude, or, quite possibly, (2) to the occasion that gives rise to the poem.

sadly] 'joylessly', rather than 'tearfully', which would clash with line 6.

3–4] 'Why do you bother to listen to something which bores you, or do you perhaps take pleasure in being bored?' ('Annoy' = '*ennuy*', Cotgrave-Sherwood, *Dictionary*, ed. 1632).

5–6] 'If the harmonious agreement of notes in tune and in just musical relation is distasteful to you.'

7 *sweetly chide*] (1) 'gently reprove'; (2) i.e. their sweetness is itself a reproof to you.

7–8 *who confounds . . . bear*] This seems to have at least two meanings: (1) Musical: 'who through ignorance of music hear only one blurred confusion where you should distinguish the separate parts'. ('In singleness' seems to carry both the sense of ignorance and the sense of failure to distinguish. As to 'bear', though the performer can only 'bear' one part at a time, it might be said that an initiated listener could 'bear' all parts simultaneously.) (2) Matrimonial: 'who, by remaining single, suppress those roles (of husband and father) which you should play'.

9–12] If the image is still that of several parts in harmony, then these are said to 'strike in' or combine to form an agreeable composition. There is, however, the possibility that the image has changed to that of instruments strung in 'courses', e.g. lutes, where one string being plucked makes its fellow resound in sympathy, and these in turn produce a harmonic which enriches the tone. Either of these interpretations can involve 'sire', 'mother', and 'child'. 'Note' may also carry a sense of 'message'. Massey aptly cites Sidney, *Arcadia*, 1590 ed., p. 262b: 'Can one string make as good music as a consort?'.

14 '*Thou . . . none*'] 'Single, and so heirless, you are doomed to extinction.' Possibly also echoing the proverb 'One is not a number.' Cf. 136. 8, note.

Harmony)

8

M<small>USIC TO</small> hear, why hear'st thou music sadly?
Sweets with sweets war not, joy delights in joy:
Why lov'st thou that which thou receiv'st not gladly,
Or else receiv'st with pleasure thine annoy?   4
If the true concord of well-tunèd sounds
By unions married do offend thine ear,
They do but sweetly chide thee, who confounds
In singleness the parts that thou shouldst bear: 8
Mark how one string, sweet husband to another,
Strikes each in each by mutual ordering,
Resembling sire, and child, and happy mother,
Who all in one one pleasing note do sing: 12
  Whose speechless song, being many, seeming one,
  Sings this to thee: 'Thou single wilt prove none'.

9 4 *makeless*] 'mateless' (as in 'I sing of a mayden that is makeles').

5 *still*] 'ever', 'continually' (a common meaning).

7 *private*] The grief of other bereavements is 'private', whereas the whole world will be his widow.

9 *Look,*] 'only consider', as often in modern colloquial usage. Cf. 11. 11. Capell added the comma, not in Q, and is followed by most modern editors.

10 *his*] 'its'.

11 *beauty's waste*] i.e. beauty wasted; perhaps, secondarily, beauty's wasting away.

12 *user*] (1) 'he who has the right to use', and probably (2) 'waster' or 'spendthrift'.

unus'd . . . user] As in 4. 7–10 and 6. 5, the primary metaphor is from usury.

11–12] These lines probably also refer to the deterioration of things or materials not duly employed. Cf. *Ham.* IV. iv. 36 ff: 'He that made us . . . gave us not . . . that . . . god-like reason To fust in us unus'd.'

14 *murderous shame*] 'shameful murder'. The construction is frequent in Elizabethan English.

9

Is it for fear to wet a widow's eye
That thou consum'st thyself in single life?
Ah! if thou issueless shalt hap to die,
The world will wail thee like a makeless wife;   4
The world will be thy widow and still weep
That thou no form of thee hast left behind,
When every private widow well may keep
By children's eyes her husband's shape in mind: 8
Look, what an unthrift in the world doth spend
Shifts but his place, for still the world enjoys it;
But beauty's waste hath in the world an end,
And kept unus'd the user so destroys it: 12
   No love toward others in that bosom sits
   That on himself such murderous shame commits.

10 1 *For shame deny*] 'Deny for very shame'. Q has no stop after 'shame'. Most modern editors insert an exclamation mark, but to read these two words as a separate exclamation both creates an abrupt and violently-broken rhythm inconsistent with Shakespeare's practice in the *Sonnets* and also distorts the idiom. Wyndham first among modern editors observed the offence to rhythm of an inserted stop.

shame . . . love] J. Q. Adams calls attention to the linkage in words and thought with 9. 13–14.

6 *stick'st not*] i.e. you do not even draw the line at. Cf. *Cor.* II. iii. 17: 'He himself stuck not to call us the many-headed multitude.'

7 *beauteous roof*] the Friend's beauty of form.

Seeking . . . ruinate] 'wilfully trying to bring to ruin'. (Human beauty can only be preserved by procreation.)

8 *repair*] 'keep in repair', 'maintain by renewing yourself in a child'. (There is no implication of a present state of *dis*repair.)

7–8] See note on 3. 3. There is no excuse for arguing, as Dowden and others have done, that the plea is for the rehabilitation of a decaying family, or that the lines imply that the Friend's father has died.

9] 'Oh, change your mind, so that I may change this opinion of you.'

11 *gracious*] Cf. note on 7. 1.

14 *still*] 'always'.

10

For shame deny that thou bear'st love to any,
Who for thyself art so unprovident!
Grant if thou wilt, thou art belov'd of many,
But that thou none lov'st is most evident: 4
For thou art so possess'd with murderous hate,
That 'gainst thyself thou stick'st not to conspire,
Seeking that beauteous roof to ruinate
Which to repair should be thy chief desire: 8
Oh change thy thought, that I may change my mind!
Shall hate be fairer lodg'd than gentle love?
Be as thy presence is, gracious and kind,
Or to thyself at least kind-hearted prove: 12
   Make thee another self for love of me,
   That beauty still may live in thine or thee.

11 2 *departest*] Usually interpreted as 'leave behind', i.e. your youth. Thus Tucker: 'You grow, in the person of one of yours begotten from that (prime) which you yourself are leaving.' This tortuous paraphrase heavily strains the construction with 'from' and 'departest'. Beeching seems nearer, taking 'departest' as 'separatest off', and 'that which thou departest' as 'a slip of thee'. 'Blood' (line 3), 'store' (line 9) and 'barrenly' (line 10), however, would seem to support Pooler's suggestion that the force of 'departest' is *seminal*. The sense of lines 1 and 2 would then be: 'Out of that seed which I am asking you to sow, you will grow, in a child of your making, as fast as you decline in yourself.' 'Departest' is, in any case, transitive here, and almost certainly = 'to share, bestow, impart' (*OED*. I. 2, —1651). Cf. Fr. *départir*. Littré gives a number of sixteenth-century instances, e.g. 'Chacun se donne si entier a son amy, qu'il ne luy reste rien a despartir ailleurs' (Montaigne). There is probably also a secondary train of associations in this sonnet, viz. investment, appearing in 'bestow'st' (line 3) and continuing in the ambiguity of 'increase', which would thus make the transition back to the seminal associations of 'store' and 'barrenly'.

3 *youngly*] 'in youth'.

bestow'st] 'Bestow' frequently means in Shakespeare 'lay out' or 'invest'.

4 *convertest*] 'turnest away'.

5, 6 *Herein . . . Without*] 'Within this course of action . . . outside of this . . .' (Pooler).

6 *cold decay*] thin-blooded, chill decline.

7 *the times should cease*] 'there would be no more generations of men'.

9 *for store*] 'for breeding' (as in 'store cattle').

9, 10 Punctuation] We have replaced Q's commas at *store* and *rude* by dashes to indicate the sense, viz. that these things are to perish *because* they are 'harsh, featureless, and rude' and thus things Nature did not want to breed from.

10 *rude*] 'uncouth'.

11 *Look,*] So Capell and most modern editors. Q and some modern editors: no comma. We take 'Look' as admonitory, as in 9. 9. Rollins takes 'Look whom' to mean 'whomever', which would certainly fit better the *second* interpretation of line 11 suggested below, though we prefer the first.

11] 'The best endowed creatures (those made for store) are also given by Nature the most generative vitality.' (Shakespeare's generalization, true or not, might be exemplified by the fact that on the day we wrote this note a photograph was published of the stallion Hyperion's first foal of the year, out of Mystification. Hyperion was then twenty-seven!) Neither punctuation of 'Look, whom' *requires* Sewell's emendation of Q's *the* to *thee*, so

II

As FAST as thou shalt wane so fast thou grow'st
In one of thine from that which thou departest,
And that fresh blood which youngly thou bestow'st
Thou mayst call thine when thou from youth convertest:
Herein lives wisdom, beauty, and increase;
Without this, folly, age, and cold decay:
If all were minded so, the times should cease,
And threescore year would make the world away.   8
Let those whom nature hath not made for store—
Harsh, featureless, and rude—barrenly perish:
Look, whom she best endow'd she gave the more;
Which bounteous gift thou shouldst in bounty cherish: 12
    She carv'd thee for her seal, and meant thereby
    Thou shouldst print more, not let that copy die.

frequently adopted by modern editors. That emendation, however, has certainly some attractions, and would allow the interpretation: 'Find whom you will that Nature has endowed most richly, and you will find that she has endowed you more richly still.'

12 *bounteous gift*] If our interpretation of line 11 be correct, the 'bounteous gift' is probably the gift of procreation.

in bounty] by being bountiful, i.e. prolific (Pooler).

13 *seal*] The stamp from which an impression is made, not the wax impressed.

14 *copy*] Primarily in Elizabethan English the original form *from* which a copy is made—the archetype. This does not make literal sense; but by transference 'copy' was also used for 'pattern' and hence 'example' ('Be copy now to men of grosser blood' (*H5*. III. i. 24) and 'Lady, you are the cruell'st she alive/If you will lead these graces to the grave/And leave the world no copy' (*TN*. I. v. 261–3); and so here. But is there perhaps also a play on the Elizabethan sense of 'plenty' (cf. Lat. *copia*), in relation to the 'bounteous gift' of line 12?

12 1–2] The clock is striking the time well on into the night. For the Elizabethans long nights were often full of fear and peril. We should also remember that the Elizabethans went to bed earlier than we do.

2 *brave*] resplendent, showily beautiful.

4 *o'er-silver'd all*] Q's reading *or siluer'd ore* was followed by a few early editors. Two emendations have found most favour: (1) Malone's (1780): *all silver'd o'er* is accepted by most editors. This seems the best alternative to the reading here adopted. It would be typically Shakespearean usage, but has two disadvantages: (a) that, as Professor Sisson points out (*New Readings in Shakespeare*, II. 209–10), the occurrence in line 7 of the monotonously similar 'all girded up in sheaves' tells against it; (b) that repetition of a word (*or . . . ore*) by a copyist or compositor is more probable than its anticipation. (2) That of all eighteenth-century editors from Gildon to Evans: *are silver'd o'er*. This Sisson supports on the ground that 'are' spelt 'ar' was often misread 'or'. We consider this reading grammatically unsatisfactory, and inconsistent with the sequence of past-participial constructions in lines 2–8. Q is supported by Tucker, who argues that the sonnet is addressed to a fair man, that the poet insistently depreciates black as a colouring, that the fur of the sable is brown, not black, that allusions to heraldry, being frequent in Shakespeare, would justify the reading *or*, and that 'or (i.e. gold) silvered with white' is 'exactly right'. We cannot agree. The hair that is silvered is not necessarily that of the Friend, but could be that of any man grown old enough, and if the allusions to heraldry justify *or*, then we are almost bound to read 'sable', heraldically, as black.

The reading here adopted was conjectured by Verity, and a similar reading, *o'er silver'd all*, was conjectured by Nicholson and printed by Aldis Wright in Cambridge[2] (1893). The reading has all the advantages of Malone's emendation, and avoids objections (a) and (b). A similar construction occurs in *V&A*. 900–1: 'The hunted boar; Whose frothy mouth, bepainted all with red . . .'.

9–10 *Then . . . That*] 'Then I begin thinking about your beauty, that . . .'.

10 *wastes of time*] 'things destroyed by time' (not 'deserts').

11 *do themselves forsake*] 'abandon themselves to decay' (cf. Lat. *sese deserere*).

12 *others*] not 'other people than you' but 'other sweets and beauties' (cf. line 11).

13 *Time's scythe*] not merely a stereotype figure, but, as Tucker observes, echoing the reaping image of lines 7–8.

14 *breed*] 'offspring'.

brave] 'defy'; but also echoing line 2, where the *adjective* has a less defiant and more elegiac tone. Cf. the variations in tone on 'state' in 29.

28

12

When I do count the clock that tells the time,
And see the brave day sunk in hideous night;
When I behold the violet past prime,
And sable curls o'er-silver'd all with white; 4
When lofty trees I see barren of leaves,
Which erst from heat did canopy the herd,
And summer's green all girded up in sheaves
Borne on the bier with white and bristly beard: 8
Then of thy beauty do I question make
That thou among the wastes of time must go,
Since sweets and beauties do themselves forsake,
And die as fast as they see others grow; 12
    And nothing 'gainst Time's scythe can make defence
    Save breed to brave him when he takes thee hence.

13 *General Note:* Obscure at first sight through the apparently complex play on pronouns, this sonnet becomes clearer when the continuity of the image is apprehended. The 'you' of line 1 is either the body and its beauty, as opposed to the 'self' or soul, or is the composite of soul and body. If the bodily beauty (or the composite) and the soul were identical, the former, like the latter, would be immortal. Shakespeare embodies what he considers the actual relationship in the image of the eternal soul inhabiting a temporal house (cf. line 9). As long as the occupier remains heirless, this house is held on a lease determinable by death. Provident economy would not allow 'so fair a house' to fall into decay through age and inoccupancy; but by 'husbandry' (line 10, with an obvious play on the word) would produce an heir who would maintain the house both during the Friend's old age (line 11) and after his death (line 12).

1 *your self*] So Q. Almost all modern editors: *yourself*. Here and at the beginning of line 7 the meaning would seem to be the 'self' or soul, and we therefore print as in Q.

5–6 *lease . . . determination*] In the Law of Property 'determination' of an estate is its ending (cf. 18. 4).

7 *Your self*] So this edition: almost all modern editors *Yourself*. Q: *You selfe*, which Tucker would retain as = 'you, the same over again', an interpretation equally consistent with our reading. We again print as two words to contrast with *yourself* later in the line, which = 'you the living person'.

9 *house*] As in 10. 7, there is no suggestion that the Friend's family estate is in a bad way. The 'house' is the personal beauty which he can propagate.

10 *husbandry*] economy and good management, also tillage (cf. 3. 6); and with a play, via 'husband', on marriage.

12 *barren rage*] probably 'barren-making ravage'. For the use of the adjective see Abbott (*Shakespearian Grammar*, s. 4), who quotes several parallels, including *AYLI*. II. vii. 132: 'Oppress'd with two weak evils, age and hunger', and Chaucer's reference to the rod of Caduceus as 'His sleepy yerde' (*Canterbury Tales*, line 1387). As to 'rage' = 'ravage', this is paralleled elsewhere in Shakespeare, who never uses the word 'ravage' itself. Cf. *R2*. II. iv. 14, 'to enjoy by rage and war'.

13–14] Q prints commas after 'unthrifts', 'know', and 'father'. The clause 'dear my love you know' could thus be read either with the preceding phrase or with the succeeding sentence; but the sense 'you know you had a father' seems platitudinous, and line 14, taken as a unit in itself, relates back more tellingly to the image of the provident head of a household (lines 5–12).

14 *You had a father*] The argument from the preterite that the Friend's father is dead has some plausibility, but is inconclusive.

30

13

OH THAT you were your self! but, love, you are
No longer yours than you yourself here live;
Against this coming end you should prepare,
And your sweet semblance to some other give: 4
So should that beauty which you hold in lease
Find no determination; then you were
Your self again after yourself's decease,
When your sweet issue your sweet form should bear.   8
Who lets so fair a house fall to decay,
Which husbandry in honour might uphold
Against the stormy gusts of winter's day
And barren rage of death's eternal cold?   12
    Oh none but unthrifts, dear my love you know:
    You had a father,—let your son say so.

14 1 *do . . . pluck*] 'do I draw my conclusions'.

2 *I have astronomy*] 'I understand astrology'. (Cf. 'He had small Latin'.)

3–8] *i.e.* I am no common omen-monger, no Regiomontanus, Partridge or Old Moore.

5 *to brief minutes*] either 'for each single minute' or possibly 'to within a few minutes'. Tucker suggests 'down to small details', quoting Jonson, *Staple of News*, I. v. 138: 'every minute of news'.

6 *Pointing to each*] appointing or assigning to each minute.

his] its.

6] i.e. saying exactly when it will thunder or rain or blow.

8] Either 'by signs, which I make it my regular habit to read in the sky' or 'by the common signs, relevant to that particular occasion, which I discover in the sky'. There are seventeenth-century examples of 'oft' as an adjective; but this is the only recorded use of 'predict' as a noun.

10 *constant stars*] i.e. 'in your eyes, *which are* constant stars'.

in . . . read] by interpreting them I arrive at.

art] specialized learning.

11 *As*] i.e. as the proposition that. . . .

11, 12, 14] To put *truth . . . convert* and line 14 in inverted commas, as many editors do, is positively misleading, for so treated 'thyself', 'thou', and 'thy' would refer to the poet and not, as they clearly must, to the Friend.

12 *store*] as in 'store cattle', cf. 11. 9.

12] 'If you would turn from self-sufficiency to breeding a son.'

14 *date*] 'end'. Cf. the modern colloquial phrase 'that's put a date to that'.

14

Not from the stars do I my judgment pluck,
And yet methinks I have astronomy—
But not to tell of good or evil luck,
Of plagues, of dearths, or seasons' quality: 4
Nor can I fortune to brief minutes tell,
Pointing to each his thunder, rain, and wind,
Or say with princes if it shall go well
By oft predict that I in heaven find: 8
But from thine eyes my knowledge I derive,
And, constant stars, in them I read such art
As truth and beauty shall together thrive
If from thy self to store thou wouldst convert: 12
    Or else of thee this I prognosticate:—
    Thy end is truth's and beauty's doom and date.

15 2 *Holds*] 'stays', as in 'Hold still!' to a horse.

3 *this . . . stage*] the familiar playhouse image for the world.

4 *the stars . . . comment*] Certainly Elizabethan audiences were given to 'commenting' during performances. They 'cheered and checked' as in line 6. Astrology held that the stars 'influenced' by their qualities and conjunctions human life and circumstance. This action, less noisy than the playhouse audience's, was known only by its effects. Some editors see a subtle contrast simultaneously distinguishing and binding together the rather disparate parts of this double metaphor: The audience comment audibly but do not influence the play's action, whereas the stars directly affect men's lives but are silent. But Tucker takes 'secret' to mean not so much 'silent' as 'occult', and points out that the 'influence' of the stars was by the emanation of an ethereal fluid—stars 'poured' (Spenser, *FQ.* I. viii. 4) or 'shed' (Milton, *PL.* VII. 375) their influence.

It is hard to say whether Shakespeare took this image directly from experience of the Elizabethan playhouse or was elaborating a further form of the ancient homiletic metaphor of the world as a stage, found, e.g., in Ralegh, 'What is our life? a play of passion', lines 5–6: 'Heaven the judicious sharp spectator is / That sits and marks still who doth act amiss'.

6 *Cheerèd*] 'encouraged', 'incited'.

check'd] (1) 'rebuked', 'chidden'; (2) 'restrained'. Both these terms have obviously a primary meaning relating to the 'plants' and the 'sky' (as = 'weather' or 'season'); a secondary meaning in reference back to the stars as occult 'influences'; and a tertiary in reference back yet again to the noisy playhouse audiences. Such multiple connotativeness is a feature of the style of the *Sonnets*.

sky] (1) weather and season affecting both the growth of plants and the welfare of men; (2) possibly also the celestial bodies again, as affecting men's fortunes, though, if present, this meaning is certainly fainter than in line 4, even if it has not, as J. Q. Adams holds, already disappeared.

7 *Vaunt*] exult and swagger. (Wyndham: 'display themselves'—probably on the analogy of birds' display.) There may be some continuity with the stage image of line 4—cf. also Macbeth's actor who 'struts and frets his hour upon the stage'.

at height decrease] when they have reached their prime, start to decline.

8 *brave state*] 'showy splendour'. Cf. *LLL.* V. ii. 364: 'trim gallants full of courtship and of state'. Alternatively, or even concurrently, 'magnificent deportment' (the V.I.P. manner).

out of memory] probably 'when other people have forgotten what important people they once were'; alternatively, though less probably, 'for ever and a day' (cf. 'time out of mind').

34

15

When I consider every thing that grows
Holds in perfection but a little moment,
That this huge stage presenteth nought but shows
Whereon the stars in secret influence comment;   4
When I perceive that men as plants increase,
Cheerèd and check'd even by the selfsame sky,
Vaunt in their youthful sap, at height decrease,
And wear their brave state out of memory: 8
Then the conceit of this inconstant stay
Sets you most rich in youth before my sight,
Where wasteful time debateth with decay
To change your day of youth to sullied night;   12
   And all in war with Time for love of you,
   As he takes from you I engraft you new.

8] It is possible that this line bears latent allusion to players' clothes. A decayed player continued to wear the finery (often originally handed over from noblemen's wardrobes) long after it had lost both gloss and fashion.

9 *conceit . . . stay*] realization, apprehension of this transience and mutability.

11 *Where*] i.e. in my sight. There seems no need for the various and ingenious explanations which editors have offered, such as 'whereas', 'while', or (as referring to 'you') 'in whose case'. (See note on lines 10–11, below.)

debateth] either (1) 'discusses', 'puts his head together with', or (2) 'disputes', arguing how they shall, or (3) 'contends', which of them shall. (3) would demand an opposition between time and decay, presumably in respect of the rapidity of their action. It is Time alone that recurs as the enemy in line 13. This could either be because Time has been victorious against decay, a suggestion which seems both absent and irrelevant, so that (3) seems improbable; or because there was no contest as to *which* shall destroy the Friend, but only a dispute (2) or discussion (1) as to *how* they shall both do it. Pooler, on the other hand, draws attention to the bare possibility that there may be no contestants or disputants at all. Q has

15 (*continued*)

no capitals in line 11 and no comma after 'decay', so that decay could be merely the instrument of time. But lines 11–12 would then be rhythmically and grammatically awkward. We should have to break up the typically alliterative phrase 'debateth with decay', and link 'with decay', across both an untypical rhetorical hiatus and a grammatical inversion, with 'to change'.

10–11] The meaning, then, seems to be: 'This apprehension of transience sets you in the height of your youthful beauty before my eyes as the subject of a discussion (or dispute) between the conspirators Time and Decay, as to how they shall despoil you'.

12 *sullied night*] probably referring rather to old age than to death.

14] 'As Time withers your features, I give you new life (by my verse).' Old trees are revivified by inserting 'grafts' which, when they have taken, replace exhausted branches. Beeching and Fort among others note this as the first reference to the immortalizing power of the poet's verse (cf. Sonnets 18 and 19).

15

WHEN I consider every thing that grows
Holds in perfection but a little moment,
That this huge stage presenteth nought but shows
Whereon the stars in secret influence comment;   4
When I perceive that men as plants increase,
Cheerèd and check'd even by the selfsame sky,
Vaunt in their youthful sap, at height decrease,
And wear their brave state out of memory: 8
Then the conceit of this inconstant stay
Sets you most rich in youth before my sight,
Where wasteful time debateth with decay
To change your day of youth to sullied night;   12
   And all in war with Time for love of you,
   As he takes from you I engraft you new.

16 1 *mightier*] than by the poet's 'engrafting' (cf. 15. 13–14).

4 *barren*] contrasting with the procreation theme. 'Verses beget nothing; you can beget a son.'

5] Not 'you are on top of life', in the modern colloquial sense, but 'you are at your zenith' (from which in due course you must decline).

6 *unset*] 'not planted', or, more appropriately here, 'not sown with seed'. The latter use was current (see Cotgrave and *OED*).

7] 'Would be only too glad to bear you children, in wedlock'. 'Would' probably means 'want to', 'are eager to', and is not merely conditional. 'Virtuous' may possibly also carry the secondary sense of fertility. (The use of 'virtue' = 'power' is frequent in Shakespeare. Cf. Lat. *virtus*.)

7 *your*] So Q. Many editors emend to *you*, but the change seems unnecessary and the arguments for it unconvincing. 'Your living flowers' surely means simply 'flowers springing from your seed'.

8 *counterfeit*] 'portrait'.

9 *lines of life*] A phrase that has proved fertile of comment. The following list contains the most noteworthy interpretations with the names of their earliest and/or chief advocates:

> (*a*) children (as 'living pictures') (Malone, who conjectured 'lives' for 'lines');
>
> (*b*) lines drawn with a pencil—a portrait (Schmidt, Dowden, Empson);
>
> (*c*) lineage, descendants (Dowden, Tyler, Beeching, Empson);
>
> (*d*) wrinkles on the brow of age (Tyler, who later rejected it for (*c*), Empson);
>
> (*e*) (from palmistry) marriage and procreation (Wyndham, Empson);
>
> (*f*) form of personal appearance in the young men . . . or in his descendants (as one speaks of the lines of someone's figure) (Pooler, Empson);
>
> (*g*) lines drawn with a pen in writing (Alden, Dowden, Empson);
>
> (*h*) lines of verse ('the kind a sonnet has fourteen of') (Wyndham, Empson);
>
> (*i*) lines of relationship in a genealogical table (Fort);
>
> (*j*) 'the line fixed in the continuum with which space–time theorists describe such reality as they allow to a particle' (Empson).

It seems reasonable to hold with Professor Empson that there is a play here on several simultaneous connotations, and that the quality of the poem would be impaired if we confined our interpretation to a single association. But some selection and priorities would seem possible. We take it that 'lines of life' is the subject, and 'that' a demonstrative adjective, and that

16

B UT WHEREFORE do not you a mightier way
Make war upon this bloody tyrant Time,
And fortify yourself in your decay
With means more blessèd than my barren rhyme?   4
Now stand you on the top of happy hours,
And many maiden gardens, yet unset,
With virtuous wish would bear your living flowers,
Much liker than your painted counterfeit: 8
So should the lines of life that life repair
Which this (Time's pencil or my pupil pen)
Neither in inward worth nor outward fair
Can make you live yourself in eyes of men: 12
  To give away yourself keeps your self still,
  And you must live drawn by your own sweet skill.

'of life' bears the emphasis, and is intended to contrast the *living* portrait
(the child) with the inanimate products of the 'pencil' or the 'pen'. This
interpretation would seem to give highest priority to senses (*a*) and (*c*),
and somewhat lower priority to (*f*), (*e*), and (*i*), in that order.

repair] cf. 'engraft you new' (15. 14), to which the poet now proposes
a better alternative. The 'mightier way' (by begetting a child) will
revivify and maintain the essential 'self' (which, as the body is mortal,
must otherwise be lost to the eyes of men) as neither the portrait nor the
poetry can do.

10 *pencil*] an artist's paint-brush, especially a small and fine one (now
archaic, see *OED*, whose earliest instance of the modern use is dated 1612).

pupil] prentice, inexperienced.

10] So Q. Editors have offered many punctuational and typographical
emendations, substantially reducible to three types: (1) interpreting 'this'
as 'this, namely', e.g. Capell: *this, —time's pencil, or . . . pen*; (2) taking
'this' as a demonstrative adjective and 'time' as 'period', e.g. *this time's
pencil or . . . pen*; (3) taking 'this' as a demonstrative adjective (cf. Lat.
iste) qualifying either 'Time', or, though less probably, 'pencil'. (1) has

16 (*continued*)

no advantage over Q, which readily affords the same sense; (2) is a radical departure, only justifiable if Q were unintelligible; (3) on either construction seems unduly strained.

11 *fair*] 'beauty'.

12 *Can . . . yourself*] 'can make you yourself live', i.e. keep you personally alive.

13 *To give away yourself*] Perhaps primarily 'to give yourself in marriage', rather than 'to produce likenesses of yourself', as Malone suggested. Malone's meaning, however, is probably also present.

yourself . . . your self] as always, Q prints both as two words. We have retained Q in the second instance, so as to reflect a possible distinction between the bodily immortality referred to in line 12, and the perpetuation of the spiritual personality which may be referred to here.

still] always.

14 *drawn*] (1) 'delineated' (in the 'living pictures'); and, just possibly, though doubtfully, (2) 'continued', 'prolonged' (cf. 'drawn out').

14] So Q. Almost all modern editors have inserted a comma after 'live', but this gives an emphasis to either 'must' or 'live' which is inconsistent with the general mood of the sonnet. The plain sense seems to be: 'And the only way in which you can perpetuate yourself is to be your own painter and poet.'

Bᴜᴛ ᴡʜᴇʀᴇꜰᴏʀᴇ do not you a mightier way
Make war upon this bloody tyrant Time,
And fortify yourself in your decay
With means more blessèd than my barren rhyme?   4
Now stand you on the top of happy hours,
And many maiden gardens, yet unset,
With virtuous wish would bear your living flowers,
Much liker than your painted counterfeit: 8
So should the lines of life that life repair
Which this (Time's pencil or my pupil pen)
Neither in inward worth nor outward fair
Can make you live yourself in eyes of men: 12
   To give away yourself keeps your self still,
   And you must live drawn by your own sweet skill.

17 1] Q places the query at the end of line 2, and is followed by nearly all modern editors, who supply a comma after 'come', and make line 2 a qualifying clause to line 1. We have accepted Tucker's emended punctuation. This, which treats lines 3 and 4 as parenthetical, links lines 2–4 with 5–8 in a paratactic sequence. It also avoids the unintelligible clash of tenses between 'will' in line 1 and 'were' (line 2), 'could' (line 5) and 'would' (line 7).

2 *If . . . with*] i.e. if it fully expressed.

deserts] then pronounced to rhyme with 'parts' (cf. 11. 4 and 14. 12).

3 *yet*] 'as yet'. (He is *still* writing with a 'pupil pen' (16. 10).)

tomb] i.e. a monument which, however imposing, can only enshrine the dead without conveying his merits to the beholder. Cf. 83. 12.

4 *parts*] bodily or intellectual merits.

6 *fresh numbers*] 'lively verses'.

11 *your true rights*] 'the praises which are your due'. It is possible that there is also a pun here (as perhaps again in 23. 6) on 'right' and 'rite' (very often spelt 'right' in the old quartos and folios).

a poet's rage] '*furor poeticus*' (cf. 100. 3).

12 *strechèd . . . song*] 'extravagances of a bygone poetical fashion'.

àntique] then always accented on the first syllable. 'Antique' was then a spelling both for 'antic' and for 'antique'. In view of lines 9–11, 'antique' = 'old' seems to be the primary meaning here, but the homophone would, in this context, almost inevitably suggest to the Elizabethan the additional connotation of the fantastic.

12] There may possibly be also a back-handed allusion to the elongated metres used by some contemporary poets but beginning to go out of fashion—e.g. Poulter's Measure (12, 14 alternate), 'fourteeners' and continuous Alexandrines.

17

Who will believe my verse in time to come?
If it were fill'd with your most high deserts—
Though yet heaven knows it is but as a tomb
Which hides your life and shows not half your parts,— 4
If I could write the beauty of your eyes,
And in fresh numbers number all your graces,
The age to come would say: 'This poet lies;
Such heavenly touches ne'er touch'd earthly faces.' 8
So should my papers, yellow'd with their age,
Be scorn'd, like old men of less truth than tongue,
And your true rights be term'd a poet's rage
And stretchèd metre of an ántique song: 12
  But were some child of yours alive that time,
  You should live twice—in it and in my rhyme.

18 1 *a summer's day*] Tucker suggests that 'day' is here used for 'season' rather than for a single day. The whole phrase could then be construed as 'a summertime'. This would make the progression of the imagery logically more compact. Line 4, with its reference to the length of summer's tenure, would appear less of a digression interposed between May's 'rough winds' (line 3) and the too hot or too cloudy weather of lines 5–6. The use of 'day' for 'season' or 'period' is, however, rare with an indefinite article, and this would make apprehension of this meaning difficult at the beginning of a poem, which would be an argument against Tucker's interpretation, though 'day' = 'period' is familiar enough usage, and the following not dissimilar instance occurs in Shakespeare: 'I saw not better sport these seven years' day' (*2H6*. II. i. 2). (Cf. also the obsolete Scottish use 'a month's day' = 'a period of a month', quoted *OED*.) Yet whatever logical difficulties may arise later in the poem from taking 'day' as meaning 'day' rather than 'period', we find, and we think most readers will find, that the impact of the first line evokes the image of a *day* in summer.

2 *lovely*] Not used in the modern, often trivial, sense, but as (1) 'kind', 'gentle', and possibly (2), in relation to the Friend, 'lovable'.

temperate] 'equable', 'even-tempered'.

3 *May*] We too easily forget that Shakespeare's May ran from our mid-May to our mid-June, and was therefore for him a part of summer.

4 *date*] terminable period. (Cf. 123. 5: 'Our dates are brief'.)

8 *untrimm'd*] stripped of its beauty.

10 *lose*] So Capell and all modern editors except Wyndham, who, without comment, retains Q's reading: *loose*. But eight times out of nine in the *Sonnets* Q spells 'lose' as 'loose'.

ow'st] 'ownest'.

11] Cf. the interesting verbal parallel in *A&C*. V. ii. 317–18: 'Now boast thee, death, in thy possession lies / A lass unparallel'd'.

12 *to . . . grow'st*] 'to grow to' is to coalesce or become incorporate in, as a graft coalesces with its parent stock; i.e. as long as time lasts the Friend will last.

18

Shall i compare thee to a summer's day?
Thou art more lovely and more temperate:
Rough winds do shake the darling buds of May,
And summer's lease hath all too short a date: 4
Sometime too hot the eye of heaven shines,
And often is his gold complexion dimm'd,
And every fair from fair sometime declines,
By chance or nature's changing course untrimm'd: 8
But thy eternal summer shall not fade
Nor lose possession of that fair thou ow'st,
Nor shall Death brag thou wander'st in his shade,
When in eternal lines to time thou grow'st: 12
  So long as men can breathe or eyes can see,
  So long lives this, and this gives life to thee.

19 2] 'And (as you habitually do) cause the earth to re-absorb the creatures which spring from her' ('sweet' suggests primarily flowers).

4] As to the longevity of the Phoenix, MSS of Pliny's *Natural History*, X. 2, give variously 40, 511, 540, and 560 years see (Bostock and Riley's translation, 1855); and Philemon Holland's translation (1601) gives 660!

4 *in her blood*] i.e. 'alive', in the way customary to Phoenixes at their appointed end, rather than Tucker's 'in full vigour of life'.

5 *fleets*] So Dyce, for the rhyme. Q: *fleet'st*. The second person singular in '-s' is historically a correct form, common in the First Folio for verbs ending in '-t' or '-d'. Abbott (*Shakespearian Grammar*, s. 340) cites this example without noting that it is an emendation. What is perhaps questionable is whether the Elizabethan reader would have been troubled by the rhyme 'fleet'st . . . sweets', whatever be the status of the former word, e.g. whether a compositor's error or no.

10 *ántique*] Cf. 17. 12, note. Here (1) 'caricaturing', from 'antic' = 'grotesque'; (2) 'immemorial'; and, possibly, but only as an overtone, (3) 'that draws pictures of old age', by adding wrinkles. Shakespeare constantly plays on (1) and (2), both senses being then spelt indiscriminately (e.g. in *R2*. III. ii. 162: 'and there the antique sits' is so spelt in all Qq and in all four Ff; in *Ham*. I. v. 172: 'an antic disposition' is variously spelt 'antike', 'anticke', and 'antick'; while *AYLI*. II. iii. 57: 'the constant service of the antique world' has 'antique' in F1 and F2, but by 1664 and 1685 the printer has printed 'antick'). We have retained Q's spelling.

11 *untainted*] Pooler's 'metaphor from tilting' may tempt some readers with its implied association with 'course'—'permit him to remain untouched or uninjured' by your onslaught; but it cannot be substantiated by firm parallels. Pooler quotes Cotgrave's 'Attaint', and claims 'taint' as aphetic from that; but both Cotgrave and *OED* give 'attaint' = 'blow or touch (e.g. in tilting)' only as a noun, and Pooler's one example (from Chapman) is also a noun. Pooler thus asks us to accept two conjectures as to linguistic extension. Either extension alone might be a possible Shakespearean freedom, but to plant a conjectural springboard in a conjectural bank makes for unsure leaping. It is safer to interpret: 'Let him in your passage remain unsullied in beauty.'

19

Devouring time, blunt thou the lion's paws,
And make the earth devour her own sweet brood;
Pluck the keen teeth from the fierce tiger's jaws,
And burn the long-liv'd phoenix in her blood; 4
Make glad and sorry seasons as thou fleets,
And do whate'er thou wilt, swift-footed Time,
To the wide world and all her fading sweets:
But I forbid thee one most heinous crime:— 8
Oh carve not with thy hours my love's fair brow,
Nor draw no lines there with thine ántique pen;
Him in thy course untainted do allow
For beauty's pattern to succeeding men. 12
    Yet do thy worst, old Time: despite thy wrong
    My love shall in my verse ever live young.

20 1 *nature's*] as opposed to 'art's', as in *TN*. I. v. 259–60: ' 'Tis beauty truly blent, whose red and white / Nature's own sweet and cunning hand laid on.'

2 *master-mistress*] So Capell and most modern editors. Q: *Master Mistris*. Interpretation is multifarious and frequently subject to editors' theories of the Friend's identity and the poet's relation to him. Relevant notes (which are the exception) are offered by Mr. J. B. Leishman (*RES*. XV. 94) and J. Q. Adams. The former writes: 'If, with Shakespeare's printer, we omit the hyphen, *Master Mistris* will mean "supreme mistress"; if we insert the hyphen it will mean that the "mistress" usually invoked by poets is in this case a man.' J. Q. Adams (*Life of William Shakespeare*, Houghton, Boston, and Constable, London, 1923) writes: 'Is not Shakespeare here thinking of the numerous mistresses celebrated in sonnet cycles (as Delia, Laura, Diella, Stella, Phillis, etc.) and meaning to comment, favourably, on the fact that he is celebrating in his cycle a *man*?'

passion] This word also appeals to pre-established theories. The three main interpretations are: (1) 'sexual passion'; (2) simply = Lat. *passio*, '(strong) feeling' (Tucker); (3) 'love poem'—recalling such a use by Watson, *Hekatompathia* (1582), where each of the hundred poems is called a 'passion'. To accept (3) would strictly require us to ask which poem of Shakespeare's is referred to. Walter Thompson (*The Sonnets of Shakespeare and . . . Southampton*, Blackwell, Oxford, 1938, 1–5) declares for *The Lover's Complaint*, and for Southampton as the Friend. Another possibility is: just this poem (Sonnet 20). Just possibly, however, the term might refer to the whole group to which Sonnet 20 belongs. We think (3) possible, while recognizing that to say that a poem is a 'love poem' is not to imply an exact description of the kind of love involved. (1), however, seems at least equally likely, and it is possible that both meanings may be present. Both senses of the word were fairly new (first instance of (1) in *OED*. 1588). A similar sense to (3) occurs in *MND*. V. i. 295–6 and 322–3, where the word means 'passionate speech'.

4 *false women's fashion*] As Tucker notes, this compares the fickleness of women in general (not only of *false* women) with the (so far) constant youth. Cf. an interesting parallel in *TN*. II. iv. 95 ff.

5 *rolling*] 'roving'. Dowden cites Spenser, *FQ*.III. i. 41: 'Her wanton eyes, ill signes of womanhed, Did roll too lightly.' Tyler compares Sonnets 139. 6 and 140. 14.

6 *Gilding*] Tucker notes that according to one of two conflicting theories of vision, the light lay in the eye itself, which emitted beams (cf. 114. 8), as in *V&A* 1051: '(her eyes) being open'd, threw unwilling light Upon the wide wound'. To regard the eye as a *source* of light would lead

20

A woman's face with nature's own hand painted
Hast thou, the master-mistress of my passion;
A woman's gentle heart, but not acquainted
With shifting change as is false women's fashion;   4
An eye more bright than theirs, less false in rolling,
Gilding the object whereupon it gazeth;
A man in hue all hues in his controlling,
Which steals men's eyes and women's souls amazeth: 8
And for a woman wert thou first created,—
Till nature as she wrought thee fell a-doting,
And by addition me of thee defeated,
By adding one thing to my purpose nothing.   12
    But since she prick'd thee out for women's pleasure,
    Mine be thy love and thy love's use their treasure.

naturally to crediting it with some of the powers of the sun, one of which
was commonly supposed to be that of transmuting baser substances on or
near the earth's surface to gold (cf. Donne, *Sermons*, ed. Simpson and Potter,
University of California Press, Berkeley and Los Angeles, Vol. I, 1953,
163–4). Such an idea would at least enrich the meaning of Sonnet 33. 4.
In *KJ*. III. i. 77–80 it is, indeed, the *eye* of the sun that effects the alchemy.
In this Sonnet the eye of the Friend is not seeing more beauty than is there,
but similarly performing a real transmutation.

7] The primary meaning of 'hue' till the middle of the seventeenth
century was not 'colour' or 'complexion' but 'form', 'appearance' or
'species' (see *OED* and *Webster's Dictionary*). In interpreting the word here
the form of the octave is significant. Each pair of the first six lines singles
out one of the Friend's features—line 1 his 'woman's face', line 3 his
'woman's gentle heart', while line 5 wholly differentiates him from women
by an eye brighter and less inconstant than theirs. To interpret the next
comment (line 7) as a mere contradiction of line 1 would be to reduce this
sequence to an absurdity. Instead, all these features which surpass those of
women are shown to be embodied in a manly form, which not only has

20 (*continued*)

at command all manliness, but epitomizes all the excellences ('hues') of both sexes. No wonder, then, that (line 8) he attracts the eyes of all men, and throws into confusion the souls of women.

hues] So most modern editors. Q: *Hews*, which, through its suggestion of a proper name, has provoked much speculation. The interpretation we offer of line 7 does not exclude the possibility of a pun here, which, however, we would not presume to explain.

8 *Which*] referring back to 'his' (hue), line 7. It is the *form* that steals and amazes, not the man or his 'controlling'.

amazeth] not 'surprises' or 'astonishes', but 'overwhelms and throws into confusion', cf. *V&A.* 634: 'eyne Whose full perfection all the world amazes'.

10–12 *a-doting . . . nothing*] at least assonantal in Elizabethan English. 'Nothing' was not then pronounced 'nuthing', but 'no-thing'.

11 *defeated*] 'deprived'.

13 *prick'd thee out*] 'selected you'.

12–14] A realization of the equivoques here on 'one thing', 'to my purpose nothing', 'prick'd', and 'use' (see Key to Word-play, pp. 360–2) is essential to an understanding of this sonnet and of the poet's relationship to the Friend, but their detailed working except in the case of 'use' should be easy to grasp for those familiar with modern bawdy and alert to innuendo.

These lines, so far from implying a physically homosexual element in the relation of the Poet to the Friend, are evidence against it.

A woman's face with nature's own hand painted
Hast thou, the master-mistress of my passion;
A woman's gentle heart, but not acquainted
With shifting change as is false women's fashion; 4
An eye more bright than theirs, less false in rolling,
Gilding the object whereupon it gazeth;
A man in hue all hues in his controlling,
Which steals men's eyes and women's souls amazeth: 8
And for a woman wert thou first created,—
Till nature as she wrought thee fell a-doting,
And by addition me of thee defeated,
By adding one thing to my purpose nothing. 12
 But since she prick'd thee out for women's pleasure,
 Mine be thy love and thy love's use their treasure.

21 *General Note:* Imitators of Petrarch employed nature symbolism and comparisons extravagantly. Passages·in this style occur in Shakespeare's poems and early plays. It also became in turn a convention to repudiate this convention, and to represent it as something the poets' sincerity rejected. Some commentators see in this sonnet such conventionality of the latter kind as warrants denial of Shakespeare's authorship. Others (e.g. Tucker), though not definitely impugning its authenticity, find its manner incompatible with the eulogistic style of its predecessors in the series, and some commentators (e.g. Pooler) would alter its position among the *Sonnets.* As to authorship, a rejection of this sonnet on the above grounds would involve rejection of a number of others, and for such a step there is no reliable evidence. As to sequence, though the sonnet does differ appreciably in tone from its predecessors, it does not really differ in either structure, imagery, movement, or diction. Now, differences of tone do not necessarily break sequence; and, in any case, it is highly questionable how far Shakespeare's *Sonnets* are to be regarded as forming a strict sequence, even throughout any group.

1 *So*] goes simply with 'as'—not a backward link with Sonnet 20.

Muse] Many parallels could be cited for the metonymous use of 'muse' for 'poet'. Whether this line represents 'the first attack on the false art of a Rival Poet' (who is to recur in Sonnets 78 ff), as Wyndham suggests, or refers, not to any particular poet, but to sonneteers in general (as Beeching and Tucker believe), may happily be left to the individual reader's choice, fancy, or theory.

4] 'And when celebrating the beauty of his subject feels himself obliged to drag in everything else that's beautiful.' ('Rehearse' = 'mention' or 'enumerate'.)

5] Primarily 'linking in splendid comparison'; but 'proud' also conveys the suggestion of flattery to the subject, and self-satisfaction in the author.

7 *rare*] 'highly treasured'.

8 *heaven's air*] space.

this . . . rondure] most probably 'this great enclosing roundness of the universe'.

13 *that . . . well*] 'who are fond of retailing second-hand praises'.

21

So is it not with me as with that Muse,
Stirr'd by a painted beauty to his verse,
Who heaven itself for ornament doth use
And every fair with his fair doth rehearse,   4
Making a couplement of proud compare
With sun and moon, with earth and sea's rich gems,
With April's first-born flowers and all things rare
That heaven's air in this huge rondure hems.   8
Oh, let me true in love but truly write,
And then believe me my love is as fair
As any mother's child, though not so bright
As those gold candles fix'd in heaven's air: 12
    Let them say more that like of hearsay well;
    I will not praise that purpose not to sell.

22 1 *I am old*] Of less help for dating the *Sonnets* than some have thought. Poets, like other men, are apt to feel very old until they have passed forty.

2 *are of one date*] 'last as long as each other' ('date' = determined end).

3 *furrows*] Cf. Sonnet 2. 2.

4 *expiate*] A puzzling use, and the only instance in Shakespeare of 'expiate' as a verb. The word itself was new in English at the time. (*OED* gives the first use as 1594.) The only use of the verb at all resembling that in this line seems to involve some idea of (1) pacification, and (2) ending, e.g. Marlowe, *Dido*, V. ii.: 'Die to expiate The grief that tires upon thine inward soul'; Tofte, *Honours Academy* (1610), 39: 'Nothing could appease and expiate this cankered rage'; T. Adams, *Lycanthropia*, (1615), 29: 'Somewhat to expiate their savage fury'. With this kind of sense the line could mean: 'Then I expect (and perhaps even hope) that death will bring peace to my days by ending them.' Steevens's conjecture: *expirate*, besides being ugly, neither has linguistic support nor makes good sense.

10 *will*,] So Q. As Pooler notes, the usual substitution of a semi-colon is unsatisfactory. It cuts the phrase 'Bearing thy heart' (line 11) off from its subject 'I' (line 10).

13 *Presume not on*] 'Do not count on being able to lay claim to.'

54

22

My GLASS shall not persuade me I am old
So long as youth and thou are of one date;
But when in thee time's furrows I behold
Then look I death my days should expiate: 4
For all the beauty that doth cover thee
Is but the seemly raiment of my heart,
Which in thy breast doth live, as thine in me,—
How can I then be elder than thou art?   8
Oh therefore, love, be of thyself so wary
As I not for myself but for thee will,
Bearing thy heart, which I will keep so chary
As tender nurse her babe from faring ill: 12
    Presume not on thy heart when mine is slain;
    Thou gav'st me thine not to give back again.

23 1 *unperfect actor*] actor who has not fully mastered his part or role. 'Perfect' is frequently used in Shakespeare for 'word-perfect', and the primary connotation here is probably of that kind, but Tucker's 'not a finished artist' may well be a secondary meaning.

The theme of *eloquentia* runs through the sonnet. Elizabethans were far more familiar than modern readers with a school training that stressed the value of clear and expressive speech, of *elocutio* and *pronunciatio*, two of the five principles of rhetoric, *pronunciatio* being 'divided into the figure of the voice and motion of the body' (J. Bulwer, *Chironomia; or, the art of manuall rhetoricke*, p. 132; published with *Chirologia*, 1644; see also Sir T. Wilson, *The Art of Rhetorique*, 1560, and many other writers). Cf. Hamlet's advice to the players, III. ii. 1 ff, especially lines 20–1. The 'perfect' actor in the secondary sense given above would fulfil the demands of lines 5–10 below. The 'unperfect', in the primary sense, would handicap his chances of being 'perfect' in the secondary sense.

2 *besides*] So Q; an alternative form to 'beside' in Elizabethan English.

3 *replete . . . rage*] i.e. helpless with excessive rage.

4 *Whose*] the antecedent is 'rage' not 'thing'.

4] 'The very excess of which stifles its impulse to action.'

5 *for fear of trust*] (1) 'lacking confidence in my reliability' (as a ministrant—cf. line 6); but possibly (2) 'overawed by the responsibility'.

5–6 *forget . . . ceremony*] forget how to say the ceremony perfectly.

6 *rite*] So Malone and almost all modern editors. Q: *right*, which is, however, the most common spelling of 'rite' in other passages in the early quartos and folios. In several instances there is a play, strong or faint, on the homonym.

1–8] Pooler rightly indicates that lines 5–6 answer to lines 1–2, and lines 7–8 to lines 3–4.

9 *books*] So Q. Sewell (1725) conjectured *looks*, and most modern editors follow him. The drift of the sestet, and so of the whole poem, will differ radically according to the reading adopted. Q's reading implies that the poet, tongue-tied in the Friend's presence, can express his love more adequately in poetry. Sewell's *looks* implies that the poet cannot express his feelings in words, but only in the silent language of looks. Objections to Q as unintelligible are unconvincing, and, indeed, we find that the reading makes for the coherence of the sonnet. The image of the nervous actor (lines 1–2) loses its force if, as in Sewell's reading, the poet as performer, albeit in dumb show, achieves *in the Friend's presence* adequate expression of his love. Secondly, the perfect tense 'hath writ' (line 13) applies more aptly to completed literary composition, expressing what the poet has experienced in absence, than to the emotions which presumably continue

23

As an unperfect actor on the stage,
Who with his fear is put besides his part,
Or some fierce thing replete with too much rage,
Whose strength's abundance weakens his own heart;   4
So I for fear of trust forget to say
The perfect ceremony of love's rite,
And in mine own love's strength seem to decay,
O'er-charg'd with burthen of mine own love's might: 8
Oh let my books be then the eloquence
And dumb presagers of my speaking breast,
Who plead for love and look for recompense
More than that tongue that more hath more express'd: 12
   Oh learn to read what silent love hath writ;
   To hear with eyes belongs to love's fine wit.

and develop in the Friend's presence—a sense which would be better expressed by the present tense 'writes'. Many of the objections to *books* are very flimsy, and mere citations of parallels for *looks* are no argument. The main objections to Q worth considering are: (1) That 'fine wit' (line 14) is not required for reading books (Tucker, Beeching) or handwriting (Beeching), and, in any case, the gifted youth was surely literate (J.G.B. in *Shakespeariana*, 1885, II, 495–7). All these points depend on taking 'read' superficially; 'reading' can involve comprehending. (2) That 'a distinction between writing and saying is not here to the point' (Beeching). This begs the question. (3) That it is doubtful that Shakespeare would have called his sonnets 'books'. But 'books' could refer to other poems, e.g. *Venus and Adonis* and *Lucrece* (as suggested by Sarrazin, *Aus Shakespeares Meisterwerkstatt* (1906), 105, and by Professor Tucker Brooke). In any case, Shakespeare sometimes uses 'book' for a paper with writing on it, e.g. in *Cymb.* V. iv. 133: 'A book? O rare one!' (referring to such a piece of paper). (4) That books cannot appropriately be called 'dumb' (line 10) or 'silent' (line 13) (Tucker). Yet surely they can? And, in any case, 'silent' (line 13) qualifies

23 (*continued*)

'love', the author of the 'books', not the 'books' themselves. (5) That 'books' cannot be 'presagers' of speech (Beeching). But they are not said to be. They are called 'presagers of my speaking breast', i.e. of the poet's heart. Besides, Beeching seems to be misinterpreting 'presagers' here (see note, below).

Both *books* and *looks* make sense—the former, in our view, the better sense; but even if it made only equally good sense we should prefer it as being the reading of the earliest known text.

10 *presagers*] Shakespeare may here be using loosely a word new to the language. Schmidt, citing this instance only, construes 'presager' as 'one who indicates'. *OED* quotes Spenser (1578) using the verb as = 'make known, point out or show'; hence Tucker explains 'presagers' as 'mouth-pieces, expounders', and Harrison takes the word to mean 'interpreters'. Perhaps the best meaning here is 'representatives' or 'ambassadors' (cf. Sonnet 26. 3: 'To thee I send this written ambassage To witness duty'). Certainly 'presagers' as 'augurs' or 'soothsayers' would not *plead*, which is their function here; and Beeching's contention, that we have here a pre-liminary dumb-show (of 'looks') maintaining the image of the 'unperfect' actor, shows a confused conception, for his actor is now plural, and far from 'unperfect'.

12] The first 'more' is adjectival (qualifying 'recompense') rather than adverbial (modifying 'look'). Of the second and third, one is a noun, meaning either 'more ardours of love' or 'more of your perfections' (Dowden), and the object of 'express'd', and the other an adverb meaning either 'more fulsomely' or 'at greater length'. Whether the 'tongue' is or is not a reference to some specific other poet (e.g. the Rival of Sonnets 78 ff) we prefer to leave to the discretion of each reader of the *Sonnets*.

13–14] i.e. the skill of reading the silent tokens of love can only be learnt by loving.

14 *eyes*] It is just possible that there may be a play here on 'ayes': cf. the (to modern ears atrocious) play on 'eye' in 104. 2.

fine wit] 'acute perceptiveness'.

23

As an unperfect actor on the stage,
Who with his fear is put besides his part,
Or some fierce thing replete with too much rage,
Whose strength's abundance weakens his own heart;   4
So I for fear of trust forget to say
The perfect ceremony of love's rite,
And in mine own love's strength seem to decay,
O'er-charg'd with burthen of mine own love's might: 8
Oh let my books be then the eloquence
And dumb presagers of my speaking breast,
Who plead for love and look for recompense
More than that tongue that more hath more express'd: 12
    Oh learn to read what silent love hath writ;
    To hear with eyes belongs to love's fine wit.

24 1 *steel'd*] Q: *steeld*. Capell emended to *stell'd*, and is followed by almost all editors, Wyndham being a notable exception. The arguments for emending or retaining Q may be summarized as follows:

For change to *stell'd*:
(1) The demand for a rhyme with 'held' (line 3).
Answer on behalf of *steeld*:
As Wyndham points out, in Sonnet 2. 4 'held' rhymes with 'field' (line 2); and in *Lucrece*, 1257 'held' (spelt in Q¹ (1594) *hild*) rhymes with 'kild' and' fulfild'.
For change to *stell'd*:
(2) 'Steld' occurs in *Lucrece*, 1444, rhyming with 'dweld' (line 1446). 'Steld' means either (*a*) 'fixed' (Dyce and many others, some of whom derive it from *ME. stellen* and *AS. stellan*, 'to place or station'); or (*b*) 'painted' (Lee); or (*c*) 'portrayed' (Tucker).
Answer on behalf of *steeld*:
'Steld' might in *Lucrece* be a form of 'steeld', and its rhyme is not conclusive (see (1) above), as Tucker admits. Moreover, the meaning 'fixed' is given in *OED* as Scottish, and in Wright's *Dictionary of Provincial English* as Northern.
For change to *stell'd*:
(3) If 'steld' in *Lucrece*, 1444 were = 'steeld', then the term could not refer with physical literalness to the artistic process. It could only refer metaphorically to such a process. This argues against *steeld* in Sonnet 24.
Answer on behalf of *steeld*:
In Sonnet 24 'steeld' would also be necessarily metaphorical.
For change to *stell'd*:
(4) The only plausible interpretation of *steeld* would be 'engraved', presumably with a steel point; but a 'painter' only works in colours with a brush (a point urged by, e.g., Beeching).
Answer on behalf of *steeld*:
At least from the time of Chaucer poets had used the terms 'to paint', 'to depaint', and even 'to grave', to some degree interchangeably. Chaucer, for instance, in *The Hous of Fame*, uses 'peynted' and 'graven' in two successive lines in what seems an identical sense (*HF.* 211–12). Likewise Ronsard, in that sonnet which Sir Sidney Lee referred to as a source of the present conceit (Ronsard, *Les Amours Diverses*, Sonnet iv, *Œuvres*, ed. P. de Nolhac, *Amours*, II. 285) uses the term 'graver' three times, and the term 'peindre' once, to refer to the representation of his beloved on the 'tablettes' of his heart. Again, Spenser, in at least one place, uses 'painted' for a figure in a tapestry. There was similar flexi-

24

Mine eye hath play'd the painter and hath steel'd
Thy beauty's form in table of my heart;
My body is the frame wherein 'tis held,
And pérspective it is best painter's art—   4
For through the painter must you see his skill
To find where your true image pictur'd lies,
Which in my bosom's shop is hanging still,
That hath his windows glazèd with thine eyes: 8
Now see what good turns eyes for eyes have done:—
Mine eyes have drawn thy shape, and thine for me
Are windows to my breast, wherethrough the sun
Delights to peep, to gaze therein on thee: 12
　　Yet eyes this cunning want to grace their art,—
　　They draw but what they see, know not the heart.

bility in the use of Fr. *peindre* (see Cotgrave and Littré) and of Lat.
pingere; and there is even evidence that the indeterminacy is traceable
still further back in philological history.

It would be rash, therefore, to assume that the use of the word
'painter' in line 1 definitively determines the medium in which he is
working.

For change to *stell'd*:

(5) There is no parallel in Shakespeare or elsewhere for the use of
'steel'd' in this or any similar sense.

Answer on behalf of *steeld*:

Shakespeare is well known to be a linguistic innovator. The word
'steel'd' can bear an intelligible and vigorous meaning, 'engraved' or
'indelibly carved'. Cf. 'Photographically lined on the tablets of my
mind / When a yesterday has faded from its page' (W. S. Gilbert, *The
Bab Ballads*). To give to old words new and powerful uses is highly
characteristic of Shakespeare. It is worth noting that the image of in-
scribing on a tablet with a stylus occurs in *Tit.A.* IV. i. 103–4: 'I will go
get a leaf of brass / And with a gad of steel will write'. It even seems to

24 *(continued)*

us likely that Shakespeare is here using 'steel'd' as meaning 'styled', i.e. inscribed or engraved on a tablet with a stylus. 'Style' used as a *noun* meaning 'stylus' could, in the sixteenth and seventeenth centuries, be spelt 'steele' (e.g. Higins, *Junius' Nomenclator, 7/2. Graphium* (1585): 'a writing wyer, or a steele wherewith to write or note'). 'Style' would, furthermore, have been so pronounced. There is admittedly no recorded use in *OED* of 'style' in the sense indicated; but Shakespeare often coins new verbs from current nouns, and some of these are nonce uses. Instances of such coinage are: 'to trench', in the sense of 'to cut or carve in or into a surface'; 'to trumpet' = 'to proclaim loudly'; 'to oar' = 'to row'; 'to wing', in the sense (1) 'to fly through or traverse by flying', (2) 'to take flight or fly'; 'to tongue' = 'to utter or articulate'; and, in the same line, 'to brain' = 'to conceive in the brain'.
For change to *stell'd*:

(6) In *Lear*, III. vii. 61, some copies of Q¹ read *steeled* for what is generally accepted to be *stellèd* ('and quench the stellèd fires', i.e. either (*a*) 'starry fires' or (*b*) 'fixed fires' = 'fixed stars').
Answer on behalf of *steeld*:

This shows that a compositor could misread *stelled* as *steeled*. But a misprint, which makes a scarcely intelligible reading, in some copies of one unreliable quarto does not prove an intelligible reading in another not always reliable quarto to be a misprint.

Conclusion: Both 'steel'd' and 'stell'd' make sense; but where, as here, the existing reading in the earliest known text makes at least as good sense as any emendation proposed, it is certainly correct policy to preserve the original reading. We suggest, moreover, that serious consideration be given to the possibility that 'steel'd' means 'styled'. In support of it we may add that the use of 'in' suggests an impression taken rather than a pigment spread.

2 *table*] 'tablet', on which the picture is engraved or painted.

1–2] 'My eye has played the artist, and delineated your picture in the tablet of my heart.'

4 *pérspective*] Used adjectivally: 'seen from the right angle' or 'seen through the appropriate optical glass', here 'through the painter' so as to 'find [the] true image' (line 6). In *H5*. V. ii. 347 'perspectively' occurs with similar sense: 'You see them perspectively, the cities turned into a maid'. The Elizabethan 'perspective' or optical glass that distorted, or readjusted a specially designed distortion, was a favourite toy, and many readers will be familiar with 'perspective' paintings which, like the skull

24

MINE EYE hath play'd the painter and hath steel'd
Thy beauty's form in table of my heart;
My body is the frame wherein 'tis held,
And pérspective it is best painter's art—   4
For through the painter must you see his skill
To find where your true image pictur'd lies,
Which in my bosom's shop is hanging still,
That hath his windows glazèd with thine eyes: 8
Now see what good turns eyes for eyes have done:—
Mine eyes have drawn thy shape, and thine for me
Are windows to my breast, wherethrough the sun
Delights to peep, to gaze therein on thee: 12
    Yet eyes this cunning want to grace their art,—
    They draw but what they see, know not the heart.

in Holbein's 'The Ambassadors', have to be viewed from one particular
angle to obtain the 'true image'. Ingenuity of interpretation is only needed
if 'it' be misread as appositional to 'perspective'. Shakespeare is not saying
that such clever projections are the highest form of pictorial art, but that
his heart's image of the Friend is a perfect portrait, though to realize this
we must see it through the poet's eye.
  8 *his*] 'its'.
  13 *cunning*] 'skill'.

25 3 *triumph*] Probably both (1) 'pomp' (cf. 'honour' and 'titles', line 2); and (2) 'exultant joy' (cf. 'boast').

4 *Unlook'd for*] Probably 'beyond expectation' rather than 'unnoticed' (in the sense of 'obscure'). The latter, redundant meaning fails to further the movement of the thought culminating in the final couplet.

that] Probably 'that person'.

5–12] Wyndham (approved by Beeching) finds these lines applicable to the fall of Essex, but falls of great men are a common occurrence, and, as W. Keller (*Shakespeares Werke*, 2 vols., Berlin, 1916, XV, 511) wisely remarks, particular interpretations are but rashly founded on writers' universal observations.

6 *But*] only.

marigold] The old English marigold is the 'pot marigold' (*Calendula officinalis*). The older Calendulas, as we can see when modern hybrids revert as self-sown seedlings, tend to close in the dark. The habit was frequently moralized in Elizabethan writing.

7] A characteristically ambiguous line where both meanings count: (1) 'Whereas, left to themselves (i.e. when the sun (of favour) does not shine), their handsome show closes on itself, and is unseen'; (2) 'And their flaunting conceit, self-centred, dies with them.'

9 *painful*] i.e. dutiful through all hardships.

9 *might*⎫ Q reads *worth* in line 9 and *quite* in line 11. Theobald first
11 *quite*⎭ suggested that it was necessary to read either *fight* in line 9 or *forth* in line 11. One or other has been customarily adopted. We follow Professor Sisson (*New Readings in Shakespeare*, II, 210) who maintains that *fight* has no graphic probability, and prefers with Capell to read *might*, *mi-* and *wo-* being confusable, and the rest of the word being perhaps mutilated in MS at the end of the line. Moreover, *quite* in line 11 seems preferable to *forth* because more emphatic (one defeat being enough to annul a thousand victories).

11 *rasèd*] So Q. Most editors follow Collier in spelling *razèd*, which in modern spelling suggests the irrelevant association of a destroyed city.

14 *remove . . . remov'd*] The transitive 'remov'd' often connoted displacement from office or favour. The intransitive 'remove' here, as in 116. 4, evidently implies inconstancy, though we have not found other instances of this figurative use.

25

Lᴇᴛ ᴛʜᴏꜱᴇ who are in favour with their stars
Of public honour and proud titles boast,
Whilst I, whom fortune of such triumph bars,
Unlook'd for joy in that I honour most.   4
Great princes' favourites their fair leaves spread
But as the marigold at the sun's eye,
And in themselves their pride lies burièd,
For at a frown they in their glory die.   8
The painful warrior famousèd for might,
After a thousand victories once foil'd,
Is from the book of honour rasèd quite,
And all the rest forgot for which he toil'd: 12
    Then happy I that love and am belov'd,
    Where I may not remove nor be remov'd.

26 *General Note:* Ever since Capell in Malone's 1780 edition saw a resemblance between the language of this sonnet and the Dedication to *Lucrece*, editors have been busy relating the two. They often happily find in an interpretation influenced by the Southampton theory 'evidence' for the theory itself. N. Drake (*Shakspeare and His Times*, 2 vols., Cadell & Davies, London, 1817, II, 63) founded the theory on this supposed resemblance, calling 'the language . . . almost precisely the same'!—a view which at least appears to overlook the existence of a common idiom in dedications.

3 *written*] Tucker comments that embassages were customarily verbal, hence the emphasis. Pooler doubts whether the reference is to this sonnet, to some accompanying MS, to the twenty-five sonnets preceding this, to those following, or to some other matter.

4–5 *wit*] = (line 4) 'literary ingenuity'; (line 5) 'intelligence'.

7 *good conceit*] 'kindly and ingenious fancy'. There is a play on (1) 'conception' and (2) 'literary conceit'—which the poet is saying (lines 4, 5) he has not the intelligence to produce.

8 *bestow*] 'give hospitable lodging' (to the poor 'naked' thing)—not, however, clothing it till line 11.

9 *moving*] Commentators have been quick to see here allusion to a proposed journey, probably an actor's tour, relating it to 27 ff; but the expression makes perfect sense in its direct association with the guiding star of the poet's actions and fortune. (We wonder no one has suggested that Shakespeare was moving house—perhaps to or from Bath or Wells: see 153. 11 and 154. 9!)

10 *Points on*] 'directs its rays on'—not 'points to'. Cf. *R2*. I. iii. 146: 'And those his golden beams . . . Shall point on me, and gild my banishment'.

fair] 'favourable'.

aspéct] in the astrological sense.

11 *totter'd*] 'tattered' (as in 2. 4).

12] 'To display me in a guise worthy of that beloved object to which they (my great duty and poor wit (line 5)) are directed.'

their] So Q. Capell emended to *thy*, and is followed by all editors before Professor Sisson. Sisson, while conceding that *their* for *thy* is a not infrequent and an easy printer's error, argues that 'worthy of thy sweet respect' (i.e. 'your kindly notice') is comparatively weak. While agreeing with Sisson that 'their sweet respect' is the Friend, we take 'their' to refer to the poet's great duty and poor wit (cf. line 5), rather than to his duty, star, and loving.

respect] 'object of regard'.

14 *prove*] bring to the test.

66

26

LORD OF my love, to whom in vassalage
Thy merit hath my duty strongly knit,
To thee I send this written ambassage
To witness duty, not to shew my wit,— 4
Duty so great, which wit so poor as mine
May make seem bare, in wanting words to shew it,
But that I hope some good conceit of thine
In thy soul's thought all naked will bestow it, 8
Till whatsoever star that guides my moving
Points on me graciously with fair aspéct,
And puts apparel on my totter'd loving
To show me worthy of their sweet respect: 12
    Then may I dare to boast how I do love thee,—
    Till then not show my head where thou mayst prove me.

27 2 *repose*] 'place of repose' (Tucker; *OED*: till 1671).

travel] So Capell in his MS correction (1766) of a copy of Lintot's edition (1711). Q: *travaill*, followed by some early editors and by Butler. *Travel* coheres with 'journey' (line 3) and with the general sense of this and the next sonnet. But the pun is present—working from 'travel' to 'travail'. Either reading may obscure the pun. Most modern editors wisely follow Capell.

3 Punctuation] So Q and a few modern editors. The comma after 'head' inserted by most modern editors seems intrusive, even if we construe with Pooler: 'then a journey begins in my head, so as to keep my mind active' (presumably = 'in such a way as to . . .'). To insert a comma only suggests the unacceptable sense 'in order to . . .'.

6 *Intend*] Not 'purpose' but 'take their way on' (cf. Lat. *iter intendere*).

8 *which . . . see*] 'which' = 'such as' (Tucker); i.e. 'utter darkness' (Pooler).

9 *imaginary*] 'imaginative'. Cf. *H5*. Prol. I. 17: 'Let us . . . on your imaginary forces work'.

10 *their shadow*] So Q; i.e. 'the insubstantial image (of you) engendered by my thoughts (line 5)'. Cf. the construction of 26. 5–12 and note on 26. 12. Capell's MS emendation (1766) *thy*, followed by most editors, is unnecessary. As Sisson, supporting Q, says, 'These are "witty" sonnets in a style alien to the eighteenth century commentators'.

11 *ghastly*] 'terrifying'; not implying the then new, and here irrelevant, suggestion of pallor.

12 *old*] for Night is a hag.

14 *For*] 'on account of'.

for] both (1) 'on account of' and (2) 'to the comfort of'. The greater density of this second 'for' gives strength to the line.

27

Weary with toil I haste me to my bed,
The dear repose for limbs with travel tir'd;
But then begins a journey in my head
To work my mind when body's work's expir'd: 4
For then my thoughts, from far where I abide,
Intend a zealous pilgrimage to thee,
And keep my drooping eyelids open wide,
Looking on darkness which the blind do see: 8
Save that my soul's imaginary sight
Presents their shadow to my sightless view,
Which like a jewel hung in ghastly night
Makes black night beauteous and her old face new.   12
    Lo, thus by day my limbs, by night my mind,
    For thee, and for myself, no quiet find.

28 5 *other's*] Q: *ethers*. Malone and all modern editors: *either's*. There are three possibilities: (1) that the Q compositor dropped an 'i'; (2) that he set an 'e' for an 'o'; (3) that the MS read *ethers* = 'either's' (*eþer* occurs in Middle English as a variant, e.g. *Romance of Sir Degrevant*, 1177). We restore *other's*, the reading of early editors till Evans (1775), and also of Capell, on two grounds: the many parallel uses in Shakespeare of 'other' = 'the other', e.g. *LLL.* I. i. 305, *A&C.* II. ii. 142; and the unhesitating acceptance by early editors of *others* (= 'other's') as a natural use.

7 *to complain*] 'by giving me cause to complain'.

8 *still . . . off*] 'always getting farther'.

9] So Q. Some editors insert a comma at 'day', making 'to please . . .' the object of 'tell'. Others isolate 'to please him' by commas, as adverbial, modifying 'tell' not 'art'. By following Q's omission of commas we leave the reader the reasonable right to choose for himself.

10 *do'st him grace*] So Q. Modern editors: *dost*, which might misleadingly suggest that 'dost' is an auxiliary and 'grace' a verb. But 'grace' is a noun and the object of 'do'st'. 'Do'st him grace' = 'confer beauty on him'.

11 Punctuation] Q has a comma at *night*, but to retain this as some editors do, or still worse, to strengthen it, as other editors do, to a semi-colon, obscures the parallel between lines 9–10 and lines 11–12.

flatter] i.e. beguile by telling. ('That . . .' is to be understood at the beginning of line 12.)

12 *twire*] 'peep'. So used by Jonson, Beaumont and Fletcher, Marston and other contemporaries of Shakespeare. As 'tweer' or 'twire' the word is still in dialect use.

gild'st] So almost all modern editors. Q: *guil'st*, followed by Benson, Lintot, and Gildon[1]. Gildon[2] and Sewell[1] emend to *guild'st*. The only possible meaning for *guil'st* would be 'beguil'st', which would parallel 'flatter' (line 11), but the real parallel is with 'do'st . . . grace' (line 10). 'Gild' = 'to ornament' occurs a few times in Shakespeare, 'guile' as a verb never.

13, 14 *longer . . . length . . . stronger*] So Q and some modern editors. Capell and most modern editors: *longer . . . strength . . . stronger*, but logic is satisfied without the emendation ('each day lengthens the period of my sorrows, and each night intensifies my awareness of its length').

28

How can I then return in happy plight
That am debarr'd the benefit of rest,
When day's oppression is not eas'd by night,
But day by night and night by day oppress'd,   4
And each, though enemies to other's reign,
Do in consent shake hands to torture me,
The one by toil, the other to complain
How far I toil, still farther off from thee?   8
I tell the day to please him thou art bright
And do'st him grace when clouds do blot the heaven;
So flatter I the swart-complexion'd night
When sparkling stars twire not thou gild'st the even: 12
   But day doth daily draw my sorrows longer,
   And night doth nightly make grief's length seem stronger.

29 *General Note:* For a good note on this sonnet as exemplifying Shakespeare's spiral development in the sonnet form see W. H. Hadow, *Music and Poetry*, Cambridge University Press, London, 1926, showing how 'state' changes from minor to major key.

1 *in disgrace*] 'out of favour' (without any implication of shame, cf. 33. 8, 34. 8, in which cases, however, the sense is physical).

Fortune] The capital is commonly removed by editors, thus reducing the personification to a mere abstraction.

6 *him . . . him*] 'This man . . . that man', *not* = the 'one' of line 5.

7 *art*] skill or learning or both.

scope] range of ability or range of opportunity or both.

11, 12] Q prints line 11 in parentheses. Some modern editors remove these, some extend the bracket to 'earth', and some close it after 'day'. Other editors use commas for the same ends. Wyndham prints and defends Q. But Q cannot stand, as neither the lark nor the poet sings 'from sullen earth'. To use parentheses in a modern recension would, in any case, be heavy. The best solution seems to be a comma at 'earth' and no stop at 'arising', allowing to the lark image the fullest possible development without suggesting (as might a complete absence of commas) that the lark's song comes 'from sullen earth'.

12 *sullen*] (1) 'dull', 'heavy', in contrast with the soaring bird and the light element, air; and probably also (2) 'sombre', in contrast with the breaking light.

29

When, in disgrace with Fortune and men's eyes,
I all alone beweep my outcast state,
And trouble deaf heaven with my bootless cries,
And look upon myself and curse my fate— 4
Wishing me like to one more rich in hope,
Featur'd like him, like him with friends possess'd,
Desiring this man's art and that man's scope,
With what I most enjoy contented least; 8
Yet in these thoughts myself almost despising
Haply I think on thee, and then my state,
Like to the lark at break of day arising
From sullen earth, sings hymns at heaven's gate: 12
　　For thy sweet love remember'd such wealth brings
　　That then I scorn to change my state with kings.

30 1, 2 *sessions . . . summon*] 'When I sit alone and meditate on the past.'
Cf. for the legal image, *Oth.* III. iii. 138–141:

> . . . who has a breast so pure
> But some uncleanly apprehensions
> Keep leets and law days, and in session sit
> With meditations lawful?

Here the 'sessions', being 'of thought', are necessarily silent. They are
'sweet' because that is the poet's mood. The atmosphere suggested by the
language of the sonnet is that of an enquiry in a manorial court, presided
over by Thought, the Lord of the Manor, or his Steward, into the con-
dition of the estate, its losses and resources. Relevant words are: 'waste',
'dateless', 'cancell'd', 'expense', 'vanish'd', 'tell o'er', 'account', 'pay',
'losses', 'restor'd'.

4] So Q. Whatever line 4 means it does not merely repeat the sense of
line 3; but does 'dear' qualify 'times' or 'waste'? And is 'times' singular
('time's') or plural ('times'' or 'times')? And is 'waste'a noun or, possibly,
a participle or even an indicative verb, as E. A. Kock attractively suggested
in *Anglia*, 31 (1908), 134? The line probably means either (1) 'by calling
to mind old misfortunes, lament afresh the passing of my precious
years'; or (2) 'grieve afresh both over my old misfortunes and over the
passing of my happy days'; or (3) 'spend my precious moments in the fresh
bewailing of old woes' (Kock). *Woes* would then need to read *Woes'*,
which would be consistent with Q printing.

new] afresh.

dear] In Elizabethan usage the word has several senses, some of which
no single modern word adequately translates. Shakespearean examples are:
R2. I. iii. 151: 'thy dear exile' (not simply = 'thy grievous exile', but also
indicating that the homeland is dear); and *Temp.* II. i. 141–2: '*Sebastian*: the
fault's / Your own. *Alonso*: So is the dearest of the loss', (not simply = 'the
direst part of the loss', but also implying that the thing lost (his son) was
most precious to him). In line 4 the sense of 'dear' depends on that of
'times' and that of 'waste' (see below).

dear times waste] So Q and early editors. Dyce (Aldine Poets) and a few
modern editors: *times'*. The rest: *time's*. That time so frequently in the
Sonnets is the destroyer would support *time's*, and make 'waste' =
'destruction'. 'Dear' would then either (1) have to qualify a compound
('time's-waste'), which is possible, but may be without parallel in Shake-
speare,—the whole phrase then meaning 'time's grievous destruction of
things dear' (cf. note on 'dear', above); or (2) qualify only 'time's', the
sense being 'destruction of the best part of my life'. Reading *times'*, sense

30

<big>W</big>HEN TO the sessions of sweet silent thought
I summon up remembrance of things past,
I sigh the lack of many a thing I sought,
And with old woes new wail my dear times waste: 4
Then can I drown an eye, unus'd to flow,
For precious friends hid in death's dateless night,
And weep afresh love's long since cancell'd woe,
And moan the expense of many a vanish'd sight: 8
Then can I grieve at grievances foregone,
And heavily from woe to woe tell o'er
The sad account of fore-bemoanèd moan,
Which I new pay as if not paid before.   12
    But if the while I think on thee, dear friend,
    All losses are restor'd and sorrows end.

(2) only is possible. Neither reading would warrant the interpretation 'waste of my precious time', which would be wholly inconsistent with the thought of the sonnet. The reading *times*, in a modern edition, could make 'waste' a participle = 'wasted' (cf. 'miscreate' *H5*. I. ii. 16; 'create' *MND.* V. ii. 35, and *R&J.* I. i. 183; though these are all formed from Latin participles). We have deliberately retained Q, not in order to suggest this meaning, but so as not to force on the reader any of the interpretations outlined. We incline to (2).

  6 *dateless*] 'endless'.

  8 *expense*] 'loss', cf. 94. 6.

  9 *foregone*] 'past and done with'.

  10 *tell*] 'count'.

31 1 *endearèd*] 'made more precious'. The conceit running through the sonnet, that the Friend embodies all those the poet has loved, springs from 30. 6 and 14, and is epitomized in this word.

3 *and all love's loving parts*] i.e. all the parts of the poet's love which have been shared among those he has lost are now united in the Friend. Cf. line 11.

5 *obsequious*] 'reverentially mourning'.

6 *dear*] 'keenly felt' (Tucker).

religious] 'devoutly assiduous'. Cf. *un religieux*, and 'a religious' in earlier (and in modern Catholic) English usage, for one who lives according to the *rule* of an order.

stol'n] The strict observance of the dues of his loving sorrow has extracted from him tears which were not really due, since the 'dead' still live in his friend.

7 *interest*] 'a right', 'a claim', a legal use still current.

which] 'who', i.e. the dead.

appear] 'are revealed as' (*not* 'seem to be').

8 *remov'd*] 'moved' from one place to another.

thee] So Gildon, followed by almost all modern editors. Q, Benson, Lintot: *there*. Wyndham defends Q, maintaining that 'there' refers back to 'thy bosom' (line 1) and to 'And there' (line 3). Q makes sense, and coheres with the rest of the octave; but *thee* provides a better sounding line, and also sums up the octave more effectively and links well with the first words of the sestet.

10 *trophies*] i.e. 'memorials of all my former loves' conquests of me (which now belong to you)'. (Cf. 'parts' (line 11) and 'due' (line 12), which would naturally grace their 'grave' (line 9).)

lovers] 'friends'. Cf. *JC*. III. ii. 49: 'I (Brutus) slew my best lover for the good of Rome.'

11 *parts of me*] 'shares in me'.

31

THY BOSOM is endearèd with all hearts
Which I by lacking have supposèd dead,
And there reigns love, and all love's loving parts,
And all those friends which I thought burièd.   4
How many a holy and obsequious tear
Hath dear religious love stol'n from mine eye
As interest of the dead, which now appear
But things remov'd that hidden in thee lie!   8
Thou art the grave where buried love doth live,
Hung with the trophies of my lovers gone,
Who all their parts of me to thee did give,—
That due of many now is thine alone.   12
   Their images I lov'd I view in thee;
   And thou, all they, hast all the all of me.

32 *General Note:* This is one of the sonnets (like 55) into which commentators have read the theory that Shakespeare regarded his plays as 'potboilers', and believed real literary fame and the regard of a patron must depend on the Sonnets. (For a lively expression of the theory see Pete the Parrot in Don Marquis's *archie and mehitabel*.) C. H. Crandall (*Representative Sonnets*, 1890, 50) even found here a prevision of the resurgence of the Petrarchan form over the Shakespearean, and considered that Shakespeare was writing his own excuse! But do such ideas help the understanding of the *Sonnets*, any more than the theory itself represents Shakespeare's attitude to his own plays? More important are Shakespeare's evident awareness that he was living at a time of great literary achievement, and his uncertainty, at the time of writing this sonnet, of his own place in that swift advance.

1 *well-contented day*] i.e. 'the day of my death, which I shall quite cheerfully welcome'. No morbid reflection, but satisfaction with life, and confidence to accept death.

2 *churl Death*] Death seen as a gravedigger (Beeching), with, however, a secondary implication of a rough, discourteous fellow.

3 *by fortune*] 'by chance', i.e. 'thou shalt happen to . . .'

4 *poor rude lines*] Contrast 'eternal lines' (18. 12). But need a many-mooded series of sonnets maintain a consistent attitude to things they treat of?

5 *the bettering of the time*] Cf. line 13: 'poets better prove'. The Elizabethans were conscious of their age as one of 'progress in poesy' ('this growing age' (line 10)).

7 *Reserve*] 'preserve', 'keep' (as something worthwhile).

rhyme] 'poetry'.

8 *happier*] Either (1) because more felicitously gifted as poets, or (2) because living in the coming years of improved poetry.

12 *in ranks . . . equipage*] i.e. in the company of poets of more splendid style (cf. lines 4 and 14).

equipage] literally 'dress'.

32

I<small>F THOU</small> survive my well-contented day,
When that churl Death my bones with dust shall cover,
And shalt by fortune once more re-survey
These poor rude lines of thy deceasèd lover,   4
Compare them with the bettering of the time,
And though they be outstripp'd by every pen
Reserve them for my love, not for their rhyme,
Exceeded by the height of happier men.   8
Oh then vouchsafe me but this loving thought:
'Had my friend's Muse grown with this growing age,
A dearer birth than this his love had brought
To march in ranks of better equipage: 12
   But since he died, and poets better prove,
   Theirs for their style I'll read, his for his love'.

33 *General Note:* Comment on this sonnet superbly illustrates the range of variation deriving from temperament and predilection. S. T. Coleridge (*Biographia Literaria*, 2 vols., Rest Fenner, London, 1817, II, 18) acclaims the opening lines as exemplifying how Shakespeare 'gives a dignity and a passion to the objects which he presents. Unaided by any previous excitement, they burst upon us at once in life and in power.' J. C. Ransom (*The World's Body*, Scribners, New York, 1938, 280) finds 'this sun . . . weakly imagined . . . only felt, a loose cluster of images as obscure as they are pleasant, furnished by the half-conscious memories attending the pretty words'. Yet G. Sarrazin (*Aus Shakespeares Meisterwerkstatt*, Berlin, 1906, 221) assured himself that the lines 'definitely indicate a long residence in a mountainous region, and that too in a land rich in sunlight'.

Sonnet 33 begins a group of 'estrangement' sonnets. Interpretation will depend on the weight and literalness accorded to certain words. J. Q. Adams lists nineteen 'strong words' from 33 and 34, e.g. 'basest', 'ugly', 'disgrace', 'stain', 'grief', 'repent', 'loss', 'cross', 'ill deeds'. But these must, of course, be given the sense primary in their context, which is often milder than the mere list would suggest.

2 *Flatter*] 'encourage and brighten', as the sovereign's glance of favour would 'flatter' the courtier (at times delusively).

4] Much has been written about this image. In itself the image was not uncommon at the time, nor would it be difficult to invent at any time. It is its *exploitation* here that is characteristic of the Shakespeare of the *Sonnets.*

5 *permit*⎫ Both infinitives, like 'flatter', are governed by 'have I seen'
7 *hide* ⎭ (line 1).

5 *basest*] Probably 'dingiest' (see *OED.* 5), with a play on 'meanest', 'shabbiest'.

6 *rack*] 'vaporous drift'.

8 *Stealing*] not primarily with *furtive* but with *imperceptible* motion. (Cf. 104. 10.) Yet the sense of furtiveness is also there.

disgrace] 'blemish', 'disfigurement', 'dis-(= loss of)-grace (beauty)'; but perhaps also 'shame' (cf. line 7).

10 *all triumphant*] Almost all modern editors hyphenate, in our view unwarrantedly. 'All' surely qualifies 'splendour' not 'triumphant'? (Cf. *R2.* V. i. 54: 'With all swift speed'.)

triumphant] 'glorious and exulting' rather than 'victorious', which would be irrelevant. Even a sense of victory over *the poet* would conflict with line 11.

12 *region*] 'of the air'. (Cf. *Ham.* II. ii. 615: 'all the region kites'.) Originally, simply any one of the layers into which the atmosphere was

33

Full many a glorious morning have I seen
Flatter the mountain tops with sovereign eye,
Kissing with golden face the meadows green,
Gilding pale streams with heavenly alchemy,— 4
Anon permit the basest clouds to ride
With ugly rack on his celestial face,
And from the forlorn world his visage hide,
Stealing unseen to west with this disgrace: 8
Even so my sun one early morn did shine
With all triumphant splendour on my brow;
But out alack, he was but one hour mine—
The region cloud hath mask'd him from me now. 12
 Yet him for this my love no whit disdaineth:
 Suns of the world may stain, when heaven's sun staineth.

theoretically divided. Something dark and unworthy has come between the
friends.
 14 *stain*] 'grow dim', 'lose brightness'. Sherwood (1632) gives 'stain:
descolourer'. Cotgrave (1611) conversely gave '*descolouré*: grown pale, wanne,
lowe; that hath lost it colour, or hue'.

34 *General Note:* Story-hunters, by literal interpretation, have here detected specific events. Thus Samuel Butler invented a waylaying and rough-handling of the poet that caused the 'lameness' he takes literally in 37. 9 and 89. 3, and F. G. Fleay (*A Biographical Chronicle of the English Drama*, 1559–1642, 2 vols., London, 1891, II, 216) interpreted line 2 as '(Make me) appear publicly as an author'.

3 *base*] See note on 'basest', 33. 5.

4 *bravery*] 'splendid show' (of friendliness).

rotten] Commonly used of unwholesome vapours. Cf. *Lucr.* 778: 'rotten damps'.

7 *well*] 'favourably'.

8 *heals*] Q: *heales*; Tucker: *heles*. Two distinct words cohere as homographs in earlier modern English: (1) ⟨Old English *hǣlan* = to heal, in the modern sense, (2) ⟨Old English *helian* = to cover, or hide. So Caxton: 'But the preest alway heled (i.e. concealed) his sin'. No subsequent editor has accepted Tucker's reading, and it is, indeed, unnecessary, for the antithesis here is not between covering the wound and healing it, but between closing the wound and leaving no scar (as in *Lucr.* 731–2).

disgrace] 'disfigurement' (cf. 33. 8).

12 *cross*] So Capell, adopted by Malone and all subsequent editors. Q: *losse*.

13 *sheds*] Q: *sheeds*, giving a more perfect rhyme. The vowel in Middle English *schēden* had been long.

34

Why didst thou promise such a beauteous day,
And make me travel forth without my cloak,
To let base clouds o'ertake me in my way,
Hiding thy bravery in their rotten smoke?   4
'Tis not enough that through the cloud thou break
To dry the rain on my storm-beaten face,
For no man well of such a salve can speak
That heals the wound and cures not the disgrace: 8
Nor can thy shame give physic to my grief;
Though thou repent, yet I have still the loss:
The offender's sorrow lends but weak relief
To him that bears the strong offence's cross.   12
    Ah, but those tears are pearl which thy love sheds;
    And they are rich, and ransom all ill deeds.

35 3 *stain*] 'dim' (cf. the intransitive use in 33. 14).

4 *canker*] the cankerworm, a caterpillar or larva devouring the bud from within.

4] Tucker credibly suggests that the meaning is that the sweeter the bud the more readily the canker chooses it. He cites parallels from Lyly and from *Two G.* I. i. 42:

> 'Yet writers say, as in the sweetest bud
> The eating canker dwells, so eating love
> Inhabits in the finest wits of all.'

But the meaning could equally well be: 'however sweet the bud you may yet find a worm inside it'.

5 *make faults*] 'commit offences', not merely 'make mistakes' (cf. line 13).

even I in this] 'even so do I in this'.

6 *Authórizing . . . with compare*] 'justifying . . . by analogy.'

7] So Q; Capell: *myself corrupt in salving*, where 'corrupt' could either be adjective or verb—an emendation which has received some support; but almost all modern editors retain Q's wording, inserting, however, a comma at *corrupting*. We consider this comma not only unnecessary but misleading, and interpret: 'corrupting my self in salving'—i.e. the would-be physician catches the disease. This line, with its religious, medical, and legal associations, is pivotal in the poem.

salving] 'palliating'.

amiss] 'offence'.

8 *their . . . their*] So Q, and all editors before Malone. Capell MS, Malone, and almost all modern editors: *thy . . . thy*. Wyndham, also Sisson (op. cit.): *thy . . . . their*. Misprints of *their* for *thy* are certainly common in Q, but this is not conclusive. Most subsequent editors, however, have found Q unintelligible. Yet it seems to us that Q may bear a coherent sense, namely: 'All men commit offences, and, in fact, I am doing so in trying to justify your misconduct by drawing those analogies (in the first quatrain), thus corrupting myself in palliating your offence, since I am by implication exonerating those natural objects from a moral turpitude they are incapable of (thus confusing the natural and the moral orders).' If we were to read *thy . . . thy*, the meaning would not be all that dissimilar, viz. that the poet is giving excessive exculpation for his friend's misconduct by reducing it, through his analogies, from a moral to a natural fault. His excuse for his friend's offence would be stretched so much wider than the offence itself that it would, if valid (which the poet knows it is not), exculpate all sins whatever. As for *thy . . . their*, this

84

35

No more be griev'd at that which thou hast done:
Roses have thorns, and silver fountains mud,
Clouds and eclipses stain both moon and sun,
And loathsome canker lives in sweetest bud;⠀⠀⠀⠀⠀⠀4
All men make faults, and even I in this,
Authórizing thy trespass with compare,
My self corrupting salving thy amiss,
Excusing their sins more than their sins are:⠀⠀⠀⠀8
For to thy sensual fault I bring in sense—
Thy adverse party is thy advocate—
And 'gainst myself a lawful plea commence:
Such civil war is in my love and hate⠀⠀⠀⠀⠀⠀12
⠀⠀That I an áccessary needs must be
⠀⠀To that sweet thief which sourly robs from me.

could give the meaning: 'excusing your sins which are more numerous (Sisson), or greater in magnitude, than the "sins" of the roses, fountains, and so on'. In view of the frequency of the undoubted misprints in Q of *their* for *thy* the two emended readings mentioned must both be considered possible. On the other hand, since Q seems to us to afford a sense no more obscure than they do, we have retained its reading.

⠀⠀9 *sensual . . . sense*] The poet is guilty of bringing reason (the distinctively human faculty) to the defence of the 'sensual fault' by casuistry. The evident homophonic play may possibly also involve a secondary meaning for 'sense', viz. 'feeling', and so 'sympathetic understanding'. Malone's emendation *incense* is unnecessary and improbable. Shakespeare always accents the noun 'íncense'. Also, among many spellings of 'incense' over the centuries, 'insence' is not recorded by *OED*, so that Malone's emendation would involve not merely closing up the words, but a most improbable spelling at some stage in the history of the text of this line. The Q text, however, may well involve a *play* on 'incense' as a sweetener of the fault.

⠀⠀11 *lawful*] Probably primarily 'in due legal form', but possibly there is also the suggestion that the plea is just.

⠀⠀14] Cf. 40. 9.

36 1 *Let me confess*] Probably simply: 'I must admit', rather than a confession of guilt, as Tucker suggests. That, such as it is, only comes later in the sonnet.

3 *those blots*] What these are is obscure. Pooler sees here a reference to the 'disgrace with fortune and men's eyes' of 29. 1, and suspects that 36 has got out of sequence. This is possible, but no more. Adams suggests that the reference may be to 'the "stain" given the poet by the friend' (33. 14, 35. 3); but this depends on a misinterpretation of 'stain' (see notes on the lines cited).

5 *respect*] 'focus of attention', as frequently in Shakespeare.

one respect] probably refers to the same unity as 'love's sole effect' (line 7).

6 *separable*] 'separating'. Shakespearean uses of adjectives in '-ble' as active are not uncommon. See Abbott, *Shakespearian Grammar*, s. 3, and W. Franz, *Shakespeare-Grammatik*, s. 131.

spite] 'injurious stroke of fortune'.

7 *love's sole effect*] i.e. the identical working of our love.

9 *not evermore*] 'never again'.

10 *my bewailèd guilt*] We agree with Beeching that 'we have no clear light from any other passage in the Sonnets upon this expression', though there may be some connexion with the 'harmful deeds' of 111. 2.

13, 14] As Malone pointed out, this couplet also concludes 96.

14 *As*] 'that'.

mine is thy good report] 'your good name belongs to me'.

36

L ᴇᴛ ᴍᴇ confess that we two must be twain
Although our undivided loves are one:
So shall those blots that do with me remain
Without thy help by me be borne alone.   4
In our two loves there is but one respect,
Though in our lives a separable spite,
Which, though it alter not love's sole effect,
Yet doth it steal sweet hours from love's delight.   8
I may not evermore acknowledge thee,
Lest my bewailèd guilt should do thee shame;
Nor thou with public kindness honour me,
Unless thou take that honour from thy name: 12
　　But do not so; I love thee in such sort
　　As, thou being mine, mine is thy good report.

37 3 *lame*] That William Shakespeare alias Francis or Anthony Bacon alias Walter Raleigh, not to mention his other names, was crook-backed (87. 8 and 90. 3), had a scar over the left eye, and was lame in the left leg (here and 89. 3), as a result of (*a*) a scuffle in which he was ambushed and beaten up, (*b*) an accident at the Fortune Theatre ('Fortune's dearest spite'), (*c*) serving as a soldier in the Low Countries, (*d*) fighting (in his role as Sir Walter Raleigh) at Cadiz in 1596, has all been triumphantly proved from the Sonnets; whence it has also been revealed that he once resided in Bath and in Wells (26, 153, 154) and in Southern Europe (33).

The reader more interested in literature than in detection may be content to take the word in a less arcanal and more metaphorical sense, as in *KL.* IV. vi. 225 (Q text): 'A most poor man made lame by Fortune's blows.'

dearest] 'most grievous'.

spite] Possibly in the now current sense of 'malice', but possibly in the obsolete sense of 'injury'. In either case the nature of Shakespeare's resulting misfortune is unclear.

4 *comfort*] Consolation and 'delight' (cf. line 1), as sometimes elsewhere in Shakespeare, e.g. *R&J.* I. ii. 26: 'Such comfort as do lusty young men feel When well-apparel'd April on the heel Of limping winter treads.'

of] 'from'.

truth] The Sonnets ring many changes on the senses and implications of 'true' and 'truth', e.g. loyalty, sincerity, genuineness, uprightness (physical or moral), closeness to an ideal pattern. Here, whatever the precise metaphorical sense of 'lame', a metaphorical sense of 'truth' must correspond to it.

7] So Q. Capell: *thy parts*, followed by nearly all modern editors. Q yields sense, and, according to whether the metaphor be (1) courtly, (2) heraldic, (3) theatrical, would mean (1) 'take precedence by virtue of quality'; (2) 'are blazoned in their parts of a crowned escutcheon'; (3)'sit on their thrones playing the sovereign parts assigned them'. Our order of preference is (1), (2), (3). (2) is elaborately explained by Wyndham, who reads *intituled*. Professor G. B. Harrison (Penguin Edition, 1938) glosses 'entitled: enrolled', but without citing any authority.

8] 'I graft my love on this abundance' (cf. line 11), i.e. on all these good qualities.

10] 'Shadow' and 'substance' were frequently contrasted at the time. Here the paradox is that it is the shadow which provides the substance.

shadow] 'image' (of the Friend), evoked by contemplating his qualities (lines 4 ff), cf. 27. 10. Beeching attractively explains: 'Here "substance" means the possession by the poet of the excellences of the Friend, and

37

As a decrepit father takes delight
To see his active child do deeds of youth,
So I, made lame by Fortune's dearest spite,
Take all my comfort of thy worth and truth;   4
For whether beauty, birth, or wealth, or wit,
Or any of these all, or all, or more,
Entitled in their parts, do crownèd sit,
I make my love engrafted to this store: 8
So then I am not lame, poor, nor despis'd,
Whilst that this shadow doth such substance give
That I in thy abundance am suffic'd,
And by a part of all thy glory live: 12
    Look what is best, that best I wish in thee;
    This wish I have—then ten times happy me!

"shadow" the imaginary possession of them.' I.e. by recalling the Friend's good qualities the poet acquires a measure of them.

11 *suffic'd*] 'adequately replenished', 'satisfied', cf. *F.Q.* I. ii. 43.

13 *Look what is best,*] So Q. The comma after *Look*, often inserted by modern editors, yields a modern idiomatic reading; but there are a number of instances in Shakespeare of 'look' = 'look for', 'seek', e.g. 'He hath been all this day to look you', *AYLI.* II. v. 33. (See Abbott, *Shakespearian Grammar*, s. 200, and Schmidt.) *Look what* is thus tantamount to 'whatever'.

38 1 *want . . . invent*] 'be at a loss for a topic'. The old academic rhetoric recognized five categories or processes of expression: *inventio, dispositio, elocutio, memoria, pronunciatio.* The first is defined by Sir T. Wilson (*The Art of Rhetorique,* 1553) as 'the finding out of apt matter . . . a searching out of things true or things likely, the which may reasonably set forth a matter'.

3 *Thine . . . argument*] 'yourself as a theme to write about'.

4 *vulgar paper*] 'commonplace piece of scribbling'.

rehearse] 'set forth'.

5 *in me*] i.e. in my writings.

6 *stand . . . sight*] 'meets your eye'.

12 *numbers*] cf. 17. 6, note.

13 *slight Muse*] The modesty here, as in, e.g., 16, is as conventional as the arrogance of, e.g., 17. 14 and of the couplets of 18 and 19.

curious] 'hypercritical', but perhaps also laboriously ingenious in composition as well as in criticism.

14 *pain*] 'pains', 'trouble'.

38

How can my Muse want subject to invent
While thou dost breathe that pour'st into my verse
Thine own sweet argument, too excellent
For every vulgar paper to rehearse? 4
Oh, give thyself the thanks if aught in me
Worthy perusal stand against thy sight;
For who's so dumb that cannot write to thee,
When thou thyself dost give invention light? 8
Be thou the tenth Muse, ten times more in worth
Than those old nine which rhymers invocate;
And he that calls on thee, let him bring forth
Eternal numbers to outlive long date. 12
 If my slight Muse do please these curious days,
 The pain be mine, but thine shall be the praise.

39 1 *with manners*] 'with decent modesty'.

2] cf. 74. 8.

3–4] The most evident meaning is: 'What benefit to myself can blowing my own trumpet bring? And what is it but blowing my own trumpet when I praise you?' (cf. line 2). But is there also a play on 'mine own self' as 'you' (as often in the *Sonnets*) with the meaning: 'What honour can praise of myself bring to you, and what is it but praise of myself when I praise you?'?

6 *dear*] Probably not only 'precious' but also 'keenly felt'.

lose . . . one] 'lose the reputation of being a union of inseparables'.

7 *separation*; 9 *absence*; 13–14] How literally these should be taken is a hard question, and it could only be answered in the context of a total view as to the biographical content of the *Sonnets* and as to their correct order.

10 *sour leisure*] 'dreary stretch of empty time' (made so by absence).

11 *entertain*] 'pass agreeably', 'beguile'. Cf. *1H4.* V. i. 24: 'to entertain the lag-end of my life With quiet hours'.

12] So Q. Capell MS: *do deceive*. Malone and almost all modern editors: *doth*, generally taken as singular, with 'love' as subject, though 'doth' could be plural in Elizabethan English, and, if plural here, would have 'time and thoughts' as subject. Wyndham and a few modern editors, including Professor Sisson, support Q. There are two possibilities for the syntax of Q: (1) to supply, as Wyndham and Sisson suggest, 'thou' (standing for 'absence') as the subject of 'dost deceive', which would entail taking 'Which time' as = 'which same time'; (2) to take 'Which' as = 'Who', with 'absence' as antecedent. (2) has the advantage that no subject need be supplied, but the disadvantage that the relative is inconveniently far from the antecedent.

so] Either merely intensive, or as = 'in this manner'.

deceive] Possibly, as Malone and others have thought, 'beguile', which seems somewhat repetitive of 'entertain'; or, as we incline to think, 'delude' (with daydreams for realities).

13–14] 'And that you teach me how to make one person into two, namely, by the device of praising him in these lines, which makes him present to me, though absent'.

39

Oʜ ʜoᴡ thy worth with manners may I sing
When thou art all the better part of me?
What can mine own praise to mine own self bring?
And what is't but mine own when I praise thee?   4
Even for this let us divided live,
And our dear love lose name of single one,
That by this separation I may give
That due to thee which thou deserv'st alone.   8
O absence, what a torment wouldst thou prove,
Were it not thy sour leisure gave sweet leave
To entertain the time with thoughts of love,
Which time and thoughts so sweetly dost deceive,   12
   And that thou teachest how to make one twain
   By praising him here who doth hence remain!

40 *General Note:* The full meaning of this sonnet is particularly dependent on ambiguities.

1 *all my loves*] 'all the kinds of love I have'—e.g. my affection and my mistress as well.

3 *No love*] Both (1) 'No mistress' and (2) 'No affection'.

true] Probably having all the following meanings: (1) 'constant'; (2) 'honest'; (3) 'genuine'.

love] again ambiguous.

3–4] The main drift would appear to be: 'You would not acquire any *true* love [in either sense], for all my affection was yours already.' The apparently deliberate restriction of the sense of love in 'mine' (line 4) would be a device of 'wit'.

5 *for my love*] (1) 'out of love for me'—being willing to love anything that is mine; (2) 'in place of my love for you'; (3) (Beeching): 'as being my love' (with, we presume, a play on (*a*) affection, (*b*) object of affection).

my love receivest] 'you "receive" my mistress'—a masterly understatement.

6 *I cannot blame thee, for . . . usest*] So Q, followed by Malone and some modern editors. Most modern editors remove the comma, the sense then being: 'I cannot blame you for using . . .'. Shakespearean parallels can be cited for this construction, e.g. *R3.* II. ii. 95: ''Tis called ungrateful . . . to be thus opposite with heaven, For it requires (= for requiring) the royal debt it lent you.' Without the comma the sexual meaning of 'for . . . usest' becomes dominant. With it the ambiguity is more balanced.

7 *this self . . .* 8 *thy self*] So Q. Gildon: *thy self . . . thy self*, which most modern editors accept, closing up the two words in each case into *thyself*. We agree with Wyndham's interpretation of *this self* as 'the poet' (cf. 39 and 42). The meaning of lines 7 and 8 could then be: 'But you are to blame if your betrayal of me is such as involves deliberate indulgence in something repellent to your deeper self ('thy self').' Possibly there is also a play on the two senses of love (cf. note on line 3) implied in 'what'— my mistress (whom you 'taste') and my affection (which you are repudiating).

Another possibility (which we have not seen suggested) is that by the not uncommon error of 'attraction' a copyist or compositor might have substituted the repetition from line 7 of *selfe* for a correct reading *sense* in line 8. The reading *sense* as = 'reason' (cf. 35. 9), in contrast to 'taste', would give a fairly typical line, which would, however, cohere better with the reading *thy* in line 7 than with Q's *this*. But the fact that this sonnet abounds in verbal repetitions weakens the argument for any emendation.

94

40

Take all my loves, my love, yea, take them all:
What hast thou then more than thou hadst before?
No love, my love, that thou mayst true love call—
All mine was thine, before thou hadst this more.   4
Then if for my love thou my love receivest,
I cannot blame thee, for my love thou usest,—
But yet be blam'd, if thou this self deceivest
By wilful taste of what thy self refusest.   8
I do forgive thy robbery, gentle thief,
Although thou steal thee all my poverty:
And yet love knows it is a greater grief
To bear love's wrong than hate's known injury.   12
  Lascivious grace, in whom all ill well shows,
  Kill me with spites, yet we must not be foes.

8 *wilful taste of*] (1) 'sexual relish for' (see 'will' in Glossary); (2) 'sexual enjoyment of'; and (3) 'deliberately perverse savouring of'. All meanings seem to be present.

10 *all my poverty*] 'all the little I have'.

11] So Q. Modern editors have variously punctuated, some isolating 'love knows' by commas, thereby weakening the sense by turning the phrase into a mere parenthesis. In fact, no commas whatever are required.

12 *hate's known injury*] 'that injury which we know hate is likely to give'.

13 *Lascivious*] Though, as Tucker observes, the word could, in Elizabethan English, mean simply 'wanton', 'sportive', yet the suggestion of oxymoron in its conjunction with 'grace' would be lost if that were the sense here. The full modern sense 'lustful' seems required.

14 *spites*] 'outrages'. (See OED for this sense applied to actions, which OED calls obsolete, but which does in fact survive in regional colloquial usage.)

41 1 *pretty*] A complex word probably involving the senses: (1) 'wanton' (Sherwood–Cotgrave for 'pretty' gives *inter alia* '*mignard*', and Cotgrave for '*mignard*' *inter alia* 'wanton'); (2) 'slight', 'venial'; (3) 'fine' (used ironically). (3) may be dominant.

liberty] Probably 'licentiousness', as Schmidt suggests, rather than merely 'lack of restraint'. The sexual meaning is more consonant with the rest of the sonnet.

3 *befits*] Third person plurals in '-s' are common in Elizabethan English, and frequently used by Shakespeare.

4 *still*] 'continually'.

5] Either (1) 'You are high-born, and therefore a prize'; or (2) 'You are kind-hearted, and therefore susceptible of conquest.' It is even *possible* that there is a play on both meanings.

6 *therefore to be assail'd*] 'therefore exposed to attempts at seduction'.

8 *sourly*] 'churlishly'.

leave her till he have prevail'd] So Q and early editors, followed by Collier[3], Wyndham, Hadow, Ridley, Harrison. Tyrwhitt conjectured: *she have . . .*, on the ground that it is the woman who is doing the wooing (line 7), and this reading is followed by Malone and by most modern editors. But Q can make sense, in more than one way, viz. (1) 'cease to respond (or actually go away) before he has achieved intercourse'; (2) 'refrain from responding till he has worn her down, and she ceases wooing him'. Sense (2) could be supported by reference to 70. 9–10, suggesting that victory for the man here would be repulse of the 'assault'.

9 *my seat*] 'the place I have a right to occupy', i.e. 'You might keep off my mistress!'

9–14] The sharp contrast of tone between the sestet and the octave of this sonnet is particularly remarkable.

10 *chide*] 'rebuke'.

11 *riot*] 'debauchery' (*OED*. 1).

12 *truth*] 'troth' (*OED*. —1650).

41

THOSE PRETTY wrongs that liberty commits
When I am sometime absent from thy heart
Thy beauty and thy years full well befits,
For still temptation follows where thou art: 4
Gentle thou art, and therefore to be won;
Beauteous thou art, therefore to be assail'd;
And when a woman woos what woman's son
Will sourly leave her till he have prevail'd?   8
Ay me! but yet thou mightst my seat forbear,
And chide thy beauty and thy straying youth
Who lead thee in their riot even there
Where thou art forc'd to break a twofold truth,—   12
   Hers, by thy beauty tempting her to thee:
   Thine, by thy beauty being false to me.

42 5 *excuse*] Not 'forgive' but 'make excuses for'.

6] The rhythm puts a stress on the first 'thou' and 'her', and on 'I', and this brings out the force of the conceit.

7 *abuse*] (1) 'misuse', (2) 'ill-use', (3) 'deceive'.

8 *approve*] Very possibly with a *double entendre*, playing on (1) 'put to the test', 'try out' (Fr. *éprouver*), a common Elizabethan and Shakespearean meaning, with sometimes also a sexual implication; (2) 'hold a good opinion of'.

9 *my love's*] A play on (1) 'my mistress's' and (2) 'my affection's'.

11 *and*] Tucker is surely right in holding 'and' to mean here 'if.' 'And' is the older spelling of 'an' = 'if'. Except in *an't, an* is found only once in the First Folio (see *OED*). The clause 'and . . . twain' would parallel 'If . . . thee' in line 9, comparing the consequences of a double loss with those of a single one.

42

THAT THOU hast her, it is not all my grief;
And yet it may be said I lov'd her dearly:
That she hath thee is of my wailing chief,
A loss in love that touches me more nearly.   4
Loving offenders, thus I will excuse ye:—
Thou dost love her because thou know'st I love her;
And for my sake even so doth she abuse me,
Suffering my friend for my sake to approve her.   8
If I lose thee my loss is my love's gain;
And losing her, my friend hath found that loss:
Both find each other, and I lose both twain;
And both for my sake lay on me this cross.   12
    But here's the joy: my friend and I are one.
    —Sweet flattery! then she loves but me alone!

43 1 *wink*] 'have my eyes closed'.

2 *unrespected*] i.e. 'unobservantly'. The force is adverbial, though literally the participle qualifies 'things'.

4 *darkly bright*] perhaps 'though shuttered, no longer dull' (cf. a dark lantern).

bright in dark directed] 'alertly directed in the darkness' (i.e. heedfully, contrast line 2). Shakespeare often uses 'bright' adverbially, and here the adverb balances 'darkly'.

5 *shadow*] 'image'.

shadows] 'darkness'.

6 *shadow's form*] The real form and substance, of which the 'shadow' is the image.

6–8] i.e. 'How your body, brighter than the day, would add a fitting splendour to the day's brightness.'

11 *thy*] So Capell's MS, adopted by Malone and all subsequent editors save Porter. Q: *their*. *Their* could be argued to make sense as referring to the 'eyes' (cf. lines 9 and 12) that see the image in the darkness, but it strains grammar, and coheres less well than *thy* with lines 6 and 8. The frequent confusion of *thy* and *their* in Q has already been noted (see 26. 12, note, and 35. 8, note, above).

imperfect] not because unclear or inexact, but because insubstantial.

13 *to see*] So Q. Malone proposed: *to me*, a reading adopted by a few editors. Q is fully capable of bearing two satisfactory senses, and possibly a play on both is intended. The senses are (1) 'in appearance', (2) 'for purposes of seeing'. Dowden rightly argues for Q that this sonnet contains a more than usual number of instances of doubling a word in the same line (lines 4, 5, 6).

14 *show thee me*] The sense 'show you to me' is clear enough without any of the transpositions that have been proposed.

43

WHEN MOST I wink, then do mine eyes best see,
For all the day they view things unrespected;
But when I sleep, in dreams they look on thee,
And darkly bright are bright in dark directed: 4
Then thou whose shadow shadows doth make bright,
How would thy shadow's form form happy show
To the clear day with thy much clearer light,
When to unseeing eyes thy shade shines so!   8
How would, I say, mine eyes be blessèd made
By looking on thee in the living day,
When in dead night thy fair imperfect shade
Through heavy sleep on sightless eyes doth stay!   12
　　All days are nights to see till I see thee,
　　And nights bright days when dreams do show thee me.

44 1 *dull*] 'heavy' (see note on line 11).

2 *Injurious*] 'cruel and unjust' (cf. 63. 2).

3 *would be*] 'should be' (conditional), *not* 'want' (or 'would want') 'to be'. He is not merely asserting that he wants (or would want) to be brought, but that he would actually be brought. He wants, and would want this, in any case, whether the substance of his flesh were 'dull' or 'nimble'. 'Then', in lines 3 and 5, supports this meaning. Abbott's assertion that Shakespeare does not use 'would' for 'should' (*Shakespearian Grammar*, s. 331) is too sweeping, and some of his examples questionable. Franz (*Shakespeare-Grammatik*, s. 616) recognizes a number of instances of the use.

4 *limits*] 'regions' (cf. Lat. *fines*).

where] 'to where'.

8 *he*] i.e. thought (personified).

9] 'I am reduced to despair by the thought that I have not the swift mobility of thought.'

11 *earth and water*] In the doctrine of the four elements earth and water were considered heavy (cf. 'dull' (line 1)), fire and air light. Thought is 'air' in 45. 3, but 'fire' in *H5*. Prol. I. 1. Cf. also *H5*. III. vii. 22: 'He is pure air and fire; and the dull elements of earth and water never appear in him . . .'; and *A&C*. V. ii. 291–2: 'I am fire and air; my other elements / I give to baser life.' The poet is largely made of earth and water, i.e. heaviness and tears; and so he cannot move like thought.

12–14] The image appears to be that of a petitioner waiting on a great man, Time (for which reason we have capitalized the *t* of Q's *time*). The petitioner is such a lowly character (being composed so largely of the 'dull' elements) that all he obtains is heavy (grievous) tears, which are the insignia of the grief of his heavy elements, which prevent him from swiftly reaching his friend.

14 *either's*] i.e. of the poet's heavy elements, *not* 'of the poet or the Friend'.

44

I F THE dull substance of my flesh were thought,
Injurious distance should not stop my way;
For then despite of space I would be brought
From limits far remote where thou dost stay: 4
No matter then although my foot did stand
Upon the farthest earth remov'd from thee;
For nimble thought can jump both sea and land
As soon as think the place where he would be.   8
But ah, thought kills me that I am not thought,
To leap large lengths of miles when thou art gone,
But that, so much of earth and water wrought,
I must attend Time's leisure with my moan;   12
    Receiving naught, by elements so slow,
    But heavy tears—badges of either's woe!

45 1–4] 'My other two elements, insubstantial air (possessing no quality of grossness) and purifying fire, are both with you wherever I may be. The first, which is my thought, and the other, which is my desire, moving swiftly, are with me and gone again at once.' If line 2 be taken strictly, as it must be, its hyperbole is already contradicted in this first quatrain, and the rest of the sonnet undermines it still further. This is by no means an isolated instance in the *Sonnets* of such a pattern of development.

4 *present-absent*] So Malone and almost all modern editors. Q, Benson, Lintot, Gildon[1], Tucker, Harrison: *present absent* . Gildon[2]—Evans: *present, absent*, Massey: *present, absent* . Some editors take the meaning to be: 'at the same time here with me and there with you'. This meaning is perfectly possible in itself, but would involve too blatant a contradiction both with the rest of line 4 and with lines 5–12, for if the thought and desires were simultaneously in both places at once no motion would be necessary. Any of the punctuations except Massey's, however, will yield the sense given in the last note.

5 *So*] Q: *For*, which has been accepted by all editors, though Tucker, dissatisfied with the awkward connexion between the quatrains which *For* provides, conjectures *Forth*. We share Tucker's dissatisfaction. Moreover, we cannot discover in Shakespeare a parallel for the use of 'For' in such a loose sense. We therefore propose the reading *So*, = 'accordingly', a frequent use in Shakespeare. In MSS of the time the initial letter of a line of verse is not invariably written with a capital. If 'Soe' were written with a small long 's' in secretary hand, it might easily be mistaken for 'For'. This emendation would therefore seem to have greater graphic plausibility than Tucker's *Forth*.

5–8] 'Accordingly, when these livelier elements have gone on a tender mission of love to you, my life, which consists of four elements, left with two only, goes into a decline [or 'declines and dies'], weighed down by melancholy.' He has only the heavy elements left, and melancholy is a condition of heaviness. Cf. *KJ*. III. iii. 42: 'Or if that surly spirit, melancholy, Had bak'd thy blood and made it heavy-thick.'

8 *melancholy*] The humour 'melancholy' was, like earth, cold and dry. Some commentators have suggested that the word here must be pronounced 'melanch'ly'; but this seems unlikely. R. E. Neil Dodge has pointed out (1) that Shakespeare always gives the word the modern accent, 'mélanchóly'; (2) that there is much Elizabethan and earlier precedent for the kind of imperfect rhyme represented by 'thee . . . mélanchóly' (*Wisconsin Shakespeare Studies*, 1916, 174 ff). There certainly seems to be no instance of a Shakespearean verse line where the word is stressed on any syllables other than the first and third. On the other hand, according to

45

THE OTHER two—slight air and purging fire—
Are both with thee wherever I abide;
The first my thought, the other my desire,
These present-absent with swift motion slide;   4
So when these quicker elements are gone
In tender embassy of love to thee,
My life, being made of four, with two alone
Sinks down to death, oppress'd with melancholy: 8
Until life's composition be recur'd
By those swift messengers return'd from thee,
Who even but now come back again assur'd
Of thy fair health, recounting it to me: 12
    This told, I joy; but then no longer glad
    I send them back again, and straight grow sad.

OED, 'down to the seventeenth century the poetical examples commonly indicate stress on the second or fourth syllable'. An example from Drayton, *Idea, the Shepheards Garland* (1593) reads: 'And being rouzde out of melancholly, / Flye whirle-winde thoughts, unto the heavens, quoth he.' Apart from such stressing being contrary to Shakespeare's practice, however, it would be very difficult to read line 8 with a stressing similar to Drayton's. To a modern ear an acceptable rhyme with line 6 can result from stressing the first and third syllables of 'melancholy', provided the stress on the third syllable is not laid heavily.

9] Either (1) 'Until the balanced blending of the elements of my life be restored', or (2) 'Until life's constitution be restored to health.' If line 8 recounts a 'death', then only (1) would apply; if merely a 'decline', then either (1) or (2). See note on lines 5–8.

11 *even but now*] 'just at this very moment'.

12 *thy*] So Gildon[2], Malone, and all subsequent editors. Q: *their*, evidently another misreading of *thy*.

13 *no longer glad*] 'He cannot maintain the joy, since he misses the beloved, becomes anxious again, and once more sends off the messengers' (Tucker).

14 *sad*] Very probably playing on (1) 'sad' = 'sorrowful', (2) 'sad' = 'heavy' (having once more lost his lively elements).

46 *General Note:* The conceit of a dispute between eye and heart is a poetical commonplace, and legal imagery as frequent. Deductions as to sources and borrowings, as to authorship, or as to Shakespeare's training or profession, are all equally discredited by these facts.

1–2] The issue here and the agreement in 47 concern a portrait.

2 *conquest*] (1) 'booty', 'spoils', the meaning naturally suggested by line 1; and, very probably, (2) 'acquisition' (by any means other than inheritance, as in the Scots law of real estate: cf. 6. 14). It may well have been this legal sense of the term that suggested to Shakespeare the transition to the legal conceit which he exploits in the rest of the sonnet.

3, 8 *thy*] So Capell, Malone, and all subsequent editors. Q: *their*. In line 3 *their* would make sense ('the picture they have acquired'), but in line 8 *their* would strain the meaning of 'appearance'. In view of the frequent misreading of *their* for *thy* in Q, and of the virtual certainty of *thy* in line 8, it seems reasonable to read *thy* in line 3.

3] 'My eye would deny my heart the right to see your picture' (lit. 'the right of ownership of the sight of your picture').

4] 'My heart would deny the eye's freedom to exercise that right'; but alternatively, 'freedom' might mean either (1) 'special privilege', or (2) 'exclusive right'.

5] 'My heart pleads that the essential "you" is located in him' (so that he is most qualified to appropriate the portrait and therefore to have the right to look at it).

6 *closet*] Could, in Elizabethan English, mean either (1) a small inner room, or (2) a cabinet or locked case. In either sense it would be private and a place for locking things up.

crystal] 'clear', with the possible implication 'penetrating'. 'Crystal' might, however, be intended to suggest that the eyes are mere lenses, which, of themselves, have no power of penetration.

8] 'And says that he possesses a clearer idea of your beautiful features' (and so is better entitled to have the portrait to look at).

9 *side*] So Q. Sewell's conjecture, adopted by Malone and most modern editors: *'cide*. 'Side' as a verb certainly existed, with other meanings than it could bear here, e.g. 'to take the part of' (Cotgrave; Wright's *Dictionary of Obsolete and Provincial English*) and 'to equal' (Wright; Nares's *Glossary*). *OED* gives, in addition to these: 'to assign to one of two sides or parties' and '(dial.) "to clear or tidy up".' Alden disputes the first of these meanings (for which *OED* cites only this one example), while Tucker glosses 'settle, arrange', referring to *OED*. In favour of *'cide* is the fact that Shakespeare quite frequently drops prefixes (see Abbott, *A Shakespearian Grammar*, s. 460), though the only possible instance of ''cide' is this one. 'Decide',

46

MINE EYE and heart are at a mortal war
How to divide the conquest of thy sight;
Mine eye my heart thy picture's sight would bar,—
Mine heart, mine eye the freedom of that right: 4
My heart doth plead that thou in him dost lie—
A closet never pierc'd with crystal eyes;
But the defendant doth that plea deny,
And says in him thy fair appearance lies.   8
To side this title is impanellèd
A quest of thoughts, all tenants to the heart,
And by their verdict is determinèd
The clear eye's moiety and the dear heart's part,   12
    As thus: mine eye's due is thy outward part,
    And my heart's right thy inward love of heart.

itself, is only used three times in Shakespeare. On linguistic grounds '*cide*
would seem somewhat the likelier reading; but it seems unlikely that a
compositor would mistake *c* for *s* in Elizabethan handwriting, and there is
no special reason to suppose that an *s* would be wrongly distributed into the
c case, though any such happening is possible. An error of *side* for '*cide*
would only be likely to occur as a result of dictation at some stage (i.e. to
copyist or to compositor). Neither the linguistic evidence for '*cide* nor the
graphic evidence against it seems decisive, and we have therefore decided
to follow Q, adopting for 'side' the meaning 'to assign to one side' (see ref.
to *OED*, above).

10 *quest*] 'jury'.

10] The jury is clearly 'packed', since it consists of 'thoughts', which
are all tenants to the heart.

12 *dear*] here probably 'deeply feeling'.

clear . . . dear] Implicit in the antithesis of these adjectives is the drift
of the final couplet.

moiety] The word was currently used to refer to any share or portion,
not necessarily a half.

46 (*continued*)

13–14] The "packed" jury, surprisingly, finds in favour of the eye's claim to the portrait; but thereby, in fact, show their bias in favour of their landlord, the heart, since they declare his right to something of far greater value—the Friend's heartfelt love, and save him from setting too much store by the external.

thy . . . thy] So Capell, Malone[1], and some other editors. Q and early editors: *their . . . their*. Malone[2] and most modern editors: *thine . . . thine*. *Their* is clearly wrong. Graphically, *their* for *thy* is a much more likely error than *their* for *thine*. Orthographically, 'thy' before a vowel is unobjectionable in the light of Shakespearean practice.

46

MINE EYE and heart are at a mortal war
How to divide the conquest of thy sight;
Mine eye my heart thy picture's sight would bar,—
Mine heart, mine eye the freedom of that right:⠀⠀⠀⠀⠀4
My heart doth plead that thou in him dost lie—
A closet never pierc'd with crystal eyes;
But the defendant doth that plea deny,
And says in him thy fair appearance lies.⠀⠀⠀⠀⠀8
To side this title is impanellèd
A quest of thoughts, all tenants to the heart,
And by their verdict is determinèd
The clear eye's moiety and the dear heart's part,⠀⠀⠀12
⠀⠀As thus: mine eye's due is thy outward part,
⠀⠀And my heart's right thy inward love of heart.

47 4 *heart in love*] 'heart in its love for you (the Friend)' (*not* 'heart in love with sighs').

5] The portrait now being in the eye's possession (cf. 46. 13).

5–8] i.e. the heart gains refreshment from contemplating the picture, and the eye in turn learns to see more deeply.

10 *Thyself, away,*] Q: *Thy self away*, a punctuation which might misleadingly suggest the construction: 'your portrait or my love for you, although you are away, is present . . .', which would be absurd, in view of 'by'. One must therefore either omit the comma after 'away' or insert another before it. Most modern editors follow the former course. We prefer the latter as making clearer the antithesis between 'away' and 'present'.

art] So Capell and almost all modern editors. Q, early editors, Butler, Hadow: *are*. 'Are' for 'art', 'will' for 'wilt', 'shall' for 'shalt', and analogous forms, occur quite frequently in early editions of Shakespeare (see W. Franz, *Shakespeare-Grammatik*, s. 152), especially where the '-t' ending, in conjunction with the following word, produced an effect which the Elizabethans may have found uneuphonious. The MS reading may well have been *are*, but the slight emendation followed here avoids drawing undue attention to a grammatical peculiarity, and obviates any possible misconstruction of lines 9–10 (see note on *Thyself, away*).

still] 'continually'.

11 *not*] So Benson (1640), followed by almost all modern editors. Q: *nor*. Capell, Lowell conj., Brooke, Neilson[2]: *no*. Graphically, *nor* could be an error by Q compositor for either *noe* or *not*. Grammatically, *not*, of course, qualifies 'canst move', and semantically it gives a greater sense of the movement of the thoughts than *no* would.

47

Betwixt mine eye and heart a league is took,
And each doth good turns now unto the other:
When that mine eye is famish'd for a look,
Or heart in love with sighs himself doth smother,   4
With my love's picture then my eye doth feast,
And to the painted banquet bids my heart;
Another time mine eye is my heart's guest
And in his thoughts of love doth share a part.   8
So, either by thy picture or my love,
Thyself, away, art present still with me:
For thou not farther than my thoughts canst move
And I am still with them and they with thee;   12
   Or if they sleep, thy picture in my sight
   Awakes my heart to heart's and eye's delight.

48 5 *to whom*] 'compared to whom'.

9–11 *chest*] For the quibble cf. *Lucr.* 761: 'Some purer chest to close so pure a mind.' Apart from these two cases, where he uses it to pun, Shakespeare only twice uses the word to mean the breast or thorax (viz. in *T&C*). According to *OED* this sense of the word was then comparatively new (first mention 1530). This might have made the pun livelier than now.

11 *gentle closure*] may involve an oxymoron.

12 *part*] 'depart'.

14 *truth*] 'honesty', i.e. honesty itself would turn thief for a prize so precious as you.

48

Hᴏᴡ ᴄᴀʀᴇꜰᴜʟ was I when I took my way
Each trifle under truest bars to thrust,
That to my use it might unusèd stay
From hands of falsehood, in sure wards of trust!   4
But thou, to whom my jewels trifles are,
Most worthy comfort, now my greatest grief—
Thou best of dearest and mine only care
Art left the prey of every vulgar thief.   8
Thee have I not lock'd up in any chest
Save—where thou art not, though I feel thou art—
Within the gentle closure of my breast,
From whence at pleasure thou mayst come and part: 12
   And even thence thou wilt be stol'n, I fear,
   For truth proves thievish for a prize so dear.

49 1 *Against*] 'In preparation for'. Cf. *à l'encontre* (Cotgrave), also *T. of S.* II. i. 306: 'to buy apparel 'gainst the wedding day'.

3 *cast . . . sum*] 'cast his final reckoning' (to close his account).

4 *advis'd respects*] 'careful considerations' (of the mutual relations that are the subject of the audit). Cf. *KJ*. IV. ii. 212: 'More upon humour than advis'd respect'.

5 *strangely*] 'as a stranger', i.e. not acknowledging me.

6 *that sun thine eye*] playing on the image of the sun as the eye of heaven (cf. 18. 5). The same image is implied in 33.

7 *converted*] 'transformed'.

8] 'Shall find reasons for behaving with starchy solemnity.' The plausible interpretation sometimes given: '. . . reasons of confirmed weight' (cf. 'advis'd respects') would require us to find what the reasons are for, and they could only be implied by doubling back on 'love converted' (line 7). The sense given here, in any case, continues the image of lines 5–6.

9–14] All the interpretations we have seen of these lines seem to us radically mistaken. The poet is not appearing as a witness for an attack on himself, or, indeed, as a witness at all. He is fortifying himself in a sense of his own worth, against any slurs the Friend might one day adduce as reasons for coldly rejecting him (see notes on lines 9, 11, 12). He recognizes the Friend's right to *leave* him at any time, but this right depends on the purely negative fact that there is no reason why the Friend should love him, and not on any positive causes for reproach. To take lines 11, 12 to refer to a witness taking an oath would make these contradict lines 9 and 10.

9 *ensconce me*] 'shelter myself', as behind an earthwork.

10 *desert*] So almost all modern editors. Q: *desart*, followed by two modern editors for the rhyme. However, in Elizabethan English the ear-rhyme would have been perfect with either spelling, and in a modern edition the old spelling looks needlessly archaic.

11 *against*] here 'in front of'.

12 *guard*] 'ward off', 'parry'.

lawful reasons] 'reasons given as if you were arguing against me in a court of law'.

part.] Q has a comma; most modern editions a colon—no doubt because of their editors' mistaken belief that the couplet is a witness's testimony. To prevent this impression we have printed a full stop.

13–14] The opposition is between 'leave' and 'love', as their alliteration and dissonance emphasize.

49

AGAINST THAT time (if ever that time come)
When I shall see thee frown on my defects,
Whenas thy love hath cast his utmost sum,
Call'd to that audit by advis'd respects: 4
Against that time when thou shalt strangely pass
And scarcely greet me with that sun thine eye,
When love converted from the thing it was
Shall reasons find of settled gravity: 8
Against that time do I ensconce me here
Within the knowledge of mine own desert,
And this my hand against myself uprear
To guard the lawful reasons on thy part.   12
    To leave poor me thou hast the strength of laws,
    Since why to love I can allege no cause.

50 1–4] 'How disconsolate I travel onwards, when what I'm looking forward to, the end of each weary day's journey, only teaches that comfort and rest (which I am seeking) to tell me that all I have done is to travel farther away from my friend.'

6 *dully*] So Benson (1640) and almost all editors. Q, Lintot, Ridley: *duly*. Q is a much tamer reading.

to bear] 'at bearing' (Pooler).

5–12] Tyler's note is excellent: 'The very beast on which he rides sympathizes with his rider, as if by instinct, and plods heavily on, answering, when spurred, with a groan, a groan which reminds the rider of his own sorrow.'

50

How HEAVY do I journey on the way,
When what I seek (my weary travel's end)
Doth teach that ease and that repose to say:
'Thus far the miles are measur'd from thy friend.' 4
The beast that bears me, tirèd with my woe,
Plods dully on to bear that weight in me,
As if by some instínct the wretch did know
His rider lov'd not speed being made from thee: 8
The bloody spur cannot provoke him on
That sometimes anger thrusts into his hide,
Which heavily he answers with a groan
More sharp to me than spurring to his side; 12
For that same groan doth put this in my mind:—
My grief lies onward and my joy behind.

51 1 *slow offence*] 'fault of slowness'.

4 *posting*] 'hasting' (cf. 'post haste'). Often used in Shakespeare in this sense, but not purely Shakespearean (cf. Cotgrave: 'to post: *poster*'; and '*poster*: to speed').

6 *swift extremity*] 'extreme speed'.

7 *Then . . . wind;*] So Gildon, and most modern editors. Q: *. . . wind*, followed by Benson (1640), Lintot and many other editors. The punctuation adopted makes line 7 a categorical conditional, and lines 7 and 8 paratactic, line 8, however, developing the hyperbole of line 7. Q's punctuation makes line 7 hypothetical. Then line 8 becomes slightly redundant and the sequence of tenses somewhat awkward.

10 *perfect'st*] So Dyce and most modern editors. Q, Benson (1640), Lintot: *perfects*. Gildon—Evans, Malone and some modern editors: *perfect*. The superlative 'perfectest' occurs in the plays, e.g. *Macb*. I. v. 2: 'the perfectest report'. If the word Shakespeare intended was the superlative, some abridgement was metrically at least advisable if not essential. (The full form would, in any case, have resulted in an irregularity wholly untypical of the *Sonnets*.) The only possible abridgement other than *perfects* would have been *perfectst* or *perfect'st*, involving an agglomeration of five consonants *ctst l*. Similar agglomerations resulting from verbs in the second person singular being followed by initial consonants were often remedied in quarto and folio editions of Shakespeare by eliding the final '-t' of the verb, e.g. *A&C*. I. iii. 71: 'thou affect'st' (F[1]: *affects*, F[2]: *affectst*). It seems likely that a similar measure was taken here. The *s* in *perfects* (Q) has, in any case, to be accounted for, and the above explanation seems to us more plausible than to have recourse to a simple mistake.

11] A line which several editors have emended, and many re-punctuated. Q and some early editors: *Shall naigh noe dull flesh in his fiery race*. Gildon[2] and a few editors: *need . . . Flesh*. Malone conjectured: *neigh to . . . flesh*. Most modern readings fall into two groups: (1) those which, either by commas or brackets, parenthesize *no dull flesh*, in which case 'race' is taken to mean 'career'; (2) those which print *no . . . race* as a single phrase, in which case 'race' = 'strain' (desire is a thoroughbred with no trace of the dull elements in him). Cf. *H5*. III. vii. 20 ff: '*Orl*. He's of the colour of the nutmeg. *Dau*. And of the heat of the ginger. It is a beast for Perseus; he is pure air and fire; and the dull elements of earth and water never appear in him. . . .' We prefer the interpretation involved in these group (2) readings, and we think our punctuation represents this most clearly. Desire (pure *eros*) cries out with impatience. The word 'neigh' was evidently suggested by the fact that the poet is riding a horse, which often neighs from the impatience of sexual desire. (Cf., indeed, *V&A*. 202, 265, 307.)

51

Thus can my love excuse the slow offence
Of my dull bearer when from thee I speed:
From where thou art why should I haste me thence?
Till I return, of posting is no need.   4
Oh what excuse will my poor beast then find
When swift extremity can seem but slow?
Then should I spur though mounted on the wind;
In wingèd speed no motion shall I know: 8
Then can no horse with my desire keep pace;
Therefore desire, of perfect'st love being made,
Shall neigh—no dull flesh in his fiery race:
But love, for love, thus shall excuse my jade:—   12
   'Since from thee going he went wilful slow,
   Towards thee I'll run and give him leave to go.'

For the application of the word to human desire cf. *Jer.*, v. 8: 'They were
as fed horses in the morning; every one neighed after his neighbour's wife.'
  12 *But love, for love,*] 'But love itself, out of its own inherent charity.'
(The contrast, in our view, is with 'desire' (line 10) which, though it con-
tains no element other than passionate love, yet, being egoistic, is less than
the whole of love.) Other interpretations of 'for love' include: (1) 'from
love to the poor beast' (Tyler); (2) 'on account of the love shown by the
horse' (cf. 50. 6) (Bernard Shaw); (3) 'for the sake of the love awaiting
me on my return' (Tyler); (4) 'on account of my affection' (Furnivall).
  14 *go*] 'walk'. The antithesis is with 'run'; cf. *Two G.* III. i. 390:
   'Thou must run to him, for thou hast stayed so long that going will
  scarce serve the turn.'

52 1 *So am I*] 'I am exactly like'.

key] The standard pronunciation till the end of the seventeenth century was 'kay' (cf. modern 'grey', 'whey').

3 *will not*] 'does not want to'.

4 *For blunting*] 'Lest it blunt'. Cf. *Two G.* I. ii. 133: 'Yet here they shall not lie, for catching cold.'

5 *solemn*] 'formal', 'ceremonious', and in a joyful sense. The word emphasizes the double association in 'rare'.

8 *captain*] 'chief', 'principal' (late Lat. *capitanus*). Cf. Mulcaster (1581): 'sound sleep, the captain cause of good digestion'.

carcanet] an ornamental collar or necklace, usually of gold and sometimes set with pearls.

9 *So is . . .*] The same construction as in line 1.

keeps] 'withholds', 'detains', bearing the sense 'imprisons' which changes to 'treasures up' (in the chest), cf. 'imprison'd pride' (line 12).

12 *his imprison'd pride*] Primarily 'its imprisoned splendour'; but possibly with a play on 'the pride of (best thing in) the wardrobe'.

14 *triumph*] 'exultant joy'.

52

So AM I as the rich whose blessèd key
Can bring him to his sweet up-lockèd treasure,
The which he will not every hour survey,
For blunting the fine point of seldom pleasure.   4
Therefore are feasts so solemn and so rare,
Since, seldom coming, in the long year set
Like stones of worth they thinly placèd are,
Or captain jewels in the carcanet.   8
So is the time that keeps you as my chest,
Or as the wardrobe which the robe doth hide,
To make some special instant special blest
By new unfolding his imprison'd pride.   12
    Blessèd are you whose worthiness gives scope
    Being had, to triumph; being lack'd, to hope.

53 *General Note:* This sonnet exemplifies one of the ways in which Shakespeare lays under contribution the philosophical vocabulary of the time (here 'substance', 'shadows', 'shade'), without exploiting it with philosophical strictness or system.

1 *substance*] Possibly (1) 'essential nature', possibly (2) 'matter'; or Shakespeare may be using the term here without either precise connotation or, even, in a comprehensive sense including either or both of these and/or (3) 'wealth' (he has many servant shadows to attend him); and/or (4) 'solid quality of mind or character'—*OED*. 19, citing *inter alia* a quotation of 1581.

2 *strange*] i.e. not your own. (Yet in one sense they must be!—another instance of the vagueness with which the words and symbols are here used.)

shadows] Here (and also in line 4) presumably not *umbrae*, in which colour, texture and detail are absent, but *imagines*, as the examples in lines 5 ff show, though the phrase 'on you tend' would more naturally apply to *umbrae*.

3 *every one hath, every one*] 'Every entity (e.g. person, object, phenomenon (line 9)) has its individual and unique shadow.' The repetition is not merely tautological. 'Every one hath one shade', alone, might imply one shadow common to all. Tucker's suggestion that the first *every one* should read *everyone* seems unacceptable, as restricting the reference to persons, contrary to line 9.

shade] Does the word here mean *umbra* or *imago*, or neither with any precision? It is hard to say.

4] 'And you, although only one person, can supply an image for every sort of excellence.'

lend] 'supply'.

5 *counterfeit*] 'picture', 'portrait'. (Cf. *M. of V*. III. ii. 115: 'What have we here? Fair Portia's counterfeit.') Not, as has been suggested, 'description', but the picture called up by it.

8 *tires*] If the portrait were of a head only, the word would mean 'headgear', the more common Elizabethan sense. If it were full-length, 'tires' could be used in the more general sense of 'attire'.

new] 'afresh', 'yet again'.

9 *spring . . . foison*] As 'foison' (plentiful harvest) emphasizes, the antithesis is not between Spring and Autumn simply as the seasons of the year, but between the active properties which characterize them, the concreteness of association being characteristically Shakespearean. The 'spring' is freshness and vitality, as the 'foison' is abundance of produce.

12] 'And we recognize you in every fine form.'

53

Wʜᴀᴛ ɪs your substance, whereof are you made,
That millions of strange shadows on you tend?
Since every one hath, every one, one shade,
And you, but one, can every shadow lend:⠀⠀⠀⠀⠀4
Describe Adonis, and the counterfeit
Is poorly imitated after you;
On Helen's cheek all art of beauty set,
And you in Grecian tires are painted new:⠀⠀⠀⠀8
Speak of the spring and foison of the year,—
The one doth shadow of your beauty show,
The other as your bounty doth appear;
And you in every blessèd shape we know:⠀⠀⠀⠀12
⠀⠀In all external grace you have some part,
⠀⠀But you like none, none you, for constant heart.

13] Not 'you share in every external beauty', but 'every external beauty partakes of you'. The sense is probably Platonic.

14] 'But in the matter of constancy you are like no one else, and no one else is a match for you.'

54 2 *truth*] Probably simply 'fidelity', cf. 53. 14. Resemblances between this sonnet and 101 have led some editors to suppose that there is here the further connotation of closeness to an ideal, but the differentiating quality of the Friend was seen in 53 to be 'constancy of heart', and the present sonnet makes perfect sense as a continuation of that thought.

5 *canker blóoms*] The blooms of the canker or dog-rose, which only smell faintly at most. Wyndham's argument that Shakespeare here means blossoms eaten by the canker-worm, because the worm is the most frequent use of 'canker' in Shakespeare, is a poor argument, and the interpretation would be inconsistent with lines 7–9 and false to fact. Eaten buds never properly develop. Steevens and Tyler allege an inconsistency on the ground that the dog-rose was pale and not wholly without scent. Though these facts might have weakened the force of the image, we must not think of cultivated Elizabethan roses as having the intense colours of modern hybrids.

6 *tincture*] Not the alchemical quintessence (anticipating line 12), which would tend to make 'perfumèd' redundant, but the colour (equivalent to the 'dye' of line 5). The emphasis is on 'perfumèd', the general sense of the image being that Nature the artist has endowed both the canker and the rose with the quality of colour, which fades when either dies, but has added to the rose the quality of scent, which may be preserved when the rose has perished. (The word 'tincture' seems to have come into use in the fourteenth century, and to have replaced 'dye' until sometime in the sixteenth century.)

8 *discloses*] 'opens up'. *OED* quotes (1577): 'It [a rosebud] discloseth it selfe and spreadeth abroad.'

9 *for*] 'because'.

only is] 'lies wholly in'.

10 *unrespected*] 'without any attention being paid to them'.

11 *to themselves*] 'without affecting anything but themselves'.

13 *lovely*] Not just 'handsome', but 'lovable', 'worthy of deep affection'.

14 *that*] 'your beauty', referring to the former of the two qualities just mentioned; as the second half of line 14 refers to the latter of the two, lovableness.

vade] So Q and many modern editors. Gildon–Evans, Malone, and many other editors: *fade*. Some of those editors who have retained *vade* have done so because the form occurs elsewhere in Shakespeare, and they regard it as a variant of 'fade'. Those who have read *fade* have adopted the same view. But N. Bailey (*Universal Etymological English Dictionary*, 1721) gives 'vade' = 'to decay, fade or wax weak' (as *OED* does) as a distinct word derived from Lat. *vadere*. T. Wright (*Dictionary of Obsolete and Provincial*

54

O H HOW much more doth beauty beauteous seem
By that sweet ornament which truth doth give!
The rose looks fair, but fairer we it deem
For that sweet odour which doth in it live.   4
The canker blooms have full as deep a dye
As the perfumèd tincture of the roses,
Hang on such thorns and play as wantonly
When summer's breath their maskèd buds discloses: 8
But for their virtue only is their show
They live unwoo'd and unrespected fade—
Die to themselves. Sweet roses do not so;
Of their sweet deaths are sweetest odours made: 12
    And so of you, beauteous and lovely youth,
    When that shall vade, by verse distils your truth.

English) quotes 'vading of waters' from Foxe's *Book of Martyrs*, as = 'failing
of waters'. In Elizabethan usage it seems that 'vade' was sometimes used
as = 'fade', and sometimes as a distinct word = intrans. 'vanish' or =
trans. 'do away with' (*R2*. I. ii. 20). Spenser twice uses 'vade' to rhyme
with 'fade' (*FQ*. III. ix. 20 and *Ruins of Rome*, xx. 13–14). Cf. also Thomas
Becon, *The Demands of Holy Scripture*, 1563 (ed. J. Ayre for the Parker
Society, 1844, p. 609) quoting from *Ps.* lxviii: 'As the wax *vadeth and
consumeth* in the fire, so shall all sinners perish before the face of God'
(glossed at foot by Ayre, 'departeth'). Here the stronger meaning 'vanish'
would seem the more appropriate, as cohering with the references to death
in lines 11 and 12.

   by] So Q. Editors are divided between retaining *by* and accepting Capell's
and Malone's *my*. The right policy would seem, first, to see if Q can have
a meaning. Alden (ed. 1916) argues that *by* cannot be justified by taking
'distils' as intransitive, because it is not found with the meaning 'is dis-
tilled', which he thinks would be the meaning required here. But this is
inconclusive, since the modern meaning 'is distilled' is not directly
required. Cotgrave–Sherwood (1632) gives 'distil: *distiller, alembiquer,*

54 (*continued*)

degoutter', and Cotgrave (1611) had given 'degoutter: to drop, distill; fall
downe by little and little', and 'distiller: to distill, trill, drop downe by
little and little'. The meaning 'to descend drop by drop' would be quite
compatible with the general sense of the sonnet, lines 13–14 meaning:
'And so with regard to you . . ., when your beauty vanishes, your con-
stancy will distil (like the dew) through verse.' Cf. *Deut.* xxxii, 2: 'My
speech shall distil as the dew, as the small rain upon the tender herb.' The
word as so used would, however, also inevitably suggest here that con-
stancy is of the essence of the rose. If we read *my verse*, 'of you' in line 13
must = 'out of you', cf. 'Of their sweet deaths' (line 12); and 'distils'
would then be transitive, the parallel with the manufacture of attar of roses
being complete. On grounds of sense *my* is perhaps preferable, but textually
it is harder to justify, and on that account we retain Q.

54

O_H H O W much more doth beauty beauteous seem
By that sweet ornament which truth doth give!
The rose looks fair, but fairer we it deem
For that sweet odour which doth in it live.　　　　　4
The canker blooms have full as deep a dye
As the perfumèd tincture of the roses,
Hang on such thorns and play as wantonly
When summer's breath their maskèd buds discloses:　　8
But for their virtue only is their show
They live unwoo'd and unrespected fade—
Die to themselves. Sweet roses do not so;
Of their sweet deaths are sweetest odours made:　　12
　　And so of you, beauteous and lovely youth,
　　When that shall vade, by verse distils your truth.

55 *General Note:* Defiance of Time, and the boast of the immortality verse alone can confer, have been a frequent theme of poets since Classical times, and we find it in the French and English sonneteers alike. The most celebrated classical exemplars are Ovid. *Met.* xv. 871:

> iamque opus exegi quod nec Iovis ira nec ignis
> nec poterit ferrum nec edax abolere vetustas.

and Horace, *Odes.* III. xxx. 1–5:

> exegi monumentum aere perennius
> regalique situ pyramidum altius. . . .

Commentators, according to their individual interests, have variously found in this sonnet material for discovering the dates, sources, or authorship of the *Sonnets*, or the nature and extent of the personal element in them. Despite some low estimates of its poetic merit, Sonnet 55 has remained a favourite of the anthologists.

1 *monuments*] So Malone and almost all modern editors. Q, early editors, and Tyler: *monument. Monuments* is required by the rhyme.

2 *this powerful rhyme*] Tucker is probably right in holding that Shakespeare is not here praising his own poetry as 'powerful' beyond that of other poets, but only acclaiming the power of poetry.

3 *these contents*] Variously explained as (1) 'the contents of my poems about you'; (2) 'this sonnet'; (3) 'my poems about you'; (4) 'the contents of this book of poems' (not necessarily by Shakespeare); (5) (Tucker) 'what is contained in writings of this kind.' (1) and (3) seem the only real possibilities.

4 *Than unswept stone*] i.e. than in a neglected monument. Cf. *Cor.* II. iii. 126: 'Dust on antique time would lie unswept.' Meticulous care and cleaning of tombs and monuments would seem to be a distinctively modern practice.

5 *wasteful*] 'destructive'.

6 *masonry*] The art or skill, not the fabric, which has already been named in 'work'.

7 *Nor . . . sword*] The omission of the verb is a typically Shakespearean ellipsis.

Mars his] An Elizabethan genitive form, often wrongly believed to be *the* original and correct English inflection. It is commonest after proper names, especially those ending in '-s' or '-ce'. The form may have originated in a confusion between the ''s' or '-es' inflection and the possessive adjective or pronoun 'his' when spoken with the aspirate suppressed.

quick] lit. 'lively', and therefore, here, 'fierce'.

55

N OT MARBLE, nor the gilded monuments
Of princes shall outlive this powerful rhyme;
But you shall shine more bright in these contents
Than unswept stone besmear'd with sluttish time.   4
When wasteful war shall statues overturn,
And broils root out the work of masonry,
Nor Mars his sword nor war's quick fire shall burn
The living record of your memory.   8
'Gainst death and all oblivious enmity
Shall you pace forth: your praise shall still find room
Even in the eyes of all posterity
That wear this world out to the ending doom.   12
  So, till the judgment that yourself arise,
  You live in this, and dwell in lovers' eyes.

9 *all oblivious enmity*] 'all hostile forces bringing things to oblivion.' This
is Q's reading, which is followed by Tyler, Walsh, Ridley. Almost all
modern editors have adopted Malone's *all-oblivious*. The advantages of Q
are: (1) that the phrase fittingly sums up the hostile forces of which
examples have already been given; (2) that it gives a better weighted line.
Moreover, on Malone's reading, 'and' would misleadingly appear to be
introducing the mention of a force not already mentioned.

A possible variant has occurred to us: *all oblivion's enmity*. There would
be no apostrophe in Elizabethan spelling, and *u* for *n* is a common typo-
graphical error. A good and typical line would result. But there is no
definite need for an emendation.

10 *pace forth*] 'stride on' (not needing to dodge the enemies).
praise] 'glory'.
still] 'always'.
find room] i.e. it will not need to jostle for a place.

12 *wear this world out*] 'will last as long as this world' (which posterity as
a whole will do).

13 *judgment*] 'Last Judgment'.

that] 'when', 'at which'. Cf. *AYLI*. III. ii. 187: 'I was never so berhymed since Pythagoras' time, that I was an Irish rat, which I can scarcely remember.'

14 *in this*] probably 'in verse' (cf. line 2) rather than specifically 'in these contents' (line 3).

lovers' eyes] (1) 'the eyes of those who will be able to conceive you properly because they are lovers'; and perhaps secondarily (2) 'the eyes of those who will love you when they read of your glory.'

14] 'You will live on in verse, and your habitation will be in the eyes of lovers.'

55

Not marble, nor the gilded monuments
Of princes shall outlive this powerful rhyme;
But you shall shine more bright in these contents
Than unswept stone besmear'd with sluttish time.   4
When wasteful war shall statues overturn,
And broils root out the work of masonry,
Nor Mars his sword nor war's quick fire shall burn
The living record of your memory.   8
'Gainst death and all oblivious enmity
Shall you pace forth: your praise shall still find room
Even in the eyes of all posterity
That wear this world out to the ending doom.   12
　　So, till the judgment that yourself arise,
　　You live in this, and dwell in lovers' eyes.

56 *General Note:* Does this sonnet refer to (1) a physical absence, (2) an estrangement, or (3) a period of apathy? Consideration of the sonnet itself suggests (3) without supporting or contradicting (1) or (2). Sonnet 57 specifically mentions absence, but an editor challenging Q's order could not use that fact to support (1) here. If there is absence, it is the Friend and not the poet who is away, in contrast to the poet's journey in 50–53. In any case, whether or not we take the *Sonnets* to be in detailed sequence autobiographical, there is no indication in those earlier 'sonnets of travel' that the poet felt his affection weakened by absence; but lines 1–8 clearly imply a touch of 'love's sad satiety'. Sonnet 58, which seems to imply an estrangement, might support (2), though this is inconclusive.

1 *Sweet love*] Not the Friend, but the feeling felt, either by both Friend and poet, or by the poet (not by the Friend alone (see lines 5–8)). The feeling is almost personified: but to capitalize would misleadingly suggest the God of Love.

3 *but*] 'only for'—emphasizing the sharp contrast with 'to-morrow'.

4 *his*] 'its'.

6 *wink*] 'close', in the sleep of repletion.

7 *see*] 'open your eyes and see'. The plea is: 'Do not atrophy the animating spirit of love by keeping it in [or alternatively 'by remaining in'] a perpetual torpor.'

9 *sad interim*] Primarily, at least, 'period of apathy' (Beeching). 'Sad' here = primarily, 'heavy', 'torpid'; though also, no doubt, 'sorrowful', because it is a pity such a period should occur.

9–12] Commentators have justifiably found the image obscure. The situation is similar to that of Hero and Leander, on whom Marlowe's poem was written before 1593. In our view 'shore' may well mean 'land' in general, which the seas divide. Moreover, the term 'return of love' would seem less appropriate to the return of either lover than to the arrival of some manifestation each awaits of the flow of feeling. (Cf. 45.) The arrival would perhaps be comparable to the arrival of a mail-boat eagerly awaited by the lovers on their respective 'banks' (i.e. 'shores', in the narrower sense).

10 *two contracted new*] 'two newly betrothed'.

13 *As*] So Q, Lintot, Hadow. Palgrave and others: *Else.* Capell, Malone (adopting Tyrwhitt's conjecture), and most modern editors: *Or.*

As would graphically be an unlikely mistake for *Or*, and *Else* (written *Els*), though, as Professor Tucker Brooke says, graphically closer to Q, would not be very close. Professor Sisson defends Q as meaning 'As (who should)' (*New Readings in Shakespeare*, II, 212), and it seems probable that Q can be given this or some similar meaning, e.g. 'As (one might)'.

56

Sᴡᴇᴇᴛ ʟᴏᴠᴇ, renew thy force; be it not said
Thy edge should blunter be than appetite,
Which but today by feeding is allay'd,
Tomorrow sharpen'd in his former might: 4
So, love, be thou; although today thou fill
Thy hungry eyes even till they wink with fulness,
Tomorrow see again, and do not kill
The spirit of love with a perpetual dulness: 8
Let this sad interim like the ocean be
Which parts the shore where two contracted new
Come daily to the banks, that when they see
Return of love more blest may be the view: 12
    As call it winter, which being full of care
    Makes summer's welcome, thrice more wish'd, more rare.

But we have not found a parallel instance to what would be a very vague
use of 'as'.

  it] the 'sad interim' (line 9).

  14 *Makes summer's welcome, thrice more wish'd, more rare*] So Q. Almost all
modern editors tacitly omit the comma after *welcome*, thus somewhat alter-
ing the sense of Q, which is that the welcome we give to summer is the
more splendid, *because* we have so much longed to give it.

57 7 *Nor think*] 'Nor dare I think' (Rollins), continuing the construction of line 5.

8 *servant*] As often in Elizabethan English, both (1) slave and (2) lover.

10 *your . . . suppose*] 'guess what you're at'.

13 *true*] Punning on (1) 'loyal' and (2) 'real'.

fool] 'simple-minded attendant'. The dog-like devotion of 'fools' even when ignored, slighted or mocked, is several times implied in Shakespeare. The shift here from 'slave' to 'fool' may, however, well imply a self-mocking overtone.

your will] So most modern editors. Q: *your Will* (*Will* not, however, being italicized), followed by some modern editors. Is there a pun? And, if so, what on? Scarcely on the name 'Will' as referring to the Friend. Again, to speak of the fool love's loyalty in thinking no ill to exist in the one who loves would be nonsense. There may, on the other hand, be a pun on (1) 'your wishes', (2) 'your waywardness' (Pooler), and/or (3) 'your lasciviousness' (an Elizabethan use). (Cf. the obscene pun in 135 and 136.) But there is also one possibility of a pun on the name. The lines could mean: 'Love is so loyal (and real) a fool that, in your William Shakespeare, he (love) can . . .' Since, however, we do not regard such a meaning as primary, we do not retain Q's capital W.

57

Being your slave, what should I do but tend
Upon the hours and times of your desire?
I have no precious time at all to spend,
Nor services to do, till you require: 4
Nor dare I chide the world-without-end hour
Whilst I, my sovereign, watch the clock for you,
Nor think the bitterness of absence sour
When you have bid your servant once adieu: 8
Nor dare I question with my jealous thought
Where you may be, or your affairs suppose,
But like a sad slave stay and think of nought
Save where you are how happy you make those.   12
    So true a fool is love that in your will,
    Though you do anything, he thinks no ill.

58 3 *to crave*] 'crave'. See Abbott (*Shakespearian Grammar*, s. 416) for examples of 'to' inserted before a second infinitive following a remote auxiliary. We should either omit the 'to' or repeat the auxiliary (here 'should').

6 *The imprison'd absence*] The Friend, 'absent', not necessarily spatially (by a journey) but perhaps by coldness (see general note on 56) is 'at liberty'. The poet is 'imprison'd' by being separated from him. The line represents what Ridley (1934) called 'a typical instance of violent compression'.

liberty] Possibly, as Tucker suggests, combining the senses (1) your own movements as a free man, (2) libertine behaviour. (Cf. 41. 1 and 57. 13–14.)

7 *And patience-tame, to sufferance bide each check*] Q, some early editors, and Harrison: *And patience tame, to sufferance bide each check*, Capell: *And patience tame to sufferance; . . .* The rest of the editors: *And patience, tame to sufferance, . . .* Modern editors have rightly refused to be satisfied with Q, which involves the weak meaning 'tame patience' and an uncharacteristic transposition of the adjective (see Abbott, *Shakespearian Grammar*, s. 419). Capell's reading makes *tame* a verb and *patience* its object. Besides radically altering Q's punctuation this would seem to involve some redundancy unless 'suffer' (line 5) be taken to mean simply 'be a victim of', and it would make a somewhat loose and slow progression. The usual reading certainly makes good sense, but at the expense of a drastic change of Q's punctuation. The reading we propose involves the minimum change of punctuation (the insertion of a hyphen), and provides what we think a better sense: '(Let me), tame as patience itself, endure to the point of acquiescent indulgence, every unresponsive coldness.' There are plenty of examples in Shakespeare of similar compounds of nouns with adjectives expressing characteristic attributes, e.g. 'giant-rude', 'marble-constant', 'wind-swift', 'snail-slow', 'flower-soft', 'stone-hard'. Mr. F. L. Lucas, adopting our proposed hyphen in *patience-tame*, has suggested to us another possible reading: *And, patience-tame to sufferance, bide each check,*. 'Sufferance' here would bear the meaning 'suffering' (*OED*, sense 4). This he feels would avoid a certain redundancy, on our interpretation, between 'sufferance' and 'bide'. The construction 'tame to' can certainly be supported from *KL*: IV. vi. 225: 'tame to fortune's blows' (F1). Mr. Lucas's very attractive reading involves, however, greater interference with Q's punctuation than ours, which still seems to us to have a Shakespearean ring, and to be interpretable without redundancy.

8 *injury*] 'injustice', 'wrong'.

9 *charter*] 'acknowledged privilege'.

136

58

THAT GOD forbid that made me first your slave
I should in thought control your times of pleasure,
Or at your hand the account of hours to crave,
Being your vassal bound to stay your leisure!   4
Oh let me suffer—being at your beck—
The imprison'd absence of your liberty,
And patience-tame, to sufferance bide each check
Without accusing you of injury!   8
Be where you list, your charter is so strong
That you yourself may privilege your time
To what you will, to you it doth belong
Yourself to pardon of self-doing crime: 12
    I am to wait, though waiting so be hell,—
    Not blame your pleasure, be it ill or well.

10–11 *privilege . . . will*] 'grant privileged freedom to your time to be employed for what purpose you will'.

10–11 *time To*] So Q, early editors, and some modern editors. Malone and many modern editors (with minor variations): *time: Do*. Malone's emendation has appealed to some editors as paralleling lines 11–12 with lines 9–10, but the parallel seems to us to have Augustan neatness rather than a Shakespearean ring.

12 *self-doing crime*] 'any offence against yourself'. The poet is professing to regard the Friend's offences as entirely his own affair, but to do this he has to repress a sense that they are also offences against himself.

59 *General Note:* The idea that at intervals the course of the world exactly repeats itself occurs frequently in ancient speculation. In the West it was elaborated most fully by some of the Pythagoreans and Stoics. Eudemus, the pupil of Aristotle, writes: 'If we are to believe the Pythagoreans, exactly the same conditions will be repeated, and I with this little rod in my hand shall some day again be addressing you my class sitting round me precisely as you sit now, and everything in like manner will recur precisely as before.' (Eudemus apud Simplic. *In Phys.*, 732, 26.) Most of the older Stoics accepted the doctrine of the complete similarity of the successive worlds. Some of the younger Stoics, however, appear to have held that there might be differences between them. The resulting controversy is perhaps reflected in lines 11–12, but, if so, it is more than possible that the idea came to Shakespeare rather through intellectual gossip than through any assiduous study of philosophy. In any case, the source of the idea with which the sonnet opens is very likely to be simply the biblical quotation cited in the note on lines 1–2, below, which is paralleled in Marcus Aurelius's saying that 'there is nothing new under the sun' (*De rebus suis*, vii, 19, xi. 1).

For further information on the Pythagorean and Stoic theories of cycles the reader may profitably consult E. Zeller, *The Stoics, Epicureans and Sceptics*, tr. Reichel, new ed., London, 1892, Ch. VII, and R. D. Hicks, *Stoic and Epicurean*, London, 1910, Ch. I, especially 32 ff.

Astronomically the Great Year was the period (variously reckoned) after which all the heavenly bodies were supposed to return to their original positions. To those who believed in stellar influence on human affairs this would naturally seem to cause a corresponding recurrence in human affairs. The periods assigned to the Great Year included 540 years and 600 years as well as far longer periods. On these smaller estimates, if a cycle were in measurable distance of its end, a regression of five hundred years (see line 6, below) would put the world back into a previous cycle.

1–2] The parallel with *Eccles.* i. 9–10 is often pointed out.

3 *invention*] The first of the five processes of rhetoric, 'the finding out of apt matter . . .' (cf. 38. 1, note).

amiss] Without this word the sense of the quatrain would be perfectly clear, namely: 'If everything is merely a repetition of what has happened before, how our brains are deluded, when they toil and labour to give birth to new matter, and only bring forth what has been created before!' But what is the sense of the word 'amiss', modifying 'bear'? If we took it to mean 'wrongly', then 'bear amiss' might suggest an abortion, which clearly does not fit the sense, since if there is exact repetition, either the new birth is not an abortion or the old one was also. Tucker's interpretation 'mistakenly, in a futile way', is loose, since the two expressions are not synony-

59

I<small>F</small> <small>THERE</small> be nothing new, but that which is
Hath been before, how are our brains beguil'd,
Which labouring for invention bear amiss
The second burthen of a former child!   4
Oh that recórd could with a backward look
Even of five hundred courses of the sun
Show me your image in some ántique book
Since mind at first in character was done!—   8
That I might see what the old world could say
To this composèd wonder of your frame,
Whether we are mended, or whe'er better they,
Or whether revolution be the same.   12
    Oh sure I am the wits of former days
    To subjects worse have given admiring praise.

mous, the first is unclear, and the second finds no support in any recorded
English usage. But 'amiss' could mean 'short or wide of a mark or objective'
(cf. OED. I: 'in a way that goes astray or misses its object', quoting Caxton,
Chronicles of England, 244–98: 'Our Archyers shet neuer arowe amys.')
The sense would then be: 'We travail to produce something new, but fail
to do so, and only reproduce material from past worlds.'

8] 'Written at any time since men first expressed thought in writing.'

10 *composèd wonder*] 'impeccably proportioned miracle'.
frame] 'form', rather than merely bone-structure or even build.

11 *mended*] 'amended', i.e. an improvement on men of that time.

Whether . . . whe'er] Q: *Whether . . . where*. All modern editors agree
that *where* = 'whether', which was frequently contracted into a mono-
syllable. Some read *whether*, most *whe'r*, a few *whe'er*, which we prefer, as
involving least alteration of Q and most readily indicating the contraction.

12] i.e. Or whether recurrence (from cycle to cycle) involves complete
qualitative similarity.

13 *wits*] 'able men', men of understanding and 'invention' (cf. line 3).

14 *admiring*] 'wondering'.

13–14] Probably an intentionally ironic understatement; otherwise the
ending would be ineffably banal.

60 1 *pebbled*] As Tucker says, not an 'idly picturesque epithet'. A rocky shore would not provide the apt image, since it would not, as a pebbly shore would, illustrate the gentle, imperceptible 'making' tide.

4] 'All press forward one after another in steady succession'. 'Contend' does not imply competition here.

5 *Nativity*] Shakespeare frequently uses abstract for concrete. So 'Nativity' here means, first, 'new-born infant', and leads to one association of 'Crawls' (line 6). But as it has also the astrological sense of the moment of birth in relation to the conjunction of planets and their position in the Twelve Houses, the imagery next moves from the sea to the heavens, from the element of water to that of light, and so to the sun (see line 7).

main] 'broad expanse', as in 'main of waters', and 'this main from Hell to that new world' (Milton, *PL*. x. 257), a transference from the primary sense 'main sea'. 'Main of light' thus implies for the child the sphere of independent existence. It would also connote to an Elizabethan the hollow sphere of the universe filled with light (Wyndham), as contrasted with the 'main of waters'. This, no doubt, led Shakespeare to the sense of 'full day', involving the sun at its height (line 6), and so to the eclipses of line 7.

7 *Crookèd*] 'malignant'.

8 *confound*] 'destroy'. Cf. 5. 5–6: 'For never-resting time leads summer on/To hideous winter and confounds him there.'

9 *transfix the flourish*] though the general meaning seems evident— 'destroy or impair the physical beauty'—no glossarist or commentator has satisfactorily explained the meanings of the individual words and how they add up to the required result. Arbitrary definitions citing this line alone for support will not do.

'Flourish', now confined to a linear embellishment in printing, an *ex gratia* ornament in calligraphy, or, in gesture, a similar wavy line made with hand, arm, and so on, originally meant (1) (*a*) 'a blossom' (still in Northern dialect), and hence (1) (*b*) 'a bloom'; thence (2) 'a gloss, varnish, or ostentatious ornament laid on'; (3) (in architecture) 'a flower-work'. 1(*b*) and (2) are both relevant to this line. For (2) cf. 'Folly Erasmus set a flourish on' (Nashe, *Summer's Last Will and Testament*) and *TN*. III. iv. 405: 'the beauteous evil / Are empty trunks o'erflourish'd by the devil'; and *LLL*. II. i. 14: 'the painted flourish of your praise.' The beauty of youth in 60. 9 is spoken of as a 'flourish', a 'bloom' regarded as a 'gloss or orna-ment' 'set on', in contrast to numerous Shakespearean references to beauty that is 'in grain'. There may, indeed, be a secondary reference to the fact that the Elizabethan gallant painted—sometimes pretty thick.

'Transfix' is nowhere recorded, except in reference to this line, with any meaning but 'pierce through', 'impale', or 'fix or fasten by piercing'.

60

Ⅼᴵᴷᴱ ᴀꜱ the waves make towards the pebbled shore,
So do our minutes hasten to their end;
Each changing place with that which goes before
In sequent toil all forwards do contend.   4
Nativity, once in the main of light,
Crawls to maturity, wherewith being crown'd,
Crookèd eclipses 'gainst his glory fight,
And Time that gave doth now his gift confound.   8
Time doth transfix the flourish set on youth,
And delves the parallels in beauty's brow,
Feeds on the rarities of nature's truth;
And nothing stands but for his scythe to mow.   12
    And yet to times in hope my verse shall stand,
    Praising thy worth, despite his cruel hand.

The last of these senses clearly does not fit here. The meaning 'Remove',
given by Schmidt and Onions without citing any other instance, cannot be
accepted without evidence, which they have not supplied. 'Pierce through'
would certainly be consonant with Time's dart, which may here be in
mind, though not hitherto named or alluded to in the sonnet. Mr. Stuart
Tunnah, of Emmanuel College, suggests that if a sharp stick or dart is pushed
through a window the cracks 'spider away', and that the 'flourish' of brittle
beauty set upon youth would 'spider away' in wrinkles when pierced by
Time's dart. Malvolio's face had split into 'more lines than are in the new
map with the augmentation of the Indies'.

   10 *delves the parallels*] Cf. 2. 1–2 and 19. 9–10. Tucker objects to the
interpretation 'digs trenches (i.e. wrinkles)' that the idea of 'trenches' is
inconsonant with 'flourish' and 'rarities', and he goes on to suggest that
'delves' means 'digs hollows in' and that 'parallels' means 'the symmetrical
lines which belong to the brow of beauty'. But to us it seems that the image
is of trenches (i.e. the furrows of an ageing face), and that this is a fresh
image, touched off by the association of the lines in the crinkled mask, and
in turn provoking the further image of destruction in line 11.

   11 *rarities*] 'choicest features'. *truth*] 'perfection'.

   13 *in hope*] 'looked for but as yet unborn'.

61 1–3 *open . . . broken*] One of the cases of assonance instead of strict rhyme in the *Sonnets*. There is another in 120, lines 9 and 11; and there are also two cases of imperfect double-rhymes (26. 13, 14 and 42. 5, 7).

4 *shadows*] mere unreal semblances.

5 *spirit*] Here the immaterial element of the Friend, temporarily dis-embodied.

7 *shames . . . me*] 'my shameful actions and what I do in my idle hours'.

8 *scope*] 'target'. Cf. Spenser, *Shepherd's Calendar*, Nov. 155: 'that . . . shooting wide, do miss the markèd scope'. The 'target' is 'me' (line 7).

tenour] Capell's emendation, adopted by most modern editors. Q: *tenure*, the most frequent spelling in Shakespeare Quartos and Folios for 'tenour'. To follow Q in a modern edition would tend to mislead a reader into taking the word to be the land-law term 'tenure'.

10–13 *awake . . . watchman . . . watch . . . wake*] These words involve a complex of puns, originating in the reference in the second quatrain to the Friend's spirit spying on the poet's actions. 'Watch' = (1) 'keep a look out', (2) 'remain awake'. 'For' (line 13), correspondingly, means (1) 'in expectation of', (2) 'on account of'. 'Wake' might naturally be taken to mean (1) 'remain awake', (2) 'be on guard', but both these meanings are here ingeniously excluded in favour of (3) 'sit up late for pleasure or revelry'. Cf. *Ham.* I. iv. 8: 'The king doth wake tonight and takes his rouse,' and, if there is a reference to the Friend's lasciviousness, (4) 'lie awake in bed too near a mistress'.

61

Is it thy will thy image should keep open
My heavy eyelids to the weary night?
Dost thou desire my slumbers should be broken,
While shadows like to thee do mock my sight?   4
Is it thy spirit that thou send'st from thee
So far from home into my deeds to pry,
To find out shames and idle hours in me,
The scope and tenour of thy jealousy?   8
Oh no! thy love though much is not so great;
It is my love that keeps mine eye awake—
Mine own true love that doth my rest defeat,
To play the watchman ever for thy sake: 12
    For thee watch I, whilst thou dost wake elsewhere,
    From me far off, with others all too near.

62 1 *self-love*] Cf. lines 13–14, and the play on the identity of the self and the beloved in 20, 36, and 39. The 'self-love' is not just selfishness, but conceit, with the features (hence 'eye', line 1) and 'worth' (hence 'soul', line 2) of the 'self'. This 'self', throughout the octave, is made to seem to be the poet; but the sestet refutes this, and reveals that the true 'self' the poet loves is the Friend.

5 *gracious*] Not simply physically but also spiritually beautiful. Cf. 7. 1 and 10. 11.

6 *true*] 'perfect'.

no . . . account] (1) No perfection is (*a*) so important in itself, (*b*) so important to me. (2) No constancy is (*a*) so praiseworthy [as mine] when you are cold, (*b*) of greater price to me [than yours, could I be assured of it]. Thus an obvious play on 'truth', springing from 'true', combines with the play between octave and sestet on the identity of the self.

7 *for myself*] probably 'in my own mind and for my own satisfaction'.

7, 8] So Q, followed by almost all modern editors, though the lines have been found puzzling, and various emendations offered, e.g. Walker and Delius conjectured: *And for myself mine own worth so define*. Lettsom conjectured: *And so myself . . . do define*, and this reading has been adopted by Hudson[2] and Tucker Brooke. Pooler conjectured: *And for myself . . . to define, I do. . . .* The chief difficulty with Q is that there seems to be no subject for 'do' (line 7), unless we understand a nominative 'I', derived from 'Methinks' (line 5). But, in the case of such originally impersonal verbs as 'methinks', instances occur as early as Chaucer of an impersonal construction followed immediately by a corresponding personal construction without a subject of the latter being supplied. O. Jespersen (*Progress in Language*, Swan, Sonnenschein & Co., London, 1894, s. 176) quotes an instance from Chaucer's *Monk's Tale*, 551–2: 'For drede of this, him thoughte that he deyde, And ran into a gardin, him to hyde.' The period during which impersonal verbs were acquiring personal construction lasted at least till Shakespeare's time. The case of 'methinks' involves, however, a further complication. In Old English there were two distinct verbs *þyncan* ('to seem') and *þencan* ('to think'), which in time came to be pronounced the same. Moreover, possibly by phonetic association, 'me' in certain syntactical contexts, from at least the fifteenth century, tends to acquire nominative force (cf. Jespersen, *op. cit.* s. 193). These two factors would readily conduce to a confusion of 'methinks' and 'I think', and make such a transition as that of the Chaucer example still more likely to occur. Lines 5–8 in Q may be an instance of just such a transition.

On the other hand, it is graphically plausible that Q's *for* is, as Professor Tucker Brooke suggests, a misreading for *soe*. In this case, *myself* would be

62

S IN OF self-love possesseth all mine eye,
And all my soul, and all my every part;
And for this sin there is no remedy,
It is so grounded inward in my heart.   4
Methinks no face so gracious is as mine,
No shape so true, no truth of such account,
And for myself mine own worth do define
As I all other in all worths surmount.   8
But when my glass shews me my self indeed,
Beated and chopp'd with tann'd antiquity,
Mine own self-love quite contrary I read—
Self so self-loving were iniquity: 12
   'Tis thee (my self) that for myself I praise,
   Painting my age with beauty of thy days.

the subject of 'do define'. For this reading the construction of 'As' in 'so
. . . as' offers no difficulty, whereas Q requires us to construe 'As' as =
'in such a way that' (Dowden) or 'as though' (Beeching) or 'in such a way
that it appears that'. Moreover, the very fact that *for* gave a possible sense
might well have prevented a proof-reader from suspecting a misreading.
The argument for *soe* is, therefore, strong; but since Q can bear a good
sense we have felt it wiser to print it. As to '*for* . . . *so*', this is graphically
just possible, but far less likely than *for* for *soe*. Pooler's conjecture, *for* . . .
to, adopting Capell's conjecture: *I do* (line 8) seems to us to involve too
drastic alterations. The general sense of the lines is: 'And in my own mind
and for my own satisfaction I define the estimate of my own value as being
that I excel all others in all respects.'

  8 *other*] The old plural form deriving from Middle English *oth(e)re*.

  9 *my self*] one of the cases where it seems justifiable to retain Q's
reading as two words.

  10 *Beated*] Many, we think unnecessary, emendations have been sug-
gested. Other weak forms of participle for strong verbs occur in Shake-
speare, e.g. 'shak'd' (*T&C*. I. iii. 101); 'weav'd' (*1H4*. V. iv. 88); 'wax'd'

145

62 *(continued)*

(*Tim*. III. iv. 11). The meaning 'beaten' provides a sense ('time-beaten')
parallel to 'weather-beaten'. Recourse by some commentators to dialect or
technical terms from turfing or the preparation of loam seems unduly
recherché.

    chopp'd] 'chapped', cf. *AYLI*. II. iv. 49; *JC*. I. ii. 245; *2H4*. III. ii. 297.
    12] i.e. 'this sort or degree of narcissism would be iniquitous.'
    13 *my self*] i.e. 'my true self.'

62

Sɪɴ ᴏꜰ self-love possesseth all mine eye,
And all my soul, and all my every part;
And for this sin there is no remedy,
It is so grounded inward in my heart.   4
Methinks no face so gracious is as mine,
No shape so true, no truth of such account,
And for myself mine own worth do define
As I all other in all worths surmount.   8
But when my glass shews me my self indeed,
Beated and chopp'd with tann'd antiquity,
Mine own self-love quite contrary I read—
Self so self-loving were iniquity: 12
    'Tis thee (my self) that for myself I praise,
    Painting my age with beauty of thy days.

63 1 *Against*] 'In preparation for the time when. . . .' Cf. *R&J*. IV. i.
113: 'against thou shalt awake'; and *MND*. III. ii. 99. The meaning is
taken up by 'For' (line 9).

2 *injurious*] More than 'destructive' or 'harmful'—unjustly or wrong-
fully so. Cf. *3H6*. III. iii. 101: 'injurious doom'.

crush'd and o'erworn] Steevens's complaint (1780) that this is like saying
a man is first killed and then wounded, misses what is probably the image
—that of a cloth whose nap is pressed upon and worn away. Cf. J. Weever,
Ancient Funeral Monuments, 1631 (quoted *OED*): 'A beaten-out pulpit
cushion, an oreworn Communion-cloth'.

5 *travail'd*] So Q and early editors (*trauaild*). Modern editors: *travell'd*.
The spellings 'travail(e)' and 'travel(l)' were pretty well interchangeable
in Elizabethan English. It is noteworthy that Shakespeare, when he clearly
intends the sense 'journey' to be primary, often strongly suggests the idea
of the toil involved, whatever the spelling in the printed text. This is not
surprising in view of the fact that 'travail' and 'travel' were originally the
same word, and that Elizabethan English was so much closer to 'origins'
than our own. Here the modern spelling, 'travell'd', might well obliterate
the sense of toil required, whereas the modern spelling 'travail'd', in this
context, does not obliterate the sense of 'journey'.

steepy night] Some modern explanations, e.g. 'the dark and steep descent
of old age', give insufficient weight to the sun metaphor. Age plunges into
dotage and oblivion, as the sun to its setting.

8 *Stealing*] We of today have lost so much the vital sense of many
common words that we may easily overlook the element of secrecy in
'steal' = 'take dishonestly *and secretly*'. Shakespeare's diction retains that
vitality, and the sense of imperceptible removal is definitely present here.

spring] So most modern editors. Q: *Spring*, which, in modern typo-
graphy, would *confine* the sense to the season. But 'spring' (without the
initial capital) could still, at least till the mid-seventeenth century, mean
'young growth' and its freshness, and that meaning seems also to be
present.

9 *fortify*] (intransitive) 'raise defence-works'. Cf. *2H4*. I. iii. 56: 'We
fortify in papers and in figures.'

10 *confounding*] 'destroying'. Cf. 5. 5–6 and 60. 8.

11, 12] i.e. The beauty of him whom I love will never be forgotten,
though he will no longer live to love me.

13 *black lines*] 'Black' is not only the black of ink, but, by its associations
of ugliness, night, death, and oblivion, establishes a paradox, for it is in
these 'black lines', in contrast with the 'lines' of age (line 4), that beauty
and freshness will be preserved.

148

63

AGAINST MY love shall be as I am now,
With Time's injurious hand crush'd and o'erworn;
When hours have drain'd his blood and fill'd his brow
With lines and wrinkles; when his youthful morn   4
Hath travail'd on to age's steepy night,
And all those beauties whereof now he's king
Are vanishing or vanish'd out of sight,
Stealing away the treasure of his spring: 8
For such a time do I now fortify
Against confounding age's cruel knife,
That he shall never cut from memory
My sweet love's beauty, though my lover's life: 12
   His beauty shall in these black lines be seen,
   And they shall live, and he in them still green.

64 2] The line works through the accumulation of meanings at the expense of some logical redundancy ('rich' / 'cost' . . . 'outworn' / 'buried'). The verbal richness includes, e.g., 'proud' as = (1) 'displaying pride', or 'in which pride is taken', and as = (2) 'showy', as in 2. 3: 'youth's proud livery'; and 'cost' as = (1) 'expense', and (2) 'ornament and display', as in 146. 5. Some editors have followed Malone in hyphenating as *rich-proud*, which weakens the line by simplification.

3 *sometime*] i.e. 'once', not 'sometimes'.

down raz'd] So Q. Malone hyphenated and has been followed by almost all modern editors. The hyphen seems unnecessary.

4 *brass eternal*] The adjective, of course, qualifies 'brass' (cf. Horace's '*aere perennius*') not 'slave'. Cf. *R2*. III. ii. 168: 'brass impregnable'. The reference is to monumental brasses and their inscriptions, as in 107, 14.

mortal rage] i.e. death's rage, the destructive fury of death. (Cf. 65. 2–3.) There is, however, also a half-realized antithesis between 'mortal' and 'eternal', corresponding to the chiastic construction.

9–10 *state . . . state*] There is characteristic play on the word as (1) = 'condition', (2) = 'territory', 'sovereignty', (3) (line 10) = 'worldly grandeur'.

10 *confounded to decay*] So Sewell[1], Malone, and most modern editors. Q: *confounded, to decay*. To retain the comma in a modern recension would force us to take 'to decay' as infinitive = 'in course of decaying', but it is at least doubtful whether that was the meaning of Q. The suggestion of a gradual process of disintegration following destruction would be an anti-climax. It therefore seems more probable that 'decay' here is a noun used in a sense nearer to the root meaning of 'toppling down' (Med. Lat. *decadere*), i.e. utter destruction.

13 *which*] 'in that it' (i.e. 'this thought'). . . .

64

WHEN I have seen by Time's fell hand defac'd
The rich proud cost of outworn buried age;
When sometime lofty towers I see down raz'd,
And brass eternal slave to mortal rage;   4
When I have seen the hungry ocean gain
Advantage on the kingdom of the shore,
And the firm soil win of the watery main,
Increasing store with loss and loss with store: 8
When I have seen such interchange of state,
Or state itself confounded to decay,
Ruin hath taught me thus to ruminate—
That Time will come and take my love away.   12
    This thought is as a death, which cannot choose
    But weep to have that which it fears to lose.

65 1] For the ellipsis of 'there is' cf. 111. 11. Ellipsis of 'It is', 'there is' and 'is' is quite common in Shakespeare. For the ellipsis of 'neither' before 'nor' cf. 86. 9 and 141. 9.

2 *sad mortality*] 'calamitous destruction', cf. *OED*. 3.

3 *this rage*] Malone's conjectural emendation *his* is unnecessary. 'Rage' here = 'destructive fury' or 'violence'. Cf. *Cymb*. IV. ii. 258–9: 'Fear no more the heat o' the sun, / Nor the furious winter's rages.'

4 *action*] 'Power of action' or 'vitality'. The *word* may possibly have been suggested to Shakespeare by 'plea' (line 3), but the image is not legal. It relates to the siege that follows (lines 6–8).

8 *time* ⎫ Q has no capitals. Most modern editors capital-
10 *Time's . . . Time's* ⎭ ize in all three instances. We feel that the incipient personification of 'time' in line 8 is not completed until line 10.

9 *fearful*] A word to be taken here in its strongest sense.

10 *Time's chest*] Ingenious emenders have been busy from Theobald and Malone (*quest*) to J. G. Orger and Kellner (*theft*). Commentators have been troubled by the apparent inconsistency of hiding *from* a chest; but the image is of a jewel, lent by Time for us to enjoy for a period, which we are anxious to hide from Time, who will take it back and lock it in his treasure-chest. The chest probably also carries the secondary association of the coffin and the grave. E. L. Hubler (*Shakespeare's Songs and Poems*, New York, 1959), moreover, rightly reminds us of Time's 'wallet' . . . 'in which he puts alms for oblivion' (*T&C*. III. iii. 145–6).

12 *of*] So Malone and almost all modern editors. Q: *or*. Gildon–Evans: *on*. Capell, Hadow have conjectured *o'er*. Q is clearly unsatisfactory. *On* seems graphically more plausible than *of*, which has, however, more linguistic probability. (See *OED* under 'spoil'.)

14 *my love*] Primarily the Friend, but perhaps also the poet's love for him, which is likewise recorded in his verses.

65

SINCE BRASS, nor stone, nor earth, nor boundless sea,
But sad mortality o'ersways their power,
How with this rage shall beauty hold a plea,
Whose action is no stronger than a flower? 4
Oh how shall summer's honey breath hold out
Against the wrackful siege of battering days,
When rocks impregnable are not so stout
Nor gates of steel so strong but time decays? 8
Oh fearful meditation! where, alack,
Shall Time's best jewel from Time's chest lie hid?
Or what strong hand can hold his swift foot back?
Or who his spoil of beauty can forbid? 12
   Oh none, unless this miracle have might—
   That in black ink my love may still shine bright.

66 *Capitals.* In Q some of the personifications are capitalized, but with no apparent system. We have capitalized all.

1 *these*] The evils enumerated below under 'As'. The line does not refer back to preceding sonnets in the Q order or in any other order.

3 *needy Nothing*] A personification of 'worthless creatures of no gifts or qualities'. There is no implication of social pity extended to the 'worthy poor'. The antithesis here is to 'Desert' (line 2). 'Nothing' as applied to persons is a strong term in Elizabethan English. (Cloten is 'that harsh, noble, simple nothing', *Cymb.* III. iv. 135; and to Hamlet Claudius is 'a thing . . . Of nothing' (*Ham.* IV. ii. 30–32)).

jollity] 'fine array' (cf. Cotgrave: '*Iolieté:* . . . gainesse, trimnesse, finenesse . . .').

4 *Faith*] Could mean (1) 'loyalty', in allegiance or love; (2) 'a trust or pledge'; (3) 'the true religion', e.g. Catholic or Protestant.

unhappily] Either (1) 'disastrously' or, more probably in view of 'shamefully' in line 5, (2) 'maliciously' (see *OED*, sense 3).

forsworn] 'abjured' (see *OED*, sense 1). Faith is the victim, not the abjuror.

5 *Honour . . . misplac'd*] 'Rank or dignity shamefully ill-conferred.' Cf. *Eccles.* x. 5, 6: 'There is an evil which I have seen . . . which proceedeth from the ruler: Folly is set in great dignity.'

6 *strumpeted*] Probably 'falsely debased with the reputation of a strumpet' (see *OED*, sense 2, quoting parallels from Massinger and Ford). This sense gives a closer parallel to line 7 than would the more literal sense 'prostituted'.

7 *right*] 'true', 'genuine'.

disgrac'd] 'cheated of reputation', 'disparaged', rather than 'depriv'd of favours', which is, indeed, a less common sense in Shakespeare.

8 *by limping Sway*] 'by the weak and uncertain rule of those in power'.

disablèd] four syllables. In Elizabethan English liquids 'are frequently pronounced as though an extra vowel were introduced between them and the preceding consonant' (Abbott, *Shakespearian Grammar*, s. 477), e.g. 'wrest(e)ler', *AYLI.* II. ii. 13; 'pilg(e)rim', *All's W.* III. v. 44; 'fidd(e)ler', *T. of S.* II. i. 158.

The word here means 'prevented from exercising its ability'.

9 *Art*] Probably here 'learning and science'; certainly not 'Art' in the more modern sense applying to the fine arts.

9, 10] 'Learning and science are silenced by those in authority, and stupid ignorance, giving itself the airs of an expert, controls and directs the real technicians.' A number of commentators have either seen or conjectured a reference here to censorship difficulties of the players; but we regard the point as inconclusive.

66

Tir'd with all these for restful death I cry,—
As to behold Desert a beggar born,
And needy Nothing trimm'd in jollity,
And purest Faith unhappily forsworn,   4
And gilded Honour shamefully misplac'd,
And maiden Virtue rudely strumpeted,
And right Perfection wrongfully disgrac'd,
And Strength by limping Sway disablèd,   8
And Art made tongue-tied by Authority,
And Folly, Doctor-like, controlling Skill,
And simple Truth miscall'd Simplicity,
And captive Good attending captain Ill: 12
    Tir'd with all these, from these would I be gone—
    Save that, to die, I leave my love alone.

11 *Truth*] 'Straightforwardness', 'honesty'.

miscall'd] Stronger than 'misnamed'; rather 'slandered as'. Cf. Holland, Plutarch's *Moralia* (1603), 124: 'They deserved to be . . . punished, for so miscalling and reviling him.'

Simplicity] 'Want of acuteness', 'simplemindedness', 'naïveté'.

12 *captain*] Either (1) 'dominant', or, if a noun used attributively, (2) 'his overlord'.

14 *to die*] i.e. 'if I die'.

alone] Possibly both 'solitary' or 'by himself', and 'simply that'.

67 1 *with infection*] 'In a corrupt and vicious world' (that of 66).

4 *lace*] 'trick out', 'embellish' (as still in gold or silver lace).

5] Primarily the line alludes to the cosmetics the Elizabethan gallant employed, and which Shakespeare seems to have found repugnant. The sense is: 'Why should others imitate with cosmetics such ideal and natural beauty as his?' But Wyndham (pp. 298–9) presents an impressive array of passages, from the *Sonnets*, where 'painting' and 'false art' symbolize the flattery of rival poets (21. 1–3; 68. 14; 82. 9–14; 83. 1, 2), arguing that both senses are here present.

6 *seeming*] This is Capell's conjectural emendation, adopted by Malone and a few modern editors. Q and most modern editors: *seeing*. Linguistic support for *seeing* is negligible. Out of the fifty-one other instances of 'seeing' in Shakespeare, none carries any sense of 'false appearance', and the verbal nouns all connote active vision. Failure to notice a nunnation mark, on the other hand, as in *seēing*, is one of the easiest of editorial or compositorial errors. (Cf. Q's *blacks* for *blancks* (*blācks*).) Again, 'seeming' is one of Shakespeare's favourite pun words. Finally, 'seeming' here provides a better antithesis to 'hue' = 'real complexion'.

of] 'from'.

7 *poor beauty*] Commentators are divided between (1) 'poor Béauty' or 'béauty' (a personified, or, as we take it, semi-personified concept), to be pitied for impoverishment (cf. lines 9–12); and (2) 'póor beauty' (inferior beauty), corresponding to 'false painting' in line 5. The strongest argument against (1) is Beeching's: 'Shakespeare is usually faithful to rhetorical parallelism within the quatrain; and here "poor beauty" corresponds to "false painting", not to "bankrupt Nature".' Beeching correctly states Shakespeare's practice; but interpretation (1) observes it, giving more weight than (2) to 'indirectly' and to the parallel between 'living hue' and the 'true' 'rose' of line 8.

indirectly] i.e. by artifice ('false painting').

8 *of shadow*] i.e. imitated in paint, and so unreal.

since] Either (1) 'seeing that' or (2) 'just because', according as we take 'poor beauty' in sense (1) or in sense (2). Case calls 'because' 'the regular but here rather awkward sense'; but there are plenty of instances in Shakespeare of sense (1).

9–10] 'Beggar'd of blood' may refer either (1) to Nature or (2) to the Friend. If (1), then it explains the nature of the bankruptcy. This sense seems more likely than (2), since there is no evidence in the sonnet that the Friend has been reduced to anaemia.

9 *bankrupt is—*] Q has a comma; but a dash makes it clearer that 'Beggar'd of blood' refers to Nature.

67

AH, WHEREFORE with infection should he live
And with his presence grace impiety,
That sin by him advantage should achieve
And lace itself with his society?   4
Why should false painting imitate his cheek
And steal dead seeming of his living hue?
Why should poor beauty indirectly seek
Roses of shadow since his rose is true?   8
Why should he live, now Nature bankrupt is—
Beggar'd of blood to blush through lively veins,
For she hath no exchequer now but his,
And proud of many, lives upon his gains?   12
    Oh him she stores, to show what wealth she had
    In days long since, before these last so bad.

10 *to blush*] Probably here applying to 'blood', and used in the obsolete sense of 'to shine' (especially red), cf. Old English *blyscan*, to shine, especially red, from *blysca*, a flame (Partridge, *Origins*, 51b).

11 *For*] Possibly either (1) 'just because', or (2) 'since' (continuing the explanation of the bankruptcy). (2) yields a sense less flattering to the Friend than (1), since it implies that even with the Friend's exchequer Nature cannot meet all her commitments. With sense (1) the implication would be that Nature meets her many obligations by perpetual recourse to the Friend's never-failing source.

12 *proud of many*] Either (1) 'proud of many offspring' (and so having to maintain them); or (2) 'swollen with many creations'; or (3) 'making an arrogant display of many handsome (but artificially handsome) children (or creations)'. Choice of meaning is hard. Suggested emendations include *prov'd* (Capell), possibly = 'witnessed'; and *priv'd* (M. R. Ridley conj.) = 'deprived' (cf. 'bankrupt', line 9) favoured by J. W. Lever.

lives upon his gains] i.e. is perpetually transferring his blood into her other offspring (or creations), he alone, as live beauty, being able to make more.

10 . . . *veins*, } So Q. Most modern editors: *veins?* . . . *gains*. They
12 . . . *gains?* } appear to be selecting sense (2) for *For*, see note on line 11, above. We have preferred to retain Q.

68 1 *map*] *OED*: '2. *fig.* A detailed representation in epitome . . .; b. the embodiment or incarnation (of a virtue, vice, character, etc.); the very picture or image *of.*'

2 *as flowers do now*] i.e. unpainted, in their natural hues.

3 *these bastard signs of fair*] The cosmetics Shakespeare loathed. (Cf. 67. 5, note.)

fair] For the substantival use (= 'beauty') cf. 16. 11 and 83. 2.

borne] So Q, Tyler, Wyndham, Pooler, Harrison. Gildon–Evans, Capell, and most modern editors: *born.* The differentiation of spelling does not arise until the late eighteenth century (see Partridge, *Origins*, 43a). The modern *born* would certainly echo 'bastard', but would also obscure the other sense 'worn', 'carried', which is not only also present here, but even primary.

5–7] Wigs and artificial coiffures were often made up from hair shorn from corpses. Characteristically, as with cosmetics, Shakespeare disapproves. Cf. *M. of V.* III. ii. 92 ff.

10 *ornament, it self*] So Q, and early editors to Gildon[1]. Gildon[2] and other early editors: *ornament it self,.* Many modern editors: *ornament, itself,* or *ornament, itself.* Pooler: *ornament itself.* Malone conjectured: *ornament, himself,.* Tucker: *ornament but self.* A notoriously difficult line, but these radical emendations seem unnecessary. The difficulty does, indeed, lie in *it*, but Malone and Tucker seem to have misunderstood *self.* 'Self' was in Old English primarily an adjective agreeing with an antecedent pronoun. Quite early it did, certainly, sometimes come to be considered a noun, and antecedent pronouns began to assume possessive inflectional forms as adjectival prefixes, e.g. 'myself'. Inconsistently, this possessive was not generally accepted for the third person, and 'hisself', 'theirselves' are today dialectal or solecistic. In the case of 'it', whose possessive form was 'his' ('its' does not occur in any Shakespearean Quarto of play or poem, and is very rare in print before 1600), this lack of acceptance is particularly evident, in that 'itself' was almost always printed as two words. This is the case, e.g. in the First Folio. Here the spelling as two words, which emphasizes the adjectival sense of 'self', makes the construction clearer and more emphatic than the modern *itself.* 'It' probably refers to 'beauty' (lines 2 and 8). 'Self' means 'the same throughout', 'consistent'. This adjectival sense survives today in the description of colours (especially of flowers)— and of whisky.

68

THUS IS his cheek the map of days outworn
When beauty lived and died as flowers do now,
Before these bastard signs of fair were borne,
Or durst inhabit on a living brow: 4
Before the golden tresses of the dead,
The right of sepulchres, were shorn away
To live a second life on second head:
Ere beauty's dead fleece made another gay.   8
In him those holy ántique hours are seen
Without all ornament, it self and true,
Making no summer of another's green,
Robbing no old to dress his beauty new: 12
    And him as for a map doth Nature store,
    To show false Art what beauty was of yore.

69 2] 'Are so perfect that the deepest thought could not conceive them better'.

2 *Want*] Lack.

the thought of hearts] the deepest thought.

mend] improve upon.

3 *due*] So Capell, Malone, and all modern editors. Q: *end*. The emendation is entirely acceptable, but Malone's explanation that 'the letters . . . were probably transposed at the press and the "u" inverted' was written before the study of palaeography was brought to bear on Shakespearean texts. In Elizabethan secretary hand a *d* and an *e*, if hastily written and hastily read, might well be confused, as might a *u* and an *n*. Another factor may have been (visual or mental) confusion by the compositor with the termination of *mend* above and *commend* below.

4 *even so as foes commend*] 'in the same way as . . .' (i.e. giving no more than your due).

5 *Thine*] So Malone (1790) and many modern editors. Q and early editors: *Their*. Capell, Malone (1780) and most editors: *Thy*. The error of *their* for *thy* or *thine* occurs quite often in Q. Here *thine* seems slightly preferable to *thy* on the ground of euphony.

outward] For the use as a noun cf. 125. 2.

outward praise] (1) 'praise of your exterior'; (2) 'publicly spoken praise; and (3) 'superficial praise' (cf. line 11). It is just possible that the similarity in Elizabethan pronunciation of 'outward' and 'uttered' might afford an additional play.

11 *churls, their thoughts,*] Q has no commas, but the sense requires them: 'Then, unlike their eyes, which rightly reported you handsome, and looked kindly, their nasty minds interpret your actions churlishly.'

12 *the . . . weeds*] i.e. an unsavoury reputation.

14 *soil*] Q: *solye*. Benson (1640), Capell, and many editors: *soyle*. Gildon–Evans: *Toil*. Most editors: *solve*. A manuscript conjecture written in an old hand in the Bodley–Caldecott copy of Q: *foil*. Dover Wilson (in *The Manuscript of Shakespeare's Hamlet*, Cambridge University Press, Cambridge, 1934, 312–13): *sully* (*The sully's this*).

Toil is unsatisfactory. It involves both (1) a strain on meaning, the only at all plausible sense being a 'snare' (*OED*, sb². 2), and also (2) a double printer's error, namely the printing of an *s* for a *T*, and a transposition of *y* and *l* (i.e. *solye* for *Toyle*).

Solve is also unsatisfactory. Malone frankly admitted that he could not find such a word (= solution) in any author, and *OED* cites only this line as amended by Malone.

Dover Wilson's *sully* is certainly possible. The past participle 'sullied'

69

Those parts of thee that the world's eye doth view
Want nothing that the thought of hearts can mend;
All tongues (the voice of souls) give thee that due,
Uttering bare truth, even so as foes commend: 4
Thine outward thus with outward praise is crown'd;
But those same tongues that give thee so thine own
In other accents do this praise confound
By seeing farther than the eye hath shown: 8
They look into the beauty of thy mind,
And that, in guess, they measure by thy deeds;
Then, churls, their thoughts, although their eyes were kind,
To thy fair flower add the rank smell of weeds.   12
   But why thy odour matcheth not thy show,
   The soil is this—that thou dost common grow.

was often spelt 'solyed' in the sixteenth century. The reading *sully* therefore
has the advantage of requiring no emendation of Q. One disadvantage of
the reading is the extra syllable, for which, however, precedents can be
found. A more serious objection is that the sense ('blemish', 'stain') is
difficult to reconcile with 'why' (line 13).

   The reading *soil* seems to us the best. It has the following attractions: (1)
that it was already adopted by Benson in 1640, which is some evidence that
Q's reading already appeared unsatisfactory; (2) that it does not involve an
extra syllable; (3), and most important, that the word 'soil' was in current
use between the fourteenth and early sixteenth centuries *as a verb* meaning
'to resolve, explain, answer (a question)' (*OED*, v.² 3). It was, moreover,
often spelt 'soyle'. A good instance, from Harsnet, *Popish Impostures*, 77,
reads: 'Now a few questions I must soyle, and then I will proceede to your
holy grace.' Moreover, although *OED* quotes no instance, except this line,
in which 'soil' is used as a *noun* meaning 'the solution of a problem' (sb. 5),
'assoil' was used as a noun, with the meaning 'solution', 'explanation', e.g.
by Puttenham, *Arte of English Poesie* (Arber reprint, 198): 'By way of riddle
(Enigma) of which the sence can hardly be picked out, but by the parties
owne assoile.'

   thou dost common grow] 'you are being too familiar with all and sundry'.

70 *General Note:* The apparent inconsistency between the portrayal of the Friend's character here and that in other sonnets (e.g. 23–25) has led some commentators to hold that different young men are addressed in different sonnets. We are not concerned in the present edition to argue biographical points, but we should perhaps pass the opinion that such conclusions are especially hazardous where poems expressing divergent attitudes may well have been written at widely separated dates.

1 *art*] So Benson (1640) and almost all modern editors. Q: *are*. The plural form with 'thou' is not merely Shakespearean, but is found elsewhere in Elizabethan usage; but the oddity to a modern reader is likely to prove distracting, and this is more important here than the claims of textual purism.

1] N.B. 'shall be' not 'is', and so 'I refuse to take the slander at its face value'.

2 *mark*] 'target'.

3 *suspéct*] Never used as an adjective or past participle in Shakespeare. Here a noun (= 'suspicion') in apposition to 'crow' (line 4).

4 *crow*] Tucker drolly suggests that the crow, deemed a filthy bird, and a bird of the devil (cf. *Lucrece*, 1009) *prefers* to fly in and pollute the purest air

5 *So*] 'provided that', a common use at the time.

approve] 'prove'—the object of the verb is 'worth' (line 6).

6 *Thy*] So Capell, Malone, and all modern editors—clearly rightly. Q: *Their*.

5–8] Not usually understood. The sense seems to be: 'If you really are good, slander will only show your worth to be all the greater, if time is showering all its gifts on you; for it is indeed the finest buds that are most likely to harbour the canker-worm, and you have already revealed yourself as a newly-opened flower without defect.' If this is correct the emendations proposed for *woo'd of time* are unnecessary. The main proposals are: A MS conjecture in the Bodley–Caldecott copy of Q, Butler, and Stopes' conjecture: *woo'd oftime*. Capell's conjecture: *wood* (frantic) *oftime* (or *of time*). Malone[1] conjectured: *void of crime*, but withdrew the conjecture in his second edition. None of these seems really satisfactory. If emendation *is* necessary we can offer a suggestion we have not seen made elsewhere: *woo'd o' th' time*. Instances of such a phrase occur elsewhere in Shakespeare, e.g. 'o' the world' (*A&C.* IV. xiii. 11), 'o' the earth' (ibid. 63), 'o' the night' (*Oth.* I. i. 124), 'out o' the way' (ibid. IV. ii. 7). The meaning here would be: 'being the favourite of the age'. Objections to this reading would be: (*a*) that such phrases seem characteristic of a style which may be later than this sonnet; (*b*) that the resulting line is metrically less satisfactory than Q's.

162

70

That thou art blam'd shall not be thy defect,
For slander's mark was ever yet the fair:
The ornament of beauty is suspéct—
A crow that flies in heaven's sweetest air.   4
So thou be good, slander doth but approve
Thy worth the greater, being woo'd of time;
For canker vice the sweetest buds doth love,
And thou present'st a pure unstainèd prime: 8
Thou hast pass'd by the ambush of young days
Either not assail'd, or victor being charg'd;
Yet this thy praise cannot be so thy praise
To tie up envy, evermore enlarg'd: 12
    If some suspéct of ill mask'd not thy show
    Then thou alone kingdoms of hearts shouldst owe.

10 *assail'd*] cf. 41. 6.
charg'd] 'attacked'.
12 *To*] 'as to'.
12] *i.e.* the beast malice, that your praise cannot tether, is always being newly set at liberty. For 'enlarg'd' cf. *H5.* II. ii. 40: 'Enlarge the man committed yesterday.'
13 *suspéct*] a noun, as in line 3.
thy show] 'the appearance you would otherwise present to "the world's eye"' (Case).
14 *owe*] 'own', 'possess'.
13–14] '*If* your true appearance were not partly obscured by some suspicion of evil, then you would be unique (cf. lines 2 and 11, 12) in having absolute sovereignty over whole kingdoms of hearts.' There may be, as Mr. Salingar has suggested to us, a latent metaphor of the sun as king of the heavens.

71 *General Note:* A sonnet where the characteristic structural treatment is particularly evident—the dragging sonority of the first quatrain, attuned to its theme, the gentleness, freer flow, and lighter stresses of the contrasted second quatrain, the interweaving of these threads in the third quatrain to reach an apparent yet not really final conclusion, and the final couplet that takes all that has gone before and not only resolves but supplements it.

4 *vildest*] So Q. Gildon and all subsequent editors: *vilest*. But 'vildest' was a common form, and its heaviness better suits the line.

7 *sweet thoughts*] probably 'the thoughts thought by you who are sweet.'

11 *rehearse*] 'repeat'.

12 *even with*] 'at the same time as'. (Cf. *AYLI.* II. iii. 61, 'And having that do choke their service up Even with the having').

decay] 'cease to exist'. Cf. *Lucrece*, 22–4: 'O happiness . . . as soon decay'd and done As is the morning's silver-melting dew.'

71

No LONGER mourn for me when I am dead
Than you shall hear the surly sullen bell
Give warning to the world that I am fled
From this vile world with vildest worms to dwell: 4
Nay, if you read this line, remember not
The hand that writ it, for I love you so
That I in your sweet thoughts would be forgot
If thinking on me then should make you woe.   8
Oh if, I say, you look upon this verse
When I perhaps compounded am with clay,
Do not so much as my poor name rehearse,
But let your love even with my life decay;   12
    Lest the wise world should look into your moan,
    And mock you with me after I am gone.

72 2 *that you should love,*] So Capell and most modern editors. Q omits the comma, but this would imply that the love challenged is only that continued after the poet's death, and this is not even in question.

4 *prove*] Not here 'find', but 'demonstrate by evidence' (cf. lines 5 and 9, 10).

5 *would*] 'want to'.

virtuous] primarily 'potent', but there is doubtless a *verbal* oxymoron deriving from the more usual sense (even in Shakespeare) of 'morally excellent'.

6 *desert*] rhyming here with 'impart' (line 8), and often in Elizabethan English spelt 'desart'.

7] 'Like a badge of honour upon a tomb' (Tucker), or a tributary verse like that which Claudio hangs on Hero's tomb, *M. Ado*. V. iii. 9–10.

7 *I*] Abbott, who quotes (*Shakespearian Grammar*, s. 209) other cases in Shakespeare of 'I' for 'me', notes that they are after dentals.

10 *untrue*] 'untruly'.

9–10] The wordplay in line 9 runs on 'true' = 'loyal', and 'false' = (1) 'untruthful', and (2) 'unfaithful' (this sense being suggested but implicitly denied); and in line 10 on the *apparent* opposition between 'well' and 'untrue'.

13] Variously explained as referring to (1) a sense that his poems were, or were thought, bad poetry; (2) a sense that all his work was, or was thought, poor work; (3) the social stigma of being a writer for the public playhouse. (3) seems to us the most likely interpretation. Shakespeare's name would be more likely to 'live' (line 12) as a playwright than simply as a bad poet or writer of any kind; and the stigma of remembered familiarity with a purveyor of public amusement would be greater than that attaching to the friend of a bad writer.

14 *should*] 'would be'.

72

O<small>H</small>, LEST the world should task you to recite
What merit lived in me that you should love,
After my death, dear love, forget me quite,
For you in me can nothing worthy prove,— 4
Unless you would devise some virtuous lie
To do more for me than mine own desert,
And hang more praise upon deceasèd I
Than niggard truth would willingly impart: 8
Oh, lest your true love may seem false in this,
That you for love speak well of me untrue,
My name be buried where my body is
And live no more to shame nor me nor you: 12
    For I am sham'd by that which I bring forth,
    And so should you, to love things nothing worth.

73 2 *or none, or few,*] So Capell and almost all modern editors. Q, followed by early editors from Benson to Evans, and by Harrison: *or none, or few* . Tucker objects to Capell's reading that it gives the 'inferior' sense 'there hang leaves which are yellow, or (there hang) none at all, or (in any case) few'. Tucker reads *or none or few*, construed to mean 'either none or few' (= 'only few, if any'). But this would really mean that only few, if any, of the leaves were yellow; and that would put the scene at the wrong end of autumn. Capell's punctuation yields a slower line than Q, consistent with the general mood. The resultant sense would reflect a brooding and unsettled state of mind, unable to rest on a definitive image.

3 *shake . . . cold*] i.e. (1) 'shake as the cold threatens' (in the autumn gales); though possibly (2) 'shiver with the coming of the cold'.

4 *Bare ruin'd choirs*] So all modern editors, following Benson (1640), who read: *Bare ruin'd quires*. Q: *Bare rn'wd quiers*. Lintot: *Barren 'wd quiers*, corrected by Capell to *Barren'd [?] of quires*. Comments on the phrase are of two types. Some sense overtones and ambiguities in Shakespeare's diction and imagery; others would tie both to uniqueness of reference. Of the first type are Malone's (1780): '*Choirs* here means that part of cathedrals where divine service is performed, to which, when . . . in ruins, . . . the poet compares the trees at the end of autumn, stripped of that foliage which at once invited and sheltered the . . . [birds]'; Steevens's, followed by J. A. Gotch (*Shakespeare's England*, 2 vols., Clarendon Press, Oxford, 1917, II. 50), seeing here a reference to 'our desolated monasteries'; and Professor Empson's, in his fine essay *Seven Types of Ambiguity*, pp. 1 ff, which cites this as an example of his first type—ambiguity of word, syntax, etc., which 'while making only one statement, is effective in several ways at once'—a feature with which any reader of Shakespeare is constantly faced. The second approach, seeking simplicity and consistency, is exemplified in Pooler's protest: '(The line's) beauty is of sound and lingering movement rather than of painting; if a picture is intended by "choir", which I do not think, it is at least instantly withdrawn, or "those boughs which shake against the cold" would contrast strangely with the stolid desolations of masonry'; and 'it is imprudent to go behind the scenes and inspect the properties'—a view from which Professor R. H. Case rightly dissented: 'As to the contrast between boughs and masonry, Shakespeare passes from image to image and metaphor to metaphor without minding the contrasts', citing *Macb.* II. ii. 36 ff on sleep. The reader alert to the diction and imagery of Shakespeare, whether in poems or plays, will have no difficulty in choosing between these critical attitudes.

5–7, 9–11] For Shakespeare's relative constructions consult Abbott, *Shakespearian Grammar*, ss. 275–89 especially s. 279.

73

THAT TIME of year thou mayst in me behold
When yellow leaves, or none, or few, do hang
Upon those boughs which shake against the cold,
Bare ruin'd choirs where late the sweet birds sang: 4
In me thou see'st the twilight of such day
As after sunset fadeth in the west,
Which by and by black night doth take away,
Death's second self that seals up all in rest: 8
In me thou see'st the glowing of such fire
That on the ashes of his youth doth lie
As the death-bed whereon it must expire,
Consum'd with that which it was nourish'd by: 12
　This thou perceiv'st, which makes thy love more strong
　To love that well which thou must leave ere long.

8 *seals up*] It is impossible to decide whether the metaphor is (1) of en-
closing in a coffin or (2) of stitching up the eyes (of a hawk). (2) is now
usually spelt 'seel' but was frequently spelt 'seal' in the sixteenth and seven-
teenth centuries, as e.g. in the *Othello* Qq.

10 *his*] 'its'.

12] 'With' is usually taken here as = 'by', and 'that' either (1) as =
the ashes which once nourished the fire but now choke it, or (2) as like a
torch turned downward, the feeder now extinguishing the flame. But
'with', surely, as L. Kellner suggests in *Englische Studien* (1933, lxviii. 72)
means 'simultaneously with', and *contrasts* with 'by'? A flame lives on the
volatilization of the fuel (e.g. wood, coal, oil), and when that substance
is itself consumed there is no more to become the flame that consumes it.

9–12] The general sense, then, seems to be that the leaping flame of
youth has died down into a quiescent glow, which seems to lie on the
ashes of his past and its vigour, and which will ultimately fade out com-
pletely at the moment when the last trace of bodily vitality is exhausted. In
each quatrain Shakespeare not only delineates an autumnal, twilight, or
glowing present, but foreshadows a winter, night, or coming extinction;
both elements are reflected in the final couplet, and constitute its point.

14 *leave*] 'part with', not 'depart from'.

74 1] Q, Benson (1640), Lintot, Gildon¹, have no stop after 'contented'. Gildon² (1714)—Evans (1775) inserted a comma. Almost all modern editors, following Malone, insert a colon, but such a redirection of the injunction from the future to the present, though possibly justifiable, does not seem really necessary. Moreover—though we should not claim the following points as conclusive—(1) save for vocatives and mild exclamations there are no cases in the *Sonnets* of opening lines, unbroken by punctuation in Q, which indubitably demand its insertion; and (2) dramatic interruption of the smooth flow of an opening line is wholly untypical of Shakespeare's practice in the *Sonnets*. We do, however, concur in the obvious removal of Q's comma from the end of the line.

1 *arrest*] There is no problem of choice between (1) 'stay', 'act of stopping' (Schmidt) and (2) seizure by an officer ('this fell sergeant, Death, Is strict in his arrest', *Ham.* V. ii. 347). The word here has both meanings, though only sense (2) is developed in line 2.

2 *all*] 'any', cf. 'without all ornament' (68. 10).

3] The metaphor is not that of interest on capital, but of a legal or equitable interest in an estate. Moreover, 'My life' is not the owner of this estate, but the property out of which the estate is carved; and 'hath' does not express ownership but inclusion (as in 'this house has three bedrooms').

4 *still*] 'always'.

1–4] The sense, then, seems to be: 'Do not distress yourself unduly when Death carries me away, and no one can go bail for me, for my life has carved out an estate from itself in the shape of this work, and this will always remain with you as a memorial of me.'

5 *When thou reviewest*] 'when you re-read'.

review] 'see again'.

7 *his*] 'its'.

8 *spirit*] i.e. the nobler, volatile elements (air and fire), as contrasted with the heavier and baser ('earth' (line 7), 'dregs' (line 9)). 'Spirit' is also the creative genius of the poet, cf. 80. 2, 85. 7, 86. 5.

11] Several problems arise:

   (1) Who is the 'wretch'?
   (2) Is it the 'body', or the 'wretch', or his action that is cowardly? (The last seems impossible on grammatical grounds.)
   (3) Does 'conquest' mean (a) what is overcome (victim), or (b) what is acquired (booty, or, just possibly, 'legal possession gained otherwise than by inheritance', cf. 6. 14 and 46. 2)?

To (1) answers have been (a) Death or Time (Furnivall, Dowden's conjecture, Verity, Wyndham, Beeching, Lee, Tucker, Tucker Brooke); (b)

74

B UT BE contented when that fell arrest
Without all bail shall carry me away:
My life hath in this line some interest
Which for memorial still with thee shall stay.   4
When thou reviewest this, thou dost review
The very part was consecrate to thee:
The earth can have but earth, which is his due;
My spirit is thine, the better part of me: 8
So then thou hast but lost the dregs of life,
The prey of worms, my body being dead,
The coward conquest of a wretch's knife,
Too base of thee to be rememberèd: 12
    The worth of that is that which it contains,
    And that is this, and this with thee remains.

Shakespeare, meditating suicide (Dowden's conjecture); (c) Marlowe's
murderer or someone who might similarly murder Shakespeare (Dowden's
conjecture, Olivieri, Ridley, contra Furnivall); (d) anyone who might kill
anybody (Dowden's conjecture, Tyler, Herford, Beeching, who sees here
only an image echoing lines 1, 2, and not a real fear); (e) a dissecting
anatomist (dissection having been recently revived by Vesalius and others
(Palgrave)).

   To support (b) strong evidence would be required that Shakespeare ever
contemplated suicide, and this is not to hand. (a) seems the most plausible,
then (d); but (c) or (e) might have been an association in Shakespeare's
mind. More than one of these meanings or associations may have been
present; but the evidence for any one or more is inadequate to command
definitive assent. If the 'wretch' is Death, then it is worth noting Beeching's
observation that line 11 develops the image of lines 1, 2, in that the officer
who arrested has now become the executioner. Alternatively, as Mr.
Salingar has suggested to us, 'wretch' and 'knife' together suggest a mean
assassin or cut-throat, and so show what a cheap 'conquest' the body is.
   To (2) the prevalent answer among scholars who have glossed the line is:

74 (*continued*)

the 'body', as yielding to the knife without courageous resistance. We agree. There is no Shakespearean parallel for the attributive use of 'coward' to qualify a noun so far distant in a sentence as is 'wretch's' (or 'knife').

As to (3), only allusions to a murderer (1 (*c*) and (*d*)) would restrict the meaning exclusively to 3 (*a*) (victim). Some element of both meanings ('victim' and 'acquisition') could be present in all other cases considered under (1) above.

12 *rememberèd*] So Gildon[2] and all modern editors. Q: *remembred*. See note on 66. 8 ('disablèd') for Shakespearean treatment of consonants followed by 'r' or 'l'.

13, 14] 'The value of the living body lies in the spirit which animates it, and, in my case, this spirit is one and the same as my poetry, which will live on with you.'

74

But be contented when that fell arrest
Without all bail shall carry me away:
My life hath in this line some interest
Which for memorial still with thee shall stay.
When thou reviewest this, thou dost review
The very part was consecrate to thee:
The earth can have but earth, which is his due;
My spirit is thine, the better part of me:
So then thou hast but lost the dregs of life,
The prey of worms, my body being dead,
The coward conquest of a wretch's knife,
Too base of thee to be rememberèd:
   The worth of that is that which it contains,
   And that is this, and this with thee remains.

75 2 *sweet season'd*] So Q. Malone and all modern editors: *sweet-season'd*. It is, indeed, often necessary in the *Sonnets* to supply a hyphen in a modern recension, and Malone's emendation affords a perfectly good Shakespearean line. With his hyphen the expression could mean (1) 'tempered with gentleness', in contrast to heavy storms; or, less plausibly, (2) 'of the sweet season, viz. April' (Pooler). Both meanings *could* co-exist. In our view, however, Q gives an equally good Shakespearean line. The expression could then mean either (1) 'gentle and opportune' (see *OED*) or (2) 'pleasant and temperate', and, in either case, a reference to the spring season would be just as possible as with the hyphen.

3 *for the peace of you*] Possible meanings are: (1) 'as a result of the peace and contentment I find in your friendship'; (2) 'in order to achieve the tranquil enjoyment of your friendship'; (3) 'in order to resolve the issue of how best to enjoy your friendship in tranquil security'; (4) 'instead of the peace which I ought to find in your friendship'; (5) 'in order to achieve undisputed possession of your friendship'. (4) does not fit well with 'And' (line 3). (5) does not convey the element of enjoyment implicit in 'peace'. (1), (2), and (3) seem equally plausible.

5 *proud . . . enjoyer*] 'exulting in having possession'.

6 *Doubting*] 'Fearing'.

the filching age] 'the sneakthief age in which we live'.

8 *better'd*] So Q (but without the apostrophe) and almost all modern editors. Capell, Conrad, Dubislav have conjectured: *better*. The emendation is unnecessary, as 'better'd' makes good sense as 'made both happier and prouder' ('in that the world can see . . .').

13 *pine*] 'starve'. Cf. the transitive use in *V&A*. 601–2:

> 'Even so poor birds, deceiv'd with painted grapes,
> Do surfeit by the eye and pine the maw.'

14 *Or . . . or*] 'Either . . . or'.

14] 'Either feasting myself on every delight, or finding the table of my pleasure empty.'

75

So are you to my thoughts as food to life,
Or as sweet season'd showers are to the ground;
And for the peace of you I hold such strife
As 'twixt a miser and his wealth is found,— 4
Now proud as an enjoyer, and anon
Doubting the filching age will steal his treasure;
Now counting best to be with you alone,
Then better'd that the world may see my pleasure; 8
Sometime all full with feasting on your sight,
And by and by clean starvèd for a look;
Possessing or pursuing no delight
Save what is had or must from you be took: 12
  Thus do I pine and surfeit day by day,
  Or gluttoning on all, or all away.

76 *General Note:* A similarity with 32. 5–8 is worth noting.

1–8] Probably a reiteration of common charges against the poet's manner of writing rather than a series of self-questionings.

1 *new pride*] 'new-fangled elaboration'.

2 *variation or quick change*] 'variety and nimbly shifting conceits'.

3 *with the time*] 'following the fashion'.

glance] 'turn'—not with the eye but in the really much more frequent and basic sense in which the word is still used, e.g. in sport (as in cricket), in ballistics, and in describing collisions.

4 *compounds strange*] 'recherché combinations of images and words'.

6 *invention*] the term of rhetoric (cf. 38. 1, note).

in a noted weed] i.e. in the same old dress (possibly the sonnet form).

7 *tell*] So Capell, Malone, and all modern editors. Q: *fel*. The misreading of a *t* as an *f* is quite possible from a contemporary script. Though Nicholson's conjecture, adopted by Aldis Wright in the second Cambridge edition: *spell*, is possible ('spel' was a quite common form in the sixteenth and seventeenth centuries, and occurs four times out of fifteen in the First Folio), yet the emendation would involve assuming a double error, reading *f* for *s*, and omitting *p*. 'Tel' still occurred in the seventeenth century, though comparatively rarely.

8 *where*] 'whence', cf. *H5*. III. v. 15: 'where have they this mettle?'

10, 14 *still*] 'ever'.

argument] 'theme'.

11, 12] Cf. 59. 1–4.

12 *spent*] playing on (1) 'dispensed', (2) 'exhausted'.

76

Why is my verse so barren of new pride,
So far from variation or quick change?
Why with the time do I not glance aside
To new-found methods and to compounds strange?   4
Why write I still all one, ever the same,
And keep invention in a noted weed,
That every word doth almost tell my name,
Shewing their birth and where they did proceed?   8
Oh know, sweet love, I always write of you,
And you and love are still my argument;
So all my best is dressing old words new,
Spending again what is already spent: 12
    For as the sun is daily new and old,
    So is my love still telling what is told.

77 *General Note:* Steevens's suggestion that this sonnet 'was designed to accompany a present of a book consisting of blank paper' seems almost certainly right. Such a gift would, both in Shakespeare's and in Steevens's time, be a much less unusual and more valuable gift than today, and examples still come into the antique market. Whether the mirror and sundial also formed part of the gift must remain uncertain, though 'thy glass' and 'thy dial' do somewhat suggest the view that they did not.

1 *wear*] So Gildon² and all modern editors. Q: *were*.

2 *dial*] 'sundial' (possibly, though not necessarily, a pocket one). Cf. 'shady stealth' (line 7), which would hardly apply to a watch or clock.

waste] 'waste away'.

3 *The*] So Q and almost all modern editors. Capell, and Malone in his second edition, conjectured *These*, and some other editors have followed this reading, which J. Q. Adams calls 'almost a necessary emendation', and which Rollins thinks has much to be said for it. The emendation is evidently designed to parallel 'These vacant leaves' with 'this book' (line 4) and 'these waste blanks' (line 10), and so avoid the uneasy isolation of 'the vacant leaves'. But, if emendation is necessary, it would seem more likely that 'Thy glass' (line 1) and 'Thy dial' (line 2) are misreadings by copyist or compositor of 'The glass' and 'The dial'. In secretary hand the dropped tail of an *h*, looped up to join a following *e*, might well, if the top of the *e* were faint, be misread as a *y*. 'The glass', 'The dial' could be either particular (paralleling 'The vacant leaves') or, less probably, general. The misreadings could, but need not necessarily, have recurred in lines 5 and 7.

4 *of*] 'from'.

this learning mayst thou taste:] Q has a full stop for the colon, and is followed by all modern editors. But elsewhere the same editors often rightly alter Q's full stops to colons, and here the sonnet evinces a more organic development if 'this learning' refers forward to the richer content of the following quatrain, rather than statically, and somewhat tamely, to lines 1 and 2 alone. And for this forward reference the colon is required.

taste] 'come to experience'.

6 *mouthèd graves*] i.e. gaping graves, ready to devour. That wrinkles would readily suggest the eventual grave is obvious. The problem is how far a *visual* parallel can be intended. The preoccupation with wrinkles is frequent in the *Sonnets*, and they are sometimes associated with furrows, trenches, and digging (2. 2, 22. 3, 60. 10, 100. 10); but even these would hardly seem to justify *seeing* the wrinkled face as analogous to a graveyard.

will give thee memory] 'will remind you'.

7 *shady stealth*] Not only referring to the slowly creeping shadow, but also, through the form of 'stealth', anticipating 'Time's thievish progress'.

77

Thy glass will shew thee how thy beauties wear,
Thy dial how thy precious minutes waste,
The vacant leaves thy mind's imprint will bear,
And of this book this learning mayst thou taste: 4
The wrinkles which thy glass will truly show
Of mouthèd graves will give thee memory;
Thou by thy dial's shady stealth mayst know
Time's thievish progress to eternity;   8
Look what thy memory cannot contain
Commit to these waste blanks, and thou shalt find
Those children nurs'd, deliver'd from thy brain,
To take a new acquaintance of thy mind.   12
   These offices so oft as thou wilt look
   Shall profit thee and much enrich thy book.

5–8] Not a mere repetition of lines 1, 2, but a development, by the Friend's creative imagination, of far-reaching and illuminating analogies.

9 *Look*] So Q. All modern editors insert a comma after *Look*. But, as in 37. 13, 'Look what' seems to be an indefinite relative = 'whatever' (cf. examples quoted in *OED*. I. 46: e.g. Hooker, *Eccl. Pol.* VII. vi. s. 9: 'He added, farther, that look what duty the Roman Consuls did execute . . . the like charge had the Bishop').

10 *waste*] 'unfilled'.

blanks] Theobald's conjecture, followed by all modern editors. Q: *blacks*. The MS almost certainly read: *blācks* = *blancks*; the compositor evidently overlooked the nunnation mark. Cf. J. Dover Wilson's *The Manuscript of Shakespeare's Hamlet*, C.U.P., London, 1934, 118, for similar examples, e.g. *Ham.* II. ii. 348: Q² 'black verse', Q¹ and F¹ 'blanke'.

10–12] 'Put your thoughts on blank leaves, and leave them as children are put out to nurse, and when you read them later they will strike you afresh with a fuller meaning, just like the children who have matured.'

13, 14] 'Look' seems to refer to the 'glass' and 'dial', and 'offices' to their functions as prompters of serious reflection. These functions will bring the Friend the profit of deepening his thought whenever he contemplates the 'glass' and 'dial'; and his thoughts will enrich the book.

78 *General Note:* Many conjectures have been offered as to the identity of the rival poet. We are not, however, concerned with such questions in the present edition.

2 *fair*] Primarily 'favourable', 'benign', but possibly also, as Tucker suggests, 'of beauty' in beautifying.

assistance] Either (1) inspiration, or (2) encouragement, or (3) patronage, or more than one of these. We find it hard to share the certainty with which some commentators adopt one particular interpretation.

3 *As*] 'That'. See Abbott, *Shakespearian Grammar*, s. 109, and Franz, *Shakespeare-Grammatik*, s. 572.

alien] Either (1) 'of those who are complete strangers to you', or (2) 'of those who have not the claim of my intimate affection for you' (outsiders).

got my use] 'adopted my practice' (of addressing you) rather than 'caught the trick of my style', which is scarcely referred to in this sonnet. The interpretation we suggest is supported by line 4.

4 *under thee*] (1) 'in your service', or (2) 'under your influence' (cf. lines 1, 10), or (3) 'under your patronage' (actual or hoped for), or (4) 'under cover of your name', e.g. in a dedication; though again more than one of the senses may be present.

disperse] 'circulate'.

5 *on high*] 'aloud'.

5–8] As Beeching says, 'the "dumb ignorant" is Shakespeare, the "gracious learned" is some other poet of whom we thus hear for the first time'.

7] A hawking metaphor. Broken or missing feathers were replaced by a form of grafting known as 'imping'.

9] The stress is clearly on 'I'.

10 *influence*] probably with an almost astrological sense.

12 *arts*] 'learning and scholarship'.

13, 14 *and . . . ignorance*] 'and you raise my barbarous ignorance to the same level as learning.'

78

So OFT have I invok'd thee for my Muse
And found such fair assistance in my verse
As every alien pen hath got my use
And under thee their poesy disperse.   4
Thine eyes, that taught the dumb on high to sing
And heavy ignorance aloft to fly,
Have added feathers to the learnèd's wing,
And given grace a double majesty.   8
Yet be most proud of that which I compile,
Whose influence is thine and born of thee:
In others' works thou dost but mend the style,
And arts with thy sweet graces gracèd be.   12
    But thou art all my art, and dost advance
    As high as learning my rude ignorance.

79 2 *had all thy . . . grace*] A subtle pun, involving at least the senses (1) 'was fully possessed of the same elegance as that of your person and character'; (2) 'gave full expression to your excellence'; and, not least, (3) 'received the whole of your favour'.

3 *gracious*] with corresponding senses to those of 'grace' in line 2 (see note, above).

decay'd] Both (1) 'declined in power', and (2) 'fallen from favour'.

5 *thy lovely argument*] 'the theme of your lovableness'. Cf. 38. 3, and 'slow offence' (51. 1).

7 *what of thee*] 'what qualities in you' (e.g. 'virtue' (line 9), 'beauty' (line 10)).

thy poet] more probably 'any poet who writes of you' (Tucker), rather than either 'myself, as your poet' or specifically the rival poet.

invent] 'discover' (as matter for writing) (cf. 38. 1, note).

9 *lends*] 'ascribes to'—not in contrast with 'give' (line 10).

11 *afford*] 'offer'. Cf. *M. Ado*, I. i. 181–2: 'This commendation I can afford her'.

14 *owes*] Either (1) as patron, or (2) for the Friend's excellent qualities.

79

Whilst i alone did call upon thy aid,
My verse alone had all thy gentle grace;
But now my gracious numbers are decay'd,
And my sick Muse doth give another place.   4
I grant, sweet love, thy lovely argument
Deserves the travail of a worthier pen;
Yet what of thee thy poet doth invent
He robs thee of, and pays it thee again: 8
He lends thee virtue, and he stole that word
From thy behaviour; beauty doth he give,
And found it in thy cheek: he can afford
No praise to thee but what in thee doth live.   12
    Then thank him not for that which he doth say,
    Since what he owes thee thou thyself dost pay.

80 1 *faint*] 'lose heart'.

2 *a better spirit*] i.e. a more gifted poet.

4 *To make*] It is impossible to say from internal evidence whether this imputes intention, records the result, or both.

4 Punctuation] So Q, but with a full-stop after *fame*. Almost all modern editors insert a comma after *tongue-tied*, probably to mark off the qualifying phrase. But this might well suggest that 'speaking' modifies 'spends' instead of qualifying 'me'. That would, indeed, be possible, but seems to us less probable, and certainly affords a less good Shakespearean line.

7 *saucy*] Involving both (1) cheekiness in comparing itself with the greater craft, and (2) venturesomeness in braving the great ocean. Cf. *T&C.* I. iii. 42:

> 'Where's then the saucy boat
> Whose weak untimber'd sides but even now
> Co-rivall'd greatness?'

8 *wilfully*] 'with willing confidence', or possibly, as Tucker suggests, 'with perverse audacity'.

9–10] The small boat can keep to the shallows, and demands less support. The 'tall' bark, which can ride the deeps, requires more water to keep it afloat.

11 *wreck'd*] So most modern editors. Q, Benson, and some other editors: *wrackt* (some: *wrack'd*).

12 *of tall building*] 'mighty', as being tall-masted, with a great hull, and of stout construction.

of goodly pride] 'of great splendour'.

14 *decay*] 'ruin'.

80

O<small>H HOW</small> I faint when I of you do write,
Knowing a better spirit doth use your name,
And in the praise thereof spends all his might,
To make me tongue-tied speaking of your fame!   4
But since your worth, wide as the ocean is,
The humble as the proudest sail doth bear,
My saucy bark, inferior far to his,
On your broad main doth wilfully appear.   8
Your shallowest help will hold me up afloat,
Whilst he upon your soundless deep doth ride;
Or, being wreck'd, I am a worthless boat,
He of tall building and of goodly pride: 12
    Then if he thrive and I be cast away
    The worst was this:—my love was my decay.

81 1, 2 *Or . . . Or*] Here 'Whether . . . or'. (See *OED* 'or', sense 3b, and cf. *M. of V.* III. ii. 64: 'Tell me where is fancy bred, Or in the heart or in the head?'). Staunton conjectured (*Athenaeum*, 3 Jan. 1874, 21): *Whe'r* = whether, and this gives the right sense, but is unnecessary.

2 *rotten*,] So Q. Almost all modern editors: *rotten*;—which makes lines 1 and 2 a platitude of high banality.

3 *From hence*] Sometimes construed (e.g. by Tyler, Pooler, and Tucker) as 'from these poems', but no reader who has only read so far in the poem could be expected to take this meaning; and, moreover, by anticipating the turn executed in lines 8–9, such a sense here would weaken the poem. A far more likely sense is 'from the world of men'.

4 *in me each part*] 'every quality I have'.

5 *from hence*] By a turn the phrase has now been given the temporal sense 'from henceforth'.

7 *but a common grave*] 'nothing but an undistinguished grave'. It is ironical, as Ivor Brown and G. Fearon (*Amazing Monument*, Cape, London, 1939, 27 ff) have pointed out, that Shakespeare was buried in an honorific place, viz. the chancel in Stratford Parish Church—not because of his works but as a lessee of tithes!

8] It is the Friend who is to have an honorific tomb.

in men's eyes] i.e. where all can see the splendid erection.

9] This is the first mention, in the sonnet, of the author's poems. By a sudden turn of wit at the start of the sestet he reveals that the 'monument', implied in line 8, is no marble sepulchre but his verses.

11 *rehearse*] 'tell of'.

81

Or I shall live your epitaph to make,
Or you survive when I in earth am rotten,
From hence your memory death cannot take,
Although in me each part will be forgotten: 4
Your name from hence immortal life shall have,
Though I, once gone, to all the world must die;
The earth can yield me but a common grave,
When you entombèd in men's eyes shall lie: 8
Your monument shall be my gentle verse,
Which eyes not yet created shall o'er-read;
And tongues to be your being shall rehearse
When all the breathers of this world are dead: 12
   You still shall live—such virtue hath my pen—
   Where breath most breathes, even in the mouths of men.

82 2 *attaint*] Either (1) 'dishonour', or (2) 'accusation of dishonour'.

o'erlook] Primarily here 'read', but, in view of lines 7–8 and 13, there may be something in Tucker's suggestion that there is a secondary hint of a young man 'casting an appraising eye over women'.

3 *The dedicated words*] Here 'words consecrated to the praise of the writer's subject'. Shakespeare never uses 'dedicate' or 'dedicated' other than = 'devote(d)', 'consecrate(d)', save in the dedication of *Venus and Adonis*. Of course, some of 'the dedicated words' may have occurred in 'dedications' in the narrower sense.

4 *blessing*] 'commending'. Cf. *H8*. III. i. 54: 'To taint that honour every good tongue blesses.' The grammatical subject of 'blessing' is 'thou', understood as the subject of 'mayst' in line 2.

5 *fair*] (1) May mean 'eminent', in which case 'Finding' will = 'And find'; or (2) may, as Tucker suggests, involve a play on (a) 'just' and (b) 'beautiful', in which case 'Finding' will = 'In finding', i.e. in *deciding* (like a judge or jury) that his value is beyond the poet's range of praises.

hue] 'appearance', not merely 'complexion', as some editors have suggested. See 20. 7, note.

8 *stamp*] Possibly an image from minting coins or striking medals. The Friend may be demanding a new 'image' of himself in the modern style of verse which Shakespeare says he does not himself practise. Cf. for a comic parallel metaphor: *TN*. III. ii. 24 ff (Fabian to Sir Andrew: 'some excellent jests, fire-new from the mint . . .').

of] 'from'.

time-bettering days] Cf. 32. 5: 'the bettering of the time'. Here: 'the days that have brought such advances in poetic style and skill'.

11 *sympathiz'd*] 'feelingly and understandingly represented'. Cf. *Lucrece*, 1113:

> 'True sorrow then is feelingly sufficed
> When with the semblance it is sympathized.'

11–12] The senses of 'truly' and 'true' played on here include: 'true to the ideal pattern', 'accurately', 'sincere', 'honest-to-goodness', 'true to the facts'.

11–12] The general sense is: '(In view of your qualities) you would be properly matched and best represented in plain words by that friend who loyally speaks the truth, and not by these sycophantic "fantastic poets".' (It is, of course, often impossible even to hint at the overtones of Shakespeare's sonnet writing, in a prose paraphrase, without prolixity.)

13 *gross painting*] In addition to the obvious sense of 'laying it on thick', there may also (cf. note on line 2, above) be a secondary association of

82

I GRANT thou wert not married to my Muse,
And therefore mayst without attaint o'erlook
The dedicated words which writers use
Of their fair subject, blessing every book: 4
Thou art as fair in knowledge as in hue,
Finding thy worth a limit past my praise,
And therefore art enforc'd to seek anew
Some fresher stamp of the time-bettering days: 8
And do so, love; yet when they have devis'd
What strainèd touches rhetoric can lend,
Thou, truly fair, wert truly sympathiz'd
In true plain words by thy true-telling friend;   12
    And their gross painting might be better us'd
    Where cheeks need blood—in thee it is abus'd.

meretricious prostitution, though, if present, this is certainly not de-
veloped into an independent image. For Shakespeare's evident contempt for
cosmetics cf. 67. 5, 83. 1–2, and *LLL*. II. i. 13. There may also be a refer-
ence here to 'larded' rhetoric. Cf. 'Colours' = rhetorical figures.

14 *in thee*] i.e. in applying it to you.

83 1–8] It seems as if the first quatrain refers to a time when Shakespeare wrote about his friend, though not, as he thinks, in an exaggerated style; whereas the second quatrain refers to a recent period of silence.

2 *to . . . set*] 'added no extra colour to your beauty'. 'Beauty' in this sonnet is not necessarily restricted to the physical (see 'worth' (line 8)), though the physical seems to be dominant (see line 13).

3 *or thought I found*] Whether this qualification is added (1) because the Friend thought it should be possible for a poet to praise him adequately (cf. line 9), or (2) because other poets considered themselves capable of doing so, seems uncertain.

4 *barren tender*] 'fruitless offering'.

debt] i.e. to his patron.

5 *therefore*] 'for the following purpose'. For a similar forward reference see *2H6*. IV. viii. 24: 'Hath my sword therefore broke through London Gates, that you should leave me at the White Hart?'

slept in your report] 'been inactive in singing your praises'.

6 *being extant*] i.e. by simply being alive.

7 *modern*] 'commonplace, trite, ordinary', as always in Shakespeare, cf. *AYLI*. II. vii. 156: 'Full of wise saws and modern instances'. Here the word either refers (1) to the limitations of Shakespeare's own pen, or (2) to the limitations of pens in general, in comparison with the reality of the Friend.

8 *Speaking of worth*] 'in speaking of value'.

what worth] 'of what value'.

10 *being dumb*] 'I being dumb' (cf. Abbott, *Shakespearian Grammar*, s. 379).

11 , *being mute*, Punctuation] Q and almost all modern editors: *being mute*, . But this might well suggest that it is the beauty not the poet who is mute.

12 *When*] 'Whereas'.

would] 'want to'.

and bring a tomb] and create (lit. 'bring forth') an elaborate structure without any life within it, and possibly, *a fortiori*, without the possibility of conferring immortality on the Friend. For the metaphor cf. 17. 3–4.

14 *both your poets*] The two possible meanings are: (1) Shakespeare and a rival, or (2) two rivals. No conclusive evidence is available. 'Others' (line 12) might suggest (2), but it is not uncommon to find it used, especially in a petulant mood, even when only one person is in question.

83

I NEVER saw that you did painting need,
And therefore to your fair no painting set;
I found—or thought I found—you did exceed
The barren tender of a poet's debt: 4
And therefore have I slept in your report,
That you yourself being extant well might show
How far a modern quill doth come too short,
Speaking of worth, what worth in you doth grow.   8
This silence for my sin you did impute,
Which shall be most my glory, being dumb;
For I impair not beauty, being mute,
When others would give life and bring a tomb.   12
    There lives more life in one of your fair eyes
    Than both your poets can in praise devise.

84 1 *most* Punctuation] So Kittredge; and Pooler as a conjecture, Q. Benson–Evans, and a few modern editors: *most*, . Malone, followed by nearly all modern editors: *most?* Q has five commas in lines 1–2, and these seem merely to mark off the clauses. The retention of Q's comma after *most* is compatible with, but does not fully suggest, what appears to us to be the right sense, viz. 'What extravagant eulogist can say more than this . . . ?' As P. Simpson writes (*Shakespeare's Punctuation*, p. 13): 'here "which" is a relative pronoun, but . . . frequently read as interrogative, and the line distorted . . .' Malone's question mark has this effect, and needlessly establishes an auction-battle of compliments between Shakespeare and a rival.

2 *are you,* Punctuation] So Q, Lintot, and some modern editors. Most modern editors: *are you?,* which does not materially alter the sense ('In whose' being construed as 'And in your'), but does needlessly break the flow of the quatrain, the whole of which forms the question.

3–4] It seems possible that the image here is of a walled garden where a unique specimen of a plant (e.g. a rose, cf. 37. 8) can alone be seen and studied. The image certainly seems to be biological rather than that of a treasury. The sense would be that the only stock from which one could learn under what conditions a person of the Friend's excellence could develop is to be found in the Friend himself.

5 *penury . . . pen*] There may be not only the obvious pun but also a pun on each word.

6 *his*] 'its', as in 9. 10. ('Its' does not occur more than eight or nine times in the Shakespearean quartos or in the First Folio; nor does it occur at all in the 1611 printing of the Authorized Version of the Bible.)

8 *so*] 'by that means'.

story: Punctuation] Q and some modern editors: *story.* Lintot, Malone and many modern editors: *story,* . Some modern editors: *story;.* To read a comma implies the sense: 'so dignifies . . . (that), let him . . .', but this cuts across the octave-sestet division, and presumably results from misunderstanding the sense of 'so'. A full stop, on the other hand, does not fully reflect the continuity. The best punctuation seems to us either a semi-colon, or the colon we have adopted for its forward look.

10 *clear*] Either (1) 'distinguished', 'glorious', or (2) 'irreproachable'.

11 *counterpart*] 'portrait' (cf. 'counterfeit', 16. 8, 53. 5).

fame] 'make famous'.

wit] So Q and modern editors. Benson (1640) and some early editors: *writ,*—probably a compositor's error from line 9. Q is quite satisfactory. 'Wit', of course, is not here used in the modern sense, but means a compound of intelligence, knowledge and skill.

84

Who is it that says most which can say more
Than this rich praise,—that you alone are you,
In whose confine immurèd is the store
Which should example where your equal grew?   4
Lean penury within that pen doth dwell
That to his subject lends not some small glory;
But he that writes of you, if he can tell
That you are you, so dignifies his story: 8
Let him but copy what in you is writ,
Not making worse what nature made so clear,
And such a counterpart shall fame his wit,
Making his style admirèd everywhere.   12
    You to your beauteous blessings add a curse,
    Being fond on praise, which makes your praises worse.

13 *your . . . blessings*] Here (1) 'your many excellent qualities', and (2)
'the commendations you give' (cf. 82. 4).

14 *fond on*] 'indiscriminately eager in respect of'.

praise] There seems to be a turn of wit depending on 'praise' meaning (1)
'praise you receive', (2) 'praise you bestow'.

, which makes your praises worse] So Q and nearly all modern editors. Tyler
and Tucker: no comma. Without the comma the whole line could mean:
'Being indiscriminately eager to receive the sort of praise which by in-
sincere extravagance cheapens the whole procedure of praising you.' This
meaning seems to us rather weak. A better meaning without the comma,
however, would be: 'Being indiscriminately eager to *give* the kind of com-
mendation which, through being undeserved, encourages the proliferation
of inferior compliments.' But a more satisfactory line results from retain-
ing Q's comma, since a double meaning in the line is rendered possible,
viz.: (1) 'Being indiscriminately eager to receive praise, the consequence
being that your commendations become of less value', and (2) 'Being in-
discriminately eager to lavish commendation, with the result that you
receive cheaper and cheaper compliments.' It may even be possible that
four meanings are present, the other two being obtained by interchanging
the first and second clauses of (1) and (2).

85 1 *in manners*] 'with becoming restraint'.

holds her still] 'keeps quiet'.

2 *comments*] 'expository treatises'.

of your praise] 'of praise of you'.

compil'd] 'composed' (cf. *LLL*. IV. iii. 134: 'Longaville / Did never sonnet for her sake compile').

3 *Reserve their*] Well over a dozen emendations have been suggested, e.g. *Preserve their*; *Rehearse thy*; *Rehearse your*; *Deserve their*; *Reserve your* (or *thy*); *Rehearse their*; *Receive their*; *Rescribe their*; *Re-serve thy*; *Treasure their*; *Rehearsers*; *Tressure their* (*sic*); *Refine their*. Some of these clearly derive from a misunderstanding of 'character', which in Shakespeare never carries its modern sense of 'personal moral and temperamental qualities', though in two or three cases it is used to connote the *outward lineaments* of such inward qualities. The dominant Shakespearean sense is always that of *writing*.

Reserve has been too easily rejected by commentators as implying 'hold back', but dictionaries down to Johnson's stress the sense 'to keep in store', 'to lay up', and Cotgrave (1611) gives Fr. *reserver* = 'to save, preserve, lay up for store'. Moreover, this is the sense the word bears in Sonnet 32. 7.

Giving the words 'reserve' and 'character' their Elizabethan senses, lines 3–4 can be interpreted: 'Store up manuscript upon manuscript, writing them in letters of gold and in choice phrases polished by learned study of the greatest poets.' Alternatively, line 3 could mean: 'lay up in permanent record their characteristic style (or styles) by writing in letters of gold choice phrases . . .'.

5 *whilst*] So Q and most modern editors. Some modern editors have needlessly emended to *while*.

others] So Gildon², followed by many modern editors. Q: *other*. For 'other' as a form of plural cf. 62. 8, Abbott, *Shakespearian Grammar*, s. 12, Franz, *Shakespeare-Grammatik*, s. 357. To retain the archaism in this case would seem to us pointlessly awkward in a modern recension.

6] It was the duty of the parish clerk to lead the responses and the amens.

still] 'always'.

7 *that*] Probably relative, not demonstrative. As Tucker suggests, the intervention of a singular, particularizing one writer, between the two plurals ('other' (line 5) and 'others' (line 13)), would be awkward.

able spirit] Either (1) 'powerful genius' (abstract), or (2) 'any talented genius' (concrete). (2) involves the ellipsis of 'some' or 'any', which is not uncommon in Shakespeare.

affords] 'offers'.

85

My TONGUE-TIED Muse in manners holds her still,
While comments of your praise richly compil'd
Reserve their character with golden quill
And precious phrase by all the Muses fil'd.   4
I think good thoughts, whilst others write good words,
And like unletter'd clerk still cry 'Amen'
To every hymn that able spirit affords
In polish'd form of well-refinèd pen.   8
Hearing you prais'd I say, "Tis so, 'tis true',
And to the most of praise add something more;
But that is in my thought, whose love to you,
Though words come hindmost, holds his rank before. 12
    Then others for the breath of words respect:
    Me for my dumb thoughts, speaking in effect.

7] The line carries on the liturgical simile of line 6.

11–12] As Tucker suggests, the metaphor seems to be that of prece-dence in a procession. The inferiority of Shakespeare's words assigns them a rank behind those of other poets, but his love for the Friend sustains the claim of his thought to rank before theirs.

12 his] 'its'.

13 respect] 'pay attention to' (not 'pay deference to').

14 in effect] 'in reality' (see OED. 8).

86 *General Note:* The language and imagery here used to describe the style of the rival poet have been the source of much speculation as to his identity, with which, however, the present edition is not concerned.

1 *proud*] To an Elizabethan the word would imply (1) stateliness and splendour, (2) the swelling of the full sails, (3) confidence.

1, 2] The image is that of a 'tall ship' bound on an expedition for booty, e.g. in the New World or on the high seas.

full sail] Three impressions are intimately bound up in these words: (1) great spread of canvas; (2) sails filled with wind; (3) powerful forward movement. All these impressions would have their corresponding features in the literary style metaphorically alluded to. (3) depends on the sense of 'sail' as 'manner of sailing', found elsewhere in Shakespeare, e.g. *Ham.* IV. vi. 17–18: 'Finding ourselves too slow of sail'.

2 *all-too-precious*] So Capell and many modern editors. Q: (*all to precious*). Many other modern editors: *all too precious*. Percy Simpson points out that in Elizabethan usage compound nouns or adjectives are enclosed within brackets where we should employ the hyphen if we used any punctuation at all.

3 *ripe*] i.e. for birth.

inhearse] 'bury'. 'Hearse' did not at the time have the modern meaning of 'funeral carriage', but was used in several senses, ranging from an erection over the bier or tomb to the coffin or tomb itself. Burial in a grave seems most likely to be the image here (cf. *R&J.* II. iii. 9–10).

3, 4] The image seems to be that of thoughts, ripe for birth, dying unborn and being buried for ever in the brain that had conceived them.

5 *spirit*] Either (1) 'vigorous mind', or (2) 'daemon', or, just possibly, a play on both. For (2) cf. *A&C.* II. iii. 18–22: 'Therefore, O Antony! stay not by his side; / Thy demon—that's thy spirit which keeps thee,—is / Noble, courageous, high, unmatchable, / Where Caesar's is not; but near him thy angel / Becomes a fear, as being o'erpower'd; . . .' and ibid. 28–30: 'I say again, thy spirit / Is all afraid to govern thee near him, / But he away, 'tis noble.'

by spirits] Whatever this means there is a play on 'spirit' and 'spirits'. Here 'spirits' may mean: (1) 'great talents of the past'; (2) 'live-witted associates'; (3) 'supernatural familiars'. We prefer (1) for reasons given below (see note on lines 5–12, page 198). There remains a further possibility: that 'spirits' is used with an indefinite singular meaning (= 'some spirit or other'), which would at least cohere readily with line 9.

6 *pitch*] 'height', the technical term in falconry.

Above . . . pitch] Probably simply hyperbolical; not at all necessarily referring to supernatural inspiration, or to a supra-heroic theme.

86

W̄AS IT the proud full sail of his great verse,
Bound for the prize of all-too-precious you,
That did my ripe thoughts in my brain inhearse,
Making their tomb the womb wherein they grew?   4
Was it his spirit, by spirits taught to write
Above a mortal pitch, that struck me dead?
No, neither he, nor his compeers by night
Giving him aid, my verse astonishèd: 8
He, nor that affable familiar ghost
Which nightly gulls him with intelligence,
As victors of my silence cannot boast,—
I was not sick of any fear from thence: 12
    But when your countenance fill'd up his line,
    Then lack'd I matter; that enfeebl'd mine.

7 *his compeers by night*] Again uncertain in meaning. We think probably
the sense is: (1) 'books (or their authors) over which he burns midnight
oil'; but it might be (2) 'a coterie of his literary associates', or, just
possibly, (3) 'supernatural familiars' (see note on line 5, above).

8 *astonishèd*] 'paralysed', as e.g. by lightning. (The ultimate root is Lat.
attonare.) The modern sense 'greatly surprised' does not seem to occur till
early in the eighteenth century.

9 *that . . . ghost*] Either (1) the one great author of the past on whose
aid the rival poet chiefly relied; or (2) one particular friend (in the coterie
(see note on line 7)); or (3) a familiar spirit who helped him with his
writing (cf. 'spirits', sense (3) in note on line 5, above).

10 *gulls*] One or both of two meanings are possible: (1) 'crams', 'gorges'
(*OED*. V¹, 2. cf. obsol. Fr. *engouler*, for which Cotgrave gives as first meaning:
'to put into, or send down, the throat'); or (2) 'deceives', 'dupes'. The
disadvantage of (2) is that it clashes with lines 1 and 5–6, unless these are
taken ironically. The disadvantage of (1) is that in the only place elsewhere
where Shakespeare uses the verb, it is in a sense definitely implying deceit
(though the deceit *is* by *stuffing* with false ideas). (The passage is *TN*. II. iii.

146–7.) Here, if lines 1 and 5–6 *are* ironical, the implication would be that the assistance the rival poet receives consists of cramming him with false ideas of form or content.

intelligence] 'information'. Shakespeare never uses the term to refer to a mental faculty or gift.

12 *of*] 'from', 'with'.

5–12] Many candidates have been suggested for the rival poet. As already mentioned, we are not concerned with such identifications in this edition; though we may perhaps venture the opinion that the question cannot be decided on the available evidence. If, however, a convincing case were made out for Chapman being the rival poet, these difficult lines could be coherently interpreted. Line 1 would fit the fourteeners of his *Iliad*. Lines 5–8 would readily apply to his labours in translating the classics and his heavy reliance on past writers. 'Above a mortal pitch' would describe well the high epic style and theme of his great translation. And lines 9–10 might refer to his rhetorical claim in his *Tears of Peace* to have been constantly prompted by the spirit of Homer. The double reference to night, moreover, might well, in this case, allude to the motto of his poem *The Shadow of Night* (1594), *Versus mei habebunt aliquantum noctis*.

13 *countenance*] Probably has two meanings here: (1) 'features'; (2) 'favourable regard'. The play on these strengthens the couplet. (1), the more obvious meaning, would leave it open to the Friend to protest that both poets could delineate his beauty and worth. Such a protest could then be countered by insisting on sense (2), and so making it clear that it was the removal of the Friend's favour that had emptied Shakespeare's verse of substance.

fill'd] So almost all modern editors. Q: *fild*, which Steevens took to mean 'polished'. Malone and many other editors: *fil'd*. We have been unable to find any instance in Elizabethan or in modern usage of the expression 'filed up'.

14 *that*] demonstrative—'that fact'.

14] 'Then' and, still more, 'that' should be stressed in reading.

86

Was it the proud full sail of his great verse,
Bound for the prize of all-too-precious you,
That did my ripe thoughts in my brain inhearse,
Making their tomb the womb wherein they grew?   4
Was it his spirit, by spirits taught to write
Above a mortal pitch, that struck me dead?
No, neither he, nor his compeers by night
Giving him aid, my verse astonishèd: 8
He, nor that affable familiar ghost
Which nightly gulls him with intelligence,
As victors of my silence cannot boast,—
I was not sick of any fear from thence: 12
    But when your countenance fill'd up his line,
    Then lack'd I matter; that enfeebl'd mine.

87 1 *dear*] Both (1) 'of great value' (generically), and (2) 'of high rank', the two senses being frequently commingled in Elizabethan and earlier usage. Cf. *T&C.* V. iii. 27: 'Life every man holds dear; but the *dear* man / Holds honour far more precious-dear than life.'

2 *estimate*] 'value'.

3 *charter*] Either (1) 'privilege' or (2) the document conferring it. The image works slightly differently in the two cases.

worth] Involves the same senses as 'dear' (line 1).

releasing] Charters usually granted exemptions from legal obligations.

4 *determinate*] 'ended'—because the charter has 'released' the Friend from the obligations the bonds had imposed.

5 *do*] Not marking a change of situation, but the indefinite or neutral present, describing the general terms of their relationship.

6 *riches*] originally singular (= Fr. *richesse*).

7] Some commentators see here a reference to the unenforceability, in English law, of contracts lacking consideration; but that doctrine only applies to contracts not under seal, and so not to bonds.

8 *my patent . . . swerving*] 'my title of possession (conferred by the bonds) reverts to you'.

9 *Thy self*] So Q: *Thy selfe*, followed by all editors from Benson (1640) to Sewell (1728). All modern editors after Sewell, excluding Tucker: *Thyself*. Q coheres better with 'it' (line 10); and gives a 'feel', frequent in the *Sonnets*, and strongly present in this sonnet, of the self as an entity.

worth] cf. note on line 3.

10 *mistaking*] 'misjudging' (by overestimating).

11 *upon misprision growing*] 'originating in a misjudgment'.

12] A difficult line. The crux is 'making', which might be either (1) a present participle, with as subject either (*a*) 'you' (understood), or (*b*) 'someone' (understood), or (*c*) 'gift', or (*d*) 'judgment'; or (2) a present participial form for a passive participle = 'being made'; or (3) part of a compound verbal noun ('judgment-making'). In case (1) (*c*) 'making' could mean either 'moving towards' [the better judgment which attracts it], or 'moving towards' [home]. (1) (*d*) would only seem sensible if the metaphor were a tide 'making' for the shore, which we think improbable and grammatically awkward. For (2) there is no exact parallel in Shakespeare, the nearest being *Ham.* III. ii. 93: 'If he steal aught the whilst this play is playing' (= 'being played'), but this is a finite form of a quasi-passive verb, whereas 'making' *may* be a quasi-passive verb but not part of a finite clause. (3) is possible, compounds often lacking hyphens in Q; but most of Shakespeare's compounds are adjectival, and very few compound nouns have a present participle as their second element. (1) (*a*) seems to us the most likely of the

87

Farewell—thou art too dear for my possessing,
And like enough thou know'st thy estimate:
The charter of thy worth gives thee releasing;
My bonds in thee are all determinate.   4
For how do I hold thee but by thy granting?
And for that riches where is my deserving?
The cause of this fair gift in me is wanting,
And so my patent back again is swerving.   8
Thy self thou gav'st, thy own worth then not knowing;
Or me, to whom thou gav'st it, else mistaking:
So thy great gift, upon misprision growing,
Comes home again on better judgment making.   12
    Thus have I had thee as a dream doth flatter—
    In sleep a king, but waking no such matter.

alternatives considered. Similar grammatical irregularities, where a subject
has to be supplied from the context, occur elsewhere in Shakespeare. (See
Abbott, *Shakespearian Grammar*, s. 144.)
  14] The 'king' is the poet—the 'I' of line 13.

88 1 *set me light*] 'hold me cheap'.

2] 'Exhibit [or, possibly, 'publicly estimate'] my deserts in such a way that others will hold them in contempt.' 'Merit' is here used in a neutral sense, cf. Book of Common Prayer, Communion service: 'Not weighing our merits, but pardoning our offences. . .'.

4] 'And prove that you are doing right, although you are being false to our friendship'.

6 *Upon thy part*] 'In support of your case'.

set down] Besides the primary meaning of writing a deposition, there may also be a metaphor from weighing or from staking at a game.

7 *faults*] Either (1) 'moral defects', or (2) 'actual offences against friendship' (cf. 89. 1).

attainted] Not 'charged' but 'besmirched', 'tainted'.

8 *That*] 'So that'.

11] i.e. in exposing his 'faults'.

12 *double*] 'doubly'. It is hard to say how precisely 'double' should be taken. It could be simply hyperbolical, in which case we need not look for an intricate mathematical conceit. But, whether or not the term be taken more strictly, the sense might be that any advantage to the Friend is welcome to the poet, because he loves him, yet, as in his love he identifies himself with the Friend, such an advantage also becomes an advantage to himself—the two making a double advantage. An alternative possibility is that it is only in the final couplet that the *double* advantage is explained, the whole of the last five lines being themselves an exposition of line 9, the first line of the sestet. The double advantage could then be (1) that, because of his love for the Friend, the poet welcomes the Friend's being justified in breaking with an unworthy friend, and (2) that, since the Friend is himself guilty of a wrong to the poet (cf. 'forsworn' (line 4)), by bearing for love the guilt of this wrong too, the poet will gain in moral stature. It would be almost as if the poet could say: 'And in this, indeed, am I glorified!'

Whichever the right interpretation, Capell's addition of a hyphen, adopted by almost all modern editors, seems unnecessary.

14 *for thy right*] 'to put you in the right'.

88

W<small>HEN</small> <small>THOU</small> shalt be dispos'd to set me light,
And place my merit in the eye of scorn,
Upon thy side against myself I'll fight,
And prove thee virtuous, though thou art forsworn. 4
With mine own weakness being best acquainted,
Upon thy part I can set down a story
Of faults conceal'd wherein I am attainted,—
That thou in losing me shall win much glory: 8
And I by this will be a gainer too—
For bending all my loving thoughts on thee
The injuries that to my self I do,
Doing thee vantage, double vantage me. 12
    Such is my love, to thee I so belong,
    That for thy right myself will bear all wrong.

89 1 *Say*] Some editors take as = 'suppose'. Shakespeare does use 'say' in that then new sense, e.g. *TN*. I. iv. 23: 'Say I do speak with her, my lord, what then?'; but, in view of 'Speak' (line 3), the ordinary sense seems far more probable.

fault] Here as usual in Shakespeare an act of transgression rather than a defect (cf. 'offence' (line 2)).

2 *comment*] 'enlarge upon'.

3] A line that has been taken literally, to prove (*a*) that Shakespeare was lame, (*b*) that he was not, (*c*) that he was not Shakespeare but, e.g., the future Lord Very Lame (Verulam) prophesying his own elevation. Editors not convinced that Shakespeare was lame see here mere rhetorical exemplification. We leave the reader to judge.

halt] 'limp'.

4 *reasons*] 'arguments'.

5 *disgrace*] Cf. line 7. A complex word. Both lines play on the senses (1) 'divest (me) of grace', whether (*a*) moral (cf. line 1) or (*b*) physical (cf. line 3), (2) 'dishonour', (3) 'remove from favour' (the Friend's or the world's).

ill] Primarily (1) 'to my disadvantage', but with the implication of (2) 'wrongfully', which would make the 'disgrace' also slander.

6 *To set*] Either (1) 'In order to set', or (2) 'In setting'.

set a form upon] 'lend colour to'.

desirèd] i.e. by *you*.

7–8 Punctuation] Q has commas after 'disgrace' and 'will', and a colon after 'strange'. Almost all modern editors print a semi-colon after 'disgrace', and lighten the stop after 'strange', thus virtually closing the octave in the middle of line 7, and forcing the reader to take 'knowing thy will' as modifying exclusively the lines that follow. We believe that the phrase is more strongly attached to the sense of the octave, and especially to line 6 ('desirèd'). Moreover, the movement resulting in a heavy caesura at 'disgrace' seems to us excessively untypical of the *Sonnets*. We believe that it is far preferable to attach 'knowing thy will' at least chiefly to what has gone before, by printing a heavier stop at 'will', such as the full stop of Kittredge and Neilson[2], or better, the colon of Capell. This does, indeed, mean virtually ending the octave at the end of line 7; but it cannot, in any case, end with finality at its usual point, and, indeed, both grammatical construction and sequence of sense demand only a light pause at the end of line 8. Q's colon there is weak authority for a greater pause, since Q has a colon after 'halt' (line 3) and 'wrong' (line 11)' where there is clearly little pause if any, and almost all editors print a comma. A light pause (at most) after line 8 is found in at least two other sonnets (19 and 132).

204

89

Say that thou didst forsake me for some fault,
And I will comment upon that offence;
Speak of my lameness, and I straight will halt,
Against thy reasons making no defence: 4
Thou canst not, love, disgrace me half so ill,
To set a form upon desirèd change,
As I'll myself disgrace, knowing thy will:
I will acquaintance strangle and look strange,   8
Be absent from thy walks, and in my tongue
Thy sweet belovèd name no more shall dwell,
Lest I, too much profane, should do it wrong
And haply of our old acquaintance tell: 12
   For thee, against my self I'll vow debate,
   For I must ne'er love him whom thou dost hate.

8] Cf. *A&C.* II. vi. 129: 'the very strangler of their amity'.

8 *look strange*] i.e. as if we did not know each other.

9 *Be . . . walks*] Not 'I shall not go for walks with you', but 'I shall avoid the places where you walk'.

11 *profane*] Probably playing on (1) 'outside the sacred circle of your intimacy', cf. Lat. *profanus*; and (2) 'blasphemous'.

wrong Punctuation] Q has a colon after *wrong*; most modern editors print a comma. A colon would clearly be inappropriate in a modern text. A comma suggests that 'and' is a copula, and that the sense of 'And haply' is 'And perhaps even'; though, alternatively, line 12 could be read as specifying the wrong. If the comma be omitted either interpretation remains possible, but the second is suggested, and this we prefer.

13 *my self*] Q always prints as two words even when the simple reflexive is intended; but here the simple reflexive would not sufficiently indicate the sense of 'true nature' or 'innermost self' that seems to be present.

debate] 'war', as often in Shakespeare, and cf. Coverdale's translation of *Luke*, xii. 51: 'Think ye that I come to bring peace upon earth? I tell you nay, but rather debate.' (Authorized Version: 'division'.)

90 3, 12 *Fortune*] Q and all modern editions we know: *fortune*. But here, as in 37. 3 'Fortune's dearest spite', where Q has a capital, personification seems intended. Q is further inconsistent in this matter in printing a lower case *f* in 111. 1 and 124. 2, where personification is quite certainly present.

4] The general sense is clear, but it is obscure what the exact image is. The explanations of 'drop in' by Schmidt ('come in') and by *OED* ('come in or call unexpectedly or casually') are unconvincing. The sense of a weighty motion or fall seems more in place.

for] 'as'.

after-loss] So Sewell and almost all modern editors. Q: *after losse*. 'A later or final disaster.' The expression seems to involve also, however, a play on (1) 'defeat' (cf. the military image in lines 6 and 11), and (2) 'loss' of the Friend (cf. 'leave' (line 9) and 'loss of thee' (line 14)).

6 *in the rearward of*] i.e. like a reserve following up earlier waves of troops whose attack has been repulsed. Cf. *R & J.* III. ii. 116–24.

8 *linger out*] 'protract', 'prolong'.

purpos'd] either (1) by Fortune, or (2) by the Friend, or (3) by both.

10 *other petty griefs*] i.e. other (and by comparison) petty griefs. There is no suggestion that this grief is petty.

11 *in the onset*] 'in the first wave of attack' (cf. 'rearward' (line 6)).

13 *strains*] The primary sense, 'kinds', seems to be combined with the secondary sense 'stresses', to reinforce the line.

90

Then hate me when thou wilt,—if ever, now—
Now, while the world is bent my deeds to cross,
Join with the spite of Fortune, make me bow,
And do not drop in for an after-loss: 4
Ah do not, when my heart hath 'scap'd this sorrow,
Come in the rearward of a conquer'd woe;
Give not a windy night a rainy morrow,
To linger out a purpos'd overthrow.   8
If thou wilt leave me, do not leave me last,
When other petty griefs have done their spite,
But in the onset come: so shall I taste
At first the very worst of Fortune's might;—   12
    And other strains of woe, which now seem woe,
    Compar'd with loss of thee will not seem so.

91 1 *skill*] 'knowledge and intelligence'. The Elizabethans used the term in far wider senses than prevail in modern times, when manual dexterity is generally implied.

3 *new-fangled ill*] The ambiguity of the phrase ((1) 'in the latest hideous fashion', (2) 'a poor example of the latest fashion') might be rendered by 'hideously cut in the latest fashion'.

4 *horse*] plural, cf. *T. of S.* III. ii. 207: ''' Grumio, my horse!" "Ay, sir, they be ready."' This was the original Old English plural (cf. 'sheep', 'deer', etc.), and remained in common use as late as the seventeenth century.

5 *humour*] 'temperament', 'disposition'. (As in the four Hippocratic humours, and Ben Jonson's elaboration of them in his 'comedy of humours'.)

his] 'its'.

7] 'These separate sources of satisfaction are none of them adequate for me' (taking 'measure' in *OED*, sense II, 10).

8 *I better*] 'I can improve upon'. Cf. *M. of V.* III. i. 78: 'it shall go hard but I will better the instruction'.

10 *prouder*] 'more splendid' (cf. 2. 3).

cost] 'display'.

10 *cost*, 12 *boast*] A perfect rhyme in Elizabethan times. The modern pronunciation of 'boast' is nineteenth century in origin. Both words would have a long vowel in Shakespeare's English, roughly equivalent to that in the modern pronunciation of 'broad'.

13 *Wretched*] Referring to his objective destiny, whereas in line 14 the reference is to his state of mind.

91

SOME GLORY in their birth, some in their skill,
Some in their wealth, some in their body's force,
Some in their garments—though new-fangled ill,—
Some in their hawks and hounds, some in their horse: 4
And every humour hath his adjunct pleasure
Wherein it finds a joy above the rest;
But these particulars are not my measure:
All these I better in one general best. 8
Thy love is better than high birth to me,
Richer than wealth, prouder than garments' cost,
Of more delight than hawks or horses be;
And having thee of all men's pride I boast: 12
    Wretched in this alone, that thou mayst take
    All this away and me most wretched make.

92 1 *But*] Three of the Sonnets (16, 74, 92) begin with a 'But', which appears to indicate a link with that which precedes. Two of these have none the less been placed by several of the rearrangers in quite different relative positions from those they occupy in Q—74 six times in a sample of twenty rearrangements, 92 four times.

2 *For term of life*] i.e. for the duration of the poet's life. Like 'assurèd', 'term of life' is a legal expression.

5–6] 'The least sign of coldness or inconstancy on your part will kill me, so I need not fear to live to endure the worst wrong of all, complete alienation.'

8 *humour*] Either (1) 'temporary mood', or (2) 'permanent disposition'.

10 *revolt*] Not 'rebellion', but, as frequently in Shakespeare, 'act of inconstancy', 'change of affection'. Cf. *KJ*. III. i. 322: 'O foul revolt of French inconstancy!'

doth lie] 'rests'.

11 *happy title*] '(1) fortunate and (2) joyful right of ownership' (cf. line 2).

13] 'But what beautiful time (here the splendid situation) is so fortunate as not to run the danger of being sullied?' The construction has been much misunderstood. Malone hyphenated *blessèd-fair* (which Q did not), and he has been almost universally followed. Schmidt and *OED* cite this line as a nonce use of a quasi-adverbial use of 'blessèd', taking 'fair' as an adjective. Yet Shakespeare not only nowhere else uses 'blessèd' as even a quasi-adverb, but frequently uses 'fair' as a noun = 'beauty' or 'beautiful thing'. The use here 'so blessèd fair' = 'so blessèd a fair' can be paralleled in the usage of that time, e.g. in the Authorized Version of the Bible, *John*, xiv. 9: 'Have I been so long time with you, and yet hast thou not known me, Philip?' (and cf. *OED* 'So', III. 14c). Again, for the present use of 'so', followed by a relative clause, cf. *Lucrece* 853: 'No perfection is so absolute / That some impurity doth not pollute.' (and cf. *OED* 'So', III. 13b).

13–14] The couplet expresses a pang of awareness of a possibility hither-to blissfully uncontemplated. On the surface the possibility is merely hypothetical, 'mayst' bearing a future meaning, and 'yet' the sense 'never-theless'. But subtly underlying this may be a darker hint, for 'mayst' could be taken as present, and 'yet', as meaning 'as yet', as frequently in Shake-speare. This more deadly meaning could be revealed by reading the line with a stress on 'be' = 'already be'. In the belief that there is probably a play on both meanings we have removed Q's comma after *false* (retained by modern editors), which would tend to suggest only the second of the above meanings.

92

B<small>UT</small> <small>DO</small> thy worst to steal thyself away,
For term of life thou art assurèd mine;
And life no longer than thy love will stay,
For it depends upon that love of thine: 4
Then need I not to fear the worst of wrongs,
When in the least of them my life hath end;
I see a better state to me belongs
Than that which on thy humour doth depend: 8
Thou canst not vex me with inconstant mind,
Since that my life on thy revolt doth lie.
Oh what a happy title do I find—
Happy to have thy love, happy to die!   12
     But what's so blessèd fair that fears no blot?
     Thou mayst be false and yet I know it not.

93 1 Punctuation] Q, followed by all modern editions we have seen, has commas after 'live' and 'true'; but in a modern text this parenthesizing of the clause can easily mislead, by suggesting the sense 'if we assume you are true', instead of the true meaning 'deceived into thinking that'.

1 *So*] Cf. 92. 1, note. Five out of twenty sample rearrangements collated by Rollins unconvincingly separate this sonnet from 92. 'So' = 'In the situation implied in 92. 14—you being false and I ignorant of it.'

2 *so*] has the same function as in line 1.

love's face] The image is of the face of the beloved; the idea is of the outward show of love.

3 *seem*] Extensively used in Shakespeare to connote hypocrisy (e.g. *Two G.* II. iv. 10–12; *M. for M.* II. iv. 76; *Lear.* IV. vi. 176–7), though also often simply as = 'appear'. Either meaning is possible here, and, correspondingly, a stronger or weaker sense can be attached to 'deceivèd'; but 'thy heart in other place' (line 4), 'false heart' (line 7), line 11, and the final couplet suggest the possibility of real desertion, and therefore of some degree of hypocrisy.

alter'd new] What is altered? Not the face, which, the whole sonnet insists, can express nothing but love; but the love itself. There appears to be an ellipsis of 'it is' after 'though' (for parallels see Abbott, *Shakespearian Grammar*, s. 403). It is therefore unnecessary to follow Malone's hyphenation, as some modern editors have done. 'New' = 'newly'.

5, 6 *For . . . Therefore*] 'Since . . . Therefore'.

7 *many's*] For such plural possessives see Abbott, *Shakespearian Grammar*, s. 12.

8 *moods*] 'outbursts of anger', or 'signs of anger' (e.g. looks and gestures). One meaning of Old English *mōd* was 'anger'. Bailey (1733) gives '*Mood: anger. Shakespeare*'. Wright (*Dictionary of Obsolete and Provincial English*) gives '*moody: angry* (cf. Old English *mōdig*)'. Palsgrave (1530) gives '*Mody, angerfull, ireux, attayneux*'. Although the centuries have mollified the sense of the adjective, it still often implies a dangerous 'mood'.

strange] 'distant', 'unfriendly', cf. 89. 8, and Painter, *Palace of Pleasure* (1569): 'Myne aduise is, that by litle and litle you do make your selfe straunge, and vse no more your wonted grace vnto him.' 'Wrinkles strange' would then connote wrinkling of the face as if to say: 'Who the devil are you?'

12 *should*] Not = 'ought to' but 'would', as in line 10. A 'That' parallel to 'That' in line 10 is to be understood at the start of line 11. Lines 11–12 are an amplification of line 10.

93

So SHALL I live supposing thou art true
Like a deceivèd husband; so love's face
May still seem love to me, though alter'd new,—
Thy looks with me, thy heart in other place: 4
For there can live no hatred in thine eye,
Therefore in that I cannot know thy change;
In many's looks the false heart's history
Is writ in moods and frowns and wrinkles strange: 8
But heaven in thy creation did decree
That in thy face sweet love should ever dwell,—
Whate'er thy thoughts or thy heart's workings be
Thy looks should nothing thence but sweetness tell. 12
 How like Eve's apple doth thy beauty grow
 If thy sweet virtue answer not thy show!

13 *Eve's apple*] For its beauty cf. *Gen.* iii. 6: 'the tree . . . was pleasant
to the eyes', and *M. of V.* I. iii. 102–3:

  'A goodly apple rotten at the heart,
  Oh, what a goodly outside falsehood hath!'

94 *General Note:* One of the chief difficulties of this somewhat elusive poem is to determine how far the portrait of the type of men described is intended as laudatory. Some commentators take it as an ideal portrait, others as a highly critical one. We feel that it is an ambivalent one, expressing admiration but also implying, particularly in lines 3 and 4, and possibly also in line 7, certain reservations. The virtue described is, in any case, a passive or negative one. Many readers may, indeed, like us, find themselves shrinking from such cold and unresponsive characters. The cold image of the stone, however, is countered by the warmer image of the summer's flower, suggesting the positive excellence of such people and their benefit to society. This positive note, nevertheless, gives rise in turn to a warning that people of this kind, once corrupted, will sink far lower than moral mediocrities.

We would suggest the following paraphrase: 'Those who (by their personality, or their physical, social or spiritual qualities) have the power to harm others, and yet have no desire to do so—who in fact do not do what they most look as if they could: who affect others strongly but themselves remain, like stone, unaffected, cold in disposition and slow to succumb to temptation—such people do indeed inherit from heaven all sorts of graces, and they do not squander irresponsibly these gifts of nature: they are (truly) the masters of the appearance they present to the world, while others are merely the stewards of qualities richly bestowed on (1) the 'lords and owners' (line 7), or (2) themselves (see notes on line 8). A flower that blooms in summer gives out its sweetness to the summer even though it blooms alone and dies alone (unpollinated and bearing no fruit) (i.e. it is nevertheless a positive addition to the summer's total worth); *but* (and here lies a warning), if that flower is attacked by disease and corruption, then the coarsest weed (in its rank vigour) makes a finer show than the (now ruined) dignity of the flower.

'(Remember), the sweetest things, when their vital force is perverted into wrong activity, become the sourest. Rotting lilies stink far worse than weeds. (Corruption of the best is ever the worst corruption.)'

5 rightly] The only use of the word in the poems. Of all the twenty-three uses of the word in the plays, not one bears the moral or legal sense of 'rightfully', 'justly', 'legitimately', or 'of right'. Here the meaning must be 'truly' or 'really' or 'indeed'. (Cf. 'I don't rightly know.')

6 husband . . . from expense] 'carefully protect from wasteful spending'.

6] The dominant tone of the line is favourable. Reminiscence of the first sonnets of the series might, however, suggest that to 'husband' the riches has an element of miserliness. This, if present, is countered by the positive assertion of lines 9, 10.

214

94

_THEY THAT have power to hurt and will do none,
That do not do the thing they most do show,
Who moving others are themselves as stone,
Unmovèd, cold, and to temptation slow—   4
They rightly do inherit heaven's graces,
And husband nature's riches from expense;
They are the lords and owners of their faces,
Others but stewards of their excellence.   8
The summer's flower is to the summer sweet,
Though to itself it only live and die;
But if that flower with base infection meet,
The basest weed outbraves his dignity: 12
   For sweetest things turn sourest by their deeds;
   Lilies that fester smell far worse than weeds.

8 *stewards*] almost always in Shakespeare the official on an estate who manages its affairs for the lord or owner.

their excellence] either, we think, the excellences of the characters of lines 1–7, or those of the 'others' (line 8).

10 *to itself it only*] 'only to itself it . . .', i.e. *not* 'selfishly', but 'unpollinated, and bearing no seed'. The position of 'only' in English sentences down to the end of the eighteenth century often misleads a modern reader. For a Shakespearean parallel cf. *M. for M.* III. ii. 243: 'Novelty is only in request' = 'only novelty is in request'.

12 *outbraves*] 'makes a finer show than'.

his] 'its'.

13 *by their deeds*] i.e. by acting in a corrupt way. This is a startling addition to what has gone before. The suggestion is that these impassive people who have sunk so low have done so by *acting* corruptly. One is reminded of the Aristotelian doctrine that one becomes what one is by what one does. (*Nicomachean Ethics*, Book I.)

14 *fester*] 'rot', cf. *H5*. IV. iii. 88: 'their poor bodies must lie and fester'.

14] This line occurs in *The Raigne of King Edward the Third*, entered in the Stationers' Register on 1 December 1595 and published in 1596 and 1599. It has been argued that Shakespeare wrote certain scenes (Act I, Scene ii and Act II) in that play. Even if that conclusion were accepted, however, no inference as to the date of the sonnet could be drawn, since the question of priority would remain open.

On the other hand, the line has far more point in the sonnet than in the play, where it comes to no more than saying that vices are more offensive in kings than in commoners. This would suggest that the sonnet was written after the date of composition of that scene in the play, provided that Shakespeare wrote that line in the play.

94

THEY THAT have power to hurt and will do none,
That do not do the thing they most do show,
Who moving others are themselves as stone,
Unmovèd, cold, and to temptation slow— 4
They rightly do inherit heaven's graces,
And husband nature's riches from expense;
They are the lords and owners of their faces,
Others but stewards of their excellence. 8
The summer's flower is to the summer sweet,
Though to itself it only live and die;
But if that flower with base infection meet,
The basest weed outbraves his dignity: 12
    For sweetest things turn sourest by their deeds;
    Lilies that fester smell far worse than weeds.

95 1 *lovely*] 'lovable' (cf. 54. 13).

2 *canker*] The canker-worm which eats the bud before it opens, and chooses the most luscious buds, which would develop into the most fragrant flowers (cf. 35. 4, 70. 7).

3] Stressing that, as the Friend is young, his reputation can still be destroyed before it is fully established.

4 *sweets*] In Shakespearean usage the primary sense of 'sweets' is 'perfume' (as here) or 'savour', though, by extension, Shakespeare sometimes uses it in the normal sense of 'delights', 'pleasures'; and here the general sense 'delightful qualities' is also present. Shakespeare does not use the word of the visual. Though in lines 9–12 the outside or 'mansion' is presented visually, in this line the closer connexion is with the 'fragrance' enclosing corruption (line 2), smothering a bad smell with a sweet one.

6 *lascivious*] 'irresponsibly ribald'.

sport] 'sexual adventures'.

7, 8 Punctuation] So Q, which we retain with some hesitation. Most editors delete the comma after *dispraise* and print a semi-colon after *praise*, and some delete the comma after *name* in line 8. If, as here, the punctuation of Q is retained, the syntax is carried through the quatrain with a continuous but somewhat meandering flow, round slight obstructions of parenthetical qualifying phrases. It antithesizes 'dispraise' against 'bless' (i.e. censure against sanctification), and oversteps the more obvious antithesis of 'dispraise . . . kind of praise', though without destroying the paradox. The usual punctuation gives a reading of line 8 immediately acceptable to a modern ear, and eases the involution of the syntax by breaking the quatrain into 3 + 1. It leaves line 7 somewhat cryptic, but explains it by the syntactically isolated line 8. With the punctuation here printed, the sense is: 'The tongue that tells rich stories of your amours cannot really besmirch your reputation, but in effect only sanctifies the scandal by attaching your name to it.' With the usual punctuation the sense is: 'The tongue . . . can only censure your deeds by in a way praising them. To bring your name into such a story sanctifies the scandal.' This also makes good sense, and we do not insist on the punctuation here adopted.

12 *turns*] So Q and some modern editors. Most modern editors: *turn*. *Turns* could be interpreted as an *s*-plural, such as is quite common in Shakespeare (see Abbott, *Shakespearian Grammar*, s. 335, Franz, *Shakespeare-Grammatik*, ss. 155 ff, and cf. Sonnet 41. 3, note). The subject would then be 'all things'. Alternatively, it could be a singular verb with 'veil' as subject.

that eyes can see] i.e. outward appearances, which might otherwise betray inward vices.

95

How sweet and lovely dost thou make the shame
Which like a canker in the fragrant rose
Doth spot the beauty of thy budding name!
Oh, in what sweets dost thou thy sins enclose!   4
That tongue that tells the story of thy days,
Making lascivious comments on thy sport,
Cannot dispraise, but in a kind of praise,
Naming thy name, blesses an ill report.   8
Oh, what a mansion have those vices got
Which for their habitation chose out thee!—
Where beauty's veil doth cover every blot
And all things turns to fair that eyes can see.   12
    Take heed, dear heart, of this large privilege:
    The hardest knife ill us'd doth lose his edge.

13 *large privilege*] the wide freedom charity concedes to beautiful youth.
14 *his*] 'its'.

96 1 *wantonness*] All the following senses are found in Shakespeare: (1) playfulness; (2) frivolity; (3) lechery. (2) or (3) or both seem most likely here.

2 *gentle*] Primarily 'aristocratic', derivatively 'high-mettled'.

1–4] The sense seems roughly as follows: 'Some people say that the trouble with you is just that you are young, but others think there is more to it, and say that you are naturally frivolous (or 'lascivious' (see note on line 1)). Other people more indulgently say that your very attraction lies in your youth and in your being a playboy (or 'in the sexual freedoms, allowable to the high-born, which you indulge in'). But whether they find these qualities attractive or blameworthy everybody likes them; for all blemishes that come your way you turn into attractions.'

8 *truths*] 'right ways of acting', as opposed to wrong ways ('errors' (line 7)).

translated] 'transformed'. Cf. *MND*. III. i. 124–5: 'Bless thee, Bottom! bless thee! thou are translated.'

deem'd] Not simply 'thought to be', but 'adjudged to be by reason'.

11 *away*] 'astray'.

12 *wouldst*] 'wanted to'. Cf. 'will' (94. 1).

the strength of all thy state] 'all the glamour at your command'. Shakespeare uses 'state' in several ways. See, e.g., 64, which plays on several senses. Here the word seems to connote (1) 'personality', (2) 'rank'.

13–14] As Malone pointed out, these lines also end 36. (For their meaning see the note above on that sonnet.) Some editors have found the lines inappropriate here, and various theories have been advanced to account for their presence. (See Rollins, I. 238.) We do not find the lines inappropriate in sense. Nor are we impressed by Beeching's objection that the rhyme clashes with those in the first quatrain. There are other instances of the repetition of rhymes within the same sonnet (e.g. 3, 4, 6, 24, 51).

96

SOME SAY thy fault is youth, some wantonness;
Some say thy grace is youth and gentle sport;
Both grace and faults are lov'd of more and less,—
Thou mak'st faults graces that to thee resort.   4
As on the finger of a thronèd queen
The basest jewel will be well esteem'd,
So are those errors that in thee are seen
To truths translated and for true things deem'd.   8
How many lambs might the stern wolf betray
If like a lamb he could his looks translate!
How many gazers mightst thou lead away
If thou wouldst use the strength of all thy state!   12
   But do not so: I love thee in such sort
   As, thou being mine, mine is thy good report.

97 *General Note:* This splendid sonnet does not too readily reveal all its secrets. The general tone is immediately evident; but the precise sense of the second and third quatrains presents difficulties: (1) the exact nature of the relation intended between the seasons; (2) the mood or tone of line 8; (3) the significance of 'Yet' (line 9); (4) the meaning of line 10. We hope to resolve these difficulties below.

1 *absence*] Probably physical absence, though some editors have suggested a reference to estrangement.

2, 3, 4, !] Q has ?, which was at that time the mark both for interrogation and for exclamation.

5 *this time remov'd*] 'this time of removal (i.e. period of separation) from you'. Cf. *R2*. II. iii. 79: 'To take advantage of the absent time'.

7] A line enriched by the variety of senses the word 'wanton' could carry, of which three seem present: (1) 'frolicsome' (of children—the 'wanton burthen'); (2) 'luxuriant', cf. *MND*. II. i. 99: 'the quaint mazes in the wanton green'; (3) by hypallage, referring to 'the prime' (= the spring), 'amorously sportive', cf. *MND*. II. i. 128–9: 'To see the sails conceive / And grow big-bellied with the wanton wind'. For 'wanton spring' see *R2*. I. iii. 214: 'Four lagging winters and four wanton springs'.

8] It seems to us important for the whole sense of the sonnet that this should not be taken as a lugubrious line. There is no suggestion of mourning for the death of the spring. Moreover, widows often cherish with special tenderness the posthumous child.

9 *Yet*] If the emphasis of line 8 had been on the *melancholy* of widowhood Pooler's comment on 'Yet' (that it is absurd to say that a mother is a widow *yet* her child is an orphan) would be valid. But if line 8 continues the emphasis of lines 6–7 on 'rich increase', then 'Yet' (= 'nevertheless') perfectly expresses the contrast between the poet's subjective reaction and the situation objectively described in the second quatrain.

9, 10] The difficulty is to see whether in the image the offspring are considered as already born (which 'issue' and 'fruit' would suggest) or as yet to come (which 'hope' would suggest). In our view the tense of 'seem'd' is conclusive. The time referred to is that of the first quatrain, i.e. the period of separation. 'At that time it seemed to me that the promised abundance would prove joyless to me if you were not with me.'

11 *his*] Possibly, as often, = 'its'; though there may be a trace of personification here.

wait on thee] 'attend upon you as your minions'.

13 *with . . . cheer*] 'with so heavy a heart'. (Cf. Sir Richard Barckley, *A Discourse of the Felicitie of Man* (1598): 'he was . . . with heavie cheare enforced to seeke an other dwelling.') 'Cheer' originally meaning 'face'

97

How LIKE a winter hath my absence been
From thee, the pleasure of the fleeting year!
What freezings have I felt, what dark days seen!—
What old December's bareness everywhere!   4
And yet this time remov'd was summer's time,—
The teeming autumn big with rich increase
Bearing the wanton burthen of the prime,
Like widow'd wombs after their lords' decease: 8
Yet this abundant issue seem'd to me
But hope of orphans, and unfather'd fruit;
For summer and his pleasures wait on thee,
And thou away the very birds are mute: 12
    Or if they sing, 'tis with so dull a cheer
    That leaves look pale, dreading the winter's near.

or 'countenance' later came to mean 'disposition' and 'frame of mind',
as here.

1–14] The time-scheme of the sonnet seems to be as follows: At what-
ever season Shakespeare may have written the poem, its 'poetical moment'
is in the autumn. The months of separation have been like winter to the
poet (lines 1–4), though by the calendar they should have been summer, as
the actual coming of autumn with its bumper crops has proved (lines 5–8).
Lines 9–10 take us back to the period of dejected separation; and there we
remain for the rest of the poem, since the present tense of the remaining
lines (11–14) is a neutral or indefinite one, describing what is *always* the
case when the Friend is absent.

98 1 *have I been absent*] Some editors (e.g. Wyndham, Pooler) have considered this to refer to a specific absence in spring, and so have found no connexion between this sonnet and 97. But 'have been' surely refers to one or more previous absences which occurred in spring, and are here cited as analogies to the 'summer' absence of 97.

2 *proud-pied*] 'splendidly many-hued'.

April . . . his] 'his' (line 2) might have meant 'its', but 'him' (line 4) makes it clear that April is here personified as a young man.

trim] 'array'.

4 *heavy Saturn*] Saturn was astrologically a cold, slow planet, increasing the black bile of melancholy. Cf. our modern adjective 'saturnine'.

6 *different flowers in*] i.e. flowers differing in . . . See Abbott, *Shakespearian Grammar*, s. 419a.

hue] probably here 'colour' rather than shape or form.

7 *summer's story tell*] There is no confusion of season. The phrase probably means 'speak (or write) happily'. For the general use of 'summer' Malone pertinently quotes *Cymb*. III. iv. 12: 'If 't be summer news, / Smile to 't before: if winterly, thou need'st / But keep that count'nance still'.

8 *proud*] 'showy'.

lap] i.e. the flower-bed.

9 *wonder at*] 'admire'.

the lily's white] So most modern editors. Q: *Lillies*. Malone and a few editors: *lilies*. Lines 9–10 concern the colours rather than the flowers as flowers. In Q, as in the First Folio, the apostrophe is not the sign of a genitive but of abbreviation, and genitives of nouns in *-y* are spelt *-ies*.

11 *They . . . sweet,*] So Q (but spelling 'were', *weare*) and most modern editors, though various emendations have been suggested, among which only Malone's deserves mention: , *my sweet,*. Malone's point that only colour is mentioned in lines 9–10, and that 'drawn' and 'pattern' in line 12 only refer to visual appearance, is valid in itself, but overlooks the reference back to lines 5–6. There is also the possibility that in line 11 'sweet' no longer refers to smell but has the general sense, common in Shakespeare, of 'pleasant' (cf. 95. 4, note). The clause would then mean roughly: 'They seemed to me superficially pleasant, but no more.' In our view, however, Shakespeare, with his typically loose use of pronouns, is now using 'They' of the lily and the rose, and not of their colour, and saying that they were just sweet-smelling flowers and nothing more deeply satisfying.

figures of delight] 'representations of the (Platonic) idea of Delight.' An instance of the derivative neo-Platonism quite frequent in Shakespeare.

11 Punctuation] Q has a comma after *sweet* and a colon after *delight*. Most modern editors change Q's colon to a comma. A few modern editors,

98

 Ｆｒｏｍ ｙｏｕ have I been absent in the spring,
When proud-pied April, dress'd in all his trim,
Hath put a spirit of youth in every thing,
That heavy Saturn laugh'd and leapt with him.   4
Yet nor the lays of birds, nor the sweet smell
Of different flowers in odour and in hue,
Could make me any summer's story tell,
Or from their proud lap pluck them where they grew: 8
Nor did I wonder at the lily's white,
Nor praise the deep vermilion in the rose;
They were but sweet, but figures of delight
Drawn after you, you pattern of all those.   12
   Yet seem'd it winter still; and, you away,
   As with your shadow I with these did play.

e.g. Butler, Tucker, print no stop after *delight*. This has the advantage
of making clear that line 12 does not refer to the first half of line 11, which
it certainly does not if 'sweet' refers to smell (see note immediately above).

12 *you . . . those*] 'and you are the pattern . . .' rather than an un-
typical vocative.

13 *and, you away,*] So Capell and almost all modern editors. Q: *and
you away,*.

14 *shadow*] 'image' or 'reflection'.

1 . . . did play] 'I toyed in my mind with these flowers'.

99 *General Note:* The only fifteen-line sonnet in the collection. Instances occur, however, in other Elizabethan collections. No line here can be removed without damage to the sense or syntax, though in point of rhyme alone line 1 or line 5 is the extra line.

Massey has pointed out that in theme and treatment the poem is somewhat similar to Sonnet 9 of Book I of Constable's *Diana* (1594).

1 *forward*] Probably punning on (1) 'seasonally forward', (2) 'cheeky'.

2 *sweet that smells*] Appears redundant, though Tucker defends it on the ground that flowers have other 'sweet' properties besides odour.

3 *purple pride*] 'highly-coloured splendour'. 'Purple' is evidently used very vaguely here. The violets which Shakespeare would have known were not of the Tyrian purple which blood could supply.

2–5 Punctuation] (1) We follow Tucker in placing these lines in inverted commas. (2) We follow most modern editors in inserting a comma after *smells*, deleting Q's comma after *pride*, and its question-mark after *dwells*, and changing its comma after *died* (= 'dyed') to a full-stop.

4 *for complexion*] 'as colour'.

5 *too grossly*] Either (1) 'too heavily', giving a coarse colour; or (2) 'too obviously' (paralleling the suggestion 'Where else could you have got it?' in lines 2, 3).

6 *I condemnèd for*] i.e. 'I condemned for stealing its whiteness from . . .'.

7] Commentators differ as to the qualities involved in the comparison; but there seems no conclusive reason to suppose that either (1) sweet scent, or (2) colour (? dark auburn), or (3) tight knots, is omitted from reference. But line 15, summing up the sonnet, mentions only scent and colour, not shape; and scent ('sweet marjoram') would be the most natural association.

8 *fearfully*] because conscious of their guilty thefts.

9 *One*] So Sewell and all modern editors. Q: *Our*.

9] 'Blushing' is an adjective. The red rose is 'blushing shame' personified, and the white rose 'white despair' personified.

10 *A third . . . white*] and therefore being a tempered pink showing neither shame nor despair.

of both] Either (1) 'from both (colours)' or, as Tucker prefers, (2) 'something of each'.

13 *canker*] 'canker-worm'.

ate] So Butler. Q: *eate*. Almost all modern editors: *eat*. The tense is, in any case, past; and is almost certainly the indefinite use of the preterite, = 'was eating' (while the poet was there).

15 *sweet*] 'sweet smell'.

99

THE FORWARD violet thus did I chide:
'Sweet thief, whence didst thou steal thy sweet that smells,
If not from my love's breath? The purple pride
Which on thy soft cheek for complexion dwells   4
In my love's veins thou hast too grossly dyed.'
The lily I condemnèd for thy hand,
And buds of marjoram had stol'n thy hair;
The roses fearfully on thorns did stand—   8
One blushing shame, another white despair;
A third, nor red nor white, had stol'n of both,
And to his robbery had annex'd thy breath,
But for his theft in pride of all his growth   12
A vengeful canker ate him up to death.
    More flowers I noted, yet I none could see
    But sweet or colour it had stol'n from thee.

100 3 *Spend'st thou*] In the full sense of: 'Are you using up . . . ?'

fury] i.e. *furor poeticus*, the 'poet's rage' of 17. 11.

4 *Darkening thy power*] The working of the image is not obvious, but we think the 'darkening' is by burning up, paralleling 'spend'st' in line 3. The 'base subjects' cannot replenish the 'power' as would the Friend as subject (see line 2).

lend] 'give'.

base] punning on (1) 'inferior', (2) 'dark'. (Cf. 33. 5.)

5 *forgetful*] i.e. of your true theme.

6 *gentle numbers*] 'noble verse', fit for a finer subject.

idly] not 'indolently' but either (1) 'uselessly', or (2) 'foolishly', or both.

7 *doth . . . esteem*] Tucker holds that 'esteem' is a noun, and that the phrase means 'imparts any value to my lays', on the analogy of 'do honour', 'do grace'. That construction does not seem impossible, but we have found no instance of 'do' used with 'esteem' in this way.

8 *argument*] 'subject-matter', in the modern sense.

9 *resty*] not 'restive', but 'slothful', 'torpid'.

9, 10 *survey, If*] i.e. 'examine to see if . . .'.

11 *If any*] 'If there be any'.

a satire to] 'a satirist of . . .'. 'Satire' was so used at the time, possibly owing to some confusion with 'satyr', for a mocking, satirical fellow.

12 *spoils*] 'acts of depredation', cf. *M. of V.* V. i. 85: 'treasons, stratagems and spoils'.

14 *prevent'st*] 'forestallest'.

scythe and crookèd knife] Tucker suggests that this is not a hendiadys (as Pooler maintained), but that the crooked knife is a pruning-knife, which would remove portions of growth during life. But the pruning-knife is properly used also to promote desirable growth, and would therefore be out of place here. More relevant would seem to be the association of 'crooked' with 'malignant', as in 'crooked fortune' (*Two G.* IV. i. 22), 'crooked malice' (*H8.* V. iii. 44), and 'crooked eclipses' (60. 7). From the curved scythe which mows down the ripe crops the image passes to that of a sinister assassin.

100

Where art thou, Muse, that thou forget'st so long
To speak of that which gives thee all thy might?
Spend'st thou thy fury on some worthless song,
Darkening thy power to lend base subjects light? 4
Return, forgetful Muse, and straight redeem
In gentle numbers time so idly spent;
Sing to the ear that doth thy lays esteem
And gives thy pen both skill and argument. 8
Rise, resty Muse, my love's sweet face survey,
If Time have any wrinkle graven there,—
If any, be a satire to decay
And make Time's spoils despisèd everywhere: 12
    Give my love fame faster than Time wastes life;
    So thou prevent'st his scythe and crookèd knife.

101 2 *truth in beauty dyed*] 'truth steeped in beauty', the dye being fast (see line 6). The meaning is that all moral perfection is steeped in all physical perfection.

3 *my love*] i.e. the Friend.

depends] Such '-s' plurals were common (Abbott, § 333).

3] The Platonic ideas of Truth and Beauty are made to depend on the Friend, thus reversing the dependence of the temporal on the eternal (cf. 98. 11, 12).

4 *dignified*] i.e. 'you (the muse) are dignified'.

6–8 Inverted commas] Nearly all modern editors place in inverted commas, which gives added life to the lines. The convention of inverted commas is never used in Q.

6 *Truth . . . colour*] A proverb (see G. L. Apperson, *English Proverbs and Proverbial Phrases*, Dent, London, 1929, 650) is here elaborated into a conceit. 'Colour' implies artifice of addition or in justification. There is probably also a pun on rhetorical 'colours' = 'ornaments', 'embellishments'.

6] i.e. Truth's colour is in grain (cf. *TN*. I. v. 257), and needs no colour of art to be applied or fixed (with a fixative). 'His' = 'its', a word which does not occur in the *Sonnets* or *Poems*.

7 *pencil*] 'brush' (cf. Fr. *pinceau*).

lay] 'apply' (as one spreads paint): the truth of beauty is inherent, for beauty is itself organic—no external application, as by an artist's brush, is required.

6, 7 *Truth . . . truth*] The former has a multiple meaning: (1) moral excellence, (2) veracity, (3) reality, whereas the latter connotes simply 'reality' or 'genuineness'.

8 *intermix'd*] i.e. adulterated with something alien.

11 *gilded*] implying another artificial elaboration, cf. lines 6–8.

13 Punctuation] Q has no comma after *office*, but commas after *Muse* and *how*. Most modern editors insert a comma after *office* and print a semicolon after *Muse*, and no stop at the end of the line. But to break the sense at 'Muse', and run the clause 'I teach thee how' in with line 14 weakens the ending of the sonnet. The real point of the ending would seem to be that simply to portray the Friend as he is now, without embellishments, will be enough to ensure his posthumous fame. There is thus a *tertium quid* between absolute silence and a eulogy which could only be superfluous. To bring out this meaning we have emended Q's punctuation. 'I . . . how' is clearly parenthetical, and line 14 defines the 'office' (duty) the Muse is to perform.

101

O TRUANT Muse, what shall be thy amends
For thy neglect of truth in beauty dyed?
Both truth and beauty on my love depends:
So dost thou too, and therein dignified.   4
Make answer, Muse: wilt thou not haply say,
'Truth needs no colour with his colour fix'd,
Beauty no pencil beauty's truth to lay,
But best is best if never intermix'd'?   8
Because he needs no praise wilt thou be dumb?
Excuse not silence so, for it lies in thee
To make him much outlive a gilded tomb
And to be prais'd of ages yet to be.   12
    Then do thy office, Muse (I teach thee how):—
    To make him seem long hence as he shows now.

102 1 *seeming*] here simply 'appearance'.

2 *appear*] 'not "seem" but "is in evidence" (Lat. *apparere*). The stress is upon "love" and "show"' (Tucker).

3 *merchandiz'd*] 'commercialized'.

whose . . . esteeming] 'the rich estimate of whose worth'.

5 *in the spring*] involving the seasonal sense, but primarily 'in its early growth'. Cf. 53. 9, 63. 8, and Glossary.

7 *in summer's front*] 'at the beginning of summer'. Cf. *WT*. IV. iii. 2, 3: 'Flora / Peering in April's front'.

8 *her*] So R. F. Housman (1835), followed by most modern editors. Q and many other modern editors: *his*. Though, as Pooler points out, it is the cock nightingale that sings, Shakespeare always correctly takes Philomel to be female. Cf., moreover, 'her' in lines 10, 13.

stops her pipe] 'breaks off her singing'.

in . . . days] i.e. in late summer.

10 *mournful*] In all the variant forms of the myth Philomela's fate is a tragic one, so that her songs were inevitably mournful.

did hush the night] i.e. silenced all other creatures with the beauty of her song. Tucker draws attention to another possible meaning, 'lulled the night to sleep' (cf. 'Hush-a-by, baby'). Both meanings may be present, though the first seems dominant.

11 *But that*] paralleling 'Not that' (line 9). 'That' is not demonstrative but a conjunctional affix.

wild] 'tumultuous' (all kinds of birds are singing now in late summer).

burthens . . . bough] 'loads every bough with its "burthen" (= "burden") of song'. 'Burthens' may also suggest the sense of the *noun* 'burthen' = 'chorus'. Shakespeare plays on the *noun* in both senses in *Two G*. I. ii. 81–2. The reference here is almost certainly to the other poets who are now singing the Friend's praises (cf. 78. 3, 4).

12 *sweets*] 'pleasant things'.

dear] 'keenly appreciated' (Tucker).

13 *sometime*] 'from time to time'.

14] 'Because I do not wish my song to pall on your senses'. The emphasis seems to be on the word 'dull'.

102

MY LOVE is strengthen'd, though more weak in seeming;
I love not less, though less the show appear:
That love is merchandiz'd whose rich esteeming
The owner's tongue doth publish everywhere.   4
Our love was new, and then but in the spring,
When I was wont to greet it with my lays;
As Philomel in summer's front doth sing,
And stops her pipe in growth of riper days: 8
Not that the summer is less pleasant now
Than when her mournful hymns did hush the night,
But that wild music burthens every bough,
And sweets grown common lose their dear delight.   12
   Therefore like her I sometime hold my tongue;
   Because I would not dull you with my song.

103 1 *poverty*] 'poor stuff'.

2 *That having*] 'In that, having', as in *R&J.* I. i. 221–2: 'Oh, she is rich in beauty; only poor / That, when she dies, with beauty dies her store' (quoted Franz, *Shakespeare-Grammatik*, 435). Cf. also *TN.* I. i. 10 and Abbott, *Shakespearian Grammar*, s. 294.

a scope] Involving the sense, primarily, of 'an ample opportunity' and, secondarily, of 'topic' (from the original sense of 'aim', 'target' present in 61. 8).

pride] 'splendour'.

3 *The argument all bare*] 'The naked theme' (i.e. that mentioned in line 12).

7 *over-goes*] 'exceeds'.

blunt] Both (1) 'coarse', i.e. not sharp enough to trace such delicate features, and (2) 'dull', as in 'blunt Thurio' (*Two G.* II. vi. 41), i.e. incapable of finding words and images with which to describe the Friend.

8 *Dulling my lines*] 'making (1) my verses, (2) the lines of my portrait of you, look lifeless by comparison'.

doing me disgrace] 'putting me to shame' (see Glossary).

9 *mend*] 'improve upon'.

11 *pass*] 'effect'.

103

Alack, what poverty my Muse brings forth,
That having such a scope to show her pride
The argument all bare is of more worth
Than when it hath my added praise beside! 4
Oh, blame me not if I no more can write!
Look in your glass, and there appears a face
That over-goes my blunt invention quite,
Dulling my lines and doing me disgrace. 8
Were it not sinful then, striving to mend,
To mar the subject that before was well?
For to no other pass my verses tend
Than of your graces and your gifts to tell: 12
    And more, much more, than in my verse can sit
    Your own glass shows you when you look in it.

104 *General Note:* This sonnet has played a large part in the controversy on the dating of the *Sonnets*.

2 *when . . . eyed*] i.e. 'when I was first brought face to face with you'. Probably there is a deliberate play of sound which might at the time have seemed witty. 'Eyed' = 'saw', cf. *Cor.* V. iii. 74: 'a great sea-mark . . . saving those that eye thee'.

3 *seems*] i.e. 'to me', cf. lines 11, 12, a central theme of the sonnet being the imperceptibility, to the close friend, of signs of decay.

winters] So Q (*Winters*) and most editors. Knight (1841) and some editors: *winters'*. There would, admittedly, be no apostrophe in Q for a possessive genitive, but to make 'cold' a noun would involve taking 'have' as a third person singular. This does occur as a dialect form in Elizabethan as in modern English, but is quite uncharacteristic of Shakespeare, who, on the contrary, frequently uses singular verb forms in 's' or 'th' with plural nouns.

4 *pride*] i.e. their glorious show, cf. 80. 12.

7] To Beeching the image seemed to be from throwing incense on a fire. Tucker, concurring, even specifies a censer. But (1) there is no other ritual image in the poem, (2) incense smells as it burns, but April perfumes do not smell in June, (3) the burning of incense is an act of worship or exaltation, whereas the parallel images of lines 3–4 and 5, and even 14, are of destruction.

8 *fresh*] i.e. in the first beauty of youth.

green] probably not intended to be contrasted with 'fresh', but to be roughly synonymous with it.

9 *dial*] 'clock' or 'watch'.

10 *his*] primarily 'its', though quite possibly with a play on 'his'.

figure] the figure on the dial marking the hour. Some editors (e.g. Tucker) have seen a play on the sense of 'figure' = 'appearance' (cf. 'hue', line 11); though, taken too strongly, such a play could destroy the 'dial hand' image.

9, 10] 'Beauty steals away as imperceptibly as the hand of a watch steals away from the figures on the dial' (Beeching).

10 *and . . . perceiv'd*] Such absolute participial constructions were far commoner in Elizabethan English than today.

11 *sweet hue*] literally 'sweetness of appearance', i.e. 'handsomeness', paralleling, for the working of the image, 'beauty' (line 9) in general.

methinks . . . stand] 'seems to me to remain unaltered' (as the clock hand seemed to stay still).

13 *For fear of which*] i.e. Because of my fear of this.

hear this] probably, as Tucker suggests, the *oyez* of a public proclamation.

236

104

To me, fair friend, you never can be old,
For as you were when first your eye I eyed
Such seems your beauty still: three winters cold
Have from the forests shook three summers' pride,   4
Three beauteous springs to yellow autumn turn'd
In process of the seasons have I seen,
Three April perfumes in three hot Junes burn'd,
Since first I saw you fresh which yet are green.   8
Ah yet doth beauty like a dial hand
Steal from his figure and no pace perceiv'd,
So your sweet hue, which methinks still doth stand,
Hath motion, and mine eye may be deceiv'd,—   12
  For fear of which hear this, thou age unbred:
  Ere you were born was beauty's summer dead.

13 *thou*, 14 *you*] Possibly, as Tucker suggests, 'thou' is collectively the age, and 'you' the individuals who will live in it.

13 *unbred*] = 'to come'.

14 *beauty's summer*] the golden time of Beauty. This was, of course, the time when the Friend, who was the embodiment of Beauty, was in his prime. The future age will, therefore, never have seen Beauty in its perfection.

105 *General Note:* J. Q. Adams (*Life of William Shakespeare*, Houghton, Boston, and Constable, London, 1923) suggests that in the octave of this sonnet the poet's attitude to the Friend is said to resemble monotheism rather than idolatry, and that in the sestet its orthodoxy is more firmly established by showing its analogy to the Christian worship of the Trinity. But see note on lines 1–4, below.

1–4] Wyndham had, before Adams, taken the meaning to be that the poet's love was not idolatry, since he worshipped at only one shrine; but, as Beeching points out, there could be monidolatry as well as monotheism.

2 *show*] intransitive verb, 'seem', 'appear'.

3 *Since*] The crux is, as Pooler suggests, whether this is the reason for the accusation or the beginning of a defence against it. We think the former. To say that the 'songs and praises' are all addressed to one person and in the same strain would be a very poor counter to an accusation of idolatry!

3–4] Wyndham is probably right in holding that there is a liturgical suggestion in these lines.

4 *still such, and ever so*] 'always of the same kind and in the same strain'; not referring, as Tucker thought, to the object of the praises. That interpretation would require the comma after 'of one' to be omitted, though Tucker does not do so.

5–8] i.e. the Friend's 'constancy' in 'excellence' is sufficient justification for the singleness of the poet's theme and the uniformity of his treatment of it.

8 *leaves out difference*] 'eschews variety (of theme)'.

9, 10, 13 *Fair, kind, and true*] Q has no inverted commas, and is followed by Tyler and a few modern editors. The Globe edition and almost all modern editors enclose the words in inverted commas in lines 9 and 10, and most modern editors do so in line 13. Beeching, Tucker, and Tucker Brooke print '*Fair*', '*kind*', and '*true*' in separate quotes in line 13, and Tucker Brooke does the same in line 10.

In our view line 13 refers to the qualities connoted by the terms, whereas lines 9 and 10 recite the terms by which the qualities may be expressed. The terms in line 10 could be taken either singly, as Tucker Brooke takes them, or collectively, as we do.

9 *argument*] 'theme'.

11 *change*] 'variety of expression'; or possibly, 'writing of variations on a theme' in a musical sense. Cf. also change-ringing.

is my invention spent] 'my inventiveness is used to the full', or even 'exhausted'.

9–12] The elliptical construction is difficult. The general sense, how-

105

L ET NOT my love be call'd idolatry,
Nor my belovèd as an idol show,
Since all alike my songs and praises be
To one, of one, still such, and ever so.   4
Kind is my love today, tomorrow kind,
Still constant in a wondrous excellence:
Therefore my verse, to constancy confin'd,
One thing expressing, leaves out difference.   8
'Fair, kind, and true' is all my argument—
'Fair, kind, and true' varying to other words;
And in this change is my invention spent—
Three themes in one, which wondrous scope affords.   12
   Fair, kind, and true have often liv'd alone,
   Which three till now never kept seat in one.

ever, seems to be: 'My whole theme is that my friend is "fair, kind, and
true", though this expression of the theme is constantly varied, and in
devising these variations I exhaust my inventiveness, for this one theme is
really three, so that there is almost no limit to what can be said about it.'
The richness of the theme derives from the rare combination of all three
qualities in one person (cf. lines 13–14).

13 *alone*] i.e. each by itself in individual persons.

14 *kept seat*] 'resided permanently'.

106 1 *wasted*] Beeching construes as 'past', Tucker as 'gone to ruin'. Both were Elizabethan uses. It is hard to estimate *how far* the figure of devastation is present here, but in some degree it certainly is.

2 *wights*] 'men and women'—without any of the tone of archaism the word came to have in Romantic poetry.

3] It seems to be the concrete images of the beautiful men and women who peopled the old poems, rather than the abstract idea of beauty, that made the old poems beautiful, whether by inspiring the poet's style or, more directly, enchanting the reader's visual imagination.

4 *lovely*] Most probably either (1) 'handsome', or (2) 'worthy of love' (largely because of their handsomeness, which is the dominant pre-occupation of the sonnet).

5 *blazon*] 'rich and precise description', as in blazoning a coat-of-arms; but also involving praise and the idea of publishing to the world. Cf. Cotgrave (1611): '*Blason*: . . . the blazing of Arms; also, praise, commendation,' etc. Also '*Blasonner*. To blaze Arms; also to praise, extoll, commend; or to publish the praises, divulge the perfections, proclaim the virtues of.'

7 *their ántique pen*] i.e. the pens of the old writers. There does not seem, in view of lines 13–14, any suggestion of quaintness or inferiority in art.

would have] 'would have liked to'.

8 *master*] 'possess', 'own' (Schmidt). Cf. *M. of V.* V. I. 174: 'the wealth / That the world masters'.

10 *all you prefiguring*] i.e. all foreshadowing you.

11 *for*] 'because'.

divining eyes] 'eyes peering speculatively into the future'.

12 *skill*] So Tyrwhitt conjectured, and the reading is adopted by Capell MS, Malone, and most other editors. Q: *still*, followed by Wyndham and a few modern editors, and supported by Professor Sisson. Wyndham interprets the argument as that the old writers had descriptive talent ('tongues') but lacked the model (the Friend's beauty), whereas the moderns had the model but lacked talent. He thinks that Tyrwhitt's emendation both destroys this antithesis and contradicts Shakespeare's customary admiration of the art of the ancients. For Wyndham the force of 'still' is that for all their talent the ancients *still* lacked the best model. Wyndham's view is supported by Porter (1912) and Ridley (1934). The crux is a hard one. But if 'skill' be taken to mean 'understanding' (*OED*. 7), Tyrwhitt's emendation can make good sense: 'The old writers, peering into the future, but not actually seeing you, had not the requisite understanding to do justice to your perfections. No wonder, since we who are alive now, though we can marvel at your beauty, are unable to express it'. It may even be possible

106

WHEN IN the chronicle of wasted time
I see descriptions of the fairest wights,
And beauty making beautiful old rhyme
In praise of ladies dead and lovely knights,   4
Then in the blazon of sweet beauty's best—
Of hand, of foot, of lip, of eye, of brow—
I see their ántique pen would have express'd
Even such a beauty as you master now: 8
So all their praises are but prophecies
Of this our time, all you prefiguring;
And for they look'd but with divining eyes
They had not skill enough your worth to sing: 12
  For we which now behold these present days
  Have eyes to wonder, but lack tongues to praise.

that the ending is stronger, viz.: 'but are struck dumb by it'. Professor Sisson (*New Readings in Shakespeare*, II, 213), supporting Q, argues somewhat similarly to Wyndham, but takes the sense to be that the ancients 'had not *yet* enough to sing' the Friend 'perfectly'. The point of the argument, he says, 'is precisely that the old poets *had* "skill", which is lacking in' the moderns. He also maintains that the emendation *skill* has little graphic plausibility. Against this last point we would urge, with respect, that in secretary hand a 'k' with a faint upper loop could easily be taken for a 't', or a 't' with a pronounced upper curve for a 'k', if the lower half of the letter were in either case laterally compressed, as frequently occurred.

Against Wyndham's and Sisson's defences of *still* there are at least four possible objections. (1) As Beeching points out, there would be no noun for 'enough' to refer to. We would add that if we were to understand a noun it would be hard to choose an appropriate one. (2) If 'tongues' (line 14) means talent or skill, the couplet results in a *non sequitur*. For what logical connexion is there between modern poets lacking talent and ancient poets lacking a model? (3) 'For' is not a suitable conjunction to introduce an antithesis (it actually introduces an *a fortiori* argument in reverse).

(4) 'Still' is not cited by *OED* in the sense 'as yet' before 1632, or in the sense 'nevertheless' or 'however' before 1722.

As a matter of mere interest, not of argument, it is perhaps worth adding that the Holgate MS version (Morgan Library MS. MA 1058) of this sonnet (probably *c.* 1630) reads *skill*.

Mr. Lucas has suggested to us a further argument for *skill*, namely that 'would have express'd' (line 7) implies that the ancient writers' efforts at expression did *not* attain quite perfect success.

WHEN IN the chronicle of wasted time
I see descriptions of the fairest wights,
And beauty making beautiful old rhyme
In praise of ladies dead and lovely knights, 4
Then in the blazon of sweet beauty's best—
Of hand, of foot, of lip, of eye, of brow—
I see their ántique pen would have express'd
Even such a beauty as you master now: 8
So all their praises are but prophecies
Of this our time, all you prefiguring;
And for they look'd but with divining eyes
They had not skill enough your worth to sing: 12
 For we which now behold these present days
 Have eyes to wonder, but lack tongues to praise.

107 *General Note:* A central sonnet in the still inconclusive arguments about the dating of the *Sonnets*, with which, however, this edition is not concerned. The chief focal problems are:

(1) the referent of the 'eclipse' of the 'mortal moon' (line 5);

(2) the identity of the 'sad augurs' and the nature of their 'presage' (line 6);

(3) the allusion implied in lines 7 and 8;

(4) whether 'confin'd doom' refers to some particular event, and, if so, to what event.

The chief answers to (1) have been:

(a) the Spanish Armada, 1588 (Butler, Hotson);

(b) the Queen's Grand Climacteric, 1595–6 (Harrison);

(c) the Queen's illness in 1599–1600 (Chambers);

(d) Essex's rebellion, 1601 (Tyler);

(e) the Queen's death, 1603 (e.g. Massey, Minto, Lee, Beeching);

(f) a lunar eclipse, e.g. in 1595 (O. F. Emerson);

(g) an eclipse of the Queen's favour (Conrad).

The chief solutions proposed for (2) relate closely to their propounders' solutions to (1), and comprise:

(a) the fears and prognostications with regard to the Spanish threat;

(b) the fears and prognostications with regard to the Queen's climacteric or illness;

(c) fears of civil war on the death of Elizabeth, or in the event of a serious rebellion (e.g. (d), above);

(d) the usual promises of political and other disasters resultant upon eclipses and other astrological portents;

(e) a specifically personal reference, relating, of course, to the commentator's partisanship for one of the contestants for identification with the Friend.

As to (3), while line 7 is very general in its reference, a political context seems to be implied by line 8. In all cases, however, the passing of a threatened cataclysm seems to evoke this sense of confident security.

With regard to (4), the view that a particular event, such as imprisonment of some individual (e.g. of Southampton, who was released on the accession of James I), is referred to would seem to involve much forcing of the sense of such words as 'lease', 'true love', and 'control'.

244

107

NOT MINE own fears, nor the prophetic soul
Of the wide world dreaming on things to come
Can yet the lease of my true love control,
Suppos'd as forfeit to a cónfin'd doom.   4
The mortal moon hath her eclipse endur'd,
And the sad augurs mock their own presage;
Incertainties now crown themselves assur'd,
And peace proclaims olives of endless age.   8
Now with the drops of this most balmy time
My love looks fresh; and Death to me subscribes,
Since spite of him I'll live in this poor rhyme
While he insults o'er dull and speechless tribes: 12
   And thou in this shalt find thy monument
   When tyrants' crests and tombs of brass are spent.

1, 2] 'Neither my own present fears, nor the premonitory dread which the world at large may have of mutability or impending disaster . . .'

3 *yet*] Most commentators ignore the word, but it poses a problem, namely, whether it is (1) temporal = 'as yet' (Tucker), or (2) = 'after all', or (3) a meaningless expletive, or (4) a word intended to emphasize the magnitude of the fears and anxieties—almost equivalent to an 'even' placed after the 'not' in line 1. We prefer (4) or (2) in that order. Each would imply that not even microcosmic and macrocosmic fears taken together could 'control' the poet's 'true love'.

the lease of my true love] 'the period for which my deep and constant love (for my friend) is to last'.

control] Could mean either (1) 'have power over', or (2) 'challenge' (*OED*. 3b), if 'forfeit' in line 4 be taken in a strict legal sense.

4 *Suppos'd as*] 'on the supposition (possibly invented by the 'fears') that it is . . .'

forfeit] Taken in legal strictness a lease could only be 'forfeit' as a penalty. What such a penalty could be for here is so obscure that one suspects that Shakespeare is using the word loosely as = 'subject', which is Schmidt's interpretation.

to a cónfin'd doom] If 'forfeit' be taken in a legal sense, 'doom' could mean 'judgment', and the phrase would then mean (1) 'by a judgment of limitation'. If 'forfeit' be taken loosely, the phrase would probably mean (2) 'subject to the fate of finitude'.

5 The mortal moon] See General Note, above.

mortal] If the reference is to the Queen's climacteric, illness, or death, the sense of the word is obvious. If the reference were to the Armada, the sense of the word would be either (1) 'deadly' (as in 'mortal foe'), or (2) 'subject to destruction or death (in the battle)', or (3) 'created by mortals'.

endur'd] Shakespeare never uses the word 'endure' in the sense of 'succumb to', but only in one or other of the senses 'undergo', 'suffer', 'survive', 'last', and (though not relevant here) 'put up with'. The 'eclipse' has not, therefore, destroyed the 'moon'. This linguistic point possibly, though if so, obscurely, implied by Dowden, would seem to weigh heavily against both the Queen's death and the defeat of the Armada as the allusions of the line.

6] In our view the most probable interpretation is given by stressing 'augurs' and 'own', thereby implying an 'even' after 'And', the sense being that the time is so joyous that even the solemn and gloomy prognosticators deride their former predictions.

sad] probably carrying the double sense of (1) 'solemn', 'grave', and (2) 'gloomy' in their prophecies.

7] 'A time full of anxious uncertainties has given place to one of triumphant confidence.'

8] The tremendous effect of this line has been long and widely recognized. As with many typically Shakespearean lines, however, the statement it makes is, in fact, a simple and not particularly remarkable one: 'We can now hope for perpetual peace.' A somewhat free paraphrase such as 'Peace blazons itself as perpetual' would better represent the actual afflatus of the line. But the working of Shakespeare's own words is worth closer examination. The effect certainly depends considerably on the interrelation and sequence of sounds, both in themselves and in their connexion with the emotional evocation of 'peace proclaims' and 'endless age'. Another factor is the associational power of the 'olives', strongly reinforced by 'endless age', it being the slow maturity and the longevity of olive orchards that has made them the symbol of peace. Typically and curiously in the present line Shakespeare reverses the normal process of symbolization. Instead of making

107

Not mine own fears, nor the prophetic soul
Of the wide world dreaming on things to come
Can yet the lease of my true love control,
Suppos'd as forfeit to a cónfin'd doom.   4
The mortal moon hath her eclipse endur'd,
And the sad augurs mock their own presage;
Incertainties now crown themselves assur'd,
And peace proclaims olives of endless age.   8
Now with the drops of this most balmy time
My love looks fresh; and Death to me subscribes,
Since spite of him I'll live in this poor rhyme
While he insults o'er dull and speechless tribes: 12
    And thou in this shalt find thy monument
    When tyrants' crests and tombs of brass are spent.

the olive announce peace, he makes Peace (as a herald) 'proclaim' the 'olives'. The line is therefore, like so many in Shakespeare, potently magical rather than cogently logical.

9–10 *Now . . . fresh*] The image is of reinvigorated plants. The happiness of the poet's love revives as plants do when moisture follows a drought. 'Balmy' in Elizabethan English contains both the element of 'sap' and that of healing or refreshment. The rise of the 'sap' would be promoted by the 'drops' (of rain or dew), and the word 'balmy' itself would readily follow from the word 'drops' by independent verbal association.

10 *My love*] Probably: 'The love I bear *you*, my friend.' Some commentators think that the phrase also means or refers to the Friend himself. We think this unlikely, partly because the transition from such a reference to the Friend in the third person, to the address to him in the second person three lines later, would be pointlessly awkward, and unparalleled in the *Sonnets*. Moreover, if, as we believe, 'my true love' in line 3 refers to the poet's affection, not to the Friend, the change of meaning here would create a marked discrepancy. Lastly, and perhaps most important, there would be the loss of an effective sequence of ideas in the sestet: (1) 'my love for you is still full of vigour'; (2) 'I myself shall outlive death in my verses'; (3) 'In these verses I am creating a lasting monument to you, my friend'.

107 (*continued*)

subscribes] 'submits', 'yields', as in *1H6*, II. iv. 44:

Vernon   Stay, lords and gentlemen, and pluck no more,
            Till you conclude that he, upon whose side
            The fewest roses are cropp'd from the tree,
            Shall yield the other in the right opinion.
Somerset   Good Master Vernon, it is well objected:
            If I have fewest I subscribe in silence.

12 *insults o'er*] 'exults over', 'triumphs over', the only meaning in Shakespeare. Of the modern transitive use ('assail with contemptuous speech') *OED* cites no instance before 1620.

dull and speechless tribes] 'the dull and inarticulate multitude'.

14 *tyrants*] 'cruel despots or usurpers', as always in Shakespeare except for Bottom's reference to 'Ercles' as a 'tyrant', i.e. a roaring, ranting character (and Bottom can hardly be regarded as a linguistic authority!). The reference here would seem therefore to be quite general, for it is hard to imagine any circumstances or time that would have prompted Shakespeare to write of Elizabeth as a 'tyrant' in his sense of the word, nor would the term seem likely to have been applied to a newly ascended monarch received with the acclamation that greeted James. The line would therefore seem to be of questionable utility for dating.

are spent] 'have perished'.

248

107

Not mine own fears, nor the prophetic soul
Of the wide world dreaming on things to come
Can yet the lease of my true love control,
Suppos'd as forfeit to a cónfin'd doom.　　　　　　4
The mortal moon hath her eclipse endur'd,
And the sad augurs mock their own presage;
Incertainties now crown themselves assur'd,
And peace proclaims olives of endless age.　　　　8
Now with the drops of this most balmy time
My love looks fresh; and Death to me subscribes,
Since spite of him I'll live in this poor rhyme
While he insults o'er dull and speechless tribes:　　12
　　And thou in this shalt find thy monument
　　When tyrants' crests and tombs of brass are spent.

108 1 *character*] 'write'.

2 *figur'd*] 'represented'.

true] 'constant'.

3 *what now to register*] So Q and some modern editors. Malone and most modern editors: *new*. We follow Q for two reasons: (1) that emendation can only be justified by a convincing objection to Q; (2) that the vowel change 'new', 'now' is both pleasing in itself and also calls more attention to these words than mere repetition would to the word 'new'.

register] 'record'.

4 *dear*] 'highly valued'.

5 *prayers divine*] i.e. a daily office in set words.

5–8] The consonance of this quatrain depends on the analogy of a daily religious office, first referred to in 'prayers divine' (line 5), developed in line 6 ('each day say o'er the very same (words)'), and reaching a climax in the daring reference to the language of the Lord's Prayer in line 8. 'Counting . . . old' thus means 'not regarding a many times repeated formula as outworn'; and 'thou . . . thine' might be this formula or the substance of it.

7 —*thou mine, I thine*—] Q reads: , *thou mine, I thine*, and is followed by most modern editors. Tucker places *thou . . . thine* in inverted commas, rightly emphasizing that the words express a formula, but his device confines interpretation to strict reportage of actual speech. Cf. *Song of Sol.*, ii. 16.

9–14] Difficult lines which have much troubled commentators. Most have taken them to refer to the Friend's growing old and losing his beauty; but we believe that the lines could also be understood to refer to the repeated formula of line 7. We think the two concurrent meanings are: (1) 'And thus a love that is eternal, in ever vigorous form, takes little account of the impairing of beauty by age, and does not concede importance to the inevitable wrinkles, but makes old age itself give way [possibly also: 'transforms old age into a youth'], since it finds the original idea it had of love perpetuated in the very place where the passage of time and the changes of outward appearance would [or even 'strive to'] make it seem dead'; (2) 'And thus a love that is eternal, expressed in a form of words that never loses its vitality, sets no store by the dusty overlay and wear and tear of time, and does not admit that words shrivel with age, but makes an ancient phrase still his youthful and vigorous servant, finding the original idea of love still perpetuated in that formula which the passage of time and the pattern of the words might seem to render obsolete'. To bring out these meanings we strengthen Q's comma at *place*, and remove that at *bred*. (Q ends each line from 9 to 13 with a comma. Modern editors variously modify.)

108

WHAT'S IN the brain that ink may character
Which hath not figur'd to thee my true spirit?
What's new to speak, what now to register,
That may express my love or thy dear merit?　　4
Nothing, sweet boy; but yet like prayers divine
I must each day say o'er the very same,
Counting no old thing old,—thou mine, I thine—
Even as when first I hallow'd thy fair name.　　8
So that eternal love in love's fresh case
Weighs not the dust and injury of age,
Nor gives to necessary wrinkles place;
But makes antiquity for aye his page,　　12
　　Finding the first conceit of love there bred
　　Where time and outward form would show it dead.

12 *his*] 'its', since love is not here personified.

109 2 *flame*] 'passion'.

qualify] 'abate'.

3 *my self*] So Q. Most modern editors: *myself*, which fails to suggest the meaning 'my true self', 'my real nature', which we take to be present here.

4 *in thy breast*] Tucker compares 22. 6–7.

5 *rang'd*] 'roamed'. Tucker suggests that there is an antithesis with 'travels' in line 6, which implies a definite destination as opposed to random wandering. There does seem to be an antithesis, though not between definiteness of destination and random wandering, but between the latter and journeying with a return to base.

7 *Just . . . time*] 'Faithfully punctual'.

time . . . time] 'hour . . . period of absence'.

with the] Either (1) 'by', or (2) 'along with', 'like'. Both meanings were current.

exchang'd] 'changed', 'altered' (a common use at the time).

8] The suggestion is that his return, punctual, and unchanged in his love, is enough to expunge any previous guilt. This fits the preceding lines better than Tucker's explanation of 'water' as 'tears of repentance'.

10 *all kinds of blood*] Probably 'all dispositions', rather than, as Tucker suggests, 'persons of every kind of sensual passion', which would be less relevant here.

12 *for nothing*] 'for the sake of something utterly insignificant'.

109

Oh NEVER say that I was false of heart,
Though absence seem'd my flame to qualify!
As easy might I from my self depart
As from my soul, which in thy breast doth lie;—   4
That is my home of love: if I have rang'd,
Like him that travels I return again,
Just to the time, not with the time exchang'd,
So that myself bring water for my stain.   8
Never believe, though in my nature reign'd
All frailties that besiege all kinds of blood,
That it could so preposterously be stain'd
To leave for nothing all thy sum of good—   12
    For nothing this wide universe I call,
    Save thou my rose: in it thou art my all.

110 1 Punctuation] Q has a comma after *true*. As Professor Sisson has pointed out (*New Readings in Shakespeare*, II, 213–14), 'editors have silently altered the punctuation to *Alas, 'tis true I have gone . . .*'. (Actually, a number of editors, including Tyler, Wyndham, and Tucker Brooke, retain Q's vital comma after *true*.) As Sisson observes, though the point is not recorded by Rollins, it is not negligible. To insert a comma at *Alas* is, in our view, not only harmless but even desirable; but to omit the comma at *true* radically alters the sense. As Sisson says, 'And pity 'tis 'tis true' is echoed in this line.

2 *motley*] 'fool', 'buffoon'. Some commentators have seen here a direct reference to Shakespeare's profession as an actor, but there seems no conclusive reason for assuming this. On the other hand, there may well be allusion to the parti-coloured costume of the buffoon, with an implication of fickleness in the poet.

to the view] 'in appearance', as contrasted with the reality.

3 *Gor'd . . . thoughts*] Most commentators take 'gor'd' to mean 'wounded'. But to create the parti-colouring in a buffoon's breeches, 'gores' (i.e. shaped pieces of material) of contrasting colours were inserted. This image would cohere better with line 2 and the rest of line 3. The poet's thoughts would thus be represented as parti-coloured. In heraldry, however, a 'gore' was a shaped area interposed between two charges, and was used as a mark of cadency or abatement of honour. There may be a play on both the last two senses here, and the word 'gore' would then stand as intermediary between 'motley' and 'sold cheap'.

what is most dear] Tucker suggests that this means the poet's connexion with, and the regard felt for him by, his friend; but we prefer Professor Tucker Brooke's suggestion, 'merchandiz'd my emotions'.

4] 'Made each new attachment into yet another instance of the old offence of infidelity.'

5 *truth*] 'constancy', 'faithfulness'.

6 *strangely*] i.e. as if it were a stranger.

7 *blenches*] Radically the same word as 'blinks' and 'blenks', meaning sidelong glances.

gave . . . youth] 'rejuvenated my passion (for you)'.

8 *worse essays*] 'experiments in poorer material'.

9 *Now . . . done*] i.e. Now that all that is over.

have . . . end] 'take what shall last for ever' (i.e. my love). Tyrwhitt needlessly conjectured: *save what . . .*, and was followed by Malone and a few other editors.

10–11] 'I will never again sharpen my affections on new material for testing in order to prove the value to me of an older friend.'

254

110

Alas, 'tis true, I have gone here and there
And made myself a motley to the view,
Gor'd mine own thoughts, sold cheap what is most dear,
Made old offences of affections new: 4
Most true it is that I have look'd on truth
Askance and strangely: but, by all above,
These blenches gave my heart another youth,
And worse essays prov'd thee my best of love.   8
Now all is done, have what shall have no end:
Mine appetite I never more will grind
On newer proof to try an older friend—
A god in love, to whom I am confin'd.   12
    Then give me welcome, next my heaven the best,
    Even to thy pure and most most loving breast.

12 *A god in love*] 'Who is a god, as far as my love is concerned.'
to . . . confin'd] Cf. the First Commandment. This forms the climax in
the progression: friend . . . a god . . . the god. For a biblical reference
with the same tendency cf. 108. 8. It may be worth mentioning that
another good meaning for the line could be obtained by omitting the comma
after *love*, viz. that the poet has passed from amorous polytheism to
amorous monotheism.
13 *next . . . best*] 'the nearest thing for me to a welcome into heaven'.

III *General Note:* Malone saw here a lament by Shakespeare at being reduced to the necessity of appearing on the stage, or writing for the theatre, and many other commentators have shared his opinion. There have, however, been dissentients. Bell, in particular (ed. 1855), taxes Malone with failing to explain why Shakespeare should say that his connexion with the theatre, from which he derived all his honours, had fixed a brand on his name. Malone's view seems plausible to us, especially in view of lines 3–4 and 6–7. Bell's objection does not seem cogent, for why should not Shakespeare complain at the disadvantages of his profession and at the low value set on it by society at the time; especially since, at the time when he wrote the *Sonnets*, it may not have brought him much honour?

1 *with*] So Gildon and all modern editors. Q, Benson, Lintot: *wish*. The emendation is obviously correct.

2] 'The goddess who is the guilty cause of my wrongdoings' (probably alluding to 110).

4 *Than public means*] Either 'Than a career involving appearance in public', or, more probably, 'Than a career dependent on public favour'.

which . . . breeds] A phrase which seems to operate on three planes: (1) 'which demands easy familiarity with all and sundry'; (2) 'which engenders in certain company excessively "free" conversation and behaviour'; (3) 'which encourages one to prostitute oneself in such ways'.

10 *Potions of eisel*] 'Draughts of vinegar' (cf. *Ham.* V. i. 299). The great French physician Paré included 'oxymel' (vinegar and honey) among his prescriptions for the plague.

11 *No bitterness*] i.e. there is no bitterness.

12 *to correct correction*] 'Nor will I consider bitter twofold penance undergone with the object of correcting me twice over.' The reading *too*, proposed by Mr. J. S. Kenyon (*TLS*, 18 Oct. 1934, p. 715) is in some ways attractive. Q often spells *too* as *to* (e.g. 38. 3, 61. 14, 74. 12, 83. 7, 86. 2); and *too* would make good sense: 'Nor will I think double penance too "just" a correction.' Unfortunately, however, 'correct' as an adjective is not recorded by *OED* before 1676.

14 *Even that your pity*] 'Even that pity of yours by itself'.

III

O_H, FOR my sake do you with Fortune chide,
The guilty goddess of my harmful deeds,
That did not better for my life provide
Than public means which public manners breeds.   4
Thence comes it that my name receives a brand,
And almost thence my nature is subdu'd
To what it works in, like the dyer's hand.
Pity me then, and wish I were renew'd;   8
Whilst like a willing patient I will drink
Potions of eisel 'gainst my strong infection—
No bitterness that I will bitter think,
Nor double penance to correct correction: 12
    Pity me then, dear friend, and I assure ye
    Even that your pity is enough to cure me.

112 1 *doth*] pl. = 'do', a common Elizabethan form.

1, 2 *doth . . . brow*] Cf. 111. 5. Tucker points out that attempts were often made to fill the hollow scars caused by branding (as in the case of ex-slaves at Rome, when *fronte notata*).

2 *vulgar scandal*] 'common reproach'.

3 *calls me well or ill*] 'gives me a good or bad name'.

4] 'As long as you cover up the evil in me, and give me credit for the good.' Whether the image is from re-turfing or from covering an ugly patch with verdure remains uncertain. No other occurrence of 'o'ergreen' is recorded in *OED*.

allow] The usual explanation, 'approve' or 'commend', though consonant with Elizabethan usage, seems too strong. 'Give credit for' and 'admit' (or 'acknowledge' (cf. Schmidt)) were also current senses.

5 *my all-the-world*] So Malone and many modern editors. Q: *All the world*, followed by other modern editors, who, however, print a lower case *a*. The phrase also occurs in *KJ*. III. iv. 104.

7–8] Steevens (1780) calls this passage 'purblind and obscure'. The sense is probably roughly: 'There being no one else who exists for me and for whom I exist in such a way that they can change my hardened sensibility either for good or for ill.'

8 *or changes right or wrong*] Emendations have been attempted, but are unnecessary. For the curious word order cf. *Lucrece* 875: 'ill-annexèd opportunity/Or kills his life or else his quality'; *Cor*. I. iii. 40: 'A harvestman that's task'd to mow / Or all or lose his hire'; *WT*. IV. iii. 42: 'Or I'll be thine, my fair, / Or not my father's'; *H. VIII*. II. iv. 87 ff: 'Her male issue / Or died where they were made or shortly after / This world had air'd them.'

10 *voices*] 'opinions'.

adder's] Cf. *T&C*. II. ii. 172: 'ears more deaf than adders', and *Ps*. viii. 4: 'the deaf adder that stoppeth her ear' (Authorized Version; 1549 Prayer Book: *ears*).

sense] Singular forms for plurals are not infrequent in Shakespeare and his contemporaries.

It might be asked why, if adders are deaf, they bother to stop their ears. Mr. Lucas has referred us to a passage from Bartholomaeus Anglicus (thirteenth century) which offers an explanation, namely that the wise reptile 'layeth *her one ear to the ground*, and *stoppeth the other with her tail*, and so she heareth not the voice of the charming'.

12] 'See how I excuse my indifference to other people's talk and opinions.' Those commentators who think the 'neglect' was the poet's for his friend seem to be mistaken. ('Neglect' could mean 'indifference' as

112

YOUR LOVE and pity doth the impression fill
Which vulgar scandal stamp'd upon my brow;
For what care I who calls me well or ill,
So you o'er-green my bad, my good allow?   4
You are my all-the-world, and I must strive
To know my shames and praises from your tongue—
None else to me nor I to none alive
That my steel'd sense or changes right or wrong.   8
In so profound abysm I throw all care
Of others' voices that my adder's sense
To critic and to flatterer stoppèd are.
Mark how with my neglect I do dispense: 12
    You are so strongly in my purpose bred
    That all the world besides methinks they are dead.

late as Steele's time. See *Tatler*, 51. 1.) For 'dispense with' = 'excuse',
'condone', cf. *Lucrece* 1070, 1279, 1704.

13] Possibly: 'You are so strongly cherished in my thought' (like a
child in the womb). For this sense of 'breed' see *OED*. 'Purpose' =
literally, subject or matter of thought, cf. Fr. *propos*.

14] A major textual crux. Q: *That all the world besides me thinkes y'are
dead*. Early editors and a few modern editors follow Q. The chief emenda-
tions proposed (variously punctuated) are:

(*a*) *besides methinks are dead* (Capell's and Steevens's conjectures,
followed by a number of modern editors);

(*b*) *besides methinks they are* (or *they're*) *dead* (Malone[2], Dyce and some
modern editors);

(*c*) *besides methinks y'are dead* (Tyler, Tucker).

We have, in substance, adopted (*b*), both (1) for its graphic plausibility (of
which presently) and (2) because it coheres with the argument (cf. note
on line 12). The letter þ (thorn) came to be written *y*; and was eventually
confused with it. The forms *y*[t] (= that) and *y*[e] (= the) are frequently
found in MSS down to the eighteenth century. Our device of printing with
a slur is designed to avoid both the dissyllabic *they are* which would spoil
the rhythm and also the modern colloquial tone of the elided *they're*.

259

113 2 *that which governs*] the physical eye which guides.

3 *part*] Most commentators take this as a verb meaning either (1) 'divide', or (2) 'depart from'. Either sense would involve a characteristic play between the verb 'part' and the adverb 'partly'. 'Divide' suggests that there are two functions, looking at, and taking in what one looks at, which is the eye's most important function, but is not being performed. 'Depart from', however, given its full sense, would wrongly suggest that the second is the eye's only function. On the other hand, Malone, followed by Beeching and Tucker, considers 'part' an adverb, cf. *Oth.* V. ii. 196: 'The wretch hath part confess'd his villainy.' This gives the substance of the passage the same meaning as (1), and the reader is, in our view, free to choose.

his] 'its': so used also in lines 7 and 8.

4 *Seems seeing*] Either (1) 'appears to see', or (2) 'affects to see', without really doing so, i.e. without fulfilling the eye's main function (see lines 5 ff).

5 *heart*] i.e. mind, as in *Ham.* I. v. 121: 'Would heart of man once think it?'

6 *latch*] So Capell, Malone[2], and all modern editors. Q: *lack*. The meaning is 'catch', cf. the latch of a door, and, for the verb, *Macb.* IV. iii. 193–5: 'words, / Which should be howl'd out in the desert air, / Where hearing should not latch them'.

which . . . latch] 'which the eye catches sight of'.

7] 'The mind has no share in the eye's momentary sense-impressions'.

8] 'Nor does the eye's vision retain what it momentarily glimpses'.

9 *rud'st*] 'most uncouth'.

gentlest] 'most elegant'.

10 *sweet favour*] So Benson and all editors except Lintot. Q and Lintot: *sweet-favor*. Delius conjectured: *sweet-favour'd*. The choice lies between (1) removing Q's hyphen and (2) with Delius changing the word to parallel 'deformedst'. There seems no adequate reason for adopting (2). 'Favour' = 'face', in any case, parallels 'creature'.

12 *feature*] 'form', not necessarily of the face.

13 *Incapable of*] 'Unable to take in'. *OED* quotes Hobbes' *Thucydides*: 'Attica being incapable of them itself, they sent our colonies into Ionia.'

14 *maketh mine eye untrue*] So Keightley, Neilson[1]. Q, Malone[2], Dyce, and most modern editors: *maketh mine untrue*. Similarly to Keightley, Lettsom conjectured, and Kittredge and Neilson[2] printed: *mak'th mine eye untrue*; and Capell and Malone[1] conjectured, and some modern editors, including Tucker and Tucker Brooke have printed: *makes mine eye untrue*. Other readings suggested are: Cartwright, *maketh m'eye untrue*; Collier's

113

S INCE I left you, mine eye is in my mind,
And that which governs me to go about
Doth part his function and is partly blind—
Seems seeing, but effectually is out: 4
For it no form delivers to the heart
Of bird, of flower, or shape which it doth latch;
Of his quick objects hath the mind no part,
Nor his own vision holds what it doth catch: 8
For if it see the rud'st or gentlest sight,
The most sweet favour, or deformèd'st creature,
The mountain, or the sea, the day, or night,
The crow, or dove, it shapes them to your feature: 12
   Incapable of more, replete with you,
   My most true mind thus maketh mine eye untrue.

conjecture, *maketh my eyne untrue*; Cartwright's conjecture, also suggested by Walsh, *maketh m'eyne untrue*; White[2], and Tyler's conjecture, *maketh mind untrue*.

Those editors who support Q maintain that 'untrue' is a noun, and cite *M. for M.* II. iv. 171: 'Say what you will, my false outweighs your true.' The supposed *parallel* is not convincing. 'False' and 'true' are there *both* adjectival nouns, whereas 'true' in line 14 is an adjective. Moreover, the transition from adjective to adjectival noun would be clumsy; and, in any case, 'untrue' is never used as a noun elsewhere in the poems or in the plays. A better argument for Q might be that 'untrue' is an adjective qualifying 'mind' (understood). The line would then mean: 'My obsessively loyal affective mind thus renders my cognitive mind inaccurate.' Such a sense would, however, not cohere with the rest of the sonnet or with 114. 1–8, for in both sonnets the relation considered is between eyes and mind, and not between types of mind or aspects of the mind. A similar objection would weigh against White's reading.

The readings *my eyne, m'eyne, m'eye* employ or imply the form 'my' in an unemphasized position before 'eyne' or 'eye', but this is not Shakespeare's customary practice. Even where the possessive adjective is not emphasized we normally find 'mine', 'my' printed in full in the old quartos and folios. Moreover, the unstressed pronunciation of 'my' (or 'm'') would give an uneuphonious line, while 'mine', pronounced 'min', would, to use Abbott's phrase, 'glide easily and unemphatically on to the following vowel', afford a most satisfying rhythm, and emphasize the antithesis between 'eye' and 'mind' which is the substance both of this sonnet and of 114. 1–8. We do, in any case, support the insertion of 'eye', which, since it might well have been spelt 'eie', as in 114. 3 and 114. 11, and would have followed a word of similar aspect, viz. 'mine', could easily have been missed by a compositor.

As to the readings *makes* (and *mak'th*) *mine eye untrue*, these involve a needless emendation of *maketh*, whose 'softened' syllable, as Abbott would have called it, provides a rhythm by no means unfamiliar in Shakespeare. Whether the printer inserted an apostrophe or not, it is evident that the fractional syllable was present. (Cf. e.g. 115. 5, where Q reads *reckening time*, with 115. 8, where Q reads *th' course of altring things*.) For the rhythm cf. *H5*. I. ii. 305: 'Be soon collected and all things thought upon', and *Cor*. II. iii. 231: 'Thinking upon his services, took from you'.

Since I left you, mine eye is in my mind,
And that which governs me to go about
Doth part his function and is partly blind—
Seems seeing, but effectually is out: 4
For it no form delivers to the heart
Of bird, of flower, or shape which it doth latch;
Of his quick objects hath the mind no part,
Nor his own vision holds what it doth catch: 8
For if it see the rud'st or gentlest sight,
The most sweet favour, or deformèd'st creature,
The mountain, or the sea, the day, or night,
The crow, or dove, it shapes them to your feature: 12
   Incapable of more, replete with you,
   My most true mind thus maketh mine eye untrue.

114 1, 3 *Or whether . . . Or whether*] i.e. Is it this ('flattery') or is it that ('alchemy')?

1 *crown'd with you*] 'made a king by having you as my friend'; or even, perhaps, more literally,—the Friend being thought of as the poet's crown.

2 *flattery*] 'pleasing deception', cf. 42. 13–14, and *Oth.* IV. i. 133 (where it = '*self*-deception'): 'she is persuaded I will marry her, out of her own love and flattery, not out of my promise'.

2, 4 Punctuation at ends of lines] Q has question marks. Most modern editors retain that in line 2, but substitute a comma in line 4. The latter measure is well taken, since lines 5–8 amplify 'alchemy'. But the question mark at the end of line 2 then makes line 2 look like an isolated question instead of the first element in a pair of alternatives, and we have therefore substituted a comma there also.

4 *your love*] More likely 'my love for you' than, as Tucker suggests, mutual love.

alchemy] 'magical transmutation of objects'.

5 *monsters*] 'monstrosities', not necessarily animate.

indigest] literally, 'shapeless', 'chaotic', cf. William Browne, *Britannia's Pastorals*, I. ii: 'a chaos rude and indigest'. Cf. *KJ.* V. vii. 26.

8] 'As fast as things on which the beams of his vision fall gather themselves into ('perfect', cf. line 7) shapes', alluding to the theory that vision consisted in the emission of beams from the eye.

9 *'tis . . . seeing*] 'seeing' is emphasized, the meaning being: 'my vision is deceptive'.

10 *my great mind*] Tucker's paraphrase 'His Greatness my mind' probably suggests the tone (cf. lines 1–2).

11 *what . . . 'greeing*] 'what pleases his taste'.

12, 13] The allusion is to the King's taster.

13, 14] Though morally questionable, the argument seems to be that even if (or perhaps 'though') the cup is poisoned the taster's offence is less because (*a*) he himself likes the drink, and (*b*) he drinks it first.

114

Or whether doth my mind, being crown'd with you,
Drink up the monarch's plague, this flattery,
Or whether shall I say mine eye saith true,
And that your love taught it this alchemy,   4
To make of monsters and things indigest
Such cherubins as your sweet self resemble,
Creating every bad a perfect best
As fast as objects to his beams assemble?   8
Oh,'tis the first!—'tis flattery in my seeing,
And my great mind most kingly drinks it up:
Mine eye well knows what with his gust is 'greeing,
And to his palate doth prepare the cup.   12
   If it be poison'd, 'tis the lesser sin
   That mine eye loves it and doth first begin.

115 2 *Even*] 'Namely'.

4 *most full*] 'very strong', not 'strongest'.

5 *reckoning Time*] 'remembering what Time can do'. The construction is taken up in lines 9, 10: 'why, fearing of Time's tyranny, / Might I not . . .'.

million'd] 'numbered by the million'.

7 *Tan*] Cf. 62. 10: 'Beated and chopp'd with tann'd antiquity'.

8 *to . . . things*] Primarily (1) 'into the *direction* dictated by things as they change'; but probably also (2) 'into the *current* of changing circumstances', fusing the two distinct and well-established senses of 'course'.

10 *then*] temporal (preceding 'when'), and stressed.

11 *o'er incertainty*] 'beyond all possibility of doubt'.

12] 'Counting that present moment supreme, and questioning whether any to come could surpass it'.

13 *not*] stressed.

14 *grow.*] So Q, Benson, Lintot, the reading being restored by Tyler, and followed by many modern editors. Gildon and all other editors before Tyler: *grow?*, which is misguidedly adopted by a few modern editors, including Tucker.

13, 14] Wyndham rightly calls this 'a contradiction, not a reiterated interrogative'. The meaning is: 'Love is a baby, and so it would be wrong at any time to say I could not love you more, for that would be to call a baby full grown, whereas it is of the essence of babies to keep growing.' 'Then', temporal in line 10, we take to be inferential in line 13.

115

THOSE LINES that I before have writ do lie,
Even those that said I could not love you dearer:
Yet then my judgment knew no reason why
My most full flame should afterwards burn clearer.   4
But reckoning Time, whose million'd accidents
Creep in 'twixt vows, and change decrees of kings,
Tan sacred beauty, blunt the sharp'st intents,
Divert strong minds to the course of altering things,—   8
Alas! why, fearing of Time's tyranny,
Might I not then say, 'Now I love you best',
When I was certain o'er incertainty,
Crowning the present, doubting of the rest?   12
   Love is a babe: then might I not say so,
   To give full growth to that which still doth grow.

116 *General Note:* In general terms it could, perhaps, be said that the poem is probably neither a plea to the Friend to be faithful, nor an apologia for the poet's own conduct, nor a defence against suspicions of his infidelity, but a meditative attempt to define perfect love.

1 *Let me not*] Not 'Don't allow me . . .' nor 'Don't cause me . . .', but simply 'May I never . . .'.

true] 'faithful'.

2 *impediments*] Alluding to the wording of the banns of marriage (and cf. the marriage service in the Book of Common Prayer): 'If any of you know cause, or just impediment, why these two persons should not be joined together in holy matrimony, ye are to declare it.'

3 *alteration*] Though the word may refer to infidelity, it could equally refer simply to the effects of time on beauty (cf. 115. 7).

4] 'Or inclines to withdraw when the other party's love withdraws'. (For 'bends' = 'inclines' see *OED* senses 14 and 16b.) A number of commentators, however, have seen in 'bends' the sense of deviation from the straight course of love. But 'bends' in that sense would be both redundant and also insufficient, since both lovers could deviate from the straight course towards the same side.

with] not 'in company with' (see note on whole line).

5 *mark*] 'sea-mark'. Cf. *Cor.* V. iii. 74: 'Like a great sea-mark, standing every flaw, / And saving those that eye thee.'

8 *his*] 'its'.

8] i.e. true love is like a guiding star by whose altitude a navigator may direct his course, but whose full value and potentialities can never be completely known. There is no need to tie the sense of 'worth' down, as a number of commentators have, to occult or astrological influence.

9 *Love's . . . fool*] 'True love cannot be made the sport of Time'. Contrast *1H4.* V. iv. 81, 'And thought's the slave of life, and life's Time's fool'; *M. for M.* III. i. 11, 'Merely, thou art death's fool'; Sonnet 124. 13, 'the fools of time', i.e. those whom Time does what he likes with, since they are (124. 3) 'subject to Time's love or to Time's hate'.

10 *bending*] not, as Tucker suggests, an idle epithet if applied to the sickle, but emphasizing the curve that gathers as well as cuts.

11 *his*] i.e. Time's.

11] Time, the menace of lines 9, 10, is here diminished to a series of petty periods.

12 *bears it out*] 'defiantly endures'.

edge] the powerful image of an abyss (as Tucker suggests).

13 *error*] probably here in the strict legal sense of a faulty judgment.

13, 14] 'If this is a false judgment (or a heresy), and this can be proved

116

Let me not to the marriage of true minds
Admit impediments: love is not love
Which alters when it alteration finds,
Or bends with the remover to remove.   4
Oh no! it is an ever-fixèd mark
That looks on tempests and is never shaken;
It is the star to every wandering bark,
Whose worth's unknown although his height be taken. 8
Love's not Time's fool, though rosy lips and cheeks
Within his bending sickle's compass come;
Love alters not with his brief hours and weeks,
But bears it out even to the edge of doom.   12
  If this be error and upon me prov'd,
  I never writ, nor no man ever lov'd.

against me, *and* by citing my own case in evidence, then I've never written
anything, and no man's love has ever been real love.' If nothing but the
correctness of the judgment were in question the ending would be less
strong. The poet is asserting not merely that his definition of true love is
right but also that true love exists, as proved by his own case.

117 1, 2 *that . . . repay*] 'that I have been utterly slack in making a return appropriate to your deserts'.

3 *to call (upon)*] 'to invoke', almost as an act of worship.

4 *bonds*] playing on the two senses (1) obligations, (2) bonds of union.

5 *frequent*] 'familiar'.

with unknown minds] possibly, 'with goodness knows who'.

6] 'And given to the passing hour that attention which is yours by right because you have paid for it the high price of giving me your love'.

7, 8] i.e. I have yielded to every distraction which was most likely to isolate me from you (both spatially and spiritually).

10] Professor Tucker Brooke's paraphrase is excellent: 'Pile on top of what you can prove all that you may suspect'. For 'accumulate' in this transitive sense cf. *Oth.* III. iii. 370: 'On horror's head horrors accumulate'.

11 *level*] far more probably 'aim' than 'range' (see *OED*, sense 9a, where all the examples quoted can mean 'aim', and most cannot mean anything else). Closer still to the sense, in our opinion, would be the phrase Mr. Lucas has suggested to us: 'field of fire'. Cf. *WT.* II. iii. 4–6.

12 *your waken'd hate*] Tucker seems to us wrong in suggesting that the Friend's hate has not yet been awakened. It may well have been ('Accuse' (line 1), 'Book . . . down' (line 9), 'surmise accumulate' (line 10), 'frown' (line 11)). It is indeed not yet fully militant: the emphasis is on 'shoot'.

13 *appeal*] 'plea by way of appeal'.

14 *virtue*] 'strength', cf. Lat. *virtus*.

117

Accuse me thus: that I have scanted all
Wherein I should your great deserts repay;
Forgot upon your dearest love to call,
Whereto all bonds do tie me day by day; 4
That I have frequent been with unknown minds
And given to time your own dear-purchas'd right;
That I have hoisted sail to all the winds
Which should transport me farthest from your sight: 8
Book both my wilfulness and errors down,
And on just proof surmise accumulate;
Bring me within the level of your frown,
But shoot not at me in your waken'd hate: 12
   Since my appeal says I did strive to prove
   The constancy and virtue of your love.

118 *General Note:* As Mrs. Winifred Nowottny rightly observes (*The Language Poets Use*, Athlone Press, London, 1962), this is a much more 'contrived' sonnet than 119.

2 *eager compounds*] 'poignant and sharp dishes (or sauces) to stimulate the appetite'.

3 *prevent*] 'forestall'.

unseen] i.e. of which there is yet no symptom.

4] The old-fashioned purges were very powerful, and could indeed make people feel extremely ill.

5 *ne'er cloying*] So, substantially, Q, Lintot: *nere cloying*, and Harrison: *ne'er cloying*. Benson, Gildon–Evans: *neare cloying*. Theobald's conjecture, Capell, and all the remaining editors: *ne'er-cloying*. The reading of Benson, and of Gildon–Evans might be tempting, in order to avoid the seeming paradox 'full'—'ne'er cloying'; but (1) Q always spells 'near' as *neare*, and (2) it is not a paradox to be replete with a food which still retains its savour for one.

A strong argument against *near* is that to say that the Friend's sweetness was 'near cloying' would be tactlessly offensive, inconsonant with Shakespeare's usual manner of address to the Friend, and also inconsistent with the argument of the rest of this sonnet.

6] i.e. I went on a diet of inferior company.

7 *sick of welfare*] 'surfeited with happiness (lit. 'fine fare')', *not* 'weary of happiness'.

9 *policy*] 'cunning (almost over-cunning) strategy'.

anticipate] 'provide against'.

10 *faults assur'd*] 'actual disorders', 'real illnesses'.

11 *brought to medicine*] 'made a pathological case out of'.

12 *rank of*] 'gross with'.

would] 'seeks to'.

14 *so*] 'in that way'.

118

LIKE AS, to make our appetites more keen,
With eager compounds we our palate urge;
As to prevent our maladies unseen
We sicken to shun sickness when we purge: 4
Even so, being full of your ne'er cloying sweetness,
To bitter sauces did I frame my feeding;
And, sick of welfare, found a kind of meetness
To be diseas'd ere that there was true needing.   8
Thus policy in love, to anticipate
The ills that were not, grew to faults assur'd,
And brought to medicine a healthful state
Which, rank of goodness, would by ill be cur'd: 12
    But thence I learn, and find the lesson true,
    Drugs poison him that so fell sick of you.

119 1 *Siren tears*] 'Tears such as Sirens weep', i.e. tears luring to destruction. Tucker aptly quotes *A Lover's Complaint*, 288: 'what a hell of witchcraft lies / In the small orb of one particular tear'. Whether the reference here is to one individual false woman (e.g. the subject of sonnets 127 onwards) or to a number of false women with whom the poet had experimented seems uncertain.

2 *limbecks*] 'alembics', 'stills', 'retorts'.

within] emphatic. For the contrast of outward and inward cf. 147. 13, 14.

3] 'Checking the sanguine hopes with draughts of fear, and cheering with draughts of hope too desperate fears'.

4 *Still*] 'Always'.

7 *spheres*] Originally the hard but transparent spheres within which were set, or moved, the celestial bodies. By Shakespeare's time the term was often applied to the cavities between 'spheres' in the original sense, in which alone the various moving bodies followed their orbits. The outer spheres were considered nobler than the inner.

7] The 'eyes' may either have been (1) displaced from their proper spheres, contrary to nature, or (2) directing their gaze towards objects in lower spheres. If (1), then 'fitted' would mean 'made to fit', out of their spheres, i.e. fitted into some baser sphere. If (2), 'fitted' would mean 'adapted to fit' (objects in lower spheres). It would seem as if Shakespeare had made no clear distinction between the relation of the eyes to their sphere and the relation of their gaze to its objects.

The closely related metaphorical use of 'sphere' in a social, moral, or spiritual sense is characteristically Shakespearean. Here the poet may be suggesting that the women he has been paying attention to were from a lower spiritual plane than his own, and by implication that his real spiritual plane was that of his friend. The line would afford no support to the view that women were low in the social scale, since Shakespeare customarily speaks of himself as of lower social standing than the Friend.

The line has justifiably proved difficult to commentators. Malone's gloss, however, has been generally accepted: 'How have mine eyes been convulsed during the frantic fits of my feverous love'. But for such a sense of 'fitted' *OED* cites only this line, and though, in view of 'fever', some play on 'fitted' is almost certainly present, we cannot accept Malone's interpretation as the primary meaning.

It is worth adding that Lettsom (1860) conjectured *flitted*, which Dyce mentions in a note, and Massey adopts. Mr. Lucas tells us that this emendation had crossed his mind independently. The verb would need to be transitive and passive. The best sense would be 'removed' (*OED*. 1), which would give a meaning for the line similar to our (1) above.

119

W<small>HAT</small> <small>POTIONS</small> have I drunk of Siren tears
Distill'd from limbecks foul as hell within,
Applying fears to hopes and hopes to fears,
Still losing when I saw myself to win!   4
What wretched errors hath my heart committed
Whilst it hath thought itself so blessèd never!
How have mine eyes out of their spheres been fitted
In the distraction of this madding fever!   8
Oh, benefit of ill! now I find true
That better is by evil still made better,
And ruin'd love when it is built anew
Grows fairer than at first, more strong, far greater: 12
   So I return rebuk'd to my content,
   And gain by ills thrice more than I have spent.

10] 'Superior things are always better [or, possibly, 'realized to be better'] after an intervening experience of evil'. The line gains force from its play on the different senses of the two words 'better'.

11–12] Mr. Lucas has suggested to us that these lines would probably remind Elizabethans of the Terentian, '*amantium irae amoris integratio est*', (*Andria* III. iii. 23).

13 *to my content*] i.e. to that relationship which fully satisfies me.

14 *ills*] So Q, Benson–Evans, and some modern editors. Malone and most modern editors: *ill*. The emendation was evidently intended to enforce a parallel with 'evil' (line 9); but, as Professor Tucker Brooke rightly suggests, Shakespeare is here speaking concretely, not abstractly as in the earlier line. Moreover, the 'potions' and the experiences referred to in the octave are all mentioned in the plural.

120 *General Note:* The sonnet could perhaps be paraphrased roughly as follows: 'The fact that you were once unkind to me serves me a friendly turn; for were I not now able to recall the anguish I then felt, I should be quite beaten down under the sense of the wrong I have done you, unless my fibre were as tough as brass or hammered steel. For if you have been shaken by my unkindness as I was then by yours, you have gone through a hellish time; and I, tyrant-like, have given no leisure to considering how I once suffered from your offence to me (and so how you must now have suffered from mine).

'Would that that time of anguish we then suffered might have put me in mind* in my deepest feelings how sharply real sorrow hurts, and so might indirectly (through impelling me to act) have offered to you now, with the same promptness as you then did to me, the salve of apology and humility which is apt for wounded hearts! But the wrong you did me then now becomes the ransom-money for my offence; for my injury to you expiates yours to me, and you must in turn allow yours to expiate mine.'

9 *remember'd*] (trans.) 'reminded', as often in Shakespeare, e.g. *Temp.* I. ii. 243: 'Let me remember thee what thou hast promis'd'.

11 Punctuation] Q has a comma after the first 'you', and Benson–Evans and several modern editors follow. Walker conjectured, and a number of modern editors, including Beeching, Pooler, and Tucker, have printed, commas after the first 'you' and after 'then'. Capell and the remaining editors have commas after the first 'you' and after 'me'. Certainly either a further comma is required besides that after the first 'you' or else none at all. Both Walker's and Capell's readings make good sense, and it seems to us that the reader is free to take his choice if all commas are removed, which we have therefore done.

tender'd] The grammatical subject is 'our night of woe' (line 9), and this works indirectly by causing the poet to act. See the paraphrase above.

13 *that*] demonstrative, not conjunctive.

* Alternatively: 'Good heavens, that time of anguish might surely have put me in mind . . .'

120

THAT YOU were once unkind befriends me now,
And for that sorrow which I then did feel
Needs must I under my transgression bow,
Unless my nerves were brass or hammer'd steel: 4
For if you were by my unkindness shaken
As I by yours, you have pass'd a hell of time;
And I, a tyrant, have no leisure taken
To weigh how once I suffer'd in your crime.   8
Oh, that our night of woe might have remember'd
My deepest sense how hard true sorrow hits,
And soon to you as you to me then tender'd
The humble salve which wounded bosoms fits!   12
    But that your trespass now becomes a fee:
    Mine ransoms yours, and yours must ransom me.

121 3–4] Two interpretations seem possible: (1) 'And the legitimate pleasure (in some comparatively innocent affair) is destroyed by the reproach that it is vile, though this is only the opinion of those looking on, and not what our own experience tells us'; or (2) 'And one hasn't had the fun, which other people would consider legitimate in such cases, though we should not do so ourselves'. 'So' in (1) would refer to 'vile', and in (2) to 'just pleasure'. It is hard to decide between the two interpretations.

5 *For why*] Possibly just 'Why'. The form survives in dialect.

adulterate] probably simply 'corrupted'.

5, 6] 'Why, just because I have a certain sexual vitality, should other people's shifty corrupted eyes greet it with knowing glances' (or, 'hail it as vicious like themselves')?

7 *frailer*] 'still frailer people than I am'.

8] 'Whose own evil desires and intents interpret conduct as bad which seems to me perfectly blameless'.

9 *I am . . . I am*] 'I admit to what I am, and I am not ashamed of it'. And, as Tucker says, the implication is that no base thinking on their part will make him anything else.

level] 'take aim at'.

10 *reckon up*] 'show the measure of'.

11 *bevel*] 'out of true'.

13, 14] Most commentators either burke the issue or offer unsatisfactory explanations which give the poem a weak ending. We tentatively offer the following interpretation as possible: Taking 'reign' to mean 'exercise authority' (*OED*, sense 2), and the authority here to be that of passing judgment, the sense would be: 'Unless they are maintaining this general proposition: that all men are evil, and that those who judge do so from the standpoint of their own badness' (in which case they are condemned out of their own mouths). Cf. the Cretan liar paradox.

A number of editors have interpreted 'reign' as = 'prosper, flourish'; but this not only gives a weaker ending to the poem but is hard to support from Elizabethan usage.

121

'TIS BETTER to be vile than vile esteem'd,
When not to be receives reproach of being,
And the just pleasure lost which is so deem'd
Not by our feeling but by others' seeing.   4
For why should others' false adulterate eyes
Give salutation to my sportive blood?
Or on my frailties why are frailer spies,
Which in their wills count bad what I think good?   8
No: I am that I am, and they that level
At my abuses reckon up their own;
I may be straight though they themselves be bevel;
By their rank thoughts my deeds must not be shown,— 12
    Unless this general evil they maintain:
    All men are bad and in their badness reign.

122 1 *tables*] 'memorandum book'. Commentators differ as to its contents.

1, 2] Although the general meaning of the quatrain is clear, there are several possibilities as to the precise working of the image in these lines: (1) that the tables contained writings by the Friend; (2) that the writings were by the poet; (3) that the leaves were blank. (1) is questionable, for it would hardly have been tactful for the poet to give away (see line 11), and to say that he had given away, anything so precious and possibly so private. An objection from discretion would also lie against (2). (3) is therefore the most probable interpretation. Such a book would then have been a more valuable gift than it might seem now. See note on 77. It is as if the poet were saying: 'You gave me a pretty book, which I have indeed given away, but in my mind I see its pages filled with eternally memorable writing.' These imagined writings might be the poet's or the Friend's, though the latter seems far less likely. The Friend is nowhere else in the Sonnets referred to as a writer, whereas there is, of course, frequent reference to the poet's recording of the Friend's virtues.

3 *idle rank*] Either (1) 'ineffectual status' of being (*a*) concrete writings, as contrasted with the mind's indelible impressions, or (*b*) unused pages; *or* (2) 'otiose rows of words set out in verses' (otiose because of the permanent record in the poet's mind). For 'rank' = 'lines of verse' cf. *AYLI*. III. ii. 104: 'it is the right butterwomen's rank to market'.

4 *Beyond all date*] 'Beyond all finite time'.

5 *brain and heart*] as seats of thought and feeling.

6 *faculty*] primarily 'capacity'. There may conceivably be an overtone from Canon Law of a 'power' granted to them (by nature).

7 *raz'd oblivion*] 'oblivion, that blots out completely'.

his] 'its'.

8 *thy . . . miss'd*] 'the record of you can never be wanting', or, just possibly, 'can never be deficient'.

9 *That poor retention*] 'That inadequate receptacle' (abstract for concrete).

10 *tallies*] sticks which were notched for reckoning.

thy . . . score] 'to make an entry of my dear love for you in my account'.

11, 12] 'And so I had the temerity to give them away, so as to rely entirely on "the tablets of my mind", on which I can record more of you (than on those you gave me).'

13 *adjunct*] 'aide-mémoire'.

14 *import*] 'imply'.

122

Thy gift, thy tables, are within my brain
Full character'd with lasting memory,
Which shall above that idle rank remain
Beyond all date even to eternity,—   4
Or at the least so long as brain and heart
Have faculty by nature to subsist;
Till each to raz'd oblivion yield his part
Of thee, thy record never can be miss'd.   8
That poor retention could not so much hold,
Nor need I tallies thy dear love to score;
Therefore to give them from me was I bold,
To trust those tables that receive thee more.   12
   To keep an adjunct to remember thee
   Were to import forgetfulness in me.

123 *General Note:* This sonnet has been used for dating the *Sonnets*, a problem with which, however, the present edition is not concerned.

2] Generally: 'Your vast buildings erected by modern techniques'; possibly also, in particular: 'Your spires and pinnacles [or 'obelisks' (Hotson)] . . .'.

3 *nothing . . . nothing*] 'in no way . . . in no way'. The Elizabethan pronunciation 'nō-thing' would bring this out.

4 *dressings . . . sight*] 're-erections of things we've seen before'. (See *OED*, 'dress' (vb.), sense 1.)

5 *Our dates*] 'the spans of our lives'.

admire] 'wonder at', 'gape at'.

7 *born*] So Gildon and almost all modern editors. Q, Benson, Lintot, Wyndham, Walsh: *borne*, which Wyndham construes as the modern 'bourn'. The modern 'bourn' is spelt *borne* in F¹ in half the cases in which it occurs. Moreover, 'bourn' would give quite a good sense here: 'the limit (or height) of our ambition'. But, in view of lines 6 and 8, *born* seems the better reading: 'we persuade ourselves that they are newly born to match our desires', 'they' being the things Time foists upon us.

8 *think*] 'call to mind'.

that . . . told] 'that we have heard all this before'.

9] 'I set no store by either your historical records or you yourself.'

11] 'And' is stressed. 'For your chronicles of the past and our present experience are both utterly deceptive.'

doth] a common early form of the plural.

12] i.e. Time is always in such a hurry that we can never get things into proper perspective. The receding past disproportionately loses significance, and the ever-new present looms disproportionately large.

123

No, TIME, thou shalt not boast that I do change:
Thy pyramids built up with newer might
To me are nothing novel, nothing strange,—
They are but dressings of a former sight.   4
Our dates are brief, and therefore we admire
What thou dost foist upon us that is old,
And rather make them born to our desire
Than think that we before have heard them told.   8
Thy registers and thee I both defy,
Not wondering at the present nor the past;
For thy recórds and what we see doth lie,
Made more or less by thy continual haste.   12
   This I do vow and this shall ever be:—
   I will be true despite thy scythe and thee.

124 1 *dear love*] 'heartfelt devotion', with the implication also of great value.

but the child of state] i.e. the mere offspring of circumstance, e.g. of the Friend's power and prosperity.

2, 3 *Fortune's* . . . *Time's*] We follow almost all modern editors in supplying initial capitals, since personification is so clearly intended.

2] 'It might as a mere capricious birth of Fortune have no proper father (as the Friend in fact is)'.

3, 4] The insecurity of the 'child of state' is compared to the effects of the caprice of Time in selecting plants to throw away as weeds or to cherish as flowers. The ellipsis of 'are' in line 4 ('(are) gathered') can readily be paralleled in Shakespeare (see Abbott, *Shakespearian Grammar*, s. 403).

5 *far from accident*] 'out of the reach of chance'.

6 *suffers not*] 'does not deteriorate'.

smiling pomp] 'happy and glorious circumstances'.

falls] 'succumbs'.

7 *thrallèd discontent*] i.e. bottled-up resentment.

6, 7] The images seem to be of courtly success, and of being waylaid by a thug. Both images, however, seem to work in a double way, viz. as referring (1) to external environment affecting the poet, and (2) to the poet's own reactions.

8] 'To which the temptations of today expose the likes of me.' (For 'fashion' = 'kind', 'sort', cf. *Two G.* V. iv. 61: 'Thou friend of an ill fashion'.)

9] It is not clear whether 'policy' is thought of as master or enemy; but the general effect is much the same.

policy] 'expediency'.

heretic] i.e. fellow of false principles.

10] 'Which acts according to a short-term view' (whereas love fixes its mind on the permanent).

11 *all alone*] i.e. in stout independence.

hugely politic] 'boldly and supremely prudent'.

12] Some commentators, e.g. Capell and Beeching, have suggested emending 'grows' in various ways so as to make the two halves of the line parallel; but, as in line 3, they are antithetical. The poet's constant love does not fluctuate with favour or disaster. ('Shower' often had a stronger sense in Elizabethan English than it does today. It often meant 'downpour'. This survives in the modern *verb*.)

13 *To this*] i.e. to the supreme satisfaction of this invulnerable attitude.

13, 14] 'I cite in support of this the cases of [or 'I call to give their testimony'] those utter time-servers [or 'those dupes of Time'] who, after

124

I F M Y dear love were but the child of state,
It might for Fortune's bastard be unfather'd,
As subject to Time's love or to Time's hate,
Weeds among weeds or flowers with flowers gather'd. 4
No, it was builded far from accident;
It suffers not in smiling pomp, nor falls
Under the blow of thrallèd discontent
Whereto the inviting time our fashion calls; 8
It fears not policy, that heretic
Which works on leases of short-number'd hours:
But all alone stands hugely politic,
That it nor grows with heat nor drowns with showers. 12
    To this I witness call the fools of time,
    Which die for goodness, who have liv'd for crime.

a life of wrong-doing, renounce their time-serving [or 'their criminal follies'] to die for permanent values'. Various allusions have been suggested, e.g. to Jesuit conspirators, to the Gunpowder Plot, to Essex and his followers, to Foxe's Martyrs; but the evidence for any of these is far too tenuous to carry conviction.

125 1 *Were it aught to me*] 'Would there be any advantage to me (as you are suggesting) if . . .?'

1 . . . canopy] Alluding to the canopy of state carried over sovereigns by important or honoured dignitaries. The poet is repudiating the informer's suggestion that in honouring the Friend he is aiming at acquiring reputation for himself.

2 *my extern*] i.e. my public tributes.

the outward] possibly (1) the Friend as a public figure, possibly (2) his physical beauty, possibly both.

3] 'Or planned an eternity of poetic fame for myself (by such merely adulatory effusions)'.

4 *proves*] So Q and a few modern editors, including Tyler, Wyndham, Butler, Tucker. Gildon² and most modern editors: *prove*. Even to achieve a plural the emendation would be unnecessary, the *-s* form being common enough in Shakespeare. But, as Tyler suggests, it is 'eternity' that 'proves more short' than 'waste or ruining'.

4] 'Which, paradoxically, turns out to be briefer than the time required to run through an estate by extravagance.' 'Waste', in the legal sense of injuring an inheritance by unauthorized acts, is frequent in the *Sonnets*, and here leads naturally to the imagery of the second quatrain.

5 *dwellers . . . favour*] 'those who attach excessive importance to outward show'. 'Dwellers', however, also continues the property image, harking back to 'waste or ruining' (line 4) and anticipating 'rent' (line 6).

6-7 *rent, . . . sweet*] So most modern editors. Q: *rent . . . sweet; Forgoing. . . .* The antithesis in line 7 is lost by Q's punctuation, which also results in an untypical movement and construction.

7] That is, forgoing the enjoyment of simplicity for cloying elaboration. 'Sweet' is probably a noun.

compound . . . simple] possibly, in view of line 6, playing on compound and simple interest.

savour—] So Tucker, bringing out the character of line 8 as a sidelong comment. Q: *savour,*.

8] 'Wretchedly prosperous people, bankrupted for love of spectacle'. Some commentators take 'thrivers' as neutral, thereby destroying the irony and paradox.

5-8] The image is of court life, but the reference is still to the false hopes of adulatory writing.

9] The sense seems to be: 'No, let me be dutiful, not with sycophancy in the court, but with genuine devotion in the intimacy of your heart.'

10 *free*] i.e. freely given.

11 *not . . . seconds*] 'unadulterated', 'entirely of the highest quality'.

286

125

W ERE IT aught to me I bore the canopy,
With my extern the outward honouring,
Or laid great bases for eternity
Which proves more short than waste or ruining?   4
Have I not seen dwellers on form and favour
Lose all and more by paying too much rent,
For compound sweet forgoing simple savour—
Pitiful thrivers in their gazing spent?   8
No, let me be obsequious in thy heart,
And take thou my oblation, poor but free,—
Which is not mix'd with seconds, knows no art
But mutual render, only me for thee.   12
    Hence, thou suborn'd informer! a true soul
    When most impeach'd stands least in thy control.

The t erm 'seconds' is still common in many trades, e.g. flour-milling glassware and pottery, textiles.

11 *art* Punctuation] So some modern editors. Q has a comma, which other modern editors retain. The disadvantage of retaining the comma in a modern edition is that it might well seem to confine the sense of 'art' to 'craftiness'; whereas, in our view, the word has here a double aspect: (1) 'craftiness' (of cooks, courtiers, and unscrupulous tradesmen); (2) simply 'skill' (of the lover who knows what is best both for himself and for his beloved).

12 *render*] 'exchange', rather than, as some commentators have suggested, 'surrender'.

13 *thou . . . informer!*] It is likely to be fruitless, and certainly unnecessary, to search for an identifiable informer. The general idea of a detractor whose accusations are imagined in lines 1–8 seems sufficient.

126 *General Note:* This sonnet differs from all the rest in length (twelve lines) and structure (couplets). Many Elizabethan 'sonnets' varied in length and structure from what is now considered a 'sonnet'. The great majority were, however, of fourteen lines. Q prints brackets round the blank space for an imaginary final couplet, the printer evidently considering that the poem must be incomplete. In fact, however, the poem (such as it is) forms a complete whole.

1 *lovely*] It is not clear which of the two then commonest senses, (1) 'lovable', (2) 'beautiful', is present or dominant here.

boy] Some commentators consider the 'boy' to be Cupid; but this would not fit well with lines 9–12. Beeching cogently urges that Cupid is immortal, whereas the point of this poem is that mortal beauty must fade at last. The 'boy' seems more likely to be the Friend. The theme (youth, beauty, and time) is that of many of the sonnets 1–17, where, indeed, the phrase 'thy sweet self' (line 4) is applied to the Friend twice, and the adjective 'sweet' some half a dozen times. There seems, indeed, some plausibility in the view of Beeching and some other commentators that 126 forms an Envoy to the poems addressed to the Friend. On the other hand, the style is not only greatly inferior to that of the immediately preceding sonnets but also no more than a pale reflection of that of sonnets 1–17, which it more closely resembles. If the poem be such an Envoy, it seems a somewhat deliberate attempt to recapture something of the spirit of the opening sonnets in the teeth of advancing age.

2] So Tyler and several modern editors. Q: *times fickle glasse, his sickle, hower* (with a long *s* for *sickle*), substantially followed by some modern editors, including Pooler and Professor Tucker Brooke. Lintot: *his fickle hower*, followed by some modern editors, including Tucker. This seems an unnecessary and even weakening emendation. Q's reading indicates three possessions of Time. It has the disadvantages (1) of demanding that we understand the possessive adjective 'his' before 'hour', and (2) of offering a third object ('hour') of an entirely different type from the other two (measure of time as contrasted with concrete object—it could not *on this reading* be 'hour-glass', since that would be the meaning of 'glasse'). The reading we have adopted makes 'sickle' characterize 'hour', indicating the hour when the sickle strikes. The Friend is then said to control the capricious passage of time, and thus the coming of the mortal hour.

3 *Who . . . grown*] A paradoxical statement of the fact that by the passage of time which should make beauty wane, the Friend has grown in beauty.

3–4 *and therein . . . withering*] 'and by this you have pointed the contrast with your lovers whose beauty has withered'.

126

O THOU my lovely boy, who in thy power
Dost hold Time's fickle glass, his sickle hour;
Who hast by waning grown, and therein show'st
Thy lovers withering as thy sweet self grow'st;   4
If Nature, sovereign mistress over wrack,
As thou goest onwards, still will pluck thee back,
She keeps thee to this purpose, that her skill
May Time disgrace and wretched minutes kill.   8
Yet fear her, O thou minion of her pleasure!
She may detain but not still keep her treasure:
Her audit, though delay'd, answer'd must be,
And her quietus is to render thee.   12

4 *lovers*] *possibly*, as Pooler suggests, just 'friends'.

5 *wrack*] 'decay'.

6 *still*] 'always', as again in line 10.

7 *to*] 'for'.

8 *Time disgrace*] 'put Time out of countenance'. See Glossary *sub* 'disgrace'.

minutes] So Capell MS, and all modern editors except Harrison. Q:
mynuit , followed by Harrison (*minute*). The minute was then the smallest
measure of time. Seconds came into use later in the seventeenth century.
The sense would be that Nature intends to obliterate even the paltriest
unit of time.

9 *fear*] 'do not rely on'.

minion] possibly at once (1) 'darling' and (2) 'slave'.

10 Punctuation] Q has a comma after *detain*. Most modern editors
add another at *keep*. Two commas or none seem called for in a modern
edition; and two seem unnecessarily heavy.

11, 12] 'However long Nature delays, she must in the end account to
Time for all her creatures, and to receive her final quittance she must
ultimately surrender you.' Cf. line 10, where 'may' = 'can'.

127 *General Note:* There is a fair measure of agreement among commentators that sonnets 127–52 form a group concerned mainly with the poet's relations (real or imaginary) with a dark woman (or lady). On the order within the group, however, very little agreement has been expressed, but no really satisfactory rearrangement has been proposed.

Some critics suggest that a number of the sonnets of this group refer to the same events as sonnets 33–42, where the poet complains of the wrong done him by the Friend.

As to the 'darkness' of the Dark Woman, it is worth bearing in mind that at least until late in the Elizabethan period, blonde beauty was the ideal in courtly and literary circles. Yet the hair of Daniel's Delia, which was golden in 1592, had become sable in 1601, and it seems possible that some general shift in taste under French and Italian influence took place (see M. Françon, *Notes sur l'esthétique*, Harvard University, Cambridge, Mass., 1939). Lines 1–4 of this sonnet may mirror such a shift, but the tone of this and other sonnets of the group (e.g. 131, 132) suggests that Shakespeare is also, in part, attacking a convention which had not yet died.

1 *In the old age*] 'Formerly'; not necessarily a long time ago.

1, 2] 'In the old days dark colouring was not considered beautiful (with a play on 'blonde'), or, if it were admired, it was not *called* beautiful.'

3 *successive heir*] 'heir by succession'.

4] 'And (blonde) beauty dubbed a bastard'.

5 *since*] Probably temporal. The sense 'because' (supported by Tucker) would result in redundancy with 'For'.

5, 6 *each . . . face*] 'everybody has usurped Nature's power and become able to paint up as a blonde'.

7, 8] 'Fresh and natural blonde beauty is held neither in repute nor in reverence, but either its appearance is profanely assumed or it is utterly discredited.'

9 *Therefore*] 'And that is the reason why . . .' the poet either (1) has in fact chosen a dark mistress, or (2) imagines a dark mistress as the object of his choice (see General Note, above).

9, 10] Q reads 'my Mistersse eyes' (line 9) and 'Her eyes' (line 10); and is followed by a number of modern editors, including Dowden, Tyler, Wyndham, and Pooler. The at least apparently lame repetition has caused scholars to emend. The chief emendations are: (1) Capell MS: *eyes* (line 9) . . . *hairs* (line 10); (2) Walker, Delius, and Conrad's conjecture, printed by Hudson[2] and Tucker: *hairs . . . eyes*; (3) Staunton and Brae's conjecture, printed by the Globe editors, and widely followed: *brows . . . eyes*; (4) Staunton's other conjecture, followed only by Tucker Brooke: *eyes . . . brows*.

127

IN THE old age black was not counted fair,
Or if it were it bore not beauty's name;
But now is black beauty's successive heir,
And beauty slander'd with a bastard shame: 4
For since each hand hath put on Nature's power,
Fairing the foul with Art's false borrow'd face,
Sweet Beauty hath no name, no holy bower,
But is profan'd, if not lives in disgrace.   8
Therefore my mistress' eyes are raven black,
Her brow so suited, and they mourners seem
At such who not born fair no beauty lack,
Slandering creation with a false esteem: 12
    Yet so they mourn becoming of their woe,
    That every tongue says beauty should look so.

The argument against *eyes* in line 9 that ravens' eyes are not black seems to us irrelevant. Secondly, if a compositor were responsible for a mistaken repetition he would be more likely to repeat *eyes* from line 9 than to anticipate it from line 10. Thirdly, Tucker's argument against *eyes* in line 9 that 'and they' (line 10) best suits the eyes, seems invalid, since 'they' can perfectly well refer back to line 9. There seems, therefore, no cogent reason to emend *eyes* in line 9. It has been suggested that *brows* would give an attractive alliteration with 'black' in line 9; but it has as great an attraction if it occurs in line 10.

As to line 10, emendation seems desirable. If *eyes* were retained, 'suited' could only mean 'clothed', but the phrase would then be redundant, since the eyes have already been called 'black'. As between *hairs* and *brows*, *brows* seems preferable (1) because it would give a richer sense to 'mourners' (line 10) and to 'look' (line 14), since 'hairs' could only have the colour of mourning, whereas 'brows' (in the common Shakespearean sense of 'countenance' (Schmidt, sense 3)) could give it emotional expression; (2) because *brows* provides a strong alliteration with 'black'; (3) because, in a remarkable parallel passage in *LLL* (IV. iii. 247–65), it is the lady's 'brows' (or 'brow', see below) that are said to be 'deck'd' in black. The passage is as follows:

King	By heaven, thy love is black as ebony.
Berowne	Is ebony like her? O wood divine!
	A wife of such wood were felicity.
	Oh! who can give an oath? where is a book?

          250

      That I may swear beauty doth beauty lack,
      If that she learn not of her eye to look:
      No face is fair that is not full so black.

King   Oh paradox! Black is the badge of hell,
      The hue of dungeons and the school of night;   255
      And beauty's crest becomes the heavens well.

Berowne Devils soonest tempt, resembling spirits of light.
      Oh! if in black my lady's brows be deck'd,
      It mourns that painting and usurping hair
      Should ravish doters with a false aspect;   260
      And therefore is she born to make black fair.
      Her favour turns the fashion of the days,
      For native blood is counted painting now;
      And therefore red, that would avoid dispraise,
      Paints itself black, to imitate her brow.   265

None of the proposed emendations could pretend to any graphic plausibility. But graphic plausibility is not in point. The mistaken repetition of *eyes* (if mistake it be) could hardly be attributed to misreading a manuscript.

Of the emendations so far proposed, *eyes . . . brows* seems to us the best. But we think that a still better reading in line 10, for a modern edition, is the singular *brow* (in the sense of whole countenance, see above). Its advantages over *brows* are as follows: (1) *brows* strongly suggests to a modern reader 'eyebrows', which (*a*) would annul the lively ambiguity of 'suited' (see below), confining its meaning to 'matched', and (*b*) would undesirably restrict the sense of the concluding lines of the sonnet; (2) *brows* would make it readily possible to misunderstand 'they' (line 10) to refer only to the 'brows'.

In connexion with our proposed reading it is worth noting two points about the passage from *LLL*: (1) As printed in the primary text (the 1598 Quarto) and in the Folio, as well as in most of the recent editions, lines 258–9 naturally raise the question whether 'It' (line 259) refers back to 'black' or to 'brows' (line 258). If to 'brows', then 'brows' must be taken as a singular. Some early editors, e.g. Theobald and Johnson–Steevens, do

127

In THE old age black was not counted fair,
Or if it were it bore not beauty's name;
But now is black beauty's successive heir,
And beauty slander'd with a bastard shame: 4
For since each hand hath put on Nature's power,
Fairing the foul with Art's false borrow'd face,
Sweet Beauty hath no name, no holy bower,
But is profan'd, if not lives in disgrace. 8
Therefore my mistress' eyes are raven black,
Her brow so suited, and they mourners seem
At such who not born fair no beauty lack,
Slandering creation with a false esteem: 12
    Yet so they mourn becoming of their woe,
    That every tongue says beauty should look so.

read *brow*; (2) lines 264–5 refer to women painting their faces 'black' (i.e. dark) to imitate Berowne's mistress's 'brow', which therefore clearly means 'countenance', not 'eyebrow' or even 'forehead'.

10 *suited*] A Janus-faced word here, looking back, with the meaning 'matched', to 'eyes' in line 9, and forward, with the meaning 'dressed', to 'mourners' in line 10.

they] Probably referring both to 'eyes' (line 9) and 'brow' (line 10) as mourners.

11 *At*] 'over the case of'.

such . . . lack] i.e. those who have artificially acquired the blonde beauty they were not born with.

12 *creation*] Despite Q's capital C, not 'the whole Creation' (first *OED* quotation 1611), but 'Nature's process of creating' (cf. 'Nature's power' (line 5)).

with . . . esteem] possibly (1) by giving the false impression that they can do what Nature does; or (2) by preferring their own creation to Nature's; or (3) by causing other people to have false standards of beauty.

13] 'Yet they mourn in a way that so graces their woe . . .'. For the construction 'becoming of', cf. 150. 5. We follow the text of Q, as Tucker does. Most modern editors insert a comma after *mourn*, which separates 'so' too sharply from 'becoming', which it modifies.

14 *look*] both (1) have that colouring, and (2) have that expression.

128 2 *that blessèd wood*] the keys of the virginals, blessed by her touch.

3 *sway'st*] 'governest', cf. a monarch's sway.

4 *that . . . confounds*] 'that amazes my ear'.

5 *envý*] The stress on the second syllable was frequent in Elizabethan English.

jacks] Strictly, the vertical pieces of wood at the far ends of the balanced keys. The jacks rose sharply when the keys were depressed, and plectra inserted in the jacks plucked the strings. But the playing hands would not touch the 'jacks'. Are 'jacks' and 'chips' (keys) being confused? Secondarily, 'jacks' may suggest 'saucy fellows', then a frequent sense.

6] The virginals were played with the fingers flatter than when we play the piano, but even so, it would be difficult for the rising keys to touch the palm of the hand. Shakespeare might, however, mean by 'tender inward' the underside of the fingers.

It may be worth mentioning that the Elizabethans attached different degrees of amorousness to touching the back of the fingers, the inner side of the fingers, or the palm of the hand, for which cf. *WT*. I. ii. 126: 'Still virginalling / Upon his palm?'

9–10 *state And situation*] Not redundant. Their 'state' is their position in the hierarchy of being, while their 'situation' is simply their physical position.

11 and 14 *thy fingers . . . thy fingers*] Q reads *their fingers* each time. First emended to *thy* by Gildon[1] (line 11) and Benson (line 14). Almost all modern editions follow.

128

How oft, when thou, my music, music play'st
Upon that blessèd wood whose motion sounds
With thy sweet fingers, when thou gently sway'st
The wiry concord that mine ear confounds,   4
Do I envý those jacks that nimble leap
To kiss the tender inward of thy hand,
Whilst my poor lips, which should that harvest reap,
At the wood's boldness by thee blushing stand!   8
To be so tickled they would change their state
And situation with those dancing chips
O'er whom thy fingers walk with gentle gait,
Making dead wood more blest than living lips.   12
    Since saucy jacks so happy are in this,
    Give them thy fingers, me thy lips to kiss.

129 1, 2] 'Lust', not 'expense', is the grammatical subject.

1 *expense*] 'expenditure', or, possibly, 'squandering' (see note on 'waste of shame', below).

spirit] Primarily 'vital energy'. The reference is probably to the subtle fluid or rarefied substance formerly supposed to course through the blood and to activate the chief organs of the body. It was of three kinds, 'animal' (springing from the brain), 'vital' (springing from the heart), and 'natural' (originating in the liver). It is impossible to say whether the reference here is to one of these exclusively, or generally to all.

There is also, however, the sense 'spirituality', this quality being thought of as dissipated in the grossness of sensuality.

waste of shame] Probably 'shameful orgy'. 'Waste' never elsewhere in Shakespeare means 'desert', except perhaps in *Ham*. I. ii. 198. Yet the lines do suggest an aftermath of spiritual desolation. In addition there may be play on 'waste/waist', as in *MW*. I. iii. 46, 2 *H4*. I. ii. 160–2. F1 spells both senses there *wast(e)*; while in *Ham*. II. ii. 236 the sense 'waist' is spelt *waste*. Indeed, the spellings 'waste/waist' overlapped into the eighteenth century.

3 *full of blame*] 'packed with guilt' or, just possibly, 'full of harm'. 'Blame', in either of these archaic senses, is a strong word here, and gathers further sense from its alliteration with 'bloody'.

4 *extreme*] Here and in line 10 evidently bearing the strong sense 'violent'.

rude] 'brutal' (Schmidt).

not to trust] i.e. 'not to be trusted' (cf. *TN*. III. iii. 18: 'What's to do?')

9 *Mad*] So Gildon[1] and all modern editions collated. Q: *Made*. Q's reading certainly makes sense, with the complement 'so' = 'mad'; but either reading requires a mental transition (e.g. either after line 8 or after line 10) from the 'taker' (the lustful man) of line 8 back to the 'lust' of line 2—which is, in any case, the required antecedent of the 'bliss', 'woe', 'joy', 'dream' of lines 11 and 12. *Made* could be a misprint, or an alternative spelling for *Mad*, which is sometimes spelt *made* in quartos and folios of the plays.

10 *in quest to have*] So Capell MS, Malone, and all modern editors. Q: *in quest, to have*. We cannot accept the interpretation of Riding and Graves in *A Survey of Modernist Poetry*, London, 1927, for while they assert that the Q punctuation makes *lust itself* 'extreme' *after* the experience (i.e. *Had*), it is the *revulsion* that is *then* extreme.

11 *prov'd, a very woe*] So Capell MS, Malone, and all modern editors except Harrison. Q: *proud and very woe*. Q follows normal contemporary practice in printing u for modern v, and omits the apostrophe in abbrevi-

129

THE EXPENSE of spirit in a waste of shame
Is lust in action; and till action, lust
Is perjur'd, murderous, bloody, full of blame,
Savage, extreme, rude, cruel, not to trust;   4
Enjoy'd no sooner but despisèd straight;
Past reason hunted; and no sooner had,
Past reason hated, as a swallow'd bait
On purpose laid to make the taker mad,—   8
—Mad in pursuit, and in possession so;
Had, having, and in quest to have, extreme;
A bliss in proof; and prov'd, a very woe;
Before, a joy propos'd; behind, a dream.   12
   All this the world well knows; yet none knows well
   To shun the heaven that leads men to this hell.

ated -ed endings. And a careless compositor could easily misread an *a* as an
ampersand.

  14 *the heaven*] Possibly, as Tucker suggests, referring both to (1) the
experience of bliss, and to (2) the woman who provides it. (2) might either
mean the poet's mistress or women in general.

  hell] Besides (1) the experience of torment, there may also be (2) a
sexual reference (cf. 144. 12).

130 *General Note:* This sonnet is not a denigration of the attractions of the poet's mistress, or even an admission that she had not the conventional beauties and graces. It is a satirical repudiation of false comparisons current in contemporary poetry ('couplements of proud (but false) compare'). The poet is affirming by implication the physical reality of the woman. In line 3, for example, he is not saying that his mistress's breasts are 'dun', but denying that the colour of snow would be appropriate to her breasts, and, perhaps, by implication, to those of any desirable woman, since 'any she' would be 'belied with' that 'false compare'. Modern scholars have collected some notable examples of such hyperboles, some of which we cite below.

It is possible that, as Mr. Lucas has suggested to us, behind Shakespeare's paradoxical praises of the Dark Lady there lies a love-hate for her 'black deeds' that makes him willing, under the flattering caresses, to wound sadistically.

1] Cf. Linche, *Diella* (1596), Sonnet 31. 3: 'Fair suns that shine when Phoebus' eyes are gone!'

2] Cf., e.g., *Diella* again, Sonnet 31. 2: 'Sweet lips of coral hue but silken softness'.

lips'] So Capell and all modern editors. Q, some early editors and Tyler: *lips*.

4] Cf. Spenser, *Epithalamion*, 154: 'Her long loose yellow locks lyke golden wyre'.

Line 4 is a more elaborate satiric turn than the preceding lines. The drift is: 'If you poets think it is praising your mistresses to say their hairs are golden wires, I'll offer you a *reductio ad absurdum*: "On my mistress's head there are black wires growing!"'

5 *damask'd*] This is the only use in Shakespeare of 'damask' as a verb. 'Damask' occurs four times in Shakespeare as an attributive adjective and twice as an adjectival noun. As a simple substantive it never occurs in Shakespeare.

The word 'damask' derives from 'Damascus', and it was already applied as a noun to three objects originating there:

(1) a silk cloth whose weave involved a pile that produced a pattern (*OED.* 1430–) or a linen whose weave produced a similar effect (*OED.* 1542–);

(2) engraved or inlaid patterning of steel (*OED.* 1603–, though 'damaskeen' occurs in this connexion as an adjective as early as 1551);

(3) a rose (*Rosa damascena*) (*OED.* 1540–).

298

130

MY MISTRESS' eyes are nothing like the sun;
Coral is far more red than her lips' red;
If snow be white, why then her breasts are dun;
If hairs be wires, black wires grow on her head: 4
I have seen roses damask'd, red and white,
But no such roses see I in her cheeks;
And in some perfumes is there more delight
Than in the breath that from my mistress reeks: 8
I love to hear her speak, yet well I know
That music hath a far more pleasing sound;
I grant I never saw a goddess go,—
My mistress when she walks treads on the ground.   12
    And yet by heaven I think my love as rare
    As any she belied with false compare.

The primary sense of the verb in line 5 would seem to derive from sense
(1) of the noun, and to be: 'patterned'. In so far as these lines would also
call up the image of the damask rose, it is worth pointing out, however,
that the original damask rose was not variegated but what we now call
'pink', a word unknown to the Elizabethans as a colour term (*OED.* 1720–).
Early botanical writers, e.g. Lyte (1578), Gerard (1597), Parkinson (1629),
Hanmer (1659), use such descriptions of the colour of *Rosa damascena* as
'pale red', 'carnation' (i.e. flesh colour), 'blush', 'deep blush', 'incarnate'.
Lyte writes of the colour as 'neither redde nor white but of a mixt colour
betwixt red and white'. It is very likely, though, that Shakespeare had in
mind not the original damask rose, but the rose referred to by Parkinson
(*Paradisi in Sole Paradisus Terrestris*, 1629) as *Rosa versicolor*, and by Hanmer
(*MS Garden Book of 1659*, ed. I. Elstob, 1933) as 'the Variegated Damaske',
and by both as 'the York and Lancaster'. This is described by several seven-
teenth-century writers as bearing sometimes self white and self blush
blooms on the same tree, sometimes striped or variegated flowers, and
sometimes even all at the same time. The image in this line would then be
the patterning of the mistress's cheeks in blush colour and white, thus

blending the image of the damasked cloth with that of the rose. A subsidiary train of associations might be of the soft texture both of silk damask and of rose petals.

Such a variegation of hue in a woman's complexion was highly esteemed in Elizabethan court circles, where an even complexion would have been considered dull. In consonance with the whole drift of the sonnet Shakespeare is saying, in effect, that he will not praise his mistress as bearing the conventional colouring.

For an example in a contemporary poet of the use of the damask rose in a hyperbole cf. Barnes, *Parthenophil and Parthenophe*, Ode 16:

> 'Her cheeks to damask roses sweet
> In scent and colour were so like,
> That honey bees in swarms would meet
> To suck!'

7, 8] Linche, *Diella*, Sonnet 31. 4, writes: 'Sweet breath that breathes incomparable sweetness!', but Shakespeare commonsensically makes it clear that there are some scents that are even sweeter than that of his mistress's breath.

8 *reeks*] Not, as Massey suggests, meant to be repulsive. The verb 'to reek' in Elizabethan usage simply meant 'to be exhaled' or 'to emanate'. The earliest instance cited by *OED* of 'to reek' as 'to emit an unwholesome or disagreeable vapour' is in Swift (1710).

11 *go*] 'walk'.

12 *treads on the ground*] i.e., as Tucker says, 'like any other human being'.

13 *my love*] here 'my mistress'.

as rare] i.e. as splendid a creature.

130

My mistress' eyes are nothing like the sun;
Coral is far more red than her lips' red;
If snow be white, why then her breasts are dun;
If hairs be wires, black wires grow on her head: 4
I have seen roses damask'd, red and white,
But no such roses see I in her cheeks;
And in some perfumes is there more delight
Than in the breath that from my mistress reeks: 8
I love to hear her speak, yet well I know
That music hath a far more pleasing sound;
I grant I never saw a goddess go,—
My mistress when she walks treads on the ground. 12
    And yet by heaven I think my love as rare
    As any she belied with false compare.

131 1 *so as thou art*] i.e. without beauty of the type that wins public acclaim.

3 *dear doting*] The phrase may be read either as (1) two adjectives, meaning 'tender and infatuated', or as (2) an adverb modifying a participial adjective, meaning 'fondly doting'. If (2), then it is possible that 'dear' might have a secondary meaning ('expensively') implying that the mistress was mercenary. In either case, it does not seem necessary to insert a hyphen, as some modern editors, following Walker's conjecture (1860), have done.

4 *fairest*] playing again on (1) 'most beautiful' and (2) the association with blonde colouring.

5 *Yet in good faith*] So Q, followed by a few modern editors, including Wyndham and Beeching. Most editors follow Capell and Malone in inserting commas after *Yet* and *faith*. The commas strongly suggest that the phrase is an expletive, though only some editors positively argue that it is. Without the commas the most natural meaning is a concession by the poet that the detractors of his mistress do at least speak in good faith; though the possibility that the phrase is expletive would not be ruled out.

7, 8] The opposition in these lines is between a public statement and a private oath.

9] 'To convince me that what I swear is not false'.

10 *but thinking*] 'if I even think'.

12] For the play on 'fairest' see note on line 4.

in my judgment's place] 'in my judgment's ranking', or 'in the order in which my judgment would place it'. The general meaning of the phrase is clear enough, but its logic will not bear close examination.

14 *as I think*] So Q. Most modern editors enclose in commas. The commas might wrongly suggest to some readers that the poet is tentative in his opinion, and we have therefore preferred to retain Q's reading.

131

Thou art as tyrannous, so as thou art,
As those whose beauties proudly make them cruel;
For well thou know'st to my dear doting heart
Thou art the fairest and most precious jewel.　　　　4
Yet in good faith some say that thee behold
Thy face hath not the power to make love groan:
To say they err I dare not be so bold,
Although I swear it to myself alone.　　　　8
And to be sure that is not false I swear,
A thousand groans but thinking on thy face
One on another's neck do witness bear
Thy black is fairest in my judgment's place.　　　　12
　　In nothing art thou black save in thy deeds,
　　And thence this slander as I think proceeds.

132 1–3] We punctuate as in the text for the reasons given below.

> Q: *Thine eies I loue, and they as pittying me,*
> *Knowing thy heart torment me with disdaine,*
> *Haue put on black, . . .*

Malone inserted a comma after *heart*, and is followed by a few modern editors. This makes 'eyes' the subject of 'torment', whereas the poet is saying that they are pitying him because the heart is tormenting him.

Benson (1640), Walker's conjecture, and almost all modern editors: *torments.* Q is, however, followed by Lintot, Malone, and a few modern editors, including Dyce in his Aldine edition of the *Poems*, and Tucker, who (rightly, we think) holds 'torment' to be an infinitive.

We have supplied the dashes as in our view the best modern device to indicate clearly the parenthetical character of line 2.

We follow all modern editors in supplying a comma after 'they'.

5 *morning*] with a phonetic echo of 'mourners' (line 3), and a phonetic and semantic play with 'mourning' (line 9).

5–9] These lines make clear that the poet saw the chief beauty of his mistress as her eyes. Indeed, the apparent parallel between 'grey cheeks' (line 6), 'sober west' (line 8), and 'thy face' (line 9) may even suggest that without the animation of her eyes the mistress's face might have been dull.

9 *mourning*] So Gildon[1], Malone[1], and almost all modern editors. Q: *morning.* There is, in any case, a multiple play (cf. note on line 5).

10 *let it*] Not the expression of a vague aspiration, but an appeal to the woman (or, possibly, the heart) to allow it to 'beseem' the heart to . . . (see note on 'beseem').

as well] 'also'.

beseem] 'be meet for'.

11 *mourn*] possibly indicating the feeling of mourning and not merely the appearance.

doth thee grace] 'gives grace to you'. 'Grace' is a noun, the object of 'doth'. Cf. 'Doth . . . that glory' (line 8).

12] i.e. once the heart really is pitying me, dress it appropriately in black, so that your pity will be clothed alike in every part of you.

14 *foul*] (1) 'ugly' and (2) 'distasteful' or 'detestable'.

complexion] playing on (1) colouring, (2) disposition, and (3) bodily constitution.

132

THINE EYES I love, and they, as pitying me,—
Knowing thy heart torment me with disdain—
Have put on black, and loving mourners be,
Looking with pretty ruth upon my pain.   4
And truly not the morning sun of heaven
Better becomes the grey cheeks of the east,
Nor that full star that ushers in the even
Doth half that glory to the sober west   8
As those two mourning eyes become thy face.
Oh, let it then as well beseem thy heart
To mourn for me, since mourning doth thee grace,
And suit thy pity like in every part.   12
   Then will I swear Beauty herself is black,
   And all they foul that thy complexion lack.

133 1] Cf. 131 and 132.2.

3 *alone*] here 'only'.

4 *slave to slavery*] 'enslaved by his slavery to you'.

6 *my next self*] 'my nearest and dearest self', i.e. the Friend. The alternatives '*alter ego*' (Tucker), '*alter ipse*' (Pooler), and 'second self' (Tucker) suggest a similarity for which there is no evidence in the *Sonnets*; and the first two expressions are also too neutral.

harder] 'more cruelly' (*OED*. 11).

engross'd] 'monopolized'.

5–8] The quatrain seems to describe a process in stages:

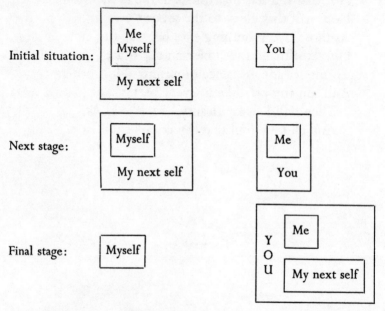

Schematic summary of final situation
(line 7): Me forsaken*   Myself * My next self You

9, 10 *my*] stressed in 'my heart' and 'my poor heart'.

9 *ward*] either (1) 'dungeon', or (2) 'strong cell', or simply (3) 'cell'.

10 *bail*] Not 'bail out of prison' but 'confine' (*OED*. V³. 1, which cites this passage). The situation asked for is like that of Chinese boxes one inside another.

11 *Whoe'er*] i.e. whoever it may be who.

keeps me] 'holds me prisoner' (*OED*. V. 25).

* N.B. Shakespeare has loosely changed terminology, putting 'me' for 'myself'.

306

133

Beshrew that heart that makes my heart to groan
For that deep wound it gives my friend and me!
Is't not enough to torture me alone,
But slave to slavery my sweet'st friend must be?   4
Me from myself thy cruel eye hath taken,
And my next self thou harder hast engross'd:
Of him, my self, and thee I am forsaken,—
A torment thrice threefold, thus to be cross'd.   8
Prison my heart in thy steel bosom's ward,
But then my friend's heart let my poor heart bail;
Whoe'er keeps me, let my heart be his guard:
Thou canst not then use rigour in my jail.   12
  And yet thou wilt; for I, being pent in thee,
  Perforce am thine, and all that is in me.

his] i.e. 'my friend's'.

guard] probably, as Tucker suggests, 'guardhouse', or even, perhaps, 'guard-room' (*OED*. sb. 17a). Place seems to be indicated rather than one or more persons.

12 *canst not*] either (1) 'you would not have the right to'; or (2) 'you would not have the power to'.

12] The 'rigour' would be intended against *the Friend*. 'My jail' means the poet's heart, in which the Friend would be imprisoned. Any other interpretation (and several have been suggested) is inconsonant with lines 13–14.

14 *and . . . me*] 'and everything that is in me is also yours'.

134 *Version A*

1 Punctuation] Q has no comma after *So*, but a comma after *thine*, and is followed by some modern editors. Other modern editors print a comma after *So*, and none after *thine*. A few modern editors, including Wyndham and Tucker Brooke, have commas in both places, as here.

The word 'So' seems to be an absolute, possibly meaning: 'Well! that being so . . .' (i.e. roughly speaking, though without pressing the metaphor, the final situation of Sonnet 133); and a comma seems required.

Editors who have removed Q's comma after *thine* evidently understood line 2 as part of the poet's 'confession'; but an alternative interpretation would be that it is a statement of fact co-ordinate with line 1. To retain the comma allows of either interpretation, whereas to remove it excludes the second, without, in the view of one of us, good warrant.

1 *now*] 'now that'.

2–3] *myself . . . My self*] Q as usual prints as two words in both cases. We print as one word in line 2 to indicate the word's merely emphatic function, as contrasted with the reference to a concrete, individual personality in line 3.

2 *mortgag'd . . . will*] 'pledged to comply with your "will", and liable to forfeiture in case of failure'.

will] Here is introduced a word which will be increasingly played on in subsequent sonnets, and with increasing obscenity (see sonnets 135 and 136). Here the play is probably restricted to (1) 'volition', (2) 'wilfulness', (3) 'carnal lust'.

3 *forfeit, so*] The poet, liable to forfeiture in any case, decides to offer it at once *on terms*. (He will become his mistress's complete slave, provided she will restore his friend to him.)

that other mine] cf. 133. 6.

6 *covetous*] i.e. 'inordinately possessive', rather than 'desirous of what you have not got'.

5, 6] 'But you do not want to restore him, because you are inordinately possessive; and he is not likely to break free because he is complaisant.' (Playing on two senses of 'will'.)

7] 'All he was instructed to do was to underwrite the bond as a surety for me' (i.e. to pledge my love and devotion to you).

8] i.e. the text of the bond, in fact, unknown to him, pledged his own love and devotion also to you.

9] i.e. you will exact the full forfeiture (namely, both my friend and me) provided for in the mortgage deed drawn because of your beauty (and the enjoyment of it (cf. line 10)).

134

So, NOW I have confess'd that he is thine,
And I myself am mortgag'd to thy will,
My self I'll forfeit, so that other mine
Thou wilt restore to be my comfort still.   4
But thou wilt not, nor he will not be free;
For thou art covetous, and he is kind;
He learn'd but surety-like to write for me
Under that bond that him as fast doth bind.   8
The statute of thy beauty thou wilt take,
Thou usurer, that putt'st forth all to use,
And sue a friend came debtor for my sake;
So him I lose through my unkind abuse.   12
    Him have I lost; thou hast both him and me:
    He pays the whole, and yet am I not free.

(Alternative punctuation of Octave)

So, NOW I have confess'd that he is thine;
And I myself am mortgag'd to thy will:
My self I'll forfeit, so that other mine
Thou wilt restore to be my comfort still.   4
But thou wilt not; nor he will not be free.
For thou art covetous, and he is kind,—
He learn'd but surety-like to write for me
Under that bond that him as fast doth bind.   8

---

10 *that . . . use*] i.e. she will give nothing except for interest. There is also an evident amatory innuendo in 'use'.

11 *came*] 'who became' (cf. *2H4*, II. iii. 57: 'So came I a widow').

12 *my unkind abuse*] Editors are divided on the sense. Some (e.g. Tyler, Wyndham, Tucker) take the phrase to refer to the poet's misuse of his friend

134 (*continued*)

as a go-between. Others (e.g. Lee, Pooler) think that it is the poet who has
been ill-used (by the woman). We prefer this view. The first view gives a
platitudinous, this a strong line, whose tone of outrage, continued in the
couplet, speaks through the stresses on 'him' and 'my'.

13, 14] We are assuming that the sexual innuendoes for the most part
need no explication.

The interrelation between the sense, the stresses, and the syntactical
variation in these lines is particularly well calculated.

14 *He . . . whole*] Two senses are dominant: (1) He is the forfeit, and
that should be enough; (2) He is giving you what ought to be full carnal
satisfaction.

Version B

We offer a second version of the octave, in which the punctuation (1)
isolates lines 1, 2 as a total statement of acknowledged defeat; (2) makes
lines 7, 8 a specification of the Friend's kindness mentioned in line 6.

134

So, now I have confess'd that he is thine,
And I myself am mortgag'd to thy will,
My self I'll forfeit, so that other mine
Thou wilt restore to be my comfort still.   4
But thou wilt not, nor he will not be free;
For thou art covetous, and he is kind;
He learn'd but surety-like to write for me
Under that bond that him as fast doth bind.   8
The statute of thy beauty thou wilt take,
Thou usurer, that putt'st forth all to use,
And sue a friend came debtor for my sake;
So him I lose through my unkind abuse.   12
   Him have I lost; thou hast both him and me:
   He pays the whole, and yet am I not free.

(Alternative punctuation of Octave)

So, now I have confess'd that he is thine;
And I myself am mortgag'd to thy will:
My self I'll forfeit, so that other mine
Thou wilt restore to be my comfort still.   4
But thou wilt not; nor he will not be free.
For thou art covetous, and he is kind,—
He learn'd but surety-like to write for me
Under that bond that him as fast doth bind.   8

135 *General Note:* Here, besides those senses of 'will' noted above (134. 2, note), there is, quite apart from any personal name allusions, the common cant sense of the *membrum pudendum*, male or female. Most commentators seem to have been innocent or reticent in respect of this meaning, for which Wright's *English Dialect Dictionary*, 1905, VI [Supplt.], and Partridge's *Dictionary of Slang* (Routledge and Kegan Paul, London, 2nd ed. 1938) offer any authority necessary. Rollins observes that *OED* gives no countenance to such glosses; but *OED* ignores all such terms on principle.

Will] We have printed Q's capitalized italics wherever they occur.

1 *wish . . . Will*] The primary contrast is between 'wish' and 'Will', but this is soon lost as the other meanings of '*Will*' flood in. 'Hath her wish' could mean either (1) 'has desires' (which might be innocuous)'; or (2) 'gets what she wants'. If (1), then 'Will' could mean 'carnal desire' and/or 'determination', though it would also have personal reference. If (2), then probably the meaning is only personal.

3 *More than enough*] If '*Will* in overplus' refers to the poet, then 'more than enough' is restorative.

4] 'Exciting you sexually in this way'. (Capitalized italics for 'will' (lower case) are markedly absent in Q in this and the immediately succeeding lines.)

4 Punctuation] Though no previous editor has, to our knowledge, taken lines 3, 4 as a question, such an interpretation would be possible, and there would be no more difficulty in converting Q's full stop at the end of line 4 into a ? than there has been in converting Q's comma at the end of line 6 or Q's colon at the end of line 8.

5 *spacious*⎫
7 *gracious*⎭ trisyllables.

10 *his*] 'its'.

13] So this edition. Q: *Let no vnkinde, no . . .*; Tyler, Beeching, Kittredge: *Let no unkind no . . .*; Dowden conj., Tyler conj., Oxford, Yale, Tucker Brooke: *Let no unkind "No" . . .*; Butler, Walsh, Pooler conj.: *Let no unkindness . . .*; Tucker: *Let 'No' unkind no. . . .* Q gives little or no guidance as to the meaning. Tyler's reading affords no satisfactory meaning as printed. Beeching's explanation 'Let no unkindness kill *any* beseechers', even as a paraphrase, disaccords with contemporary (and, indeed, present) usage of 'unkind'. Dowden's conjecture is attractive, but demands a stress on 'No' which would make a line more typical of Donne than of Shakespeare's *Sonnets*. Tucker's emendation seems to us the best, but it needs supplementing by commas at 'No' and 'unkind', to give due weight to 'unkind' as an adjective qualifying 'No'.

fair beseechers] 'genuine aspirants', perhaps even 'honest customers'.

135

Whoever hath her wish, thou hast thy *Will*,
And *Will* to boot, and *Will* in overplus:
More than enough am I that vex thee still,
To thy sweet will making addition thus.   4
Wilt thou whose will is large and spacious
Not once vouchsafe to hide my will in thine?
Shall will in others seem right gracious,
And in my will no fair acceptance shine?   8
The sea, all water, yet receives rain still,
And in abundance addeth to his store:
So thou being rich in *Will* add to thy *Will*
One will of mine to make thy large *Will* more.   12
    Let 'No', unkind, no fair beseechers kill;
    Think all but one, and me in that one *Will*.

14] Possibly, primarily, 'think of them all as one composite lover, and
that that composite lover includes me'; though in the last word of the
sonnet every meaning of '*Will*' already alluded to would seem to be present.

136 1 *check*] 'reproves'.

come so near] (1) 'come so near your conscience' (with my reproaches for your neglect of me in your promiscuity); (2) 'come so close to your bed'. Both meanings may be present.

2 *blind soul*] (1) Tyler thinks the soul is considered blind here because it is 'within the body and destitute of eyes'; (2) Tucker takes 'blind' as proleptic, the meaning being that the soul becomes blind by deliberately shutting its eyes.

thy Will] Could mean (1) 'Will, your former lover' (which he was); or (2) 'the Friend'; or (3), as Adams suggests, the woman's husband, which requires us to assume that the husband's name was 'Will'. (1) would only fit with interpretation (1) of 'blind soul', but (2) and (3) with either interpretation.

3] Meaning accordingly either (1) 'Your soul knows quite well that you admit lovers to your bed', or (2) 'Your soul knows that it is quite permissible for you to sleep with your husband'.

4 *for love*] 'out of love', rather than, as Tucker suggests, 'in return for love', which would be redundant.

, sweet,] So almost all modern editors. Q and early editions to Evans: no commas. Capell: (*sweet*).

5 ff] Innuendoes of a similar kind to those in 135 abound here, especially on 'will', 'fulfil', 'nothing', and 'something'. We feel no obligation to elucidate them.

7 *things . . . receipt*] The meaning seems to shift rapidly, from a *physical* reference to the great capacity of the woman's lust, to an accounting image.

prove] 'verify by experience'.

8] It was a long-established principle of mathematics, which had passed into a proverb, that one was no number. The point is made in Macrobius (*Somnium Scipionis*, II. ii): '*sicut punctum corpus non est sed ex se facit corpora, ita monas numerus esse non dicitur sed origo numerorum*'. In lines 8–12 the reference to this principle is only a passing one, the thought shifting immediately to the insignificance of one small item in a large account.

9 *untold*] Primarily (1) 'uncounted', but there may also be a secondary sense (2) 'unrecounted' or 'undivulged'.

10 *store's*] So most modern editors. Q: *stores*. Malone and many modern editors: *stores'*. Q does not apostrophize genitives. Malone and editors following him seem not to have realized that the collective plural 'stores' (see *OED*. 1c) did not come into use until after Shakespeare's death.

account] 'reckoning'.

9–10] 'Then, though I do help to complete your score, let me pass among the crowd without individual notice'.

314

136

If THY soul check thee that I come so near,
Swear to thy blind soul that I was thy *Will*,
And will, thy soul knows, is admitted there;
Thus far for love my love-suit, sweet, fulfil.   4
Will will fulfil the treasure of thy love,—
Ay, fill it full with wills, and my will one.
In things of great receipt with ease we prove
Among a number one is reckon'd none: 8
Then in the number let me pass untold,
Though in thy store's account I one must be;
For nothing hold me, so it please thee hold
That no-thing me a some-thing, sweet, to thee,   12
    Make but my name thy love, and love that still,—
    And then thou lov'st me, for my name is *Will*.

12 *no-thing . . . some-thing*] So this edition. Q: *nothing . . . some-thing*.
All other modern editors: *nothing . . . something*. We thought of following
them, but decided that the evident emphasis on the first element in each
word (which would be pointed by the Elizabethan pronunciation of 'nō-
thing') is insufficiently expressed by the normal modern typographical
practice.

   , *sweet*,] So Walker's conjecture (1860), followed by a few modern
editors. Q and most modern editors: no commas. The antithesis between
'no-thing' and 'some-thing', on which the line depends, would be weakened
without a comma after 'some-thing'. An alternative to our reading would,
however, be to retain that comma, but read *sweet to thee* (i.e. that is sweet to
thee).

  13, 14] The primary conceit is: Love me for my *name* (something not
physical), but my name is *Will* (something very physical indeed); though
there may conceivably also be specific personal references, as some editors
have suggested.

137 3 *lies*] Primarily 'rests', 'dwells'; but there is an underplay of 'deceives', 'is false (or counterfeit)'.

3] The line refers to the poet's eyes' general knowledge of beauty true and false, which, according to line 4, they fail to apply to this particular case.

5 *corrupt*] 'corrupted' (past participle).

6 *bay . . . ride*] cf. line 10. The equivocation is as definite as it is savage and nasty.

7 *hooks*] The god of love has, out of the deceptiveness of the poet's vision, forged hooks to anchor his judgment.

9 *that*] demonstrative ('that place').

several plot] 'enclosed, private plot', as contrasted with unenclosed common land.

13, 14] The answer to all the preceding questions. His eyes had previously failed to recognize the true beauty of some other woman; and as a punishment the god of love has afflicted his heart and eyes with the plague of deception. Wyndham confusingly takes the 'plague' to be the woman, which was, in any case, unnecessary, since there are plenty of parallels in the *Sonnets* for the construction 'this false plague', e.g. 51. 1: 'slow offence' (offence of being slow), and 127. 4: 'bastard shame' (shame of being a bastard).

137

Thou blind fool, Love, what dost thou to mine eyes,
That they behold, and see not what they see?
They know what beauty is, see where it lies,
Yet what the best is take the worst to be.   4
If eyes corrupt by over-partial looks
Be anchor'd in the bay where all men ride,
Why of eyes' falsehood hast thou forgèd hooks
Whereto the judgment of my heart is tied?   .   8
Why should my heart think that a several plot
Which my heart knows the wide world's common place?
Or mine eyes, seeing this, say this is not,
To put fair truth upon so foul a face?   12
    In things right true my heart and eyes have err'd,
    And to this false plague are they now transferr'd.

138 *General Note:* This is one of the two Sonnets of Shakespeare printed by Jaggard in *The Passionate Pilgrim*, 1599. The text of this version in the copy in the Library of Trinity College, Cambridge, reads:

> When my Loue sweares that she is made of truth,
> I doe beleeue her (though I know she lies)
> That she might thinke me some vntutor'd youth,
> Vnskilfull in the worlds false forgeries.
> Thus vainly thinking that she thinkes me young,
> Although I know my yeares be past the best:
> I smiling, credite her false speaking toung,
> Outfacing faults in Loue, with loues ill rest.
> But wherefore sayes my Loue that she is young?
> And wherefore say not I, that I am old?
> O, Loues best habite is a soothing toung,
> And Age (in Loue) loues not to haue yeares told.
> > Therfore Ile lye with Loue, and Loue with me,
> > Since that our faults in Loue thus smother'd be.

Commentators in general have been divided as to whether the version in *The Passionate Pilgrim* is an early draft or a garbled version of the text eventually printed in Q.

1 *truth*⎫ In both cases there is clearly a play on different senses of the
2 *lies* ⎰ word.

2 *I do believe her*] This element in a brilliant poetic paradox is soon revealed, by the conjunction 'that' (line 3) = 'in order that', to be a mere purposeful façade.

5 *vainly*] (1) 'in unfounded self-deception', and possibly (2) 'self-flatteringly'.

7 *Simply*] 'In assumed simplicity' (in ironic contrast with 'simple' in line 8).

9 *unjust*] Primarily (1) 'unreliable', but also (2) 'untruthful', paralleling the senses of 'truth' in line 1.

11 *love's . . . in*] 'love is best dressed up in'.

seeming] a favourite word of Shakespeare's for deceptive appearance.

seeming trust] In point of symmetry the quatrain would seem to demand that line 11 answers line 9 and line 12 line 10. But the phrase 'seeming trust' seems such a strong echo of 'Simply I credit' (line 7) and 'I do believe' (line 2) that it may be that Shakespeare was more concerned with sense than with symmetry.

12 *age in love*] Either (1) 'age, when in love . . .'; or (2) consonant with Tucker's suggestion, 'age, in the matter of love . . .'. Q has a comma

318

138

W HEN MY love swears that she is made of truth
I do believe her, though I know she lies,
That she might think me some untutor'd youth
Unlearnèd in the world's false subtleties.   4
Thus vainly thinking that she thinks me young,
Although she knows my days are past the best,
Simply I credit her false-speaking tongue:
On both sides thus is simple truth suppress'd.   8
But wherefore says she not she is unjust?
And wherefore say not I that I am old?
Oh, love's best habit is in seeming trust,
And age in love loves not to have years told.   1 2
    Therefore I lie with her, and she with me,
    And in our faults by lies we flatter'd be.

after *love*, which we follow almost all modern editors in omitting. Q's punctuation might suggest interpretation (1) but cannot be taken as conclusive support.

   told] Primarily (1) 'reckoned', but possibly with a play on (2) 'divulged', as in 136. 9.

   1 3] Here, by substituting 'with' for 'to', Shakespeare, with extravagant ingenuity, executes an equivoque in reverse!

   14 *in our faults*] 'in respect of our shortcomings'.

139 1] To excuse or justify a mistress's unkindness was a common practice in the sonnet convention.

3] 'Do not wound me by turning your eyes on others in my presence, content yourself with *telling* me of your infidelity.' The image is *not*, as it *is* at the end of the sonnet, that of the fatal stare of the basilisk.

4] 'Use your power with brutal force, and do not kill me by strategy.' There seems no reason to accept Schmidt's suggestion that 'Art' may here mean 'magic'.

5 *Tell*] stressed.

6 *glance . . . aside*] 'cast a sidelong glance'. 'Aside' is not redundant. The verb 'to glance', in this sense of 'to dart a quick look', was a comparatively new use (*OED*. 5 (1583)).

7 *What*] 'Why'. There are a number of instances in Shakespeare of this use, e.g. 'What should I stay?' (*A&C*. V. ii. 315).

8 *o'erpress'd*] Rather, as Dowden suggests, 'too hard pressed' than 'overpowered', as Pooler glosses.

9–12 Inverted commas] We follow Tucker's insertion of inverted commas, which seem necessary in a modern recension to bring out the texture of direct speech.

10 *pretty*] 'artfully attractive' (but cf. 41. 1 and note).

have been] i.e. when they used to be directed at *me*.

14 *and rid my pain*] i.e. 'and so destroy by violence my pain also'. (For 'rid' in this sense see *OED*. II. 6.)

139

OH CALL not me to justify the wrong
That thy unkindness lays upon my heart!
Wound me not with thine eye but with thy tongue;
Use power with power and slay me not by art: 4
Tell me thou lov'st elsewhere; but in my sight,
Dear heart, forbear to glance thine eye aside—
What need'st thou wound with cunning, when thy might
Is more than my o'erpress'd defence can bide?   8
Let me excuse thee: 'Ah, my love well knows
Her pretty looks have been mine enemies;
And therefore from my face she turns my foes,
That they elsewhere might dart their injuries'.   12
    Yet do not so; but since I am near slain,
    Kill me outright with looks, and rid my pain.

140 1 *wise as*] 'as wise as'.

2 *tongue-tied*] Some editors have had the misfortune to believe that Shakespeare stammered.

4 *pity-wanting*] i.e. that gets no pity from you (cf. 'cruel' in line 1).

5 *wit*] i.e. a little practical wisdom.

6, *love,*] So all modern editors except Harrison. Q and all editions up to and including Evans: no commas, which, however, the vocative obviously requires.

so] i.e. that you *do* love me.

8 *know*] i.e. 'are told'.

11 *ill-wresting*] that twists anything to the bad.

13 *That . . . so*] 'So that I may not be believed', as he would be if he were to despair and utter mad slanders.

14] It seems likely that there is an image from archery here. The difficulty is to see its exact working.

140

Be wise as thou art cruel: do not press
My tongue-tied patience with too much disdain;
Lest sorrow lend me words, and words express
The manner of my pity-wanting pain. 4
If I might teach thee wit, better it were,
Though not to love, yet, love, to tell me so;—
As testy sick men, when their deaths be near,
No news but health from their physicians know. 8
For if I should despair, I should grow mad,
And in my madness might speak ill of thee.
Now this ill-wresting world is grown so bad
Mad slanderers by mad ears believèd be: 12
   That I may not be so, nor thou belied,
   Bear thine eyes straight though thy proud heart go wide.

141 3 *despise*] 'set little store by'. There is a phonal play with 'despite' in line 4.

4 *Who*] 'Which', as frequently in Shakespeare.

view] 'visual impression'.

5, 6 Punctuation] Q has commas at *delighted* and *prone*. Most modern editors print a semi-colon at *delighted*, a comma at *feeling*, and a comma at *prone*. Such punctuation is not unreasonable, but it has the disadvantage of awkwardly marking off the sense of hearing from the senses of touch, taste, and smell. Our punctuation avoids such an awkward asymmetry in the second quatrain. The objection to it might be that in line 5 the verb 'are' is plural; but there is nothing un-Shakespearean in a singular verb being understood in a clause following one containing a plural verb. An implication of the usual punctuation, moreover, is that 'to base touches prone' qualifies 'tender feeling'; but we agree with Beeching in thinking that the poet is saying that his feeling is *not* 'prone to base touches', not that it is. On our interpretation, line 6 parallels both line 5 and lines 7–8.

5 *tongue's tune*] 'voice's timbre'.

6 *tender feeling*] i.e. sensitive tactile responses.

base touches] playing on both (1) the moral, and (2) the 'geographical' senses of 'base', both of which are frequent in Shakespeare.

8 *alone*] Not 'tête-à-tête', but 'exclusively of other women'.

9 *five wits*] The intellectual faculties as contrasted with the five senses. They were also sometimes reckoned as five, as in the poem of Stephen Hawes (referred to by Malone in his 1790 edition of the *Sonnets*), 'The Passetyme of Pleasure, or History of Graunde Amoure and la Bel Pucel', 1509. The relevant lines are:

> These are the five wittes remouing inwardly,
> First commen witte, and then ymagination,
> Fantasy, and estimation truely,
> And memory.

10 *serving*] i.e. as a lover. This idea is curiously rare in the *Sonnets* as contrasted with the plays.

11 *Who*] 'Which', as in line 4.

11] 'Which leaves me ungoverned (by the heart, as reason), and so the mere semblance or shell of a man'.

13 *plague*] 'affliction', of love.

13, 14] It seems probable that these lines are not usually well understood. It might appear, on the surface, that there could be little advantage in the seductress making the poet suffer for his 'sin' with her. But Samuel

141

In FAITH, I do not love thee with mine eyes,
For they in thee a thousand errors note;
But 'tis my heart that loves what they despise,
Who in despite of view is pleas'd to dote: 4
Nor are mine ears with thy tongue's tune delighted,
Nor tender feeling to base touches prone;
Nor taste nor smell desire to be invited
To any sensual feast with thee alone.   8
But my five wits nor my five senses can
Dissuade one foolish heart from serving thee,
Who leaves unsway'd the likeness of a man,
Thy proud heart's slave and vassal wretch to be: 12
    Only my plague thus far I count my gain,
    That she that makes me sin awards me pain.

Butler, alone among commentators, reveals real point in the lines. He
paraphrases: 'I shall suffer less for my sin hereafter, for I get some of the
punishment coincidently with the offence.'

142 1–4] The chiastic structure of line 1 is a clue to the meaning of the whole quatrain, which we take to be as follows: 'This sin of mine [that of 140. 14] is *love*: the "precious virtue" with which you resist it, is simply its opposite, *hate*—hate for my "sin" (i.e. love), (*a*) really stemming from your sinful loving of others, and (*b*) based on an allegation (hypocritical coming from you) that my love for you is sinful [there is probably a play on the two meanings]. You only need to compare your own moral condition with mine, and you will find that mine does not deserve any rebuke from you.' The case is the familiar one of the pot and the kettle.

3 *but*] 'only'.

6 *scarlet ornaments*] 'scarlet attire', which should be reserved for special occasions and not cheapened by promiscuous use.

Malone[2] noted that the same expression is found in the anonymous play *The Raigne of King Edward the Third* (1596), where it refers to blushes: 'His cheekes put on their scarlet ornaments'.

Some scholars (e.g. A. Platt, in *MLR*, VI (1911), 511–13, and J. W. Mackail (*Lectures on Poetry*, Longmans, London, 1911, 186 ff)) maintain that in the sonnet the expression refers to the scarlet wax with which deeds (e.g. the bond in line 7) are sealed. Some modern editors adopt this interpretation, but we doubt whether the image has developed into that of sealing before line 7. It would be more Shakespearean for the lips to suggest the seal image directly rather than through the intermediary of wax; and, moreover, this sonnet is one of those in which one image grows out of another (as that of line 8 does out of that of line 7), not one in which a single image is sustained.

7 *as mine*] 'as mine have done'.

7 Punctuation] Q has a comma after *mine*, and is followed by most modern editors. Some editors strengthen the comma to a semi-colon, apparently with the same intention as ours in printing a dash, namely, to show that line 8 is extensionally appositional to line 7, not mincing words. In our view, however, the semi-colon obscures rather than indicates the connexion of thought. Those few editors, such as Tucker, who read no stop at *mine*, possibly agree with his view that to isolate line 8 creates 'a wholly intolerable asyndeton'. Against this we would urge (1) that our punctuation does not isolate line 8, and (2) that, even if it did, this would be far less intolerable than the inconsistency of tenses which would result from Tucker's reading.

8] Asserting clearly what had been the veiled insinuation of line 7, that the woman was not merely promiscuous but an adulteress.

11, 12 *pity*] As in many folk-songs, probably a euphemism for complaisance with a lover's desire.

142

Love is my sin, and thy dear virtue hate—
Hate of my sin, grounded on sinful loving:
Oh, but with mine compare thou thine own state
And thou shalt find it merits not reproving;   4
Or if it do, not from those lips of thine,
That have profan'd their scarlet ornaments
And seal'd false bonds of love as oft as mine—
Robb'd others' beds' revénues of their rents.   8
Be it lawful I love thee as thou lov'st those
Whom thine eyes woo as mine importune thee:
Root pity in thy heart, that when it grows
Thy pity may deserve to pitied be.   12
  If thou dost seek to have what thou dost hide,
  By self-example mayst thou be denied!

12] The modern equivalent which preserves the essential, rather curious
feature of construction, would be: 'Your pity may deserve pity in return.'
  13 *what*] i.e. pity.
  hide] 'refuse to show'.
  14 *By self-example*] 'By the example you yourself set'.
  mayst] optative.
  denied] i.e. denied pity.

143 1] The Q spelling *huswife* indicates the Elizabethan, and still correct, pronunciation 'hussif': *careful* = 'anxious'.

8 *Not prizing*] 'Not holding as of any account'.

9 *that which flies*⎫ i.e. the 'pity' of 142. 11, 12, which, in effect, =
11 *thy hope*   ⎭ the 'will' punned on in line 13 below.

13 *thy Will*] Punning on (1) the proper name, (2) 'what you want', which is (3) 'the satisfaction of your lust'.

14 *my*] stressed, as Tucker suggests.

13, 14] Three persons are involved in the sonnet, and the poet is willing that the woman should have her other love (the 'feather'd creature') provided she will give him (the 'neglected child') satisfaction too.

143

L o, as a careful housewife runs to catch
One of her feather'd creatures broke away,
Sets down her babe and makes all swift dispatch
In púrsuit of the thing she would have stay: 4
Whilst her neglected child holds her in chase,
Cries to catch her whose busy care is bent
To follow that which flies before her face,
Not prizing her poor infant's discontent: 8
So runn'st thou after that which flies from thee,
Whilst I thy babe chase thee afar behind;—
But if thou catch thy hope, turn back to me
And play the mother's part,—kiss me, be kind: 12
   So will I pray that thou mayst have thy *Will*,
   If thou turn back and my loud crying still.

144 *General Note:* This is one of the two Sonnets of Shakespeare printed by Jaggard in *The Passionate Pilgrim*, 1599. The text of this version in the copy in the Library of Trinity College, Cambridge, reads:

> Two Loues I haue, of Comfort, and Despaire,
> That like two Spirits, do suggest me still:
> My better Angell is a Man (right faire)
> My worser spirite a Woman (colour'd ill.)
> To winne me soone to hell, my Female euill
> Tempteth my better Angell from my side,
> And would corrupt my Saint to be a Diuell,
> Wooing his purity with her faire pride.
> And whether that my Angell be turnde feend,
> Suspect I may (yet not directly tell:
> For being both to me: both, to each friend,
> I ghesse one Angell in anothers hell:
>> The truth I shall not know, but liue in doubt,
>> Till my bad Angell fire my good one out.

In fact, the only major differences between this version and Q are: (1) *The Passionate Pilgrim* prints *side* in line 6, which gives a more satisfactory rhyme and sense than Q's *sight*; (2) *The Passionate Pilgrim's faire* (line 8) lacks both the strong oxymoron afforded by Q's *fowle* and also its allusion to the woman's unhandsomeness by conventional standards; (3) *The Passionate Pilgrim's* line 11 makes easier sense than Q's.

Q's version has the advantages of expressing the grounds of the poet's suspicion that he is being deceived, namely (*a*) their intimacy, and (*b*), as Professor F. T. Prince points out (Shakespeare's *Poems*, Arden edition, 1960), the opportunities afforded by their absence from him.

1 *Two loves*] It seems reasonable to assume, as many commentators have, a reference to the situation which forms the subject of Sonnets 40–2.

1 *Punctuation*] Like a number of modern editors, including Beeching and Tucker, we print a comma after *have*, as in *The Passionate Pilgrim*, making it clear that one quality belongs to each love.

comfort] Modern usage seems to have lost the etymological element of *support*, present, for instance, in *Ps.* xxiii. 4: 'thy rod and thy staff they comfort me' (Authorized Version 1611).

2 *do suggest me still*] 'work on my soul continuously'. The use of 'suggest' as transitive with a personal direct object is frequent in Shakespeare. Most often he uses the verb with a derogatory sense, but sometimes, as here, he uses it neutrally, and occasionally he even uses it in a favourable sense.

144

Two loves I have, of comfort and despair,
Which like two spirits do suggest me still:
The better angel is a man right fair,
The worser spirit a woman colour'd ill.   4
To win me soon to hell, my female evil
Tempteth my better angel from my side,
And would corrupt my saint to be a devil,
Wooing his purity with her foul pride.   8
And whether that my angel be turn'd fiend
Suspect I may, yet not directly tell;
But being both from me, both to each friend,
I guess one angel in another's hell: 12
    Yet this shall I ne'er know, but live in doubt
    Till my bad angel fire my good one out.

4 *colour'd ill*] i.e. with the colouring of a brunette, considered inferior at the time. Cf. Sonnets 127, 132.

5 *To . . . hell*] 'In order to give me a "hell of time" (120. 6)', neither (1) meaning 'to tempt me to sin', nor probably (2) carrying the allusions that will arise in line 12, though some editors disagree.

6 *side*] So *Pass. Pilg.* and all editors except Lintot. Q and Lintot: *sight*.

8 *foul pride*] 'ugly physical fascination' (cf. 141). 'Foul' has not the modern moral sense, and 'pride', as often in Shakespeare, means, literally, 'show', and also provides an oxymoron with 'foul'.

10 *directly*] Some or all of the following senses seem to be present: (1) 'by direct evidence', (2) 'completely' (see *OED*. 4), and (3) 'as yet' (literally, 'immediately', in time); though (1) is probably primary.

11 *from me*] 'absent from me'.

both . . . friend] a redundancy intensifying the idea of intimacy.

12] Several meanings appear to be present: (1) they are both in the 'Hell' or middle-den of a game of barley-break; (2) as contemporaries averred, such a position was often used as a pretext for a sexual tumble; (3) 'Hell' is probably also, as in Boccaccio's story of Rustico and Alibech

(*Decameron*, III, 10), the female sexual organ. In the case of senses (1) and (2) 'one in another's' = 'each in the other's', and in the case of sense (3) 'one angel' is the man, and 'another' is the woman.

14] Evidently a gross insult to the woman, though veiled under the innocent meaning of 'casting off'. The underlying sense is that the poet will not know whether the Friend has slept with the woman until he sees whether he has contracted venereal disease. ('Fire out' was common usage for 'infect with a venereal disease'.)

144

Two loves I have, of comfort and despair,
Which like two spirits do suggest me still:
The better angel is a man right fair,
The worser spirit a woman colour'd ill.   4
To win me soon to hell, my female evil
Tempteth my better angel from my side,
And would corrupt my saint to be a devil,
Wooing his purity with her foul pride.   8
And whether that my angel be turn'd fiend
Suspect I may, yet not directly tell;
But being both from me, both to each friend,
I guess one angel in another's hell: 12
    Yet this shall I ne'er know, but live in doubt
    Till my bad angel fire my good one out.

145 *General Note:* These trivial octosyllables scarcely deserve reprinting. Some editors have considered the poem spurious on account of its feeble childishness. It would seem arbitrary, however, to rule out the possibility that one of Shakespeare's trivia should have found its way into a collection not approved by him. But the question of this sonnet's authenticity is as unimportant as the poem itself, which only has one touch of imagination, the image of lines 10–12.

7 *us'd in*] Either (1) 'employed in', or (2) 'experienced in' *(OED.* 3). It seems impossible to determine which is the correct meaning.

doom] 'judgments' (literally 'judgment').

13] i.e. she flung the *words* away to a distance from any *feeling* of hate for the poet.

145

THOSE LIPS that Love's own hand did make
Breath'd forth the sound that said 'I hate'
To me that languish'd for her sake:
But when she saw my woeful state,   4
Straight in her heart did mercy come
Chiding that tongue that ever sweet
Was us'd in giving gentle doom,
And taught it thus anew to greet: 8
'I hate' she alter'd with an end
That follow'd it as gentle day
Doth follow night, who like a fiend
From heaven to hell is flown away: 12
   'I hate' from hate away she threw,
   And sav'd my life, saying—'Not you'.

146 1 *centre*] Most editors cite *R&J*. II. i. 2: 'turn back, dull earth, and find thy centre out'; but do not offer to elucidate the meaning of 'centre' there either. Both here and there it refers to what is, or ought to be, the centre of attraction, the being which should be served, in the one case by Romeo, in the other by the body. In this sonnet conflicting forces are frustrating this (see note on line 2, below).

2] Q reads: *My sinfull earth these rebbell powres that thee array*. Most commentators, though not all, have agreed that the line is clearly corrupt. A number of reputable editors have left the beginning of the line blank. A few commentators have defended Q as making good sense, which, indeed, it can do; but the difficulty, which seems to us a very severe one, is that Q's line contains twelve syllables, which is without parallel in the *Sonnets*. This fact seems to make some emendation desirable, if a suitable one can be found. The essential requirements are:

(1) two syllables instead of four;
(2) (*a*) a good sense, and, moreover, (*b*) a good Shakespearean sense.

It would seem also desirable that:

(3) (*a*) the words should be words used elsewhere by Shakespeare, and (*b*) in the sense required here.

To work towards a list of possibilities fulfilling these requirements, we first considered every word recorded as used by Shakespeare, and then selected those words or combinations of words which seemed to make any kind of sense, and fitted the metrical pattern. These came to about 400. From these we discarded some 300 as failing to fulfil one or more of requirements 2 (*a*), 2 (*b*) 3 (*a*), 3 (*b*). The remaining possibilities (nearly 100) are listed on pp. 358–9. About fifty of these (printed in italic on the list) seemed to us to fulfil these requirements better than the others. In our view it is from these fifty readings that any editor of the *Sonnets* wishing to print an emendation would have to choose. It is here that we respectfully differ from Professor Sisson, who suggests *fenced by*, in the sense of 'beset by', 'besieged by' (*New Readings in Shakespeare*, II, 214). The word 'fenced' occurs only once elsewhere in Shakespeare, namely at *AYLI*. IV. iii. 78: 'A sheepcote fenc'd about with olive-trees', where the sense entirely conflicts with Professor Sisson's interpretation of the sense here. Moreover, no siege metaphor seems to us present in this sonnet.

Choice among the fifty possibilities seems to us inseparable from choice among possible meanings of 'array'. Misled by the military associations of 'rebel powers', and possibly of 'walls', and of 'array' used as a noun (in writers other than Shakespeare), some commentators have taken 'array'

146

Poor soul, the centre of my sinful earth,
[Foil'd by] these rebel powers that thee array,
Why dost thou pine within and suffer dearth,
Painting thy outward walls so costly gay? 4
Why so large cost, having so short a lease,
Dost thou upon thy fading mansion spend?
Shall worms, inheritors of this excess,
Eat up thy charge? Is this thy body's end? 8
Then, soul, live thou upon thy servant's loss,
And let that pine to aggravate thy store;
Buy terms divine in selling hours of dross;
Within be fed, without be rich no more: 12
    So shalt thou feed on Death, that feeds on men,
    And Death once dead there's no more dying then.

here to mean 'beleaguer'; but such a sense is not to be found in English, either in Shakespeare or elsewhere. To meet this difficulty some scholars have suggested the emendation *warray*, an archaism employed by Spenser, but not otherwise recorded later than 1513. The two senses of 'array' that seem to us relevant here are (1) 'to dress', 'to attire'; (2) 'to defile', (*OED.* 10c). Very probably there is a play on the two senses. Sense (1) coheres with line 4, and sense (2) with the implication of man's baser elements in 'sinful earth' and 'rebel powers'. The absence of any military image in 'array' entails the exclusion of such suggestions for the beginning of the line as Dowden's *Press'd by* and Furnivall's *Hemm'd with*. Seeking among the fifty possibilities for an emendation with superior claims to consideration, one of us was considering *fil'd* = 'defiled' (as in Palsgrave, *Lesclaircissement de la langue françoise*, 1530), in view of sense (2) of 'array'; and the other of us, scanning emendations already proposed, was struck by Massey's note, based on a parallel with a Sidney sonnet, in favour of *foil'd*, which, apparently unknown to Massey, had already been printed by Palgrave in his *Shakespeare's Songs and Sonnets* (Macmillan, London) in 1865.* It then occurred

* In the first edition of his *Golden Treasury* in 1861 Palgrave had printed *fool'd*. Later editions vary between *fool'd* and *foil'd*.

to one of us that the vowels 'oi' and 'i' = 'ee' became very similar in the sixteenth century, and continued to provide rhymes such as 'join' and 'nine' at least into the eighteenth century. Checking the two words *file* and *foil* in *OED* we then found under *file*, vb. sense 5: 'to sully the honour of', a passage where Davenant, in *The Siege of Rhodes* (1668), converted to his own use lines 9–11 of Shakespeare's Sonnet 25:

> The painful warrior famousèd for might,
> After a thousand victories once foil'd,
> Is from the book of honour rasèd quite.

The result in Davenant is this:

> The bold warrier, that hath deserv'd / Fame . . . once feel'd [modern editions *fil'd*] his victories / Are quite forgot.

The fact that Davenant probably took Shakespeare's *foild* (so Q and Benson) in Sonnet 25 as *fild* suggests that to the seventeenth-century ear a pun on *foil* and *file* in Sonnet 146 would have been possible. If we adopt Palgrave's *Foil'd by*, therefore, we may then have a pun paralleling, strengthening, and deriving strength from the pun on 'array'.

To adopt some emendation seems to us better than either leaving a blank, which gives this fine poem the air of a curious fragment, or printing the line as it stands in Q with its unmetrical repetition. *Foil'd by* attracts us for the reasons stated; but it cannot be too strongly emphasized that any emendation must be regarded as highly tentative. Some names of first proposers of other suggestions are entered in the list on pp. 358–9, against the words they proposed. Finally, it should be emphasized that the reasons we have suggested in favour of Palgrave's reading are our own. What his reasons were for adopting it are entirely unknown to us.

2 *these*] So Q and most editors. Malone, followed by some modern editors: *those*. *These* suggests, rightly in our view, something closer to the soul than *those*, which would cohere better with the siege metaphor whose presence we have already denied.

4] Probably not merely bodily adornment is meant, but all earthly show and indulgence.

5 *cost*] 'outlay'.

6 *fading mansion*] i.e. the body, subject to decay.

7 *excess*] 'extravagance'.

8 *charge*] i.e. 'what you have spent so much on', and perhaps also 'what has been entrusted to you'.

146

Poor soul, the centre of my sinful earth,
[Foil'd by] these rebel powers that thee array,
Why dost thou pine within and suffer dearth,
Painting thy outward walls so costly gay?   4
Why so large cost, having so short a lease,
Dost thou upon thy fading mansion spend?
Shall worms, inheritors of this excess,
Eat up thy charge? Is this thy body's end?   8
Then, soul, live thou upon thy servant's loss,
And let that pine to aggravate thy store;
Buy terms divine in selling hours of dross;
Within be fed, without be rich no more: 12
    So shalt thou feed on Death, that feeds on men,
    And Death once dead there's no more dying then.

8 *end*] Possibly punning on (1) 'purpose', (2) 'final end'.

7, 8] These two questions, in contrast with those preceding, are meditations rather than real questions.

9] He expects the soul to gain in health and strength by mortifying the body.

10 *that*] = 'thy servant' (line 9), i.e. the body.

aggravate] 'increase'.

thy store] 'your resources'.

11 *terms*] in the legal sense of 'terms of years' (cf. 'lease', line 5), here contrasted with the brevity of 'hours'.

12 *Within . . . without*] i.e. inside and outside the *soul*, not the body.

13, 14] 'In this way you will feed on mortification and mortality [both ideas are probably present], and so on death itself, who feeds on men, and once death [(1) your mortal body, (2) Death itself] is dead, there will be no more death for you to fear.'

147 1 *still*] 'incessantly'.

2 *nurseth*] 'nourishes' (*not* 'nurses').

3 *ill*] 'illness'.

3, 4] If Dowden were right in believing that there is a sequential connexion, particularly through these lines, with 146, then 'that which doth preserve the ill' would presumably be the bodily love of this false woman, which would be one of the 'rebel powers' of 146. 2.

4] i.e. to pander to the patient's fickle and unhealthy appetite.

6 *prescriptions*] 'instructions', 'orders' (not necessarily for medicaments).

7 *I desperate*] 'I, in a state of desperation'.

approve] 'realize by experience'.

8] Some editors, including Dowden and Beeching, take 'physic' as the object of 'did except'. The inversion, however, seems un-Shakespearean. We prefer Case's view that 'physic' is the subject, and take the meaning to be: 'in a state of desperation I am now learning by experience that desire, which medical skill proscribed, means death'.

9] Malone and many other commentators have referred to the proverbial saying 'past cure, past care'; but Shakespeare is here not merely reproducing the proverb (as he does in *LLL.* V. ii. 28), but playing with it, for, as Pooler has pointed out, he has here inverted it. The case is past cure, because the physician has ceased to care.

10 *evermore*] for the adjectival use Tucker aptly compares 14. 8: 'By oft predict'.

11 *discourse*] Probably 'speech' rather than 'reasoning', since a contrast between 'thoughts' and 'speech' seems to be continued in lines 12 and 13, whereas no contrast between 'thoughts' (concepts) and reasoning seems to be developed.

12] 'Wide of the mark and senselessly uttered'.

13, 14] In 'fair', 'bright', 'black', 'dark', the play on the physical and moral senses can be regarded as certain.

147

My LOVE is as a fever, longing still
For that which longer nurseth the disease,
Feeding on that which doth preserve the ill,
The uncertain sickly appetite to please.   4
My reason, the physician to my love,
Angry that his prescriptions are not kept,
Hath left me, and I desperate now approve
Desire is death, which physic did except.   8
Past cure I am now reason is past care,
And frantic mad with evermore unrest;
My thoughts and my discourse as madmen's are,
At random from the truth, vainly express'd: 12
  For I have sworn thee fair, and thought thee bright,
  Who art as black as hell, as dark as night.

148 1–2 Punctuation] So this edition. Q: *O Me! . . . sight,* . Gildon changed Q's comma to an exclamation mark, and has been widely followed. A few modern editors print a semi-colon at *sight*. Lines 1–2 could certainly be read as an exclamation, and lines 3–4 as a question suggested by it. It is more natural, however, to take the two couplets as expressing alternative questions, and therefore to punctuate as here.

2 *correspondence*] 'congruity', i.e. the eyes do not see properly.

4 *censures falsely*] 'forms a false estimate of' ('censures' has no derogatory sense here). Cf. *KJ*. II. i. 3 2 8: 'your armies; whose equality / By our best eyes cannot be censurèd'.

5 *fair*] (1) 'beautiful', and (2) 'honourable'. Cf. a similar play in 147. 1 3. *false*] distorting, and so, untrustworthy.

7 *then . . . denote*] 'the fact that I love clearly indicates that . . .'.

8 *all men's: No;*] Q: *all mens: no,* . Modern editors, faced with Q's strange punctuation, have either enthusiastically adopted it (e.g. Wyndham, Pooler) or rejected it as rhythmically untypical of the *Sonnets*. Some scholars, moreover, following Lettsom, have suggested that Shakespeare is punning in line 8 (or line 9 (Beeching)) on 'eye' and 'ay' = 'yes'. The chief editorial device to indicate the pun has been the deletion of the colon after 'men's'. Those editors who retain Q's punctuation forfeit the pun, and take 'No' to mean 'No, it is not'.

We believe that Shakespeare may have intended two readings of the line to be possible, and that the strange punctuation of Q was designed to permit a syntactical play in addition to the pun on 'eye'. The two meanings would be: (1) 'Love's eye does not see so correctly as everyone else's'; (2) 'Love's affirmation is not so true as everyone else's denial'. Beeching acutely observed that if there was a pun on 'eye' in line 8 it would require two in-consistent punctuations (that of Q and that of Lettsom). We believe that a semi-colon after *No* avoids any such objection, making it possible to read the line in the two ways. Such a change is entirely justifiable, since Q's commas are often equivalent to modern semi-colons.

1 0 *watching*] 'wakefulness'.

1 1 *mistake my view*] 'see amiss'.

1 3 *love*] In line 1 'love' could only mean either (1) the act of loving or (2) the god of love. In lines 7, 8, and 9 sense (1) prevails. In line 1 3, however, as a stroke of wit, a new reference of the word—to the mistress —is introduced; for in line 1 4 'thy foul faults' clearly refers primarily to the mistress. Concurrently, however, the whole couplet probably alludes to the way in which Love (the god) deludes men.

1 4 *foul faults*] Both defects of physical appearance and moral obliquities.

148

Oꜰ ᴍᴇ! what eyes hath love put in my head,
Which have no correspondence with true sight?
Or if they have, where is my judgment fled,
That censures falsely what they see aright? 4
If that be fair whereon my false eyes dote,
What means the world to say it is not so?
If it be not, then love doth well denote
Love's eye is not so true as all men's: No; 8
How can it? Oh, how can love's eye be true,
That is so vex'd with watching and with tears?
No marvel then though I mistake my view—
The sun itself sees not till heaven clears. 12
O cunning love! with tears thou keep'st me blind,
Lest eyes, well seeing, thy foul faults should find.

149 2 *partake*] 'side' (*OED*, sense 5). Q has *pertake*, a common sixteenth-and seventeenth-century spelling.

3, 4 *Do . . . myself*] It seems difficult, if not impossible, to decide which of two meanings is intended: (1) 'Can you really say I forget about you when, in fact, it is myself that I have forgotten?' or (2) 'Can you really say I have no consideration for you when it is my own interests and preferences that I neglect?' Both senses of 'forgot' ((1) oblivious, (2) neglected) might be present, sense (1) looking back to 'say I love thee not' (in line 1), sense (2) looking both back to 'partake (against)' (line 2) and forward to the rejections of lines 5 and 6.

4 *all tyrant,*] So Malone and most modern editors. Q: *all tirant*. Sewell's first edition, and Capell: *all, Tyrant,*. Hazlitt, Keightley, Beeching, Tucker: *all-tyrant,* . The main division of opinion among editors is as to whether the term refers (1) to the poet, as, e.g., Tyler, Wyndham, and Alden believe, or (2) to the woman (the view of most modern editors, following Malone). (1) would be certain if a meaning had to be extracted from Q's punctuation on the assumption that Q's punctuation was indisputably authentic, and correct for a modern reader, which there is no reason to believe. (2) seems to cohere better with the rest of the sonnet, and, particularly, with 'cruel' (line 1) and 'Commanded' (line 12).

7 *spend*] 'mete out'.

8 *with present moan*] 'by immediate complaint (against *myself*)'.

9 *respect*] 'discern'.

10 *to despise*] 'as to despise'.

11 *defect*] 'lack of good qualities'.

13, 14] Tucker finds the point of the couplet 'either very obscure or very impotent'. We share his scepticism as to the silence of commentators betokening understanding; but the conclusion, though obscure, does not seem to us impotent. Massey quotes aptly from Sidney's *Astrophel and Stella*, 62: 'That love she did, but lov'd a love not blind'. The sense of the couplet would seem to be that the poet, seeing that the woman loves those who can see all her defects, urges that her hate is the best tribute to the strength of his blind passion.

149

Canst thou, O cruel, say I love thee not,
When I against myself with thee partake?
Do I not think on thee, when I forgot
Am of myself, all tyrant, for thy sake?   4
Who hateth thee that I do call my friend?
On whom frown'st thou that I do fawn upon?
Nay, if thou lour'st on me, do I not spend
Revenge upon myself with present moan?   8
What merit do I in myself respect
That is so proud thy service to despise,
When all my best doth worship thy defect,
Commanded by the motion of thine eyes?   12
   But, love, hate on; for now I know thy mind:
   Those that can see thou lov'st—and I am blind.

150 1 *power*] i.e. supernatural power.

2 *With insufficiency*] 'By your very defects'.

4] 'And swear that it is not brightness that makes a day fine'.

5 *this . . . ill*] i.e. the gift of making defects seem attractive.

7 *strength and warrantise of skill*] 'potency and assurance of expertise'.

13, 14] The surface meaning is that in loving even the meanest in her his generosity deserves the return of her love for him; but beneath this there may well lie the harsh innuendo, playing on the two senses of 'worthy', that in loving someone so foul he shows himself a suitable person (because foul enough) to be loved by the foul one herself.

150

O<small>H, FROM</small> what power hast thou this powerful might
With insufficiency my heart to sway,
To make me give the lie to my true sight
And swear that brightness doth not grace the day?   4
Whence hast thou this becoming of things ill,
That in the very refuse of thy deeds
There is such strength and warrantise of skill
That in my mind thy worst all best exceeds?   8
Who taught thee how to make me love thee more
The more I hear and see just cause of hate?
Oh, though I love what others do abhor,
With others thou shouldst not abhor my state!   12
    If thy unworthiness rais'd love in me,
    More worthy I to be belov'd of thee.

151 *General Note:* The numerous double meanings in this sonnet are too obvious to need explanation.

1–2] The moral sense of 'conscience' is played on together with the physical, as in line 13.

3 *cheater*] 'deceiver', 'betrayer', both (perhaps) of the poet lover and of her husband (cf. 152).

amiss] 'fault', 'sin'.

3] cf. 142. 3–4.

8 *stays . . . reason*] 'doesn't need telling twice' (cf. 'tell' in line 7). (For 'reason' = 'talk' see *OED*, sense 3.)

10 *triumphant prize*] Either (1) 'triumphal prize', or (2) simply, 'splendid prize'; but in either case the reward of the triumphant flesh referred to in the carnal innuendo.

151

LOVE IS too young to know what conscience is,—
Yet who knows not conscience is born of love?
Then, gentle cheater, urge not my amiss,
Lest guilty of my faults thy sweet self prove: 4
For, thou betraying me, I do betray
My nobler part to my gross body's treason;
My soul doth tell my body that he may
Triumph in love: flesh stays no farther reason,
But rising at thy name doth point out thee
As his triumphant prize. Proud of this pride,
He is contented thy poor drudge to be,
To stand in thy affairs, fall by thy side.   12
    No want of conscience hold it that I call
    Her 'love' for whose dear love I rise and fall.

152 1–4] Commentators have differed as to how many parties are involved. Wyndham mentions four—the woman, her husband, the Friend, and the poet—leaving unmentioned the question whether line 1 refers to the poet's own marriage-vow. Other commentators, e.g. Beeching, Pooler, and Tucker, hold that the Friend is not referred to. It seems to us impossible to decide the point from the lines alone. 'Forsworn', in line 1, would seem, in the context, to refer most naturally to the poet's marriage-vow (though it *might* refer to protestations made to some other women). 'Bed-vow' (line 3) certainly *suggests* that the woman has a husband. As to the Friend, whether he is implicated would appear to depend on whether 152 refers to the triangular situation present, for instance, in Sonnets 41, 42, 134–6, and 144.

2] Two interpretations seem possible: (1) 'But you are forsworn for the second time in swearing that you love me'; (2) 'But you who swear (or have sworn) that you love me are twice forsworn already'.

3 *broke*] 'broken'.

new faith] 'new promises of love'.

torn] Tucker aptly suggests that the image is of a torn contract.

3 Punctuation] So Tucker. Q has no comma at *broke*, but a comma at *torn*. Most modern editors print commas after both words. A few modern editors, e.g. Wyndham, Beeching, Herford, print no commas.

The crucial question is whether lines 3 and 4 are intended as complete parallels, line 3 expressing what the woman has *done*, viz. broken her marriage-vows by adultery, and been false also to a newly plighted faith either to the poet or to another lover (see note on 3, 4, below), and line 4 what she is now averring, newly felt hate for the man she had only recently taken to loving. This interpretation would be brought out if commas were placed after *act* (line 3) and *vowing* (line 4) and if Q's comma after *torn* were strengthened to a semi-colon. Even without the extra pointing, however, this interpretation remains possible. To attempt to establish a parallelism of the lines with 'hate' as the grammatical object of 'vowing' founders on a resultant extreme disparity of construction. An alternative possibility, however, is that 'In . . . broke' describes the first form of the mistress's perjury, and the whole clause 'and . . . bearing' the second form. Editors who have held this view have removed Q's comma after *torn*. There would be plenty of precedent for such a measure. Q often prints commas at the ends of lines which modern readers would rightly regard as enjambed. Such cases occur in about forty sonnets out of 154. Either interpretation seems to us acceptable, but we slightly prefer the second because of the pleasing chiastic structure of line 4 when so read.

152

In LOVING thee thou know'st I am forsworn;
But thou art twice forsworn to me love swearing,—
In act thy bed-vow broke, and new faith torn
In vowing new hate after new love bearing.   4
But why of two oaths' breach do I accuse thee,
When I break twenty? I am perjur'd most:
For all my vows are oaths but to misuse thee,
And all my honest faith in thee is lost.   8
For I have sworn deep oaths of thy deep kindness—
Oaths of thy love, thy truth, thy constancy;
And to enlighten thee gave eyes to blindness,
Or made them swear against the thing they see: 12
    For I have sworn thee fair,—more perjur'd eye,
    To swear against the truth so foul a lie!

In our view the interpretation comes out more clearly if a comma be inserted after *broke*, which we have therefore done.

3, 4] Whether these lines refer simply (1) to the woman's husband and to the poet, or also (2) to another lover, e.g. the Friend, would seem to depend on whether the 'swearing' in line 2 is to be understood as past (as Pooler and Tucker Brooke believe) or as present (as Wyndham thinks). If (1), then the 'torn faith', 'new hate', and 'new love' all relate to the poet; if (2) they all relate to the other lover.

7 *misuse*] Shakespeare uses the verb elsewhere in four senses: (1) to use wrongly or for a bad purpose; (2) to treat badly; (3) to revile; (4) to deceive (in *M. Ado*. II. ii. 28: 'Proof enough to misuse the prince, to vex Claudio, to undo Hero'). (3) does not fit here. (4) fits very well. (1) and (2) may also be present as undertones, though, if so, the 'misusing' referred to may be more specific. In the sixteenth century, indeed, the verb was still being used to mean 'to debauch' (*OED*, sense 2b). There certainly seems to be no need to invent a further sense, 'to speak falsely of, to misrepresent', as do Schmidt and *OED*, both quoting this line as a nonce use. Nor is there need to take line 7 and the following lines (as Tucker

does) to imply that the woman is being used by the poet as an object to swear by.

8] Probably 'In my relationship with you I have entirely lost my integrity' (a heavily modified form of a paraphrase suggested by Tucker Brooke).

9 *deep oaths*] A rich phrase which seems to involve the following meanings of 'deep': (1) 'weighty and solemn'; (2) 'resounding', 'mouth-filling'; (3) 'apparently deeply felt'; (4) 'deeply committing'. 'Deep' here contrasts with the less rich, and probably somewhat ironical, use in 'deep kindness'.

9–14] An account of the poet's loss of integrity (see note on 8) through deliberate self-deception, and insincerity towards the woman.

10 *truth*] probably both 'loyalty' and 'genuineness', neither of which is redundant with 'constancy', as Tucker, arguing for 'veracity', alleges.

11 *enlighten*] 'make you seem bright', 'add lustre to you'. For 'enlighten' Cotgrave refers to 'inlighten', for which he gives '*enluminer*', and among the meanings for *enluminer* he gives 'to sleek or burnish'. Burnishing may be the metaphor here.

11, 12] Since clear sight would see the woman's defects, the poet made his blind imagination see her as better than she was, or else forced his eyes to swear that they saw the opposite of what they did see.

13 *I . . . eye,* Spelling] So Q, Benson (1640), Lintot, Gildon, and a few modern editors. Almost all modern editors adopt Sewell's emendation (1725) of *eye* to *I*. Q's reading is favourably mentioned by Wyndham, and supported by Professor Sisson. It provides a phonal play, 'I' echoing in sound, but not in sense, the 'eyes' of lines 11 and 12, and 'eye' not only taking up the phonal play but providing a pun. The 'eyes' had been either given to blindness or made to swear the opposite of what they saw. What this was was left uncertain, but was set in the *moral* context of lines 9 and 10. Shakespeare now suddenly shows his hand, and insults the woman's physical appearance, making it clear that his oath that she was beautiful would only be caused by deliberately tampering with his vision. The force of the pun on 'eye' would seem to depend on the word 'truth' in line 14. The poet is a more perjured kind of 'eye' than his falsely swearing eyes were. They swore the opposite of what they saw. He has sworn the opposite of what he knows to be the truth. The poet is, however, also asserting that he is a 'more perjured *I*'—more perjured in this particularly foul lie than in any he has admitted to in the rest of the sonnet.

14 *foul*] A characteristic Shakespearean contrary opposite to 'fair'; but the implication here is that the 'foul' lie is about a 'foul' woman.

152

IN LOVING thee thou know'st I am forsworn;
But thou art twice forsworn to me love swearing,—
In act thy bed-vow broke, and new faith torn
In vowing new hate after new love bearing.   4
But why of two oaths' breach do I accuse thee,
When I break twenty? I am perjur'd most:
For all my vows are oaths but to misuse thee,
And all my honest faith in thee is lost.   8
For I have sworn deep oaths of thy deep kindness—
Oaths of thy love, thy truth, thy constancy;
And to enlighten thee gave eyes to blindness,
Or made them swear against the thing they see: 12
    For I have sworn thee fair,—more perjur'd eye,
    To swear against the truth so foul a lie!

153 *General Note:* This and the next sonnet are evidently versions of the same conceit. The conceit itself is to be found in many other poems, ranging from an epigram by the fifth-century Byzantine Marianus Scholasticus (IX. 627 in the Palatine Anthology) to various poems in different languages (e.g. Latin, Italian, French) published in the sixteenth century and even later. (A considerable number of such poems are cited by James Hutton in an interesting article in *Modern Philology*, 1941, XXXVIII. 385.) Shakespeare's authorship of the two poems has been doubted, but on no very substantial grounds. Whoever the poet, we do not know the immediate source on which he drew. Marianus's epigram was first printed in the Planudean Anthology, Florence, 1494. The text in Henri Estienne's celebrated edition (1566) (IV. xix. 35), p. 354, is as follows:

Τάσδ' ὑπὸ τὰς πλατάνους ἀπαλῷ πεπεδημένος ὕπνῳ
Εὗδεν ἔρως, νύμφαις λαμπάδα παρθέμενος.
Νύμφαι δ' ἀλλήλῃσι, τί μέλλομεν; αἴθε δὲ τούτῳ
Σβέσσαμεν (εἶπον) ὁμοῦ πῦρ κραδίης μερόπων.
Λαμπὰς δ'ὡς ἔφλεξε καὶ ὕδατα, θερμὸν ἐκεῖθεν
Νύμφαι ἐρωτιάδες λουτροχοεῦσιν ὕδωρ.

'Under these plane trees Eros was resting, held in gentle sleep, having given his torch to the nymphs to take care of. "What are we waiting for?" said the nymphs to one another. "If only we could quench together with this the same fire in human hearts!" But as the torch set the waters also on fire, since then the love-nymphs pour hot water into the bath.'

6 *still*] 'always'.

7 *grew*] 'became'.

seething] 'foaming hot'.

yet] 'still'.

prove] 'find to be', 'experience to be'.

8 *strange*] So Benson (1640), followed by most editors. Q: *strang* . Tyler and Stopes conjectured, and Tucker printed: *strong* . The spelling 'strang' occurred for 'strange' from the fourteenth until the seventeenth century. On the other hand, 'strong' was sometimes spelt 'strang' from the thirteenth to the sixteenth century, but that spelling only survived later in Scotland and the North. Tucker finds 'strange' not clearly appropriate, but the word was often used to mean 'exceptionally great, extreme' (*OED*, sense 9), and in that sense does not differ greatly from 'strong'.

9 *new fir'd*] 'having been lit afresh'.

10 *for . . . breast*] i.e. 'must needs try it out on me'.

11 *bath*] So Q. Capell and Steevens conjectured: *Bath*. Other editors have argued for and against a reference to the city. Bath was certainly

354

153

Cupid laid by his brand and fell asleep.
A maid of Dian's this advantage found,
And his love-kindling fire did quickly steep
In a cold valley-fountain of that ground;   4
Which borrow'd from this holy fire of Love
A dateless lively heat, still to endure,
And grew a seething bath which men yet prove
Against strange maladies a sovereign cure.   8
But at my mistress' eye Love's brand new fir'd,
The boy for trial needs would touch my breast.
I, sick withal, the help of bath desir'd,
And thither hied, a sad distemper'd guest;   12
    But found no cure: the bath for my help lies
    Where Cupid got new fire—my mistress' eyes.

visited for its curative waters in Elizabethan times, and 'thither hied' might
allude to such a visit. On the other hand, Bath had no pre-eminence among
spas such as it was to attain in the eighteenth century, and the line might
refer to any curative spa in use at the time.

   12 *sad distemper'd*] Either (1) 'miserable and out of sorts', or (2)
'wretchedly out of sorts'. The closest parallels, such as *Tit. A.* V. iii. 82:
'Love-sick Dido's sad attending ear', and as *Lucrece* 1590–1: 'Which when
her sad beholding husband saw, / Amazedly in her sad face he stares', are
equally ambiguous grammatically.

   14 *eyes*] So Benson (1640), followed by almost all modern editors. Q,
Lintot: *eye*. The plural is required by the rhyme.

154 9 *well*] So most modern editors. Q: *Well*. Pooler notes that no commentator had suspected a reference to Wells, which, however, seems to him as likely as any reference to Bath in 153.

11 *Growing*] 'becoming'.

13 *this*] i.e. the following maxim (of line 14).

that] the remarkable event described in lines 1–12.

prove] Quite probably a play on (1) 'demonstrate' and (2) 'find by experience'.

14] As Sonnets 153 and 154 may well be alternative handlings of the same conceit rather than both members of a series, it would seem idly speculative to seek subtle reasons for the divergence of their endings. If one felt confident of the presence of something more than light fancy in these lines, there might be some point in considering Miss Porter's suggestion (*Sonnets and Minor Poems by Shakespeare*, New York, 1912) that this line sums up the two series of Sonnets by saying that 'Love's fire heats genially the cold valley fountain of Platonic love, but no such water is cold enough to cure the fever-heat of sexual love'.

154

THE LITTLE Love-god lying once asleep
Laid by his side his heart-inflaming brand,
Whilst many nymphs that vow'd chaste life to keep
Came tripping by; but in her maiden hand   4
The fairest votary took up that fire
Which many legions of true hearts had warm'd,
And so the General of hot desire
Was sleeping by a virgin hand disarm'd.   8
This brand she quenchèd in a cool well by,
Which from Love's fire took heat perpetual,
Growing a bath and healthful remedy
For men diseas'd. But, I, my mistress' thrall,   12
  Came there for cure; and this by that I prove:
  Love's fire heats water, water cools not love.

Amid
Bay'd by
Bound to (or *by*)
Breeding
Brooking
Check'd by
Cheering
Clogg'd by
Cloying
Craz'd by
Cross'd by
Crush'd by
Dear to
Deck'd by
Dogg'd by
Dress'd by (or with)
Drudge to
Dull'd by
Fatting
Feasting
Feeding (Sebastian Evans conj.)
Fil'd by
Flatt'ring
Flaw'd by
Foil'd by (Palgrave)
Fond on
Food of
Fool to
Fool'd by (Malone)
Foul'd by
Friend to
Gall'd by
Gilding
Girt by (Dodd conj.)

Gracing
Griev'd by
Gull to
Gull'd by
Held by
Hiding
House of
Housing
Jest of
Join'd with
Joying
Kin to
Kind to
King of (or to) (Fort)
Knave to
Leagued with (Brae conj.)
Lent to
Lord of (Herford conj.)
Lov'd of
Lull'd by
Maim'd by
Masking
Mir'd by
Mirth of
Mock of
Mock'd by
Prey to (or *of*)
Prince to (or *of*) (Fort conj.)
Rob'd by
Robb'd by
Rul'd by
Seat of
Slave to (or of) (Cartwright)
Smear'd by

Smirch'd by	Throng'd by
Soil'd by	*Tied to* (or *by*)
Sour'd by	Toil'd with
Spent with	*Torn by*
Spoil of (Courthope conj.)	Trick'd by (Latham Davis conj.)
Spoil'd by (R. M. Spence conj.)	Trimm'd by
Sport of (Sharp)	*Urg'd by*
Spurn'd by	Vaunt of
Stain'd by	Vaunting
Starv'd by (or *of*) (Steevens: *starv'd*	Vex'd by (W. L. Rushton conj.)
by the)	Ward of
Sway'd by	Waste of
Task'd by	*Worn by*
Thrall to	*Wrong'd by*
Thrall'd by (Kinnear conj.)	*Wrung by*
Throne of	*Yok'd to*

Professor Philip Brockbank of the University of York has suggested to us the possibility of 'Brav'd by', bearing the senses (1) 'defied by' and (2) 'decked out by'. Both senses accord well with Shakespearean usage, but we think the reading open to one of the objections we made to Professor Sisson's conjecture 'fenced by', namely that we do not believe that there is any siege metaphor in this sonnet (see p. 336, above).

Professor Brockbank's interesting conjecture subsequently appeared in a letter to *TLS*, 7 October 1977, p. 1150.

A KEY TO WORD-PLAY IN THE SONNETS

These are some of the words deliberately (and some of them frequently) played on in the Sonnets through their ambiguity in Elizabethan usage. Without recognizing these varying senses, and the way in which the presence of two or even more senses of a word (or sound) in the one line enriches the verbal and emotional pattern, it is not possible fully to appreciate the texture of the poems concerned. Some of the senses are now obsolete; some poems of lighter and even trivial quality abuse this device; but some of the greatest also depend on it for their full impact. A mistake of many seventeenth- and eighteenth-century annotators was to prescribe a single sense, only, for each word, phrase, or line.

Antic; antique: spelt in Q, without discrimination, *antique*; meaning (1) 'grotesque', 'quaint', but carrying at times the association (2) of 'belonging to an older time'. [17. 12; 19. 10]

Arrest: primarily 'an act of stopping', but our modern 'seizure by an officer' can also be present. [74. 1]

Art: conveys first the idea 'technical or specialised skill or learning', but may also imply 'trickery', 'cunning'. [frequent]

Assail: (1) 'to attack by force' and hence (2) 'to tempt' or 'attempt to seduce'. [41. 6; 70. 10]

Base: primarily here 'dark', 'gloomy'; but carrying also the implication of 'low' or 'inferior'. [33. 5; 34. 3; 100. 4]

Chest: is used with a play on (1) a coffer (e.g. for treasure); and (2) the thorax, the 'bone box' of the ribs, as in 48. 9.

Conscience: can have both senses of 'consciousness'—the mental and the physical, as well as that of 'involuntary moral self-judgment'. [151. 1, 2, 13]

Dear: this, which in English is a coalescence of two Old English words, (*déor*, 'severe, grievous', and *déore*, 'glorious, noble', and hence both 'costly' and 'held in high esteem'), has a wide variety of possibilities for word-play: e.g. 30. 4 (see note); 48. 14; 87. 1; 110. 3. Instances are frequent, and the alert reader will readily recognize them.

Eye—I—Ay: these, often with a confusion of spelling 'I' for modern 'Ay', are frequent in Shakespeare, as probably in 148. 8.

Fair: (1) light-haired and -complexioned; (2) handsome or beautiful; (3) honest and faithful. [frequent, but see especially Sonnets 127 ff]

Figure: (1) a numerical symbol; (2) shape, appearance or face. [104. 9, 10 (see note)]

Fool: (1) a servile attendant, one mocked with impunity; (2) a foolish creature. [57. 13, 14; 124. 13, 14 (see note)]

Husband(ry): may involve an evident play on the marital relation and on tillage for crops, as in 3. 6, as well as the idea of good estate management, as in 13. 10.

Lovely and *loveliness:* (1) beautiful; (2) lovable; (3) *-ness:* object of affection. [frequent]

Morn and *mourn (ing):* an obvious opportunity for word-play, as in 132.

Pretty: (1) wanton, artful and 'free' (see glossary); (2) attractive; (3) fine (ironical); (4) slight, venial. [41. 1; 132. 4; 139. 10]

Pride: as well as the moral, this carries an alternative sense of 'showiness', 'display of splendour'. [frequent] Also sometimes sexual.

Proud: (1) self-esteeming; (2) gorgeous; (3) high-mettled, lascivious, and sensually excitable or excited; (4) selfish, cold, or unkind. [frequent]

Rare and *rarity:* it is doubtful whether in the *Sonnets* the word ever simply means 'uncommon'. The stress is rather on the excellence that makes things precious.

Right; rite: the former spelling is very common for the latter sense in contemporary texts, and in several instances in the Sonnets and in the plays there is a (stronger or weaker) implied pun on the two words. [17. 11; 23. 6 (see notes)]

Sad(ly): in most cases the word means 'sober(ly)', 'dull(y)', solemn(ly)', 'drear(il)y', rather than 'sorrowful(ly)', and the latter sense if present is only a secondary meaning.

Servant; serve; service: this group, with its double sense of (1) 'to love' and (2) 'to wait on', 'work for', 'be obedient to', so frequently played on by Elizabethans and in Shakespeare's plays, occurs little in the Sonnets: *servant* only once, *service* twice (once unambiguously in sense (2)) and the verb twice.

Shadow(s): the Elizabethan primary sense of 'image' provides the play in 43. 5.

Son; sun: there is just possibly a phonal play in 33. 14.

State: (1) condition (a neutral sense); (2) rank; (3) splendid estate. The several senses are played on a number of times, markedly in Sonnet 29.

Steal: used consciously in two or three of the mingled senses of gradualness, secretiveness and theft. [33. 8; 63. 8; 92. 1; 104. 10]

Suit (vb.): (1) dress; (2) match. [127. 10; 132. 12]

Travail and *travel:* these were often indiscriminately spelt *travail(e)* or (*l*) until long after Shakespeare's time: the modern distinction of spelling is frequently bound to obscure one element in the doublet of senses, as in 27. 2.

True (truly and *truth)*: (1) loyal and faithful; (2) truth-speaking; (3) real; (4) right, or properly proportioned; (5) correct, accurate; (6) reliable, safe. The several senses are variously and frequently played on.

Use(r) (n. and vb.): (1) employ(ment); (2) (legal) right of use: sometimes played on in conjunction with 'usurer'; (3) sexual employment. [4. 7–8 and 14; 6. 5; 9. 12; 48. 3; 134. 10]

Virtuous: (1) morally commendable; (2) potent, or powerful. [16. 7; 72. 5]

Wake (vb.): (1) keep awake; (2) be on guard; (3) sit up late for revelry. [61. 13]

Watch (vb.): (1) keep looking; (2) keep awake. [61. 13]

Waste: (1) useless expenditure, or things so wasted; (2) fading away, or things so faded. [9. 11 and elsewhere]

Will: (1) desire, wish or purpose; (2) physical lust; (3) a cant or slang term for the *membrum virile* or *pudendum.* [134. 2; 135 and 136 throughout]

There are in addition frequent plays on other words which, being so utilized only once, are not listed here but discussed in the relevant notes.

GLOSSARY

The glossary lists only those uses in the Sonnets that might cause difficulty for a modern reader.

Numbers refer to the Quarto (1609) order of the poems.

K = see 'Key to Word-play', where other senses may be listed.

Some words occurring in isolated cases needing discussion (e.g. *expiate*, 22. 4; *rondure*, 21. 8) are treated fully in the notes to the poems, and are therefore not included here.

Abuse (n.): (1) misuse; (2) maltreatment, ill-usage; (3) lapse of conduct (sometimes milder than today); (4) sometimes also 'deceit'. [121. 10 (3); 134. 12 (1, 2, 4)]

Abuse (vb.): (1) misuse; (2) maltreat, use ill; (3) sometimes also 'deceive'. [4. 5 (1); 42. 7 (1, 2, 3); 82. 14 (1)]. The word is never used by Shakespeare in the modern sense of 'verbal(ly) insult'.

Adjunct (adj.): attendant. [91. 5]

Adjunct (n.): *aide-mémoire*. [122. 13]

Admire: wonder at (with or without, but usually with, delight). [84. 12; 123. 5]

Adulterate (adj.): corrupted by lewd thoughts or even conduct. [121. 5]

Afford: offer. [79. 11; 85. 7; 105. 12]

Against (exceptional sense): (1) exposed to; (2) in front of; (3) in preparation for. [38. 6 (1); 49. 1, 49. 5, 49. 9 (3); 49. 11 (2); 73. 3 (1)]

Aggravate: increase, enlarge (the only meaning in Shakespeare, with extension to 'exaggerate'). [146. 10]

Alone: only (except in a few cases, e.g. 29. 2). Usually placed after the words it qualifies and hence apt to mislead a modern reader.

Annoy (n.): boredom, rather than infuriation or harm. [8. 4 (see note)]

Antic, antique (n. and adj.): grotesque, caricaturist, quaint. Spelt indiscriminately, but usually 'antique'. [17. 12 (secondarily); 19. 10; K]

Approve: know by experience, or prove true by trial [42. 8 (see note) 70. 5; 147. 7]

Argument: theme, subject matter (in Rhetoric—cf. *invention*). [38. 3; 76. 10; 79. 5; 100. 8; 103. 3; 105. 9]

Arrest (n.): (1) check, stay, act of stopping; (2) seizure by an officer. [74. 1; K]

Art: (1) technical skill, specialised learning; (2) trickery, cunning. [frequent; K]

As: sometimes = that (conjunction). [36. 13–14; 78. 3]

Assail: tempt, attempt to seduce (derivative from the military 'assault'). [41. 6; 70. 10; K]

Astonish: stun (into silence). [86. 8]

Attaint (n.): stain, slight touch of dishonour; or accusation of dishonour. [82. 2]

Attaint (vb.): besmirch. [88. 7]

Base: dark, gloomy (not without a consciousness of the sense 'low, inferior'). [33. 5; 34. 3; 100. 4; K]

Bear (it) out: endure, last out. [116. 12]

Becoming (n.): power of making seemly, of supplying grace. [150. 5]

Bettered: made happier. [75. 8]

Blazon (n.): full description in rich terms. [106. 5 (see note)]

Blench (n.): a glance aside, or glimpse askant (Warwickshire), but Wright's *Dictionary of Obsolete and Provincial English*, also gives Northern 'fault'. [110. 7]

Brave (adj.): showy, resplendent. [12. 2; 15. 8]

Canker (n).: (1) larva of caterpillar in bud; (2) the wild rose or dog-rose (*Rosa canina*). [35. 4 (1); 54. 5 (2); 70. 7, 95. 2, 99. 13 (1)]

Captain (adj.): chief, principal, commanding. [52. 8; 66. 12 (see note)]

Carcanet: necklace, or ornamental collar. [52. 8]

Censure (vb.): judge or interpret. [148. 4]

Character (vb. or n.): write, writing. [59. 8; 85. 3; 108. 1; 122. 2]

Charge (n.): (1) cost, expense, but perhaps also (2) thing or responsibility entrusted. [146. 8 (see note)]

Charter: privilege, licence, right of free action. [58. 9; 87. 3]

Check (n.): repulse, harsh words and treatment. [58. 7]

Check (vb.): chide, reprove. [136. 1; (for 15. 6 see note)]

Chopped: chapped. [62. 10]

Churl: miser [1. 12 (see note)] (but not in 32. 2 or 69. 11).

Closet: small inner room, or cabinet, or locked case. [46. 6]

Comfort: sometimes carries the etymological sense (now lost) of *support* or *strengthening*, as in the Authorized Version of the Bible. [37. 4; 48. 6; (possibly 134. 4); 144. 1]

Comment (n.): expository treatise. [85. 2]

Comment (vb.): expound and moralise upon; make critical exposition of, enlarge by way of discourse. [89. 2]

Compare (n.): comparison or analogy. [21. 5; 35. 6; 130.14]

Composed: perfectly composed, impeccably proportioned. [59. 10] deriving from—

Composition: balanced constitution, coherence and consistency. [45. 9]

Conceit: concept, realization, thought, apprehension, idea. [15. 9; 26. 7; 108. 13]

Confined: having a fixed and limited or settled date or term. [107. 4 (see note)]

Confound: destroy, ruin (a strong term). [frequent; but see note on 128. 4]

Conquest: real estate acquired otherwise than by inheritance—opposed to 'heritage' (Scottish law). [6. 14; 46. 2 (see note); 74. 11 (see note)]

Conscience: (1) consciousness (a) mental, (b) physical; (2) involuntary moral self-judgment (with obvious play on meanings). [151. 1, 2, 13; K]

Consent: a making of common cause, a being of one mind (cf. Latin *consentio*). [28. 6]

Control (vb.): (legal) to set a term to, limit the period of. [107. 3]

Convert: turn—in a simple, non-specialized sense now lost. [7. 11; 11. 4; 14. 12]

Correct (vb.): see note on *correction*, 111. 12

Correction: punishment. [111. 12]

Cost: (1) ornament, display; (2) expense, outlay. [91. 10 (1); 146. 5 (2); 64. 2 plays on both senses]

Count (n.): account, audit. [2. 11]

Counterfeit: portrait. [16. 8; 53. 5]

Counterpart: portrait (cf. *counterfeit*). [84. 11]

Couplement: conjunction (of ideas). [21. 5]

Crooked: malignant—a sense carried secondarily in 100. 14. [60. 7; 100. 14 (see note)]

Damasked: see 130. 5 note.

Date: appointed final time, *terminus ad quem* (hence *dateless*) [frequent]

Dear: see note on 30. 4. [frequent; K]

Debate (n. and vb.): dispute, quarrel, strife, war (*not* the modern polite and regulated discussion). [15. 11 (see note); 89. 13]

Defeat (vb.): (1) deprive, cheat; (2) destroy. [20. 11 (1); 61. 11 (2)]

Determinate (p. part.): expired, or perhaps 'determinable'. [87. 4]

Determination: date fixed for expiry. [13. 6]

Disable: frustrate, prevent from using ability, incapacitate or pronounce incapable. [66. 8]

Disclose: unfold, unclose (*not* 'show' or 'display' or 'reveal'). [54. 8]

Disgrace (n. and vb.): the sense is more simply active than the modern 'ignominy'—'*loss* or *deprivation* of grace, of beauty or reputation'. [frequent]

Disperse: disseminate, publish. [78. 4]

Doom: sentence of judgment. [145. 7; see also 107. 4, note]

Doubt (vb.): sometimes = (to) fear, be distrustful of. [75. 6; For a possible instance of a corresponding noun see 144. 13]

Eager: sharp, poignant, pungent. [118. 2]

Eisel (Q. *Eysell*): vinegar (Lat. *acetillum*, O. Fr. *aisil*)—then believed to be a preventative, especially of plague. [111. 10]

Engross: monopolise, 'make a corner in'.]133. 6]

Enjoyer: (legal): one in possession. [75. 5]

Enlarge: set at liberty. [70. 12]

Entertain: pass (agreeably); beguile. [39. 11]

Essays: experiments, trials [110. 8]

Example: (vb. tr.): give instance of. [84. 4]

Exchanged: changed, altered (especially for the worse). [109. 7]

Expense: (1) loss; (2) squandering, wasteful spending (stronger than to-day). [30. 8 (1); 94. 6, 129. 1 (2)]

Faculty (to): authority (to), power (to)—cf. the modern ecclesiastical use. [122. 6 (secondarily, see note)]

Fair (adj.): see Key to Word-play.

Fair (n.): beauty. [frequent]

Fault: an *act* of transgression or offence (as in dialect today) rather than a defect. [frequent]

Favour: appearance, especially outward features of a person. [frequent]

Figure: a likeness or imperfect copy (i.e. not the real thing). [98. 11]

Filed: polished, refined (with a derogatory sense, as in the modern colloquial 'smooth'). [85. 4]

Foison: harvest plenty. [53. 9]

Fond: foolish, doting, [3. 7]

hence

Fond on: foolishly or excessively fond of, doting on (stronger than today). [84. 14]

For: sometimes = against, to prevent (as in 'spraying roses *for* mildew').

Foul: ugly. [frequent]

Frank: liberal, bountiful. [4. 4]

Free: open-handed, ungrudging or ungrudged, freely giving or freely given. [4. 4; 125. 10]

Gentle: cf. M.E. *gentil*; besides 'noble' this might also imply 'liberal', of vigorous and quick disposition, e.g. 96. 2 (secondarily).

Glance: (vb. tr. or intr.): to turn (aside)—not restricted to the eye, but as in cricket, or of a bullet. [76. 3; 139. 6 (see note)]

Glass: mirror. [frequent]

Go: walk (as distinct from, e.g., run). [51. 14; 130. 11]

Gore(d): see note on 110. 3.

Gracious: more than merely 'charming', expressing also spiritual grace. [7. 1; 10. 11] *graciously:* 'benignantly'. [26. 10]

Guard—in Q. garde (n.): guard house, guard room, detention room. [133. 11 (see note)]

Guard (vb.): ward (off), parry. [49. 12]

Gull (vb.): (1) deceive or dupe, but possibly (2) cram. [see note on 86. 10]

Gust (n.): taste. [114. 11]

Habit: dress, attire. [138. 11]

Halt (vb.): limp. [89. 3]

Happy; Happily: sometimes in the older sense of 'fortunate(ly)'—with 'joyful' only as the implied result. [32. 8; 66. 4 ('unhappily'; but see note)]

Hue: (1) external appearance, form or shape; (2) colour. [20. 7 (see note), 67. 6, 82. 5 (1); 98. 6 (2); 104. 11 (1)]

Imaginary: imaginative. [27. 9]

Indigest (adj.): shapeless, formless, chaotic. [114. 5]

Inhearse: lock up as in a tomb. (A hearse was a tomb, cenotaph, or monument hung with 'achievements': it only secondarily came down to meaning the wagon for the coffin.) [86. 3]

Injurious: doing injustice, causing *injuria* as contrasted with mere harm (*damnum*)—not with modern sense of *physical* harm [44. 2; 63. 2] hence

Injury: injustice done. [40. 12; 58. 8; 139. 12 (possibly)]

Insufficiency: shortcoming, defect. [150. 2]

Insult (vb.): exult and triumph over an enemy. (This seems to be the only meaning in Shakespeare.) [107. 12]

Intelligence: information (as in 'Intelligence Corps (or Service)' today). [86. 10]

Intend: take (one's) way. Cf. Lat. *iter intendere.* [27. 6]
Invention: art of finding matter to write (a term in Rhetoric). [frequent] hence
Invent (vb.): to find matter for writing. [38. 1; 79. 7]

Jack: erroneously used here for the wooden key of the virginals, though strictly the upright moved by the key and fitted with a quill that plucked the string. [128. 5, 13]
Jollity: fine array. [66. 3]

Lace (vb.): adorn, trick out with applied ornament sewn or stuck on. [67. 4]
Large: wide, broad (the old sense: conveying a less general 'bigness' than it suggests today. [44. 10; 95. 13; 135. 5, 12]
Latch: catch, take hold of. [113. 6]
Leese: lose. [5. 14]
Level (n.): field of fire. [117. 11]
Level (vb.): take aim at. [121. 9]
Limits: regions (the Lat. *fines*). [44. 4]
Lovely: lovable (a less trivial and casual word than as now used). [frequent; K]
Lusty: full of animal spirits and joy, or of vitality. [2. 6; 5. 7]

Main: broad expanse (transf. from 'the main sea'). [60. 5; cf. 64. 7 and 80. 8 for literal sense]
Mark: target, point of aim—and hence 'sea-mark' in 116. 5. [70. 2]
Masonry: art or skill of masons (not the stone). [55. 6]
Memory: (1) reminder; (2) record, memorial, memento, recorded note of memorandum. [1. 4 (2); 77. 6 (1); 122. 2 (senses (1) and (2))]
Miscalled: slandered as. [66. 11]
Misprision: misjudgment. [87. 11]
Mistake (vb.): (1) misjudge; (2) involuntarily falsify. [87. 10; 148. 11]
Modern: commonplace, trite. [83. 7]
Moiety: any portion, not necessarily an even half. [46. 12]
Moods: outbursts of anger—a sense fiercer and more specific than that used today. [93. 8]

Noted: familiar, well known, commonly recognized. [76. 6]
Nothing: a 'no-thing', worthlessness, a thing of no value. [20. 12; 66. 3; 136. 11–12]
Numbers: lines of verse. [17. 6; 38. 12; 79. 3; 100. 6]

Obsequious: (1) mourning, paying due respect or 'obsequy' to the dead; (2) paying due and dutiful service. [31. 5 (1); 125. 9 (2)]

Or . . . or: frequent for modern 'either . . . or'.

Outbrave: make a finer show than (cf. *brave*). [94. 12]

Outgoing: outlasting. [7. 13]

Owe: own, possess. [18. 10; 70. 14]

Pain: labour and toil (as in modern 'take pains'). [38. 14]
hence
Painful: said of one who undergoes great labour dutifully. [25. 9; K]

Part (vb.): see note on 113. 3.

Partake: take sides, confederate with. [149. 2]

Pencil: fine brush (for painting)—*not* the modern lead pencil. [16. 10; 101. 7]

Perspective: see note on 24. 4.

Policy: (1) scheming, stratagem, cunningly considered or highly careful management of affairs; (2) expedience. [118. 9 (1); 124. 9 (2)]

Politic: prudent, wise in disposing. [124. 11]

Prescription: direction, orders, especially medical but not necessarily 'recipe' or 'medicine' (147. 6). Four out of six examples occurring in the plays are rather orders and directions than 'recipes'.

Pretty: (1) pert, wanton; (2) slight, venial—and perhaps (3) 'fine' used ironically (O.E. *praettig* = artful); (4) attractive. [41. 1 (1, 2, 3); 132. 4 (1, 4); 139. 10 (1, 3, 4); K]

Prevent: forestall, hinder by anticipation and 'preventative' measures. [100. 14; 118. 3]

Pride: showiness, display of elaboration, show of splendour—cf. *proud*. [frequent; K]

Profane: as in Latin *profanus*, of an outsider, one not entitled to enter a sacred place. [89. 11 (partly)]

Proud: (1) gorgeous, resplendent, splendid in show; (2) high-mettled, lascivious (in the modern sense, and see also the entry of this word above), sensually excitable or excited; (3) selfish, cold or unkind. [frequent in sense (1); K]

Prove: put to the test. [frequent]

Qualify: temper, moderate, allay, abate. [109. 2]

Quest: inquisition made by a sworn jury; hence (derivatively) the jury. [46. 10]

Quick: (1) live, lively, vigorous, active. [55. 7; 76. 2] (2) momentary. [113. 7]

369

Quietus: quittance, discharge from an audit (ex *quietus est* = he is quit). [126. 12]

Range (vb.): wander, rove, stray—and hence 'be inconstant'. [109. 5]
Rank (adj.): coming from 'overabundant', the word seems to mean 'corrupt from excess'. [118. 12]
Rare: excellent and sometimes also highly treasured. [56. 14; 130. 13 and cf. 21. 7 and 52. 5]
hence
Rarity: a thing 'rare' in this sense. [60. 11]
Reeks: exhales, ascends as vapours (not requiring the modern repulsive association 'stinks'). [130. 8]
Refuse (n.): used literally as 'that which is cast aside as worthless', regarded as of no account. [150. 6]
Rehearse: mention, set forth, tell of (*not* 'practise'). [21. 4; 38. 4; 71. 11; 81. 11]
Remember: several times used transitively by Shakespeare (= remind). [120. 9]
Remove, removed, remover: the sense can be of change either of place or of affection, and hence imply inconstancy as well as absence. [25. 14; 116. 4]
Render: (1) exchange; (2) surrender, yield up, hand over. [125. 12 (1); 126. 12 (2)]
Repair (n.): condition (as in the modern 'in good repair'). [3. 3]
Repair (vb.): keep in good repair (not 'mend because broken'). [10. 8]
Reserve: preserve, keep, store up. [32. 7; 85. 3]
Respect (n.): point of focus and of attention, direction of vision, way of looking (cf. modern 'in that respect'). Cf. *unrespected* (43. 2) (= literally 'not clearly focused upon'). [26. 12; 36. 5]. But see 49. 4, note.
Respect (vb.): discern, observe. [149. 9]
Resty: torpid, heavy with sloth. [100. 9]
Review: look at again (the literal 're-view'). [74. 5]
Revolt: change of allegiance of affection—hence 'act of inconstancy'. [92. 10]
Revolution: recurrence in a cycle. [59. 12]
Riot: dissipation, loose living. [41. 11]
Rotten: commonly used then of damps and noisome vapours. [34. 4]
Rude(ly): rough(ly), uncouth(ly). [11. 10; 32. 4; 66. 6; 78. 14; 129. 4]

Sad(ly): sober(ly), solemn(ly), dull(ly), heavy, dreary. [frequent; K]
Satire: satirist ('a satire: a quipping fellow'—Harington, *Ulysses upon Ajax*, 1596). [100. 11]

Scope: aim or mark (61. 8)—the etymological meaning retained. In 105. 12 and perhaps 103. 2 the word is extended to the modern sense of 'range', as in 29. 7.

Seeming (adj.): deceptively apparent—the sense in Shakespeare usually tending to the pejorative. [138. 11]

Seeming (n.): appearance, outward show. [67. 6; 102. 1]

Servant: lover, as well as subject or slave and attendant. [57. 8; K] Cf. *service,* 149. 10 and see note in Key to Word-play.

Several: particular, privately owned (contrasted with 'common'). [137. 9]

Shadow: image, reflection in a mirror, image in the mind, etc., opposed to reality. [frequent]

Side (vb.): probably 'assign to one party'. [see note on 46. 9]

Simplicity: half-wittedness, ignorant folly. [66. 11]

Skill: knowledge, discernment (not primarily the modern technical sense, though it sometimes carries this). [frequent]

Soil (Q. 1609 *solye*): see note on 69. 14.

Solemn: joyously ceremonious—the old sense quite lacks our lugubriosity. [52. 5]

Sourly: (1) bitterly, mortifyingly (for the victim) and similarly *sour* (adj.) in 39. 10; (2) churlishly. [35. 14; 41. 8 (2)]

Spirit(s): (1) the volatile element(s) of air and fire, as opposed to the heavy earth and water, which four together composed a man; (2) vital energy. [56. 8, 74. 8 (partly) (1); see note on 129. 1 (2)]

Sport: amorous dalliance or intercourse. [95. 6; 96. 2]

hence

Sportive: amorously wanton. [121. 6]

Spring (of the year): the word then carried much more literal consciousness of the time of rising sap. [53. 9; 63. 8; 102. 5]

Stain (vb.): (intr.) grow dim, lose colour and brightness, (tr.) dim. [33. 14; 35. 3]

Statute: security against a debt. [134. 9]

Still (adv.): always, constantly. [frequent]

Store: breeding (as still of cattle), increase—but in 37. 8 ='abundance', and also in 64. 8. [11. 9; 14. 12]

Strange: belonging to others, alien to the person—but in 89. 8 and 93. 8 just 'as (of) a stranger'—and see note on 153. 8. [53. 2]

Subscribe (to): submit (to), acknowledge as victor or superior. [107. 10]

Sufficed: satisfied, given sufficient. [37. 11]

Suggest: prompt, tempt (with a person as object). [144. 2]

Suit (vb.): dress, clothe. [127. 10 (see note); 132. 12]

371

Suspect (n.): suspicion. [70. 3, 13]
Sympathized: feelingly or duly expressed. [82. 11]

Table: a tablet for (writing) memoranda. [24. 2; 122. 1, 12]
Tallies: sticks notched and then split longitudinally, the halves providing a checkable record. [122. 10]
Tell: sometimes = count, enumerate (the original meaning in 'tell the time'), reckon. [12. 1; 14. 5; 30. 10]. In 138. 12 ('told') there is a play on two senses: (1) 'count'; (2) the ordinary sense 'utter'.
Totter'd: tattered. [2. 4; 26. 11]
Translate: transform. [96. 8, 10]
Triumph(ant): exult(ing) as in a public triumph (not 'conquer'). [frequent]
True, truth: more frequent with the sense of fidelity than of verity of fact, but often played on. [frequent; K]
Twire: peep. [28. 12]
Tyrannous: cruel, pitiless. [131. 1]

Unbless (vb.): fail to bless. [3. 4]
Unfair (vb.): deprive of beauty. [5. 4]
Unjust: faithless, perfidious, false in loyalty or in love, possibly also untruthful. [138. 9 (see note)]
Unrespected: unattended to, not looked at, unfocused on, not clearly seen and apprehended. [43. 2 (see note); 54. 10] Cf. *respect* (= point of attention).
User: one who has the right of use (legal)—but see note. [9. 12; K]

Vainly: (1) unfoundedly; (2) emptily, unreasonably, idly; (3) fruitlessly. [138. 5 (1–3); 147. 12 (2)]
Vaunt: exult, swagger (rather than the modern 'boast'). [15. 7]
Virtuous: (1) potent—and hence perhaps (2) implying fertility. [16. 7 (senses (1) and (2)); 72. 5 (1); K]
Vulgar: commonplace, common. [38. 4; 48. 8; 112. 2]

Want: lack. [frequent]
Wanton, hence *wantonly:* gaily irresponsible—a word lighter, less pejorative than its popular use today. But see note on 97. 7 and on *wantonness,* 96. 1. [54. 7; 97. 7; K]
Warrantise: guarantee, assurance. [150. 7]
Waste(s): thing(s) wasted or destroyed—see note. [12. 10; K]
Watch: keep awake. [6. 13; 148. 10; K]
Weed: dress. [2. 4; 76. 6]

Whether . . . whether (sometimes contracted to *Whe'er*): used in correlative interrogatives either subordinate or direct. [59. 11–12; 114. 1–3]

Will: as well as volition and determination the word is played on in the senses of: (1) sexual desire; (2) the *membrum pudendum*. [frequent in 134–6, K (1)]

Wink: droop with sleepiness, close. [43. 1; 56. 6]

Wit: (1) wisdom, common sense; (2) intelligence; (3) clever mind, intellectual person. [140. 5 (1); frequent (2); 59. 13 (3)]

Wonder (vb.): admire (in the modern sense). [98. 9; 106. 14]

Would: would want to, would like to or wish to. [frequent] *N.B.* Shakespeare seldom uses *would*, which expresses resolve or desire, for the less forceful *should*, as modern American and some Midland and Northern English dialects do, though in 72. 14 *should* = modern *would*, and see 44. 3, note.

DETAILS OF CHIEF REFERENCE BOOKS AND
LINGUISTIC AUTHORITIES REFERRED TO
IN THE NOTES

Bailey, N. *An Universal Etymological English Dictionary* (1721). 8th edn, 2 vols, Midwinter and others, London, 1737.

Cotgrave, R. *A French and English Dictionary*, 1611, with English–French Supplement by R.S. (Robert Sherwood). A. Islip, London, 1632; also another edn revised and enlarged by James Howell, A. Dolle, London, 1673.

Halliwell, J. O. *A Dictionary of Archaic and Provincial Words.* 11th edn, 2 vols, Routledge, London, 1889.

Harris, W. T. and Allen, F. Sturges. *Webster's New International Dictionary of the English Language.* Merriam, Springfield, Mass., 1920.

Johnson, S. *A Dictionary of the English Language.* 4th edn, Longmans, London, 1773.

Murray, Sir J. A. H. & others. *A New English Dictionary on Historical Principles.* Clarendon Press, Oxford, 1883–1933.

Nares, R. *A Glossary . . . of Words, Phrases . . . and Allusions. . . which . . . Require Illustration in . . . English Authors, Particularly Shakespeare and his Contemporaries.* Routledge, London, 1822.

Onions, C. T. *An Oxford Shakespeare Glossary.* 2nd edn, Clarendon Press, Oxford, 1919.

Partridge, E. *Origins.* Routledge & Kegan Paul, London, 1958.

Schmidt, A. *Shakespeare–Lexicon* (1874–5). 3rd edn with Supplement, translated and edited by G. Sarrazin. Georg Reimer, Berlin, 1902.

Skeat, W. W. *A Glossary of Tudor and Stuart Words.* Edited with Additions by A. L. Mayhew. Clarendon Press, Oxford, 1914.

Wright, T. *Dictionary of Obsolete and Provincial English.* 2 vols, Bell, London, 1904.

Abbott, E. A. *A Shakespearian Grammar.* Macmillan, London, 1878.

Franz, W. *Shakespeare–Grammatik.* 2nd edn, Carl Winter, Heidelberg, 1909.

Kellner, L. *Historical Outlines of English Syntax.* Macmillan, London, 1892.

Morris, R. *Historical Outlines of English Accidence.* Macmillan, London, 1894.

Wyld, H. C. *A Short History of English.* Murray, London, 1914.

Pollard, A. W. *Shakespeare's Fight with the Pirates and the Problem of Transmission of the Text.* Cambridge University Press, London, 1920–37.

Simpson, P. *Shakespearian Punctuation.* Clarendon Press, Oxford, 1910.

Sisson, C. J. *New Readings in Shakespeare.* 2 vols., Cambridge University Press, London, 1956.

Wilson, J. Dover. *The MS of Shakespeare's 'Hamlet'.* Cambridge University Press, Cambridge, 1934.

Other works of reference employed in preparing the edition have included:

Bartlett, J. *A Concordance to Shakespeare.* Macmillan, London, (1894) 1906.

Dobson, E. J. *English Pronunciation, 1500–1700.* 2 vols., Clarendon Press, Oxford, 1957.

Ellis, A. J. *Early English Pronunciation.* Early English Text Society, Extra Series, Kegan Paul, London, and Oxford University Press, 1867–89.

Furness, Mrs. H. H. *A Concordance to Shakespeare's Poems.* Lippincott, Philadelphia, 1874.

Grieve, Hilda E. P. *Examples of English Handwriting.* Essex Record Office Publications No. 21, 1954.

Vietor, W. *Shakespeare Pronunciation.* Marburg, 1906.

SELECTED FURTHER READING

From the copious literature about and around the Sonnets we list a very few titles, selected to aid the general reader and the student seeking guidance. For further bibliographical information the reader should consult Alden, R. M., *The Sonnets of Shakespeare*, Houghton, New York, 1916; Ebisch, W. and Schücking, L. L., *A Shakespeare Bibliography*, Clarendon Press, Oxford, 1931; Tannenbaum, S. A., *Shakspere's Sonnets (A Concise Bibliography)*, Tannenbaum, New York, 1940; and Rollins, H. E., *A New Variorum Edition of The Sonnets*, Vol. II, Lippincott, Philadelphia, 1944. Details of more recent work are provided in *Shakespeare Survey*, ed. A. Nicoll, Cambridge University Press, London, 1948 and thereafter annually; *The Year's Work in English Studies*, Oxford University Press, London (for the English Association), 1919 and annually, and *The Shakespeare Association Bulletin*, published annually by the Shakespeare Association of America, New York. There is also very useful bibliographical information on the *Sonnets* in Smith, G. R., *A Classified Shakespeare Bibliography, 1936–1958*, Pennsylvania State University Press, 1963. Helpful Selected Bibliographies are included in Hilton Landry's *Interpretations* and in J. Dover Wilson's edition of the *Sonnets* (for both of which see below).

Editions

Beeching, H. C. Ginn & Co., Boston and London, 1904.
Tucker, T. G. Cambridge University Press, London, 1924.
Pooler, C. K. (Arden Edition) Methuen, London, 1918, 1931, 1943.
Rollins, H. E. (New Variorum Edition) 2 vols., Lippincott, Philadelphia, 1944.
Seymour-Smith, M. Heinemann, London, 1963.
Wilson, J. Dover. Cambridge University Press, Cambridge, 1966.
Herrnstein Smith, B. New York State University Press, 1969.

Reference Books

Abbott, E. A. *A Shakespearian Grammar.* Macmillan, London, 1878.
Donow, H. S. *A Concordance to the Sonnet Sequences of Daniél, Drayton, Shakespeare, Sidney, and Spenser*, Southern Illinois University Press, Carbondale, Ill., 1969.

Onions, C. T. *An Oxford Shakespeare Glossary*. Clarendon Press, Oxford, 1911, 1919, 1953.

Schmidt, A. *Shakespeare–Lexicon* (1874–5). 3rd edn with Supplement, translated and edited by G. Sarrazin, Georg Reimer, Berlin, 1902.

Life and Background

Chambers, E. K. *William Shakespeare*. 2 vols., Oxford, 1930.

Harrison, G. B. *The Elizabethan Journals*. Routledge, London, 1938–55.

Hotson L. *Mr. W. H.* Hart-Davis, London, 1964.

Rowse, A. L. *The England of Elizabeth*. Macmillan, London, 1950.

Shakespeare's England, 2 vols., Clarendon Press, Oxford, 1916.

The Elizabethan Sonnet

John, L. C. *Elizabethan Sonnet Sequences*. Columbia University Press, New York, 1938.

Lee, Sir Sidney. *Elizabethan Sonnets*. 2 vols., Constable, London, 1904.

Lever, J. W. *The Elizabethan Love Sonnet*. Methuen, London, 1956.

Scott, Janet. *Les sonnets élisabéthains*. Honoré Champion, Paris, 1929.

Shakespeare's Sonnets

Baldwin, T. W. *On the Literary Genetics of Shakespeare's Poems and Sonnets*. University of Illinois, Urbana, 1950.

Booth, S. *An Essay on Shakespeare's Sonnets*, Yale University Press, New Haven and London, 1969.

Herrnstein, B. (ed.). *Discussions of Shakespeare's Sonnets*, Heath, Boston, 1964.

Hubler, E. *The Sense of Shakespeare's Sonnets*. Princeton University Press, 1952.

Knight, G. Wilson. *The Mutual Flame*. Methuen, London, 1955.

Krieger, M. *A Window to Criticism: Shakespeare's Sonnets and Modern Criticism*. Princeton University Press, 1964.

Landry, H. *Interpretations in Shakespeare's Sonnets*. University of California Press, Berkeley, 1963.

Landry, H. (ed.). *New Essays on Shakespeare's Sonnets*, AMS Press, New York, 1976.

Leishman, J. B. *Themes and Variations in Shakespeare's Sonnets*. Hutchinson, London, 1961.

Melchiori, G. *L'uomo e il potere*, Turin, 1973.

A somewhat modified English version appeared in 1976 as:

Melchiori, G. *Shakespeare's Dramatic Meditations: An Experiment in Criticism*, Oxford, 1976.

Ransom, J. C. *The World's Body*. Scribners, New York, 1938.

Schaar, Claes. *An Elizabethan Sonnet Problem (Lund Studies in English* No. 28), Lund University, 1960.

Willen, G. and Reed, V. B. (eds.). *A Casebook on Shakespeare's Sonnets*, Crowell, New York, 1964.

Language and Style

Bradbrook, M. C. *Shakespeare and Elizabethan Poetry*. Chatto and Windus, London, 1951.

Empson, W. *Seven Types of Ambiguity*. Chatto and Windus, London, 1950.

Empson, W. *Some Versions of Pastoral*. Chatto and Windus, London, 1935–50.

Gordon, G. *Shakespeare's English*. Society for Pure English. Tract No. 29, Oxford, 1928.

Sister Miriam Joseph. *Shakespeare's Use of the Arts of Language*. (Studies in English and Comparative Literature, 165.) Columbia University Press, New York, 1947.

Kökeritz, H. *Shakespeare's Pronunciation*, Yale University Press, New Haven, 1953.

Mahood, M. M. *Shakespeare's Word-play*. Methuen, London, 1957.

Smith, H. *Elizabethan Poetry*, Harvard University Press, Cambridge, Mass., 1952.

Willcock, Gladys D. 'Shakespeare and Rhetoric.' *Essays and Studies of the English Association*, Vol. XXIX, Clarendon Press, Oxford, 1943.

Dating of the Sonnets

Bateson, F. W. see below, Articles in Periodicals.

Hotson, L. *Shakespeare's Sonnets Dated*. Rupert Hart-Davis, London, 1949.

Schaar, Claes. *Elizabethan Sonnet Themes and the Dating of Shakespeare's Sonnets (Lund Studies in English* No. 32). Lund University, 1962.

Textual Problems and Editorial Method

Pollard, A. W. *Shakespeare's Fight with the Pirates and the Problem of Transmission of the Text*. Cambridge University Press, London, 1920–37.

Sisson, C. J. *New Readings in Shakespeare*, Vol. II. Cambridge University Press, London, 1956.

Articles in Periodicals

Alden, R. M. 'The 1640 Text of Shakespeare's Sonnets.' *MP*, XIV, May 1916, pp. 17–30.

Alden, R. M. 'The Punctuation of Shakespeare's Printers.' *PMLA*, XXXIX, 1924, pp. 557–80.

Bateson, F. W. 'Elementary, My Dear Hotson', *Essays in Criticism*, Vol. 1, January 1951.

Hunter, G. K. 'The Dramatic Technique of Shakespeare's Sonnets', *Essays in Criticism*, III (1953), 152–64.

Knights, L. C. 'Shakespeare's Sonnets.' *Scrutiny*, III, 1934, pp. 133–60 (reprinted in *Explorations*, London, 1946).

Lee, Sir Sidney. 'Ovid and Shakespeare's Sonnets.' *The Quarterly Review*, CCX, 1909, pp. 455–67 (reprinted in *Elizabethan and Other Essays*, Clarendon Press, Oxford, 1929).

Masson, D. 'Free Phonetic Patterns in Shakespeare's Sonnets', *Neophilologus*, 37 (Oct. 1954), 277–89.

Mizener, A. 'The Structure of Figurative Language in Shakespeare's Sonnets', *Southern Review*, V (1940), 730–47.

Nowottny, W. 'Formal Elements in Shakespeare's Sonnets I–VI', *Essays in Criticism*, II (1952), 76–84.

INDEX OF FIRST LINES

10